GERMANY

PRESIDENT AND FEDERAL GOVERNMENT HANDBOOK

STRATEGIC INFORMATION, ORGANIZATION, REGULATIONS, CONTACTS

International Business Publications, USA
Washington DC, USA - Germany

GERMANY

PRESIDENT AND FEDERAL GOVERNMENT HANDBOOK

STRATEGIC INFORMATION, ORGANIZATION, REGULATIONS, CONTACTS

UPDATED ANNUALLY

Cover Design: **International Business Publications, USA**

We express our sincere gratitude to all government agencies and international organizations which provided information and other materials for this handbook

2018 Edition Updated Reprint International Business Publications, USA
ISBN 1-4330-1756-3

This handbook provides basic information for starting or/and conducting business in the country. The extraordinary volume of materials covering the topic, prevents us from placing all these materials in this handbook. For more detailed information on issues related to any specific investment and business activity in the country, please contact Global Investment Center, USA
Please acquire the list of our business intelligence and marketing reports and other business publications. We constantly update and expand our business intelligence and marketing materials. Please contact the center for the updated list of reports on over 150 countries.

For additional analytical, business and investment opportunities information, please contact Global Investment & Business Center, USA at (703) 370-8082. Fax: (703) 370-8083. E-mail: ibpusa3@gmail.com
Global Business and Investment Info Databank - www.ibpus.com

Printed in the USA

GERMANY

PRESIDENT AND FEDERAL GOVERNMENT HANDBOOK

STRATEGIC INFORMATION, ORGANIZATION, REGULATIONS, CONTACTS

TABLE OF CONTENTS

BUSINESS AND DEVELOPMENT PROFILES

STRATEGIC PROFILE

Capital and largest city	Berlin 52°31′N 13°23′E52.517°N 13.383°E
Official languages	German
Ethnic groups	80.8% Germans 10.8% Other Europeans 3.3% Turks 3.7% Asians 0.5% Americans 0.7% Africans 0.2% Other/Unknown
Demonym	German
Government	Federal parliamentary constitutional republic
- President	Joachim Gauck
- President of the Bundestag	Norbert Lammert
- Chancellor	Angela Merkel
- President of the Bundesrat	Stephan Weil
- President of the Bundesverfassungsgericht	Andreas Voßkuhle
Legislature	
- Upper house	Bundesrat
- Lower house	Bundestag
Formation	
- Holy Roman Empire	2 February 962
- German Confederation	8 June 1815
- Unification	18 January 1871
- Federal Republic	23 May 1949
- Founded the EEC (now the European Union)	1 January 1958
- Reunification	3 October 1990
Area	
- Total	357,168 km^2 (63rd) 137,847 sq mi
- Water (%)	2.416
Population	
- 2014 estimate	80,716,000 (16th)
- 2011 census	80,219,695 (16th)
- Density	226/km^2 (58th) 583/sq mi
GDP (PPP)	2014 estimate
- Total	$3.621 trillion (5th)
- Per capita	$44,741 (17th)
GDP (nominal)	2014 estimate
- Total	$3.820 trillion (4th)
- Per capita	$47,201 (16th)
Gini (2011)	29.0

		low
HDI (2013)		0.911 very high · 6th
	Currency	Euro (€) (EUR)
	Time zone	CET (UTC+1)
- Summer (DST)		CEST (UTC+2)
	Drives on the	right
	Calling code	49
	ISO 3166 code	DE
	Internet TLD	.de

Germany officially the **Federal Republic of Germany** is a federal parliamentary republic in western-central Europe consisting of 16 constituent states, which retain limited sovereignty. Its capital and largest city is Berlin. Germany covers an area of 357,021 square kilometres (137,847 sq mi) and has a largely temperate seasonal climate. With 80.6 million inhabitants, it is the most populous member state in the European Union. Germany is a major economic and political power of the European continent and a historic leader in many cultural, theoretical and technical fields. After the United States, Germany is the second most popular migration destination in the world.

Various Germanic tribes have occupied what is now northern Germany and southern Scandinavia since classical antiquity. A region named Germania was documented by the Romans before AD 100. During the Migration Period that coincided with the decline of the Roman Empire, the Germanic tribes expanded southward and established kingdoms throughout much of Europe. Beginning in the 10th century, German territories formed a central part of the Holy Roman Empire.

During the 16th century, northern German regions became the centre of the Protestant Reformation. The rise of Pan-Germanism inside the German Confederation, which had been occupied during the Napoleonic Wars, resulted in the unification of most of the German states in 1871 into the Prussian dominated German Empire.

As a result of the military defeat in World War I, and the German Revolution of 1918–1919, the Empire was replaced by the parliamentary Weimar Republic, and lost some of its territory. This was codified in the Treaty of Versailles. Despite its prominence in many scientific and cultural fields at that time, Germany experienced significant economic and political instability, which intensified during the Great Depression. The establishment of the Third Reich, or Nazi Regime, in 1933 eventually led to World War II and the Holocaust.

In 1945, after the military forces of Germany and her allies had suffered a comprehensive military defeat, the remnants of the Nazi regime surrendered to the Allied Powers. Over the next few years, Germany lost some additional territory and was divided by the victors Allied occupation zones, and evolved into two states, East Germany and West Germany. In October 1990, the country was reunified, regaining full sovereignty about six months later.

Germany has the world's fourth-largest economy by nominal GDP and the fifth-largest by purchasing power parity. As a global leader in several industrial and technological sectors, it is both the world's third-largest exporter and third-largest importer of goods. It is a developed country with a very high standard of living, featuring comprehensive social security that includes the world's oldest universal health care system. Known for its rich cultural and political history, Germany has been the home of many influential philosophers, artists, musicians, cineasts, entrepreneurs, scientists and inventors. Germany was a founding member of the European Community in 1957, which became the EU in 1993. It is part of the Schengen Area, and has been a member of the eurozone since 1999. Germany is a great power in the world, and is a member of the United Nations, NATO, the G8, the G20, the OECD and the Council of Europe.

Background: Germany—first united in 1871—suffered defeats in successive world wars and was occupied by the victorious Allied powers of the US, UK, France, and the Soviet Union in 1945. With the beginning of the Cold War and increasing tension between the US and Soviet Union, two German states were formed in 1949: the western Federal Republic of Germany (FRG) and the eastern German Democratic Republic (GDR). The newly democratic FRG embedded itself in key Western economic and security organizations, the EU and NATO, while the Communist GDR was on the front line of the Soviet-led Warsaw Pact.

The decline of the Soviet Union and end of the Cold War cleared the path for the fall of the Berlin Wall in 1989 and German re-unification in 1990. Germany has expended considerable funds—roughly $100 billion a year—in subsequent years working to bring eastern productivity and wages up to western standards, with mixed results. Unemployment—which in the east is nearly double that in the west—has grown over the last several years, primarily as a result of structural problems like an inflexible labor market. In January 1999, Germany and 10 other members of the EU formed a common European currency, the euro, and the German government is now looking toward reform of the EU budget and enlargement of the Union into Central Europe.

GEOGRAPHY

Location: Central Europe, bordering the Baltic Sea and the North Sea, between the Netherlands and Poland, south of Denmark
Geographic coordinates: 51 00 N, 9 00 E
Map references: Europe

Area:
total: 356,910 sq km
land: 349,520 sq km
water: 7,390 sq km
note: includes the formerly separate Federal Republic of Germany, the German Democratic Republic, and Berlin, following formal unification on 3 October 1990

Area—comparative: slightly smaller than Montana

Land boundaries:
total: 3,621 km
border countries: Austria 784 km, Belgium 167 km, Czech Republic 646 km, Denmark 68 km, France 451 km, Luxembourg 138 km, Netherlands 577 km, Poland 456 km, Switzerland 334 km

Coastline: 2,389 km

Maritime claims:
continental shelf: 200-m depth or to the depth of exploitation
exclusive economic zone: 200 nm
territorial sea: 12 nm

Climate: temperate and marine; cool, cloudy, wet winters and summers; occasional warm, tropical foehn wind; high relative humidity

Terrain: lowlands in north, uplands in center, Bavarian Alps in south

Base 802330 (R00002) 7-94

Elevation extremes:
lowest point: Freepsum Lake -2 m
highest point: Zugspitze 2,962 m

Natural resources: iron ore, coal, potash, timber, lignite, uranium, copper, natural gas, salt, nickel

Land use:
arable land: 33%
permanent crops: 1%
permanent pastures: 15%
forests and woodland: 31%
other: 20%

Irrigated land: 4,750 sq km
Natural hazards: flooding

Environment—current issues: emissions from coal-burning utilities and industries and lead emissions from vehicle exhausts (the result of continued use of leaded fuels) contribute to air pollution; acid rain, resulting from sulfur dioxide emissions, is damaging forests; pollution in the Baltic Sea from raw sewage and industrial effluents from rivers in eastern Germany; hazardous waste disposal

Environment—international agreements:
party to: Air Pollution, Air Pollution-Nitrogen Oxides, Air Pollution-Sulphur 85, Air Pollution-Sulphur 94, Air Pollution-Volatile Organic Compounds, Antarctic-Environmental Protocol, Antarctic Treaty, Biodiversity, Climate Change, Desertification, Endangered Species, Environmental Modification, Hazardous Wastes, Law of the Sea, Marine Dumping, Nuclear Test Ban, Ozone Layer Protection, Ship Pollution, Tropical Timber 83, Tropical Timber 94, Wetlands, Whaling
signed, but not ratified: Air Pollution-Persistent Organic Pollutants, Climate Change-Kyoto Protocol

Geography—note: strategic location on North European Plain and along the entrance to the Baltic Sea

PEOPLE

Population: 82,087,361
Age structure:
0-14 years: 15% (male 6,495,882; female 6,172,359)
15-64 years: 69% (male 28,687,267; female 27,526,698)
65 years and over: 16% (male 4,990,090; female 8,215,065)

Population growth rate: 0.01%
Birth rate: 8.68 births/1,000 population
Death rate: 10.76 deaths/1,000 population
Net migration rate: 2.12 migrant(s)/1,000 population
Sex ratio:
at birth: 1.06 male(s)/female
under 15 years: 1.05 male(s)/female
15-64 years: 1.04 male(s)/female
65 years and over: 0.61 male(s)/female
total population: 0.96 male(s)/female

Infant mortality rate: 5.14 deaths/1,000 live births
Life expectancy at birth:
total population: 77.17 years

male: 74.01 years
female: 80.5 years

Total fertility rate: 1.26 children born/woman
Nationality:
noun: German(s)
adjective: German
Ethnic groups: German 91.5%, Turkish 2.4%, Italians 0.7%, Greeks 0.4%, Poles 0.4%, other 4.6% (made up largely of people fleeing the war in the former Yugoslavia)
Religions: Protestant 38%, Roman Catholic 34%, Muslim 1.7%, unaffiliated or other 26.3%
Languages: German
Literacy:
definition: age 15 and over can read and write
total population: 99%
male: NA%
female: NA%

GOVERNMENT

Country name:
conventional long form: Federal Republic of Germany
conventional short form: Germany
local long form: Bundesrepublik Deutschland
local short form: Deutschland
former: German Empire, German Republic, German Reich

Government type:
federal republic

Capital:
name: Berlin
geographic coordinates: 52 31 N, 13 24 E
time difference: UTC+1 (6 hours ahead of Washington, DC, during Standard Time)
daylight saving time: +1hr, begins last Sunday in March; ends last Sunday in October

Administrative divisions:
16 states (Laender, singular - Land); Baden-Wuerttemberg, Bayern (Bavaria), Berlin, Brandenburg, Bremen, Hamburg, Hessen (Hesse), Mecklenburg-Vorpommern (Mecklenburg-Western Pomerania), Niedersachsen (Lower Saxony), Nordrhein-Westfalen (North Rhine-Westphalia), Rheinland-Pfalz (Rhineland-Palatinate), Saarland, Sachsen (Saxony), Sachsen-Anhalt (Saxony-Anhalt), Schleswig-Holstein, Thueringen (Thuringia); note - Bayern, Sachsen, and Thueringen refer to themselves as free states (Freistaaten, singular - Freistaat)

Independence:
18 January 1871 (establishment of the German Empire); divided into four zones of occupation (UK, US, USSR, and France) in 1945 following World War II; Federal Republic of Germany (FRG or West Germany) proclaimed on 23 May 1949 and included the former UK, US, and French zones; German Democratic Republic (GDR or East Germany) proclaimed on 7 October 1949 and included the former USSR zone; West Germany and East Germany unified on 3 October 1990; all four powers formally relinquished rights on 15 March 1991; notable earlier dates: 10 August 843 (Eastern Francia established from the

division of the Carolingian Empire); 2 February 962 (crowning of OTTO I, recognized as the first Holy Roman Emperor)

National holiday:
Unity Day, 3 October (1990)

Constitution:
previous 1919 (Weimar Constitution); latest drafted 10 to 23 August 1948, approved 12 May 1949, promulgated 23 May 1949, entered into force 24 May 1949; amended many times, last in 2012 (2012)

Legal system:
civil law system

International law organization participation:
accepts compulsory ICJ jurisdiction with reservations; accepts ICCt jurisdiction

Suffrage:
18 years of age; universal

Executive branch:
chief of state: President Frank-Walter STEINMEIER (since 19 March 2017; inaugurated 22 March 2017)
head of government: Chancellor Angela MERKEL (since 22 November 2005)
cabinet: Cabinet or Bundesminister (Federal Ministers) recommended by the chancellor, appointed by the president

elections/appointments: president indirectly elected for a 5-year term (eligible for a second term) by a Federal Convention consisting of the 630-member Federal Parliament (Bundestag) and 630 delegates indirectly elected by the state parliaments; election last held on 12 February 2017 (next to be held February 2022); chancellor indirectly elected by absolute majority by the Federal Parliament for a 4-year term; Federal Parliament vote for chancellor last held on 17 December 2013 (next to be held following the general election, 24 September 2017)
election results: Frank-Walter STEINMEIER elected president; Federal Convention vote count - Frank-Walter STEINMEIER (SPD) 931, Christopher BUTTERWEGGE (Left Party) 128, Albrecht GLASER (Alternative for Germany AfD) 42, Alexander HOLD (Free Voters FW) 25, Engelbert SONNEBORN (Pirates Party) 10; Angela MERKEL (CDU) reelected chancellor; Federal Parliament vote - 462 for, 150 against, 49 abstentions

Legislative branch:
description: bicameral Parliament or Parlament consists of the Federal Council or Bundesrat (69 seats; members appointed by each of the 16 state governments) and the Federal Diet or Bundestag (631 seats - total seats can vary each electoral term; approximately one-half of members directly elected in multi-seat constituencies by proportional representation vote and approximately one-half directly elected in single-seat constituencies by simple majority vote; members serve 4-year terms)
elections: Bundestag - last held on 22 September 2013 (next to be held on 24 September 2017); most postwar German governments have been coalitions; note - there are no elections for the Bundesrat; composition is determined by the composition of the state-

level governments; the composition of the Bundesrat has the potential to change any time one of the 16 states holds an election

election results: Bundestag - percent of vote by party - CDU/CSU 41.5%, SPD 25.7%, The Left 8.6%, Greens 8.5%, FDP 4.8%, other 10.9%; seats by party - CDU/CSU 311, SPD 193, The Left 64, Greens 63

Judicial branch:
highest court(s): Federal Court of Justice (court consists of 127 judges including the court president, vice-presidents, presiding judges, and other judges, and organized into 25 Senates subdivided into 12 civil panels, 5 criminal panels, and 8 special panels; Federal Constitutional Court or Bundesverfassungsgericht (consists of 2 Senates each subdivided into 3 chambers, each with a chairman and 8 members)
judge selection and term of office: Federal Court of Justice judges selected by the Judges Election Committee, which consists of the Secretaries of Justice from each of the 16 federated States and 16 members appointed by the Federal Parliament; judges appointed by the president of Germany; judges serve until mandatory retirement at age 65; Federal Constitutional Court judges - one-half elected by the House of Representatives and one-half by the Senate; judges appointed for 12-year terms with mandatory retirement at age 68

subordinate courts: Federal Administrative Court; Federal Finance Court; Federal Labor Court; Federal Social Court; each of the 16 German states or Land has its own constitutional court and a hierarchy of ordinary (civil, criminal, family) and specialized (administrative, finance, labor, social) courts

Political parties and leaders:
Alliance '90/Greens [Cem OEZDEMIR and Simone PETER]
Alternative for Germany or AfD [Frauke PETRY and Joerg MEUTHEN]
Christian Democratic Union or CDU [Angela MERKEL]
Christian Social Union or CSU [Horst SEEHOFER]
Free Democratic Party or FDP [Christian LINDNER]
The Left or Die Linke [Katja KIPPING and Bernd RIEXINGER]
Social Democratic Party or SPD [Martin SCHULZ]

Political pressure groups and leaders:
other: business associations and employers' organizations
trade unions; religious, immigrant, expellee, and veterans groups

International organization participation:
ADB (nonregional member), AfDB (nonregional member), Arctic Council (observer), Australia Group, BIS, BSEC (observer), CBSS, CD, CDB, CE, CERN, EAPC, EBRD, ECB, EIB, EITI (implementing country), EMU, ESA, EU, FAO, FATF, G-5, G-7, G-8, G-10, G-20, IADB, IAEA, IBRD, ICAO, ICC (national committees), ICCt, ICRM, IDA, IEA, IFAD, IFC, IFRCS, IGAD (partners), IHO, ILO, IMF, IMO, IMSO, Interpol, IOC, IOM, IPU, ISO, ITSO, ITU, ITUC (NGOs), MIGA, MINURSO, MINUSMA, NATO, NEA, NSG, OAS (observer), OECD, OPCW, OSCE, Pacific Alliance (observer), Paris Club, PCA, Schengen Convention, SELEC (observer), SICA (observer), UN, UNAMID, UNCTAD, UNESCO, UNHCR, UNIDO, UNIFIL, UNMISS, UNRWA, UNWTO, UPU, WCO, WHO, WIPO, WMO, WTO, ZC

Diplomatic representation in the US:
chief of mission: Ambassador Hans Peter WITTIG (since 21 May 2014)
chancery: 4645 Reservoir Road NW, Washington, DC 20007

telephone: (202) 298-4000
FAX: (202) 298-4249
consulate(s) general: Atlanta, Boston, Chicago, Houston, Los Angeles, Miami, New York, San Francisco

Diplomatic representation from the US:
chief of mission: Ambassador (vacant); Charge d'Affaires Kent LOGSDON (since 20 January 2017)
embassy: Pariser Platz 2
mailing address: Clayallee 170, 14191 Berlin
telephone: [49] (30) 8305-0
FAX: [49] (30) 8305-1215
consulate(s) general: Duesseldorf, Frankfurt am Main, Hamburg, Leipzig, Munich

Flag description:

three equal horizontal bands of black (top), red, and gold; these colors have played an important role in German history and can be traced back to the medieval banner of the Holy Roman Emperor - a black eagle with red claws and beak on a gold field

National symbol(s):
golden eagle; national colors: black, red, yellow

National anthem:
name: "Das Lied der Deutschen" (Song of the Germans)
lyrics/music: August Heinrich HOFFMANN VON FALLERSLEBEN/Franz Joseph HAYDN
note: adopted 1922; the anthem, also known as "Deutschlandlied" (Song of Germany), was originally adopted for its connection to the March 1848 liberal revolution; following appropriation by the Nazis of the first verse, specifically the phrase, "Deutschland, Deutschland ueber alles" (Germany, Germany above all) to promote nationalism, it was banned after 1945; in 1952, its third verse was adopted by West Germany as its national anthem; in 1990, it became the national anthem for the reunited Germany

ECONOMY

The German economy - the fifth largest economy in the world in PPP terms and Europe's largest - is a leading exporter of machinery, vehicles, chemicals, and household equipment and benefits from a highly skilled labor force. Like its Western European neighbors, Germany faces significant demographic challenges to sustained long-term growth. Low fertility rates and a large increase in net immigration are increasing pressure on the country's social welfare system and necessitate structural reforms.

Reforms launched by the government of Chancellor Gerhard SCHROEDER (1998-2005), deemed necessary to address chronically high unemployment and low average growth, contributed to strong growth and falling unemployment. These advances, as well as a government subsidized, reduced working hour scheme, help explain the relatively modest increase in unemployment during the 2008-09 recession - the deepest since World War II. The German Government introduced a minimum wage in 2015 that increased to $9.79 (8.84 euros) in January 2017.

Stimulus and stabilization efforts initiated in 2008 and 2009 and tax cuts introduced in Chancellor Angela MERKEL's second term increased Germany's total budget deficit - including federal, state, and municipal - to 4.1% in 2010, but slower spending and higher tax revenues reduced the deficit to 0.8% in 2011 and in 2016 Germany reached a budget surplus of 0.6%. A constitutional amendment approved in 2009 limits the federal government to structural deficits of no more than 0.35% of GDP per annum as of 2016, though the target was already reached in 2012.

The German economy suffers from low levels of investment, and a government plan to invest 15 billion euros during 2016-18, largely in infrastructure, is intended to spur needed private investment. Following the March 2011 Fukushima nuclear disaster, Chancellor Angela MERKEL announced in May 2011 that eight of the country's 17 nuclear reactors would be shut down immediately and the remaining plants would close by 2022. Germany plans to replace nuclear power largely with renewable energy, which accounted for 29.5% of gross electricity consumption in 2016, up from 9% in 2000. Before the shutdown of the eight reactors, Germany relied on nuclear power for 23% of its electricity generating capacity and 46% of its base-load electricity production. Domestic consumption, bolstered by low energy prices and a weak euro, and exports are likely to drive German GDP growth again in 2017.

GDP (purchasing power parity):

$3.979 trillion (2016 est.)
$3.911 trillion (2015 est.)
$3.854 trillion (2014 est.)
note: data are in 2016 dollars
country comparison to the world: 6

GDP (official exchange rate):
$3.495 trillion

GDP - real growth rate:
1.7% (2016 est.)
1.5% (2015 est.)
1.6% (2014 est.)
country comparison to the world: 148

GDP - per capita (PPP):
$48,200 (2016 est.)
$47,600 (2015 est.)
$47,500 (2014 est.)
note: data are in 2016 dollars
country comparison to the world: 30

Gross national saving:
27.9% of GDP (2016 est.)
27.7% of GDP (2015 est.)
27% of GDP (2014 est.)
country comparison to the world: 34

GDP - composition, by end use:
household consumption: 53.7%
government consumption: 19.5%
investment in fixed capital: 20.1%
investment in inventories: -1%
exports of goods and services: 45.7%

imports of goods and services: -38% (2016 est.)

GDP - composition, by sector of origin:
agriculture: 0.6%
industry: 30.3%
services: 69.1%
(2016 est.)

Agriculture - products:
potatoes, wheat, barley, sugar beets, fruit, cabbages; milk products; cattle, pigs, poultry

Industries:
among the world's largest and most technologically advanced producers of iron, steel, coal, cement, chemicals, machinery, vehicles, machine tools, electronics, automobiles, food and beverages, shipbuilding, textiles

Industrial production growth rate:
1.5% (2016 est.)
country comparison to the world: 133

Labor force:
45.3 million (2016 est.)
country comparison to the world: 15

Labor force - by occupation:
agriculture: 1.4%
industry: 24.2%
services: 74.3%

Unemployment rate:
4.3% (2016 est.)
4.6% (2015 est.)
country comparison to the world: 46

Population below poverty line:
16.7%

Household income or consumption by percentage share:
lowest 10%: 3.6%
highest 10%: 24% (2000)

Distribution of family income - Gini index:
27 (2006)
30 (1994)
country comparison to the world: 137

Budget:
revenues: $1.523 trillion
expenditures: $1.497 trillion (2016 est.)

Taxes and other revenues:
43.6% of GDP (2016 est.)
country comparison to the world: 27

Budget surplus (+) or deficit (-):
0.7% of GDP (2016 est.)
country comparison to the world: 23

Public debt:
68.2% of GDP (2016 est.)
71.2% of GDP (2015 est.)

note: general government gross debt is defined in the Maastricht Treaty as consolidated general government gross debt at nominal value, outstanding at the end of the year in the following categories of government liabilities (as defined in ESA95): currency and deposits (AF.2), securities other than shares excluding financial derivatives (AF.3, excluding AF.34), and loans (AF.4); the general government sector comprises the sub-sectors of central government, state government, local government and social security funds; the series are presented as a percentage of GDP and in millions of euro; GDP used as a denominator is the gross domestic product at current market prices; data expressed in national currency are converted into euro using end-of-year exchange rates provided by the European Central Bank
country comparison to the world: 51

Fiscal year:
calendar year

Inflation rate (consumer prices):
0.5% (2016 est.)
0.3% (2015 est.)
country comparison to the world: 50

Central bank discount rate:
0.25% (31 December 2016)
0.3% (31 December 2010)
note: this is the European Central Bank's rate on the marginal lending facility, which offers overnight credit to banks in the euro area
country comparison to the world: 133

Commercial bank prime lending rate:
1.7% (31 December 2016 est.)
1.84% (31 December 2015 est.)
country comparison to the world: 180

Stock of narrow money:
$2.049 trillion (31 December 2016 est.)
$1.923 trillion (31 December 2015 est.)
note: see entry for the European Union for money supply for the entire euro area; the European Central Bank (ECB) controls monetary policy for the 18 members of the Economic and Monetary Union (EMU); individual members of the EMU do not control the quantity of money circulating within their own borders
country comparison to the world: 5

Stock of broad money:
$4.347 trillion (31 December 2014 est.)
$4.451 trillion (31 December 2013 est.)

country comparison to the world: 5

Stock of domestic credit:
$4.327 trillion (31 December 2016 est.)
$4.452 trillion (31 December 2015 est.)
country comparison to the world: 5

Market value of publicly traded shares:
$1.716 trillion (31 December 2015 est.)
$1.739 trillion (31 December 2014 est.)
$1.936 trillion (31 December 2013 est.)
country comparison to the world: 7

Current account balance:
$294.3 billion (2016 est.)
$280.3 billion (2015 est.)
country comparison to the world: 2

Exports:
$1.283 trillion (2016 est.)
$1.309 trillion (2015 est.)
country comparison to the world: 3

Exports - commodities:
motor vehicles, machinery, chemicals, computer and electronic products, electrical equipment, pharmaceuticals, metals, transport equipment, foodstuffs, textiles, rubber and plastic products

Exports - partners:
US 9.6%, France 8.6%, UK 7.5%, Netherlands 6.6%, China 6%, Italy 4.9%, Austria 4.8%, Poland 4.4%, Switzerland 4.2%

Imports:
$987.6 billion (2016 est.)
$1.017 trillion (2015 est.)
country comparison to the world: 3

Imports - commodities:
machinery, data processing equipment, vehicles, chemicals, oil and gas, metals, electric equipment, pharmaceuticals, foodstuffs, agricultural products

Imports - partners:
Netherlands 13.7%, France 7.6%, China 7.3%, Belgium 6%, Italy 5.2%, Poland 5%, US 4.7%, Czech Republic 4.5%, UK 4.2%, Austria 4.2%, Switzerland 4.2% (2015)

Reserves of foreign exchange and gold:
$173.7 billion (31 December 2015 est.)
$173.7 billion (31 December 2015 est.)
country comparison to the world: 15

Debt - external:
$5.326 trillion (31 March 2016 est.)
$5.21 trillion (31 March 2015 est.)

country comparison to the world: 5

Stock of direct foreign investment - at home:
$1.416 trillion (31 December 2016 est.)
$1.36 trillion (31 December 2015 est.)
country comparison to the world: 6

Stock of direct foreign investment - abroad:
$2.08 trillion (31 December 2016 est.)
$1.972 trillion (31 December 2015 est.)
country comparison to the world: 3

Exchange rates:
euros (EUR) per US dollar -
0.9214 (2016 est.)
0.885 (2015 est.)
0.885 (2014 est.)
0.7634 (2013 est.)
0.7752 (2012 est.)

ENERGY

Electricity - consumption:
582.5 billion kWh
country comparison to the world: 7

Electricity - exports:
66.81 billion kWh
country comparison to the world: 2

Electricity - imports:
46.27 billion kWh
country comparison to the world: 2

Electricity - installed generating capacity:
178.4 million kW
country comparison to the world: 7

Electricity - from fossil fuels:
51% of total installed capacity
country comparison to the world: 154

Electricity - from nuclear fuels:
7% of total installed capacity
country comparison to the world: 21

Electricity - from hydroelectric plants:
6% of total installed capacity
country comparison to the world: 123

Electricity - from other renewable sources:
36% of total installed capacity
country comparison to the world: 3

Crude oil - production:
169,500 bbl/day
country comparison to the world: 42

Crude oil - exports:
14,260 bbl/day
country comparison to the world: 58

Crude oil - imports:
1.876 million bbl/day
country comparison to the world: 6

Crude oil - proved reserves:
254.2 million bbl
country comparison to the world: 56

Refined petroleum products - production:
2.198 million bbl/day
country comparison to the world: 8

Refined petroleum products - consumption:
2.4 million bbl/day
country comparison to the world: 9

Refined petroleum products - exports:
376,600 bbl/day
country comparison to the world: 18

Refined petroleum products - imports:
758,100 bbl/day
country comparison to the world: 9

Natural gas - production:
9 billion cu m
country comparison to the world: 44

Natural gas - consumption:
75.2 billion cu m
country comparison to the world: 9

Natural gas - exports:
18.17 billion cu m
country comparison to the world: 19

Natural gas - imports:
87.96 billion cu m
country comparison to the world: 4

Natural gas - proved reserves:
125 billion cu m
country comparison to the world: 52

Carbon dioxide emissions from consumption of energy:
814 million Mt

COMMUNICATIONS

Telephones - main lines in use:
50.7 million
country comparison to the world: 4

Telephones - mobile cellular:
107.7 million
country comparison to the world: 11

Telephone system:
general assessment: Germany has one of the world's most technologically advanced telecommunications systems; as a result of intensive capital expenditures since reunification, the formerly backward system of the eastern part of the country, dating back to World War II, has been modernized and integrated with that of the western part
domestic: Germany is served by an extensive system of automatic telephone exchanges connected by modern networks of fiber-optic cable, coaxial cable, microwave radio relay, and a domestic satellite system; cellular telephone service is widely available, expanding rapidly, and includes roaming service to many foreign countries
international: country code - 49; Germany's international service is excellent worldwide, consisting of extensive land and undersea cable facilities as well as earth stations in the Inmarsat, Intelsat, Eutelsat, and Intersputnik satellite systems

Broadcast media:
a mixture of publicly operated and privately owned TV and radio stations; national and regional public broadcasters compete with nearly 400 privately owned national and regional TV stations; more than 90% of households have cable or satellite TV; hundreds of radio stations including multiple national radio networks, regional radio networks, and a large number of local radio stations

Internet country code:
.de

Internet hosts:
20.043 million
country comparison to the world: 6

Internet users:
65.125 million
country comparison to the world: 5

TRANSPORTATION

Airports:
539
country comparison to the world: 13

Airports - with paved runways:
total: 318
over 3,047 m: 14
2,438 to 3,047 m: 49
1,524 to 2,437 m: 60
914 to 1,523 m: 70
under 914 m: 125 (2013)

Airports - with unpaved runways:
total: 221
1,524 to 2,437 m: 1
914 to 1,523 m: 35
under 914 m:
185 (2013)

Heliports:
23

Pipelines:
condensate 37 km; gas 26,985 km; oil 2,826 km; refined products 4,479 km; water 8 km

Railways:
total: 41,981 km
country comparison to the world: 6
standard gauge: 41,722 km 1.435-m gauge (20,053 km electrified)
narrow gauge: 220 km 1.000-m gauge (75 km electrified); 39 km 0.750-m gauge (24 km electrified)

Roadways:
total: 645,000 km
country comparison to the world: 11
paved: 645,000 km (includes 12,800 km of expressways)
note: includes local roads

Waterways:
7,467 km (Rhine River carries most goods; Main-Danube Canal links North Sea and Black Sea)
country comparison to the world: 19

Merchant marine:
total: 427
country comparison to the world: 24
by type: barge carrier 2, bulk carrier 6, cargo 51, carrier 1, chemical tanker 15, container 298, liquefied gas 6, passenger 4, passenger/cargo 24, petroleum tanker 10, refrigerated cargo 3, roll on/roll off 6, vehicle carrier 1
foreign-owned: 6 (Finland 3, Netherlands 1, Switzerland 2)
registered in other countries: 3,420 (Antigua and Barbuda 1094, Australia 2, Bahamas 30, Bermuda 14, Brazil 6, Bulgaria 12, Burma 1, Cayman Islands 3, Cook Islands 1, Curacao 25, Cyprus 192, Denmark 9, Dominica 5, Estonia 1, France 1, Gibraltar 123, Hong Kong 10, Isle of Man 56, Jamaica 10, Liberia 1185, Luxembourg 9, Malta 135, Marshall Islands 248, Morocco 1, Netherlands 86, NZ 2, Panama 24, Papua New Guinea 1, Philippines 2, Portugal 14, Saint Vincent and the Grenadines 3, Singapore 32, Slovakia 3, Spain 4, Sri Lanka 8, Sweden 3, UK 59, US 5, Venezuela 1)

Ports and terminals:
major seaport(s): Baltic Sea - Rostock; North Sea - Wilhelmshaven
river port(s): Bremen (Weser); Bremerhaven (Geeste); Duisburg, Karlsruhe, Neuss-Dusseldorf (Rhine); Brunsbuttel, Hamburg (Elbe); Lubeck (Wakenitz)
oil/gas terminal(s): Brunsbuttel Canal terminals
container port(s): Bremen/Bremerhaven (5,915,487), Hamburg (9,014,165)

MILITARY

Federal Armed Forces (Bundeswehr): Army (Heer); Navy (Deutsche Marine, includes naval air arm); Air Force (Luftwaffe); Joint Support Services (Streitkraeftebasis, SKB); Central Medical Service (Zentraler Sanitaetsdienst, ZSanDstBw) (2013)

Military service age and obligation:
17-23 years of age for male and female voluntary military service; conscription ended 1 July 2011; service obligation 8-23 months or 12 years; women have been eligible for voluntary service in all military branches and positions since 2001

Manpower available for military service:
males age 16-49: 18,529,299
females age 16-49: 17,888,543
Manpower fit for military service:
males age 16-49: 15,027,886
females age 16-49: 14,510,527
Manpower reaching militarily significant age annually:
male: 405,438
female: 384,930
Military expenditures:
1.35% of GDP
country comparison to the world: 77
1.34% of GDP (2011)
1.35% of GDP (2010)

TRANSNATIONAL ISSUES

none

Refugees and internally displaced persons:

refugees (country of origin): 40,230 (Iraq); 24,449 (Turkey); 24,203 (Afghanistan); 21,253 (Syria); 17,150 (Iran); 8,410 (Serbia)
stateless persons: 5,683

Illicit drugs:

source of precursor chemicals for South American cocaine processors; transshipment point for and consumer of Southwest Asian heroin, Latin American cocaine, and European-produced synthetic drugs; major financial center

ADMINISTRATIVE STRUCTURE

Germany comprises sixteen states that are collectively referred to as *Länder*. Due to differences in size and population the subdivision of these states varies, especially between city states (*Stadtstaaten*) and states with larger territories (*Flächenländer*). For regional administrative purposes five states, namely Baden-Württemberg, Bavaria, Hesse, North Rhine-Westphalia and Saxony, consist of a total of 22 Government Districts (*Regierungsbezirke*). As of 2009 Germany is divided into 403 districts (*Kreise*) on municipal level, these consist of 301 rural districts and 102 urban districts

State	Capital	Area (km²)	Population
Baden-Württemberg	Stuttgart	35,752	10,717,000
Bavaria	Munich	70,549	12,444,000
Berlin	Berlin	892	3,400,000
Brandenburg	Potsdam	29,477	2,568,000
Bremen	Bremen	404	663,000
Hamburg	Hamburg	755	1,735,000
Hesse	Wiesbaden	21,115	6,098,000
Mecklenburg-Vorpommern	Schwerin	23,174	1,720,000
Lower Saxony	Hanover	47,618	8,001,000
North Rhine-Westphalia	Düsseldorf	34,043	18,075,000
Rhineland-Palatinate	Mainz	19,847	4,061,000
Saarland	Saarbrücken	2,569	1,056,000
Saxony	Dresden	18,416	4,296,000
Saxony-Anhalt	Magdeburg	20,445	2,494,000
Schleswig-Holstein	Kiel	15,763	2,829,000
Thuringia	Erfurt	16,172	2,355,000

Germany is made up of sixteen ***Länder*** (singular *Land*, colloquially called ***Bundesland***, for "federated state"), which are partly sovereign constituent states of the Federal Republic of Germany. *Land* literally translates as "country", and constitutionally speaking, they are constituent countries. Often referred to in English by German speakers as "states", the term "Land" (with an uppercase 'L') is used in the official English version of the Basic Law and in UK parliamentary proceedings. However, it is sometimes translated as "federal states" in other publications.

Although the term *Land* applies to all states, some are also described as "states" in German. Each of the states of Bavaria, Saxony, and Thuringia officially describes itself as a "state" (*Staat*) and more specifically as a "free state" (*Freistaat*).

Berlin and Hamburg are frequently called *Stadtstaaten* (city-states), also the Free Hanseatic City of Bremen, which includes both the city of Bremen and Bremerhaven. The remaining 13 states are called *Flächenländer* (literally: area states).

The institution of the Federal Republic of Germany in 1949 was through the unification of the western states (which were previously under American, British, and French administration) created during after World War II. Initially, in 1949, the states of the Federal Republic were Baden, Bavaria, Bremen, Berlin (with special status), Hamburg, Hesse, Lower Saxony, North Rhine Westphalia, the Rhineland Palatinate, Schleswig-Holstein, Württemberg-Baden (also known as Baden-Württemberg), and Württemberg-Hohenzollern. Saarland was added in 1957. In 1957, the Saarland rejoined western Germany. Reunification (with the GDR, East Germany, declaring accession into the Federal Republic) in 1990 then resulted in the addition of the eastern states (through the re-division of eastern Germany into various states) as well as the reunification of Berlin and its establishment as a city-state and as a full and equal Land.

Brandenburg, Mecklenburg-Vorpommern, Saxony, Saxony-Anhalt, Thuringia, as well as Berlin (reunified, equal status) were added in 1990 through the re-division of the GDR once it acceded to the Federal Republic. Federalism is one of the entrenched principles of the Federal Republic as established in the Basic Law.

REUNITED GERMANY 1990-PRESENT

The debate about a territorial revision started again shortly before the German reunification. While scientists (Rutz and others) and politicians (Gobrecht) suggested introducing only two, three or four Länder in the GDR, legislation reintroduced the five Länder that existed until 1952, however, with slightly changed boundaries.

Article 118a was introduced into the Basic Law and provided the possibility for Berlin and Brandenburg to merge *without regard to the provisions of Article 29, by agreement between the two Länder with the participation of their inhabitants who are entitled to vote.*

Article 29 was again modified and provided an option for the Länder to *revise the division of their existing territory or parts of their territory by agreement without regard to the provisions of paragraphs (2) through (7).*

The state treaty between Berlin and Brandenburg was approved in both parliaments with the necessary two-thirds majority, but in the popular referendum of 5 May 1996 about 63% voted against the fusion.

SUBDIVISIONS

The city-states of Berlin and Hamburg are subdivided into boroughs. The state Free Hanseatic City of Bremen consists of two urban districts, Bremen and Bremerhaven, which are not contiguous. In the other states there are the following subdivisions:

AREA ASSOCIATIONS (*LANDSCHAFTSVERBÄNDE*)

The most populous state of North Rhine-Westphalia is uniquely divided into two area associations (*Landschaftsverbände*), one for the Rhineland, and one for Westphalia-Lippe. This arrangement was meant to ease the friction caused by uniting the two culturally different regions into a single state after World War II. The *Landschaftsverbände* now have very little power.

The constitution of Mecklenburg-Vorpommern at §75 states the right of Mecklenburg and Vorpommern to form *Landschaftsverbände*, although these two constituent parts of the *Land* are not represented in the current administrative division.

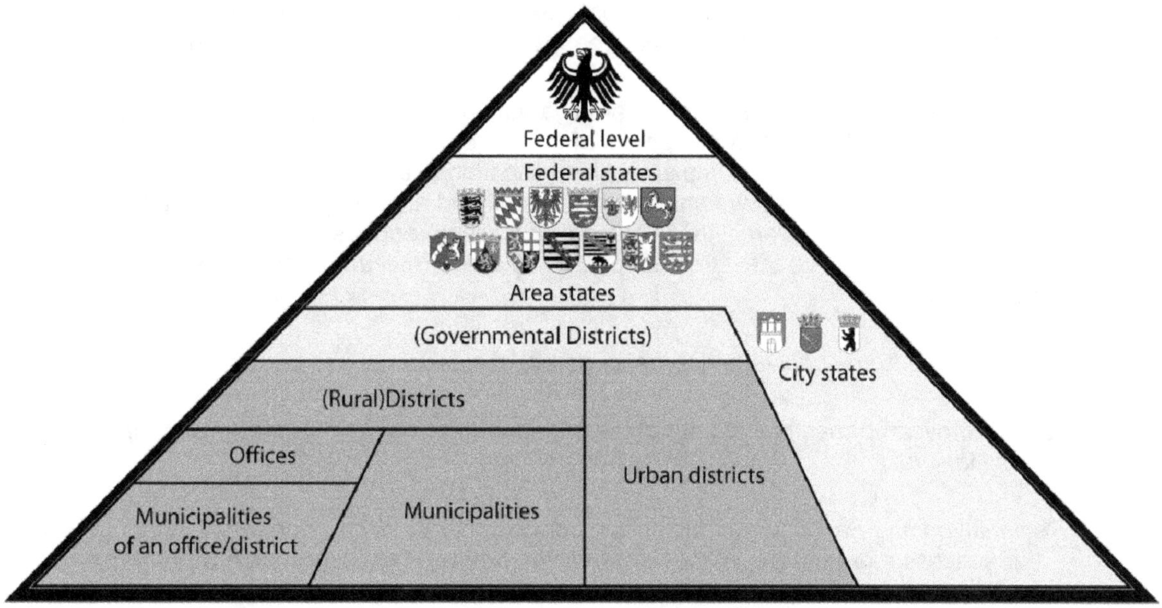

GOVERNMENTAL DISTRICTS (*REGIERUNGSBEZIRKE*)

The large states of Baden-Württemberg, Bavaria, Hesse, North Rhine-Westphalia and Saxony are divided into governmental districts, or *Regierungsbezirke*.

In Rhineland-Palatinate, these districts were abolished on January 1, 2000, in Saxony-Anhalt on January 1, 2004 and in Lower Saxony on January 1, 2005.

ADMINISTRATIVE DISTRICTS (*KREISE*)

The districts of Germany are known as German: ***Landkreise***, except in the states of North Rhine-Westphalia and Schleswig-Holstein where they are known simply as German: "***Kreise"*** (singulars: ***Landkreis*** and ***Kreis***). It would make them second level administrative subdivisions in 12 of the 16 states and third level administrative subdivisions in 4 of the 16 states.

The districts are at an intermediate level of administration between the *Länder* (German states) and the municipal governments (*Gemeinden*). They are not to be confused with the larger Regierungsbezirk. They correspond to level 3 administrative units of the Nomenclature of Territorial Units for Statistics (NUTS 3). The title German: *"Reichskreis"* (Imperial Circle) was given to groups of states in the Holy Roman Empire.

The Districts of Germany *(Kreise)* are administrative districts, and every state except the city-states of Berlin, Hamburg and Bremen consists of rural districts *(Landkreise),* District-free Towns/Cities (*Kreisfreie Städte*, in Baden-Württemberg also called urban districts, or *Stadtkreise*), cities that are districts in their own right, or local associations of a special kind

(Kommunalverbände besonderer Art), see below. The state Free Hanseatic City of Bremen consists of two urban districts, while Berlin and Hamburg are states and urban districts at the same time.

There are 313 *Landkreise* and 116 *Kreisfreie Städte*, making 429 districts altogether. Each consists of an elected council and an executive, which is chosen either by the council or by the people, depending on the state, the duties of which are comparable to those of a county executive in the United States, supervising local government administration. The *Landkreise* have primary administrative functions in specific areas, such as highways, hospitals, and public utilities.

Local associations of a special kind are an amalgamation of one or more *Landkreise* with one or more *Kreisfreie Städte* to form a replacement of the aforementioned administrative entities at the district level. They are intended to implement simplification of administration at that level. Typically, a district-free city or town and its urban hinterland are grouped into such an association, or *Kommunalverband besonderer Art*. Such an organization requires the issuing of special laws by the governing state, since they are not covered by the normal administrative structure of the respective states.

In 2010 only three *Kommunalverbände besonderer Art* exist.

District of Hanover. Formed in 2001 out of the previous rural district of Hanover and the district-free city of Hanover.

Regionalverband Saarbrücken (district association Saarbrücken). Formed in 2008 out of the predecessor organization *Stadtverband Saarbrücken* (city association Saarbrücken), which was already formed in 1974.

City region of Aachen. Formed in 2009 out of the previous rural district of Aachen and the district-free city of Aachen.

OFFICES (*ÄMTER*)

Ämter ("offices" or "bureaus"): In some states there is an administrative unit between the districts and the municipalities, called *Ämter* (singular *Amt*), *Amtsgemeinden*, *Gemeindeverwaltungsverbände*, *Landgemeinden*, *Verbandsgemeinden*, *Verwaltungsgemeinschaften* or *Kirchspiellandgemeinden*.

MUNICIPALITIES (*GEMEINDEN)*

Municipalities (*Gemeinden*): Every rural district and every Amt is subdivided into municipalities, while every urban district is a municipality in its own right. There are 12,141 municipalities, which are the smallest administrative units in Germany. Cities and towns are municipalities as well, also having city rights or town rights (*Stadtrechte*). Nowadays, this is mostly just the right to be called a city or town. However, in former times there were many other privileges, including the right to impose local taxes or to allow industry only within city limits.

The municipalities are ruled by elected councils and by an executive, the mayor, who is chosen either by the council or directly by the people, depending on the *Bundesland*. The "constitution" for the municipalities is created by the states and is uniform throughout a *Bundesland* (except for Bremen, which allows Bremerhaven to have its own constitution).

The municipalities have two major policy responsibilities. First, they administer programs authorized by the federal or state government. Such programs typically relate to youth, schools, public health, and social assistance. Second, Article 28(2) of the Basic Law guarantees the municipalities "the right to regulate on their own responsibility all the affairs of the local community within the limits set by law." Under this broad statement of competence, local governments can justify a wide range of activities. For instance, many municipalities develop and expand the economic infrastructure of their communities through the development of industrial trading estates.

Local authorities foster cultural activities by supporting local artists, building arts centres, and by holding fairs. Local government also provides public utilities, such as gas and electricity, as well as public transportation. The majority of the funding for municipalities is provided by higher levels of government rather than from taxes raised and collected directly by themselves.

In five of the German states, there are unincorporated areas, in many cases unpopulated forest and mountain areas, but also four Bavarian lakes that are not part of any municipality. As of January 1, 2005, there were 246 such areas, with a total area of 4167.66 km² or 1.2 percent of the total area of Germany. Only four unincorporated areas are populated, with a total population of about 2,000.

DEMOGRAPHICS OF GERMANY

The **demography of the Federal Republic of Germany** is monitored by the "Statistisches Bundesamt" (Federal Statistical Office of Germany). The population of Germany is approximately 81,859,000 (November 30, 2011), making it the 16th most populous country in the world. Germany's population is characterized by zero or declining growth, with an aging population and smaller cohort of youths. The total fertility rate has been rated around 1.4 in 2010 (the highest value since 1990) and has recently even been estimated at 1.6 after accounting for the fact that older women contribute more to the number of births than in previous statistic models, and total fertility rates increased in younger generations. Fertility was closely linked to educational achievement (with the less educated women having more children than the educated ones). Persons who adhere to no religion have fewer children than Christians, and studies also found that among Christians the more conservative ones had more children than the more liberal ones.

The United Nations Population Fund lists Germany as host to the third-highest number of international migrants worldwide. More than 16 million people are of foreign/immigrant descent (first and second generation, including mixed heritage and ethnic German repatriates and their descendants). 96.1% of those reside in western Germany and Berlin. About seven million of them are foreign residents, which is defined as those not having German citizenship. The largest ethnic group of non-German origin are the Turkish. Since the 1960s, West and later reunified Germany has been attracting migrants primarily from Southern and Eastern Europe as well as Turkey, many of whom (or their children) over time acquired German citizenship. While most of these migrations had an economic background, Germany has also been a prime destination for refugees from many developing countries, in part because its constitution long had a clause giving a 'right' to political asylum, but restrictions over the years have since made it less attractive.

Germany has one of the world's highest levels of education, technological development, and economic productivity. Since the end of World War II, the number of students entering universities has more than tripled, and the trade and technical schools are among the world's best. With a per capita income of about $36,850 Purchasing power parity (in 2009), Germany is a broadly middle class society. However there has been a strong increase in the children living in poverty in Germany. While in 1965 one in 75 children was on the welfare rolls in 2007 one in 6 was. Those children live in relative poverty, but not in absolute poverty however. Germans also are very mobile; millions travel abroad each year. The social welfare system provides for universal health care, unemployment compensation, child benefits and other social programmes. Due to Germany's aging population and struggling economy, the welfare system came under a lot of strain in the 1990s. This led the government to adopt a wide-ranging programme of belt-tightening reforms, Agenda 2010, including the labour market reforms known as Hartz I - IV.

About 1.7 million people have left the new federal states since the fall of the Berlin Wall, or 12% of the population, a disproportionately high number of them were women under 35.

After 1990, the total fertility rate (TFR) in the East dropped to 0.772 in 1994. In the following years, it started rising again, surpassing 1.0 in 1997 and 1.3 in 2004, reaching the West's TFR in 2007 (1.37). In 2010, the East's fertility rate (1.459) now clearly exceeds that of the West (1.385), while Germany's overall TFR has risen to 1.393, the highest value since 1990 - which is still far below the natural replacement rate of 2.1 . Since 1989, about 2,000 schools have closed because of a scarcity of children.

In some regions the number of women between the ages of 20 and 30 has dropped by more than 30%. In 2004, in the age group 18-29 (statistically important for starting families) there were only 90 women for every 100 men in the new federal states (including Berlin).

With an estimated more than 81.8 million inhabitants in late 2011, Germany is the most populous country in the European Union and ranks as the 16th largest country in the world in terms of population. Its population density stands at 229.4 inhabitants per square kilometer.

STATES

Germany comprises sixteen states that are collectively referred to as *Länder*. Due to differences in size and population the subdivision of these states varies, especially between city states (*Stadtstaaten*) and states with larger territories (*Flächenländer*). For regional administrative purposes five states, namely Baden-Württemberg, Bavaria, Hesse, North Rhine-Westphalia and Saxony, consist of a total of 22 Government Districts (*Regierungsbezirke*). As of 2009 Germany is divided into 403 districts (*Kreise*) on municipal level, these consist of 301 rural districts and 102 urban districts

State	Capital	Area (km²)	Population
Baden-Württemberg	Stuttgart	35,752	10,717,000
Bavaria	Munich	70,549	12,444,000
Berlin	Berlin	892	3,400,000
Brandenburg	Potsdam	29,477	2,568,000
Bremen	Bremen	404	663,000
Hamburg	Hamburg	755	1,735,000
Hesse	Wiesbaden	21,115	6,098,000
Mecklenburg-Vorpommern	Schwerin	23,174	1,720,000
Lower Saxony	Hanover	47,618	8,001,000
North Rhine-Westphalia	Düsseldorf	34,043	18,075,000
Rhineland-Palatinate	Mainz	19,847	4,061,000

State	Capital	Area (km²)	Population
Saarland	Saarbrücken	2,569	1,056,000
Saxony	Dresden	18,416	4,296,000
Saxony-Anhalt	Magdeburg	20,445	2,494,000
Schleswig-Holstein	Kiel	15,763	2,829,000
Thuringia	Erfurt	16,172	2,355,000

LARGEST CITIES

Rank	City	Pop. 1990	Pop. 2000	Pop. 2009	Pop. 2010	Area [km²]	Density per km²	Growth [%] (2000–2010)	surpassed 100,000	State (Bund
1.	Berlin	3,433,695	3,382,169	3,442,675	3,460,725	887,70	3,899	2.32	1747	Be
2.	Hamburg	1,652,363	1,715,392	1,774,224	1,786,448	755,16	2,366	4.14	1787	Ha
3.	Munich / München	1,229,026	1,210,223	1,330,440	1,353,186	310,69	4,355	11.81	1852	Ba
4.	Cologne / Köln	953,551	962,884	998,105	1,007,119	405,17	2,486	4.59	1852	No Rhine-Westph
5.	Frankfurt am Main	644,865	648,550	671,927	679,664	248,31	2,737	4.80	1875	He
6.	Stuttgart	579,988	583,874	601,646	606,588	207,35	2,925	3.89	1874	Ba Württer
7.	Düsseldorf	575,794	569,364	586,217	588,735	217,22	2,710	3.40	1882	No Rhine-Westph
8.	Dortmund	599,055	588,994	581,308	580,444	280,71	2,068	−1.45	1894	No Rhine-Westph
9.	Essen	626,973	595,243	576,259	574,635	210,32	2,732	−3.46	1896	No Rhine-Westph
10.	Bremen	551,219	539,403	547,685	547,340	325,42	1,682	1.47	1875	Bre
11.	Dresden	490,571	477,807	517,052	523,058	328,31	1,593	9.47	1852	Sa
12.	Leipzig	511,079	493,208	518,862	522,883	297,36	1,758	6.02	1871	Sa

Rank	City	Pop. 1990	Pop. 2000	Pop. 2009	Pop. 2010	Area [km²]	Density per km²	Growth [%] (2000–2010)	surpassed 100,000
13.	Hanover / Hannover	513,010	515,001	520,966	522,686	204,14	2,560	1.49	1875
14.	Nuremberg / Nürnberg	493,692	488,400	503,673	505,664	186,38	2,713	3.53	1881

PRESIDENT OF GERMANY - STRATEGIC INFORMATION

Politics of Germany takes place in a framework of a federal parliamentary representative democratic republic, whereby the Federal Chancellor is the head of government, and of a pluriform multi-party system. Executive power is exercised by the government. Federal legislative power is vested in both the government and the two chambers of parliament, Bundestag and Bundesrat. Since 1949, the party system is dominated by the conservative Christian Democratic Union and the Social Democratic Party of Germany.

The Judiciary of Germany is independent of the executive and the legislature. The political system is laid out in the 1949 constitution, the *Grundgesetz* (Basic Law), which remained in effect with minor amendments after 1990's German Reunification.

Frank-Walter Steinmeier
since 19 March 2017

Style	His Excellency (in international relations only)
Residence	Schloss Bellevue (Berlin) Villa Hammerschmidt (Bonn)
Appointer	Federal Convention
Term length	Five years Renewable once, consecutively
Constituting instrument	Basic Law for the Federal Republic of Germany
Precursor	The Reichspräsident
Formation	24 May 1949
First holder	Theodor Heuss
Website	www.bundespraesident.de

ELECTION OF THE PRESIDENT

The president is elected for a term of five years by secret ballot, without debate, by a specially convened Federal Convention which mirrors the aggregated majority position in the Bundestag (the federal parliament) and in the parliaments of the 16 German states. The convention consists of all Bundestag members, as well as an equal number of electors elected by the state legislatures in proportion to their respective population. Since reunification, all Federal Conventions have had more than 1200 members, as the Bundestag has always had more than 600 since then. It is not required that state electors are chosen from the members of the state legislature; often some prominent citizens are chosen.

FEDERAL CONVENTION

The **Federal Convention**, also known as the **Federal Assembly** (German: *Bundesversammlung*), is a special constitutional body in the political and federal institutional system of Germany, convened solely for the purpose of electing the President of the Federal Republic of Germany (*Bundespräsident*), either every five years or within 30 days of the premature termination of a presidential term. The Federal Convention mirrors the aggregated majority situation of the Bundestag and the parliaments of the 16 German federal states.

The Basic Law mandates that a maximum of three votes can be held. On the first two rounds, a candidate must receive an absolute majority of delegates to be elected. After that, in the third round, a plurality of all delegates voting is sufficient for election to the office of Federal President. Any delegate may nominate candidates; usually, every parliamentary group puts forth candidates, and there may sometimes be consensus candidates who are supported by several of the major parties.

PROCEDURE

Each member of the *Bundesversammlung* may suggest candidates for the office of the Federal President. In practice, however, only the candidates designated in advance by the parliamentary groups are suggested.

The procedure of the election of the *Bundespräsident* consists of a maximum of three secret votes by written ballot. If one of the first two votes ends with an absolute majority for one of the candidates, this candidate is elected immediately. If the first two votes do not lead to an absolute majority, a plurality is sufficient in the third and final vote. According to the *Grundgesetz*, the President is elected without a debate at the Federal Convention. The candidates are usually nominated by one or more parties but do not generally run a campaign. The candidate whose party or parties have the majority in the Bundestag is considered to be the likely winner and, in the main, has achieved the necessary majority – however, the Assembly can be turned around by state delegates (if the Bundestag opposition has done well in state elections), this can indicate the result of an upcoming general election (*"If you can create a president, you can form a government"*). The President of the *Bundestag* closes the session of the *Bundesversammlung* once the elected candidate accepts.

The *Bundesversammlung* is chaired by the President of the Bundestag (or one of the Vice-Presidents, if the President stands as a candidate – as was the case with Karl Carstens in 1979). The *Bundesversammlung* is dissolved once the elected President declares that they accept their election, which decision may be delayed for up to two days (however, no would-be president-elect has ever done so).

MEMBERSHIP

The *Bundesversammlung* includes the entire membership of the *Bundestag*, and an equal number of state delegates elected by the state or 'Länder' parliaments specifically for this purpose, proportional to their population. The Länder representatives are not solely politicians. It is common that the parties nominate several notable people from television, sports, and the music industry. Still, most of the Länder representatives are politicians. Especially those in the state cabinet are often nominated. From the time of their nomination until the closing of the session of the Federal Convention its members enjoy parliamentary immunity with regard to prosecution by public authorities in very much the same way as members of the Bundestag do.

The German constitution, the Basic Law, requires that the convention be convened no later than 30 days before the regular expiration of the sitting president's term or 30 days after a premature expiration of a president's term. The body is convened and chaired by the President of the Bundestag. From 1979 to 2009, all these conventions were held on 23 May, the anniversary of the foundation of the Federal Republic in 1949. However, the two most recent elections before 2017 were held on different dates after the incumbent presidents, Horst Köhler and Christian Wulff, resigned before the end of their terms, in 2010 and 2012 respectively.

In the first two rounds of the election, the candidate who achieves an absolute majority is elected. If, after two votes, no single candidate has received this level of support, in the third and final vote the candidate who wins a plurality of votes cast is elected.

The result of the election is often determined by party politics. In most cases, the candidate of the majority party or coalition in the Bundestag is considered to be the likely winner. However, as the members of the Federal Convention vote by secret ballot and are free to vote against their party's candidate, some presidential elections were considered open or too close to call beforehand because of relatively balanced majority positions or because the governing coalition's parties could not agree on one candidate and endorsed different people, as they did in 1969, when Gustav Heinemann won by only 6 votes on the third ballot. In other cases, elections have turned out to be much closer than expected. For example, in 2010, Wulff was expected to win on the first ballot, as the parties supporting him (CDU, CSU and FDP) had a stable absolute majority in the Federal Convention. Nevertheless, he failed to win a majority in the first and second ballots, while his main opponent Joachim Gauck had an unexpectedly strong showing. In the end Wulff obtained a majority in the third ballot. If the opposition has turned in a strong showing in state elections, it can potentially have enough support to defeat the chancellor's party's candidate; this happened in the elections in 1979 and 2004. For this reason, presidential elections can indicate the result of an upcoming general election. According to a long-standing adage in German politics, "if you can create a President, you can form a government."

Presidential elections Results

Election	Date	Site	Ballots	Winner (endorsing parties)	Electoral votes (percentage)	Runner-up (endorsing parties)	Electoral Votes (percentage)
16th Federal Convention	12 February 2017	Berlin	1	Frank-Walter Steinmeier (SPD, CDU, CSU, Alliance 90/Greens, FDP, SSW)	931 (74.3%)	Christoph Butterwegge (The Left)	128 (10.2%)

governing parties in bold

OATH

On taking office the president must take the following oath, stipulated by Article 56 of the Basic Law, in a joint session of the Bundestag and the Bundesrat (it is the only event that demands such a joint session constitutionally). They are permitted to omit the religious references if so desired.

> I swear that I will dedicate my efforts to the well-being of the German people, enhance their benefits, avert harm from them, uphold and defend the Constitution and the statutes of the Federation, fulfil my duties conscientiously, and do justice to all. (So help me God.)

As German constitutional law does not consider oaths of office as *constitutive* but only as *affirmative*, the president does not have to take the oath at the moment of entering office in order to be able to execute the powers of the office. The oath is usually administered during the first weeks of a president's term on a date convenient for a joint session of the Bundestag and the Bundesrat. Nevertheless, a president persistently refusing to take the oath could face an impeachment. If a president is re-elected for a second term, they do not take the oath again.

QUALIFICATIONS

The office of president is open to all Germans who are entitled to vote in Bundestag elections and have reached the age of 40, but no one may serve more than two consecutive five-year terms. As yet (2017), only four presidents (Heuss, Lübke, von Weizsäcker and Köhler) have been elected for a second term and only two of them (Heuss and von Weizsäcker) finished those terms, while Lübke and Köhler resigned during their second term. The president must not be a member of the federal government or of a legislature at either the federal or state level.

THE ROLE OF THE FEDERAL PRESIDENT

The Basic Law devotes an entire chapter to the role of the Federal President but the duties of the "first man of the state" both at home and abroad go far beyond those bestowed upon him by the constitution.

The titles "supreme federal notary", "first representative of the State" and "figure of integration" all describe aspects of the role of the Federal President. Consult this heading to find out more.

OFFICIAL FUNCTIONS

FORMING GOVERNMENT/APPOINTING, DISMISSING

In accordance with the **Basic Law** the Federal President is involved in the forming of the government as he proposes the Federal Chancellor for election (Article 63 (1) of the Basic Law) and appoints the person elected (Art. 63 (2) of the Basic Law).

The Federal Ministers are also appointed and dismissed by him upon the proposal of the Federal Chancellor (Art. 64 (1) of the Basic Law). Furthermore he appoints and dismisses federal judges, federal civil servants, and commissioned and non-commissioned officers, except as may otherwise be provided by a law (Art. 60 (1) of the Basic Law). In many cases it is incumbent upon him to appoint committees and other bodies - often upon the proposal of the Federal Government or other state agencies (for example appointing the members of the **German Council of Economic Experts**, nominating the board of the **President Friedrich Ebert Memorial**).

PROMULGATING LAWS

After countersigning by the relevant Federal Minister and the Federal Chancellor, the federal laws are signed by the Federal President (promulgation).
Before doing so he has to check that they have been adopted in line with the provisions of the Basic Law. Practice and prevailing opinion mean this procedure has formal aspects (procedural provisions in the Basic Law) and material aspects (fundamental rights, definition of the aims of the state, the right of organization of the state). To date there have been eight occasions on which a Federal President has declined to promulgate a law.

After promulgation by the Federal President, the laws are published in the Federal Law Gazette (Art. 82 (1) of the Basic Law).

The Federal President decides the day on which the election to the German Bundestag will be held (Art. 16 sentence 1 of the Federal Electoral Law).

He approves the rules of procedure of the **Federal Government** and possible amendments (Art. 65 sentence 4 of the Basic Law). Furthermore he is responsible for promulgating the determination of the Bundestag or the Joint Committee of the **Bundestag** with the consent of the **Bundesrat** that the state of defence has begun or been terminated. (Art. 115a (3), Art. 115 l (2) of the Basic Law).

POWER TO PARDON

According to Article 60 (2) of the Basic Law the Federal President exercises the power to pardon. This means he has the authority to revoke or commute penal or disciplinary sentences in individual cases.

The Federal President cannot, however, issue an amnesty waiving or commuting sentences for a whole category of offences. That requires a law enacted by the German Bundestag in conjunction with the Bundesrat.

Due to the federal structure of Germany the Federal President is only responsible for dealing with certain criminal matters (e.g. espionage and terrorism) and disciplinary proceedings against

federal civil servants, federal judges and soldiers.
For other offences, the power to pardon lies with the federal Land which exercises jurisdiction.

REPRESENTING AND INTEGRATING

REPRESENTING THE STATE

As head of state, the Federal President is particularly well placed to embody the state, represent it and integrate the various social groups within it. All activities in this field, above all decisions on designating state symbols, fulfilling representational duties, becoming a patron of organizations, delivering addresses, making speeches and ordering official ceremonies and state funerals can be summarized under the heading representing the state. This is a very broad field for which there is often no legal basis.
National anthem

NATIONAL ANTHEM

The Federal President designates state symbols in so far as the legislator does not assume the role (cf. Art. 22 of the Basic Law: the federal flag shall be black, red and gold). Alongside the federal flag, the national anthem is the most well-known state symbol. Back in 1922 Friedrich Ebert, at that time President of the Reich, by decree declared the "Song of the Germans" written in 1841 by August-Heinrich Hofmann von Fallersleben for Haydn's Austrian Imperial Anthem, to be the German national anthem.

In 1952 the then Federal President Theodor Heuss decided to take it over as the national anthem of the Federal Republic of Germany, but instructed that only the third stanza be sung on state occasions. After German reunification President von Weizsäcker, in an exchange of letters on the matter with the Chancellor, Helmut Kohl, declared the third stanza to be the national anthem of the German people.

FLAGS, COATS OF ARMS, UNIFORMS

Flags, coats of arms, uniforms and judges' robes are also state symbols. The Federal President has given relevant instructions published in the Federal Law Gazette.

OFFICIAL CEREMONIES, STATE FUNERALS

The Federal President can order a state funeral or an official ceremony to be held on the death of a public figure who has rendered distinguished services to Germany. A state funeral usually includes a military and a religious ceremony. Official ceremonies are political acts that take place in a ceremonial setting and cannot simply be ordered to pay tribute to someone who has passed away. On the occasion of German reunification on 3 October 1990 the then Federal President, Richard von Weizsäcker, ordered an official ceremony to take place at the Berlin Philharmonic.

OTHER WAYS OF REPRESENTING AND INTEGRATING

Apart from such formal occasions, the Federal President represents our country in many different ways and at many different events.

The President embodies the state every time he appears in public, every time he participates in an event, assumes a patronage, makes a speech, conveys congratulations, takes part in a tour or a wide range of other activities. He thus sets an example of recognition, goodwill or particular support.

Nevertheless there is a limit to what events the Federal President can take part in. They have to be of national relevance and special significance.

SPEECHES AND ADDRESSES

The written and spoken word is one of the most effective ways the Federal President has to act politically.
Through his speeches he can focus the attention of the public as well as government, party and community leaders on particular issues and problems in political life and society as a whole, he can generate debate and encourage new ideas.

LETTERS AND REQUESTS

Many people write to the Federal President with requests, questions or complaints. Their letters testify to the great trust people place in him to help with their problems and concerns. Given the constitutional limits to his competences and scope for action, however, people often expect more than the Federal President can deliver.

All letters addressed to the Federal President are attentively read and any points raised considered on their merits. Should such action be justified, the Federal President will pursue all avenues open to him to help.

Depending on the circumstances, the Federal President will take the problem up with the relevant federal, Land or municipal authorities - particularly the Social Security Offices - as well as charity or other organizations.

Often the mere fact that the Federal President himself or an aide acting on his instructions has asked the relevant officials for information about a particular case is sufficient to ensure a citizen's problem is taken seriously or gets the attention it deserves.

PATRONAGE AND SUPPORT

In agreeing to become a patron, the Federal President as head of state is expressing the state's special interest in a particular organization, event or initiative and highlighting its importance.
The Federal President can only become a patron if the relevant organization or event has a beneficial impact on the whole country and stands on a secure legal, administrative and financial footing.

By reason of his constitutional position, the Federal President will normally be the sole patron of an organization or event. Only in conjunction with another head of state can he be a joint patron. The decision to become a patron is always the personal decision of the Federal President and valid only for his own term of office. He is in no way bound by his predecessors' decisions, nor can he influence the decisions of his successors in this respect.

THE ORDRE POUR LE MERITE FOR SCIENCES AND THE ARTS HISTORY

The Ordre Pour le mérite for Sciences and the Arts was instituted by King Frederick William IV of Prussia in 1842 to honour services to science and the arts.

The first Chancellor of the Order was Alexander von Humboldt. The adoption of the 1919 Weimar constitution abolishing all orders and decorations threatened the Order's existence. Under its Chancellor Adolf von Harnack the Order in 1922 reconstituted itself by decision of its Chapter as a "free association of outstanding scholars and artists", a decision approved by Prussia in 1924. In 1952 at the initiative of Theodor Heuss the Order was once again reconstituted as a free self-renewing community under the protection of the Federal President.

STATUTES AND STRUCTURE

The task the Order has set itself is not to pursue some common scientific or artistic goal but to elect from among distinguished scientists and artists "whose work has earned them an outstanding reputation" those who, in the spirit and tradition of the Order, are worthy of such a high honour.

The Chapter of the Order may not exceed 40 (German) members elected for life and drawn equally from the humanities, science and the fine arts. Following the death of a member, a new member is elected. At the end of the Second World War there were only three surviving members of the Order, as no elections were held during the period of National Socialism.
Also foreign nationals may be elected to the Order, although their number should not exceed that of the German members.

Members of the Order have included such outstanding figures as Professor Golo Mann, Professor Theodor Eschenburg, Professor Emil Schuhmacher and Andrzej Szczypiorski.

FOUNDATIONS

Many people are prompted by a sense of civic responsibility to take on tasks they believe the state does not or cannot perform or cannot perform satisfactorily. Establishing a foundation is one way for people to assume such responsibility in the service of a common cause.

By tradition the Federal President promotes the work of a large number of foundations in Germany by becoming their patron, meeting people working on their behalf or supporting specific foundation projects. He encourages representatives of such foundations to brief him personally on the work done by their organizations.

People prompted to set up foundations are people who want to get things moving. Such civic commitment is no substitute for action by the state and nor should it be. It does, however, in important ways complement such action, since both for financial reasons and by its very nature there are limits to what the state can do.

There exist in Germany both private and public foundations as well as foundations that have close links with the political parties.

ANNIVERSARIES

The Federal President congratulates both Germans and foreigners living in Germany on reaching their centenary as well as on their 105th and all following birthdays. He congratulates couples on their 65th, 70th and 75th wedding anniversaries.

To be able to offer his congratulations, the Federal President has to rely on the local authorities to forward information on upcoming birthdays and wedding anniversaries to the Office of the Federal President. Usually the Federal President's congratulations are delivered by the local mayor.

HONORARY GODPARENTHOOD

At the parents' request, the Federal President may act as godfather to a family's seventh or any subsequent child but only to one child in the family. To submit such a request, the family must have at least seven living children, including adopted children, who share one or both parents. The godchild must be German as defined by Article 116(1) of the Basic Law.

The institution of honorary godparent is primarily symbolic and not to be compared with the godparenthood assumed at a child's christening. In becoming a child's godparent, the Federal President is highlighting the state's special responsibility for the welfare of large families as well as the importance of the family and children to the community as a whole. The intention is also to focus attention on the problems of large families - finding suitable accommodation, for instance - and encourage cities and local communities to offer help and support. Another purpose is to raise the social status of families with a large number of children.

Parental requests for the Federal President to become a child's godfather must be submitted to the Office of the Federal President via the local authority. If the requirements for honorary godparenthood are met, the Federal President issues a certificate of acceptance which is presented to the parents along with a gift (currently Euro 500) by a representative of the local authority.

Since 1949 the Federal Presidents have become godfather to some 79.825 children (31.12.2016).

INTERNATIONAL REPRESENTATION

Under Article 59 (1) of the Basic Law, the Federal President represents the Federal Republic of Germany in matters of international law, concludes treaties with foreign states on its behalf, accredits German diplomats posted abroad and receives all foreign ambassadors to Germany.

Many challenges of the 21st century can only be mastered through international cooperation. The Federal President uses his contacts abroad and with international institutions to support the efforts to resolve global problems. These include the preservation of peace, the fight against terrorism, protection of the environment and the climate, financial and monetary issues, energy supply and international trade.

The Federal President's activities in the foreign policy realm often give rise to projects and initiatives for which he assumes the patronage. Examples of this are the "Potsdam Encounters" between Germany and Russia as well as German-Israeli and German-African youth exchange programmes.

The dialogue among cultures and religions is close to the Federal President's heart. Particularly in the age of global communications, the exchange among cultures as well as different religious and ideological groups is especially vital for removing reservations and fostering mutual understanding.

The Federal President cultivates very close relations with European neighbours, as well as the unique relationship with Israel. He wants Europe to promote its values and convictions with one voice and boost global cooperation. To this end, he focuses on the common ground among countries at different stages of development and regards development policy as a long-term commitment.

REPRESENTING GERMANY IN MATTERS OF INTERNATIONAL LAW

The first sentence of Article 59 (1) of the Basic Law grants the Federal President the authority to represent the Federal Republic of Germany in matters of international law. The Federal President thus has sole responsibility to act on behalf of the Federal Republic of Germany in the sphere of international law. A distinction has to be made here from the conduct of foreign policy, which is largely the task of the Federal Government. That the Federal President acts for the Federal Republic in matters of international law is in keeping with the German constitutional tradition and international state practice, under which, in most cases, heads of state have the authority to represent their state in this realm.

Representing Germany in matters of international law means acting on behalf of state organs or the state as a whole. Under the first sentence of Article 59 (1) of the Basic Law, therefore, the Federal President officially represents Germany in the international sphere. Although other constitutional organs can be active in the foreign policy field, their actions must either be authorized by the Federal President or relate to tasks formally anchored in the Basic Law.

Alongside the examples referred to in the second and third sentences of Article 59 (1) of the Basic Law, these include unilateral actions of relevance to international law – for instance, the termination of agreements, protests or renunciations, as well as speeches abroad, messages, receiving state guests and state visits to other countries.

The official recognition of foreign states is also granted by the Federal President. However, the political decision on recognition is made by the Federal Government.

INTERNATIONAL TREATIES

Pursuant to Article 59 (1), second sentence, of the Basic Law, the Federal President concludes treaties with foreign states on behalf of Germany.

However, he usually grants the requisite full powers to the Minister for Foreign Affairs, a State Secretary or a German Ambassador so that they may act on his behalf.

Treaties by which the Federal Republic of Germany enters into a binding agreement with another state must be ratified by the head of state. Ratification denotes the formal declaration of approval by the head of state that makes a treaty binding on the Federal Republic of Germany. This is given in an "instrument of ratification" issued by the Federal President.

The Federal President is also responsible for declaring Germany's recognition of foreign states. However, the political decision on whether to recognize a state or not is made by the Federal Government.

Treaties between states are concluded in the name of the President of the Federal Republic of Germany. In certain cases the Federal Government or federal ministries may conclude agreements that are binding under international law – intergovernmental or interministerial agreements, for example – but they do so on the basis of powers delegated by the Federal President. Where the Federal President does not act himself, the Federal Minister for Foreign Affairs is responsible for supervising and coordinating the conclusion of such agreements.

STATE VISITS

State visits by the Federal President abroad and incoming state visits by foreign Heads of State to Germany express the quality of bilateral relations and provide an opportunity to enhance cooperation. As a rule, such visits take place on an alternating schedule and at intervals of several years. Despite the permanent international presence of the Federal Republic of Germany through its embassies abroad and the numerous bilateral and multilateral conferences which the German Government takes part in, personal encounters between Heads of State continue to hold a special significance.

When he makes a state visit the Federal President is accompanied by representatives of the political and business spheres as well as prominent academic and cultural figures. A press delegation reports back to Germany.

The entire spectrum of the two countries' relations features on the agenda of talks between Heads of State. The conversation might address coordinating policy, explaining German interests, or clearing up any issues clouding the bilateral relationship. Depending on the country in question, the visit might focus on political or economic topics or human rights.

Along with state visits the Federal President also makes official visits and working visits abroad, which entail less elaborate protocol arrangements.

APPOINTMENT OF GERMAN AMBASSADORS

A German Ambassador is the personal representative of the Federal President to the head of state of the receiving country. There are several steps to be taken before an Ambassador can take up his or her duties:

The initial decision on an ambassadorial appointment is taken by the Federal Cabinet following a recommendation by the Federal Foreign Office.

The Federal President is asked to approve the decision.

The Federal Foreign Office asks the country in question whether it is willing to accept the proposed appointment, i.e. whether it will grant the "agrément".

Once the agrément has been issued, the Federal President appoints the person Ambassador and signs a Letter of Credence to that effect.

The Ambassador presents his or her Letter of Credence to the head of state of the receiving country. This act, known as accreditation, allows the new Ambassador to begin work in the receiving country.

ACCREDITATION OF FOREIGN AMBASSADORS

When a country wishes to appoint a person ambassador to the Federal Republic of Germany, the same procedure applies as when Germany appoints an ambassador abroad. To establish whether the Federal Republic approves the appointment, the country requests the Federal President's agrément.

For the act of accreditation in Germany, the ambassador-designate is greeted in front of the Federal President's official residence with military honours. He or she then signs the visitors book in the gallery and proceeds, accompanied by several high-ranking members of the embassy, to the Langhanssaal at Schloss Bellevue, where he or she presents his or her Letter of Credence to the Federal President and the outgoing ambassador's Letter of Recall.

The new ambassador and the Federal President then withdraw for a first talk, which not only gives them the opportunity to get to know one another but often also to convey political messages. Leave is taken of the ambassador again with military honours, this time including the hoisting of his or her country's national flag to show that the ambassador is now legally entitled to perform his or her duties. The ambassador is driven to and from the Federal President's official residence in a presidential limousine with an escort of honour of 5 police motor-cycles.

HONOURS AND DECORATIONS

Honouring individuals who have rendered distinguished services to the nation has traditionally been one of the head of state's duties. In the Federal Republic of Germany, as in nearly all countries in the world, honours and decorations are awarded as a way of paying public tribute to an outstanding individual. The Federal President awards

the Order of Merit of the Federal Republic of Germany

the Silver Laurel Leaf

other decorations.

The Federal President also has supreme authority in all matters concerning honours and decorations in the Federal Republic of Germany.
He may, for instance, grant a German citizen permission to accept and wear foreign honours and decorations or to accept foreign titles. In carrying out this aspect of his duties the Federal President is assisted by the Honours and Decorations Chancellery in the Office of the Federal President, which provides relevant information and in cooperation with the State and Senate Chancelleries of the 16 Federal Länder prepares and implements the Federal President's decisions in this area.

GERMAN POLITICAL AND GOVERNMENT SYSTEM - STARTEGC INFORMATION AND DEVELOPMENTS

GERMAN PARLIAMENT - BUNDESTAG

The **Bundestag** is the German federal parliament. It can be compared to the lower house of parliament along the lines of the United States House of Representatives, the Irish Dáil Éireann or the House of Commons of the United Kingdom, with the Bundesrat, though a separate institution, having a similar role to the upper house of a bicameral parliament.

The Bundestag was established by chapter III of the Basic Law for the Federal Republic of Germany (Constitution) in 1949 as one of the legislative bodies of Germany and thus the historical successor to the earlier Reichstag.

Since 1999 it has met in the Reichstag Building in Berlin. Wolfgang Schäuble is the current President of the Bundestag. Members of the Bundestag (*Mitglieder des Bundestages*) are usually elected every four years by all adult German citizens in a mixed system of constituency voting and list voting. The constitutional minimum number of seats is 598; with overhang and leveling seats there are currently 709 seats. The Election Day can be called earlier than four years after the last if the Federal Chancellor (*Bundeskanzler*) loses a vote of confidence and asks the Federal President (*Bundespräsident*) to dissolve the Bundestag in order to hold new general elections.

In the 19th century the name Bundestag was the unofficial designation for the assembly of the sovereigns and mayors of the Monarchies and Free Cities which formed the German Confederation (1815–1866). Its seat was in the Free City of Frankfurt on the Main.

Established	1949
Preceded by	Reichstag 1933–1945 Volkskammer (East Germany) 1949–1990
	Leadership
President of the Bundestag	Wolfgang Schäuble, CDU Since 24 October 2017
Vice Presidents of the Bundestag	Thomas Oppermann, SPD Since 24 October 2017
	Hans-Peter Friedrich, CSU Since 24 October 2017
	Vacant, AfD
	Wolfgang Kubicki, FDP Since 24 October 2017
	Petra Pau, The Left Since 7 April 2006
	Claudia Roth, Alliance 90/The Greens Since 22 October 2013

	Structure
Seats	709
Political groups	Government (398) Union (246) CDU (200) CSU (46) SPD (152) Opposition parties (311) AfD (92) FDP (80) The Left (69) The Greens (67) Non-inscrits (3)
	Elections
Voting system	Mixed-member proportional representation (MMP)
Last election	24 September 2017

TASKS

Together with the Bundesrat, the Bundestag is the legislative branch of the German political system.

Although most legislation is initiated by the executive branch, the Bundestag considers the legislative function its most important responsibility, concentrating much of its energy on assessing and amending the government's legislative program. The committees (see below) play a prominent role in this process. Plenary sessions provide a forum for members to engage in public debate on legislative issues before them, but they tend to be well attended only when significant legislation is being considered.

The Bundestag members are the only federal officials directly elected by the public; the Bundestag in turn elects the Chancellor and, in addition, exercises oversight of the executive branch on issues of both substantive policy and routine administration. This check on executive power can be employed through binding legislation, public debates on government policy, investigations, and direct questioning of the chancellor or cabinet officials. For example, the Bundestag can conduct a question hour *(Fragestunde),* in which a government representative responds to a previously submitted written question from a member. Members can ask related questions during the question hour. The questions can concern anything from a major policy issue to a specific constituent's problem. Use of the question hour has increased markedly over the past forty years, with more than 20,000 questions being posed during the 1987-90 term. Understandably, the opposition parties are active in exercising the parliamentary right to scrutinize government actions.

Constituent service does also take place in the form of the Petition Committee. In 2004, the Petition Committee received over 18,000 complaints from citizens and was able to negotiate a mutually satisfactory solution to more than half of them. In 2005, as a pilot of the potential of internet petitions, a version of e-Petitioner was produced for the Bundestag. This was a collaborative project involving The Scottish Parliament, International Teledemocracy Centre and the Bundestag 'Online Services Department'. The system was formally launched on 1 September 2005, and in 2008 the Bundestag moved to a new system based on its evaluation.

ELECTION

The Bundestag is elected for four years, and new elections must be held between 46 and 48 months after the beginning of its electoral term. Unless the Bundestag is dissolved prematurely, its term ends when the next Bundestag convenes, which must occur within 30 days of the election. Prior to 1976, there could be a period where one Bundestag had been dissolved and the next Bundestag could not be convened; during this period, the rights of the Bundestag were exercised by a so-called "Permanent Committee".

Members serve four-year terms, with elections held every four years, or earlier in the relatively rare case that the Bundestag is dissolved prematurely by the president. The Bundestag can be dissolved by the president on the recommendation of the chancellor if the latter has lost a vote of confidence in the Bundestag, if the recommendation is made and accepted before the Bundestag acts to elect a new Chancellor. This has happened three times: 1972 under Chancellor Willy Brandt, 1983 under Chancellor Helmut Kohl and 2005 under Chancellor Gerhard Schröder. The procedures for these situations are governed by Articles 67 and 68 of the Basic Law of the Federal Republic of Germany. The Law regarding the election procedure itself is the Federal Election Act 1956 (Bundeswahlgesetz/BWahlG)

All candidates must be at least eighteen years old; there are no term limits. The election uses the MMP electoral system. In addition, the Bundestag has a minimum threshold of either 5% of the national party vote or three (directly elected) constituency representatives for a party to gain additional representation through the system of proportional representation. Thus, small minority parties cannot easily enter the Bundestag and prevent the formation of stable majority governments as they could under the Weimar constitution. The most recent election, the German federal election, 2017, was held on 24 September 2017.

DISTRIBUTION OF SEATS IN THE BUNDESTAG

Accordingly, each voter has two votes in the elections to the Bundestag. The first vote, allowing voters to elect their local representatives to the Bundestag, decides which candidates are sent to Parliament from the constituencies.

The second vote is cast for a party list; it determines the relative strengths of the parties represented in the Bundestag.

At least 598 Members of the Bundestag are elected in this way. Parties that gain more than 5% of the second votes or win at least 3 direct mandates are allocated seats in the Bundestag in proportion to the number of votes it has received (d'Hondt method until 1987, largest remainder method until the 2005 election, now Sainte-Laguë method).

In addition to this, there are certain circumstances in which some candidates win what are known as overhang seats when the seats are being distributed. If a party has gained more direct mandates in a Land than it is entitled to according to the results of the second vote, it does not forfeit these mandates because all directly elected candidates are guaranteed a seat in the Bundestag. The other parties are then compensated by getting additional seats as well, the *balance seats*, so proportionality is preserved.

ELECTION RESULT

The last Federal elections were held on Sunday, 24 September 2017, to elect the members of the 19th Bundestag.

The election saw the CDU/CSU win 33% of the vote, a drop of more than 8% and its lowest share of the vote since 1949, while the SPD achieved its worst result since the Second World War with just 20% of the vote. Alternative for Germany (AfD)—which was previously unrepresented in the Bundestag—became the third party in the Bundestag with 12.6% of the vote and a plurality of the vote in Saxony. No party won an outright majority in any state, including Bavaria, where the CSU often wins majorities and won a majority of the vote in 2013.

Party	Constituency			Party list			Total seats	+/–
	Votes	%	Seats	Votes	%	Seats		
Christian Democratic Union (CDU)	14,030,751	30.2	185	12,447,656	26.8	15	200	−55
Social Democratic Party (SPD)	11,429,231	24.6	59	9,539,381	20.5	94	153	−40
Alternative for Germany (AfD)	5,317,499	11.5	3	5,878,115	12.6	91	94	+94
Free Democratic Party (FDP)	3,249,238	7.0	0	4,999,449	10.7	80	80	+80
The Left (DIE LINKE)	3,966,637	8.6	5	4,297,270	9.2	64	69	+5
Alliance 90/The Greens (GRÜNE)	3,717,922	8.0	1	4,158,400	8.9	66	67	+4
Christian Social Union in Bavaria (CSU)	3,255,487	7.0	46	2,869,688	6.2	0	46	−10
Free Voters	589,056	1.3	0	463,292	1.0	0	0	0
Die PARTEI	245,659	0.5	0	454,349	1.0	0	0	0
Human Environment Animal Protection	22,917	0.0	0	374,179	0.8	0	0	0
National Democratic Party	45,169	0.1	0	176,020	0.4	0	0	0
Pirate Party Germany	93,196	0.2	0	173,476	0.4	0	0	0
Ecological Democratic Party	166,228	0.4	0	144,809	0.3	0	0	0
Basic Income Alliance	–	–	–	97,539	0.2	0	0	New
V-Partei[3]	1,201	0.0	0	64,073	0.1	0	0	New
German Centre	–	–	–	63,203	0.1	0	0	New
Democracy in Motion	–	–	–	60,914	0.1	0	0	New
Bavaria Party	62,622	0.1	0	58,037	0.1	0	0	0
AD-DEMOCRATS	–	–	–	41,251	0.1	0	0	New
Animal Protection Alliance	6,114	0.0	0	32,221	0.1	0	0	New
Marxist–Leninist Party of Germany	35,760	0.1	0	29,785	0.1	0	0	0

Healthresearch	1,537	0.0	0	23,404	0.1	0	0	New
German Communist Party	7,517	0.0	0	11,558	0.0	0	0	New
Human World	2,205	0.0	0	11,661	0.0	0	0	New
The Greys	4,300	0.0	0	10,009	0.0	0	0	New
Bürgerrechtsbewegung Solidarität	15,960	0.0	0	6,693	0.0	0	0	0
The Humanists	–	–	–	5,991	0.0	0	0	New
Magdeburger Garden Party	2,570	0.0	0	5,617	0.0	0	0	New
Alliance for Germany	6,316	0.0	0	9,631	0.0	0	0	0
you.	772	0.0	0	3,032	0.0	0	0	New
The Right	1,142	0.0	0	2,054	0.0	0	0	New
Socialist Equality Party	903	0.0	0	1,291	0.0	0	0	0
Bergpartei, die "ÜberPartei"	672	0.0	0	911	0.0	0	0	New
Party of Reason	242	0.0	0	533	0.0	0	0	0
The Violets – for Spiritual Politics	2,176	0.0	0	–	–	–	0	0
Alliance C	1,717	0.0	0	–	–	–	0	New
New Liberals	884	0.0	0	–	–	–	0	New
The Union	371	0.0	0	–	–	–	0	New
Family Party	506	0.0	0	–	–	–	0	0
The Women	439	0.0	0	–	–	–	0	New
Renter's Party	1,352	0.0	0	–	–	–	0	New
Others	100,889	0.2	0	–	–	–	0	–
Independents	2,458	0.0	0	–	–	–	0	0
Invalid/blank votes	586,726	–	–	460,849	–	–	–	–
Total	46,976,341	100	299	46,976,341	100	410	709	+78

ORGANISATION

PARLIAMENTARY GROUPS

The most important organisational structures within the Bundestag are parliamentary groups (*Fraktionen*; sing. *Fraktion*), which are traditionally formed by political parties who win at least 5% of the "second vote." The CDU and CSU have always formed a single united *Fraktion*. The size of a party's *Fraktion* determines the extent of its representation on legislative committees, the time slots allotted for speaking, the number of committee chairs it can hold, and its representation in executive bodies of the Bundestag. The *Fraktionen,* not the members, receive the bulk of government funding for legislative and administrative activities.

The leadership of each *Fraktion* consists of a parliamentary party leader, several deputy leaders, and an executive committee. The leadership's major responsibilities are to represent the *Fraktion,* enforce party discipline, and orchestrate the party's parliamentary activities. The members of each *Fraktion* are distributed among working groups focused on specific policy-related topics such as social policy, economics, and foreign policy. The *Fraktion* meets every Tuesday afternoon in the weeks in which the Bundestag is in session to consider legislation before the Bundestag and formulate the party's position on it.

Parties that do not cross the 5% threshold but win at least three seats by direct elections (i.e. which have at least three MPs representing a constituency seat) can be granted the status of a *group* in the Bundestag. This applied to the Party of Democratic Socialism (PDS) from 1990-1998. This status entails some privileges which are in general less than those of a *Fraktion.* In the current Bundestag, there are no such groups (the PDS had only two constituency MPs in parliament until 2005 and could thus not even considered a group anymore; the party—now The Left—has held full *Fraktion* status in the Bundestag since 2005).

Executive bodies

The Bundestag's executive bodies include the Council of Elders and the Presidium. The council consists of the Bundestag leadership, together with the most senior representatives of each *fraktion*, with the number of these representatives tied to the strength of the Parliamentary groups in the chamber. The council is the coordination hub, determining the daily legislative agenda and assigning committee chairpersons based on Parliamentary group representation. The council also serves as an important forum for interparty negotiations on specific legislation and procedural issues. The Presidium is responsible for the routine administration of the Bundestag, including its clerical and research activities. It consists of the chamber's president (usually elected from the largest *fraktion*) and vice presidents (one from each *fraktion*).

Committees

Most of the legislative work in the Bundestag is the product of standing committees, which exist largely unchanged throughout one legislative period. The number of committees approximates the number of federal ministries, and the titles of each are roughly similar (e.g., defense, agriculture, and labor). There are, as of the current eighteenth Bundestag, 23 standing committees. The distribution of committee chairs and the membership of each committee reflect the relative strength of the various Parliamentary groups in the chamber. In the current eighteenth Bundestag, the CDU/CSU chaired twelve committees, the SPD seven, The Left (Die Linke) two, and the Greens (Bündnis 90/Die Grünen), two. Members of the opposition party can chair a significant number of standing committees (e.g. The budget committee is always chaired by the biggest opposition party). These committees have either a small staff or no staff at all.

PRINCIPLE OF DISCONTINUATION

As is the case with some other parliaments, the Bundestag is subject to the *principle of discontinuation*, meaning that a newly elected Bundestag is legally regarded to be a body and entity completely different from the previous Bundestag. This leads to the result, that any motion, application or action submitted to the previous Bundestag, e.g. a bill referred to the Bundestag by the Federal Government, is regarded as void by non-decision (German terminology: "*Die Sache fällt der Diskontinuität anheim*"). Thus any bill that has not been decided upon by the beginning of the new electoral period must be brought up by the government again, if it aims to uphold the motion, this procedure in effect delaying the passage of the bill. Furthermore, any newly elected Bundestag will have to freshly decide on the rules of procedure (*Geschäftsordnung*), which is done by a formal decision of taking over such rules from the preceding *Bundestag* by reference.

Any Bundestag is considered dissolved only once a newly elected Bundestag has actually gathered in order to constitute itself (Article 39 sec. 1 sentence 2 of the Basic Law), which has to happen within 30 days of its election (Article 39 sec. 2 of the Basic Law). Thus, it may happen (and has happened) that the old Bundestag gathers and makes decisions even after the election of a new Bundestag that has not gathered in order to constitute itself. For example, elections to the 16th Bundestag took place on 18 September 2005, but the 15th Bundestag still convened after election day to make some decisions on German military engagement abroad, and was entitled to do so, as the newly elected 16th Bundestag did not convene for the first time until 18 October 2005

LEVELS OF THE EXECUTIVE GOVERNMENT -BASIC INFOPRMATION

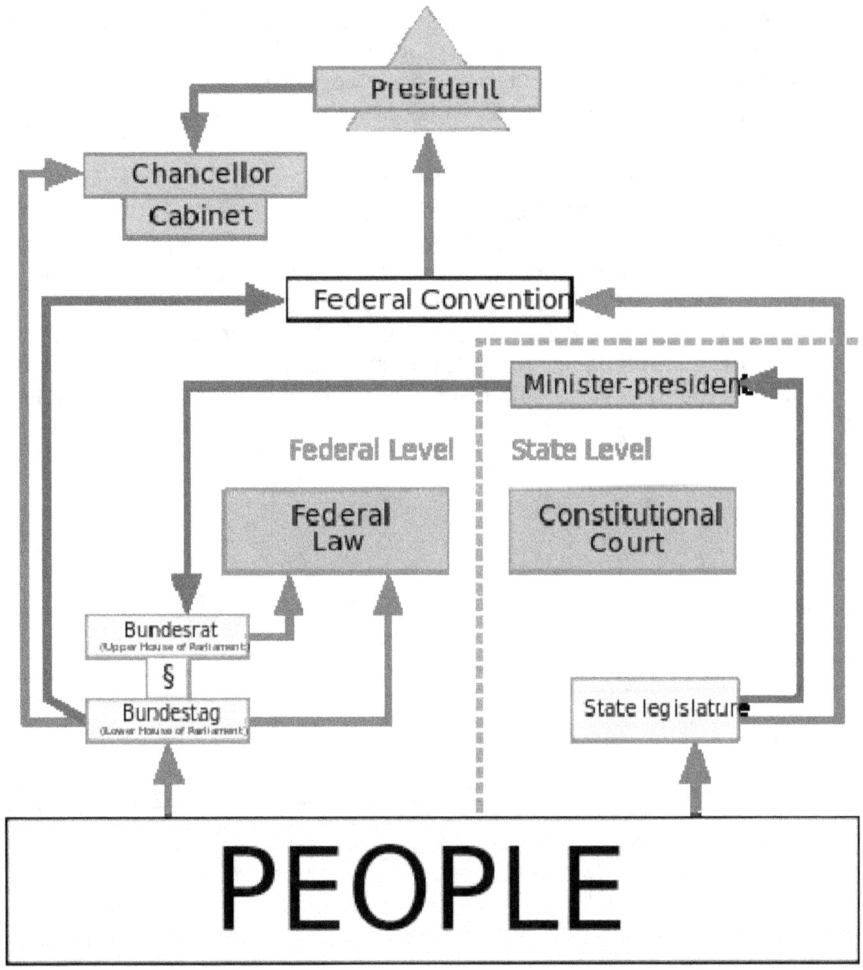

Germany is a federal parliamentary democracy governed under the *Basic Law for the Federal Republic of Germany* ("*Basic Law*"), the *Constitution* of Germany. The *Basic Law* consists of 11 chapters which set out the rights of the German people and outline in considerable detail the political and legal system of Germany. In particular, the President is the head of state and the Federal Chancellor the head of government. The *Basic Law* also enshrines the principle of the tripartition of powers into the Executive, Legislative and Judicial Branches.

EXECUTIVE BRANCH

1 In Germany, executive power is vested in the Cabinet formed by the Federal Chancellor [1] and other Ministers. The President only holds a ceremonial role with limited reserve powers. For example, he or she can dissolve the Parliament if the Federal Chancellor loses a motion of confidence and asks the President to do so.

THE PRESIDENT

2.2 Being the head of state, the President is empowered, among other things, to:

(a) propose a candidate to the Bundestag (lower House of the German Parliament) for the office of Federal Chancellor;

1 In Germany, the Federal Chancellor is the head of government and equivalent to the Prime Minister in many other countries.

(b) appoint and dismiss the Federal Chancellor, other Ministers and Federal judges;

(c) dissolve the Bundestag upon the request from the Federal Chancellor if the Bundestag are not supportive of the Federal Chancellor's policies through the vote of confidence;

(d) promulgate legislation that has been passed by the Legislative Branch;

(e) represent Germany both at home and abroad, accredit and receive envoys, and conclude treaties with foreign states; and

(f) pardon individual offenders and award honours on behalf of Germany.

3 The President is indirectly elected for a five-year term, renewable once, by the Federal Convention established solely for the presidential election. The Federal Convention is made up of all Members of the Bundestag and an equal number of representatives elected by the state legislatures. [2] The President is elected by secret ballot without any prior debate. If none of the candidates receives an absolute majority (i.e. more than half of the votes) in the first and second rounds of voting, a third round will be held. The candidate receiving the most votes in the third round will be elected. New candidates can also be nominated for the second and third rounds. Joachim Gauck, a former Lutheran pastor, was elected the President in March 2012. The next election will take place in 2017.

THE FEDERAL CHANCELLOR

4 The Federal Chancellor is the head of government. According to the *Basic Law*, the Federal Chancellor is empowered, among other things, to:

(a) propose ministerial candidates for appointment by the President to the Cabinet;

(b) chair the Cabinet and reconcile the difference among Ministers;

(c) determine the government policies; and

(d) command the armed forces in case the country is under attack.

The number of representatives which the individual states may send to the Federal Convention is calculated based on the population of each state.

To be elected as the Federal Chancellor, the candidate has to obtain an absolute majority of votes in the Bundestag in order to receive the formal appointment from the President. The election is often preceded by extensive negotiations between those parties that plan to govern together, and the leader of the party or coalition of parties winning the Bundestag election usually becomes the Federal Chancellor. Angela Merkel of the Christian Democratic Union has served as the Federal Chancellor since 2005, and she was re-elected for a third term in December 2013.

LEGISLATIVE BRANCH

1 The German Parliament is a bicameral legislature that consists of the elected Bundestag and the appointed Bundesrat (upper House of the German Parliament).

2 As a directly elected body, the Bundestag is empowered to:

(a) enact and amend legislation;

(b) elect the Federal Chancellor;

(c) monitor the performance of the Federal government based on the rights and instruments set out in the *Basic Law,* including interpellations and debates on matters of public interest;

(d) approve federal budget and scrutinize its implementation by the Federal government;

(e) determine the amount of public funding that parties are entitled to receive under the *Act on Political Parties*; and

(f) elect the President together with the appointed Members from the state legislatures at the Federal Convention.

3 Another House of the German Parliament, the Bundesrat, is composed of appointed Members representing the 16 states of Germany at the national level. To counterweight the power of the Bundestag, the Bundesrat is granted with a number of legislative and scrutiny powers. For example, the *Basic Law* provides for the Bundesrat to make initial comments on the draft law before it is submitted to Parliament for scrutiny and vote. The Bundesrat may also veto a bill that substantially affects the state interests.

4 Since bills must be approved by both Houses to become legislation, the *Constitution* allows for convening a mediation committee with 16 Members of the Bundestag and an equal number of Members of the Bundesrat to resolve the difference between the two Houses.

Election of the Bundestag

5 Election of the Bundestag is held once every four years unless it is dissolved earlier. The last election was held on 22 September 2013 in which Christian Democratic Union won 255 seats to become the largest party in the Bundestag. The next election will take place in 2017.

6 The Bundestag consists of 598 regular seats elected under a mixed electoral system. One half of the seats are elected directly in 299 constituencies based on a majority vote, while the other half are filled through the proportional representation system using the party list. The latter arrangement aims to allocate extra seats to political parties so that the make-up of the Bundestag reflects the support for these parties across the country.

7 In Germany, each voter has two votes: a first vote for an individual candidate in one of the constituencies, and a second vote to select the party list drawn up for each of the 16 states by the campaigning parties. If parties win more constituency seats than their share of seats determined by the party vote, they can keep the extra seats which are known as the "overhang seats". In case some parties obtain "overhang seats", "balance seats" are added to other parties to ensure complete proportionality of the share of votes for all parties as stipulated under the *Federal*

Electoral Act in 2013. Hence, the number of seats will be over 598 if there are "overhang seats" and "balance seats". In the 2013 election, there are four "overhang seats" and 29 "balance seats", bringing the total membership of the Bundestag to 631.

Current division by parliamentary group

8 As at 10 January 2015, the composition of the Bundestag by parliamentary group was as follows:

(a) Christian Democratic Union/Christian Social Union Alliance (311 Members);

(b) Social Democratic Party of Germany (193 Members);

(c) The Left Party (64 Members); and

(d) Alliance 90/The Greens (63 Members).

9 Norbert Lammert of the Christian Democratic Union has been the President of the Bundestag since October 2005.

Appointment to the Bundesrat

10 The Bundesrat is made up of 69 Members appointed by the state governments. In other words, the appointed Members concurrently hold office in the state and federal institutions. The number of seats for each state is based on the population size of a state, ranging from three to six seats. There is no definite term of office for Members of the Bundesrat. The state governments may recall or replace their representatives anytime.

Composition of the Bundesrat

11 The composition of the Bundesrat by state is as follows:

(a) six Members for each of Baden-Württemberg, Bavaria, Lower Saxony and North Rhine-Westphalia;

(b) five Members for Hesse;

(c) four Members for each of Berlin, Brandenburg, Rhineland-Palatinate, Saxony, Saxony-Anhalt, Schleswig-Holstein and Thuringia; and

(d) three Members for each of Bremen, Hamburg, Mecklenburg-Vorpommern and Saarland.

The presidency of the Bundesrat rotates annually among the 16 states, beginning with the Minister-President[3] of the most populous state. Volker Bouffier, the Minister-President of Hesse, has been the President of the Bundesrat since November 2014.

JUDICIAL BRANCH

1 Germany practises civilian system whose highest source of law is the *Basic Law.* The German court system has two levels comprising the federal and state courts. The Federal Constitutional Court is the highest court dealing with constitutional matters. At the federal level, there are also

(a) ordinary courts dealing with criminal and civil cases, and (b) specialized courts dealing with administrative law, taxation matters, labour disputes and social security cases. At the state level, a number of courts operate with jurisdictions corresponding to those of the federal courts.

Germany is a **federal, parliamentary, representative democratic republic.** The German political system operates under a framework laid out in the 1949 constitutional document known as the Grundgesetz (Basic Law). By calling the document Grundgesetz, rather than Verfassung (constitution), the authors expressed the intention that it would be replaced by a proper constitution once Germany was reunited as one state.

Amendments to the Grundgesetz generally require a two-thirds majority of both chambers of the parliament; the fundamental principles of the constitution, as expressed in the articles guaranteeing human dignity, the separation of powers, the federal structure, and the rule of law are valid in perpetuity. Despite the original intention, the Grundgesetz remained in effect after the German reunification in 1990, with only minor amendments.

The third-highest official and the head of government is the Chancellor, who is appointed by the *Bundespräsident* after being elected by the *Bundestag.* The chancellor, currently Angela Merkel, is the head of government and exercises executive power, similar to the role of a Prime Minister in other parliamentary democracies.

Federal legislative power is vested in the parliament consisting of the *Bundestag* (Federal Diet) and *Bundesrat* (Federal Council), which together form the legislative body. The *Bundestag* is elected through direct elections, by proportional representation (mixed-member). The members of the *Bundesrat* represent the governments of the sixteen federated states and are members of the state cabinets.

Since 1949, the party system has been dominated by the Christian Democratic Union and the Social Democratic Party of Germany. So far every chancellor has been a member of one of these parties. However, the smaller liberal Free Democratic Party (which has had members in the *Bundestag* since 1949) and the Alliance '90/The Greens (which has had seats in parliament since 1983) have also played important roles. Minor parties such as The Left, Free Voters and the Pirate Party are represented in some state parliaments.

The Basic Law of the Federal Republic of Germany, the federal constitution, stipulates that the structure of each Federal State's government must "conform to the principles of republican, democratic, and social government, based on the rule of law" (Article 28). Most of the states are governed by a cabinet led by a *Ministerpräsident* (Minister-President), together with a unicameral legislative body known as the *Landtag* (State Diet). The states are parliamentary republics and the relationship between their legislative and executive branches mirrors that of the federal system: the legislatures are popularly elected for four or five years (depending on the state), and the Minister-President is then chosen by a majority vote among the *Landtag*'s members. The Minister-President appoints a cabinet to run the state's agencies and to carry out the executive duties of the state's government.

The governments in Berlin, Bremen and Hamburg are designated by the term Senate. In the three free states of Bavaria, Saxony and Thuringia the government is referred to as the *State Government (Staatsregierung)*, and in the other ten states the term *Land Government (Landesregierung)* is used. Before January 1, 2000, Bavaria had a bicameral parliament, with a popularly elected *Landtag*, and a Senate made up of representatives of the state's major social and economic groups. The Senate was abolished following a referendum in 1998. The states of Berlin, Bremen, and Hamburg are governed slightly differently from the other states. In each of those cities, the executive branch consists of a Senate of approximately eight selected by the state's parliament; the senators carry out duties equivalent to those of the ministers in the larger states. The equivalent of the Minister-President is the *Senatspräsident* (President of the Senate) in Bremen, the *Erster Bürgermeister* (First Mayor) in Hamburg, and the *Regierender Bürgermeister* (Governing Mayor) in Berlin. The parliament for Berlin is called the *Abgeordnetenhaus* (House of Representatives), while Bremen and Hamburg both have a *Bürgerschaft*. The parliaments in the remaining 13 states are referred to as *Landtag* (State Parliament).

CHANCELLOR OF GERMANY

ANGELA MERKEL

	Angela Merkel since 22 November 2005
	German Cabinet
Style	Madam Chancellor Her Excellency (in international correspondence)
Member of	German Federal Cabinet European Council
Seat	Federal Chancellery Berlin, Germany (primary) Palais Schaumburg Bonn, Germany (secondary)
Appointer	President of Germany
Term length	4 years; renewable
Inaugural holder	Otto von Bismarck
Formation	1 July 1867 21 March 1871 24 May 1949
First holder	Konrad Adenauer
Salary	€247,000 p.a.
Website	bundeskanzlerin.de

The title **Chancellor** has designated different offices in the history of Germany. It is currently used for the Chancellor of the Federal Republic of Germany (German: *Bundeskanzler(in) der Bundesrepublik Deutschland*), the head of government of Germany. The term, dating from the Early Middle Ages, is derived from the Latin term *cancellarius.* The modern office of chancellor evolved from the position created for Otto von Bismarck in the North German Confederation in 1867; this federal state evolved into a German nation-state with the 1871 Unification of Germany.

The role of the chancellor has varied greatly throughout Germany's modern history. Today, the chancellor is the country's effective leader, although in formal protocol, the *Bundespräsident* and *Bundestagspräsident* are ranked higher.

In German politics, the chancellor is the equivalent of a prime minister in many other countries. The chancellor is elected by the Bundestag.

The current, official title in German is *Bundeskanzler(in)*, which means "federal chancellor", and is sometimes shortened to *Kanzler(in)*. The 8th and current chancellor is Angela Merkel, who is serving her fourth term in office. She is the first female chancellor

Angela Dorothea Merkel Kasner, born 17 July 1954) is a German politician serving as Chancellor of Germany since 2005 and leader of the centre-right Christian Democratic Union (CDU) since 2000. Merkel has been widely described as the *de facto* leader of the European Union, the most powerful woman in the world, and the leader of the Free World.

Merkel was born in Hamburg in then-West Germany and moved to East Germany as an infant when her father, a Lutheran clergyman, received a pastorate in Perleberg. She obtained a doctorate in quantum chemistry in 1986 and worked as a research scientist until 1989. Merkel entered politics in the wake of the Revolutions of 1989, and briefly served as a deputy spokesperson for the first democratically elected East German Government headed by Lothar de Maizière in 1990. Following German reunification in 1990, Merkel was elected to the Bundestag for the state of Mecklenburg-Vorpommern, and has been reelected ever since. As the protégée of Chancellor Helmut Kohl, Merkel was appointed as the Federal Minister for Women and Youth in Kohl's government in 1991, and became the Federal Minister for the Environment, Nature Conservation and Nuclear Safety in 1994. After her party lost the federal election in 1998, Merkel was elected Secretary-General of the CDU before becoming the party's first female leader two years later in the aftermath of a donations scandal that toppled Wolfgang Schäuble.

Following the 2005 federal election, Merkel was appointed Germany's first female chancellor at the head of a grand coalition consisting of the CDU, its Bavarian sister party, the Christian Social Union (CSU), and the Social Democratic Party of Germany (SPD). In the 2009 federal election, the CDU obtained the largest share of the vote and Merkel was able to form a coalition government with the Free Democratic Party (FDP). At the 2013 federal election, Merkel's CDU won a landslide victory with 41.5% of the vote and formed a second grand coalition with the SPD, after the FDP lost all of its representation in the Bundestag. In the 2017 federal election the CDU again became the largest party, and she was reelected to her fourth term on 14 March 2018.

In 2007, Merkel was President of the European Council and played a central role in the negotiation of the Treaty of Lisbon and the Berlin Declaration. One of Merkel's consistent priorities has been to strengthen transatlantic economic relations. Merkel played a crucial role in managing the financial crisis at the European and international level, and she has been referred to as "the decider." In domestic policy, health care reform, problems concerning future energy development and more recently her government's approach to the ongoing migrant crisis have been major issues during her Chancellorship. On 26 March 2014, Merkel became the longest-serving incumbent head of government in the European Union and she is currently the senior G7 leader.

In October 2018, Merkel announced that she would not seek reelection as leader of the CDU at the party convention in December 2018 and as Chancellor in 2021

DOMESTIC POLICY

IMMIGRATION

In October 2010, Merkel told a meeting of younger members of her conservative Christian Democratic Union (CDU) party at Potsdam that attempts to build a multicultural society in Germany had "utterly failed", stating that: "The concept that we are now living side by side and are happy about it" does not work and "we feel attached to the Christian concept of mankind, that is what defines us. Anyone who doesn't accept that is in the wrong place here." She continued to say that immigrants should integrate and adopt Germany's culture and values. This has added to a growing debate within Germany on the levels of immigration, its effect on Germany and the degree to which Muslim immigrants have integrated into German society.

REFUGEE AND MIGRATION POLICY

During the Syrian Civil War, Merkel pledged to give refuge in Germany to Syrians in fleeing the fighting, discontinuing the enforcement of EU regulations for asylum seekers. This policy is widely regarded as having set off the 2015 European migrant crisis. During the crisis, the number of people coming from African nations as well as from countries in the Middle East, outside the war zone, such as Afghanistan and Iran, rose significantly.

On 1 July 2018, German Interior minister Horst Seehofer offered to resign after rejecting Chancellor Angela Merkel's EU migration deal.

FOREIGN POLICY

Merkel's foreign policy has focused on strengthening European cooperation and international trade agreements. Merkel has been widely described as the *de facto* leader of the European Union throughout her tenure as Chancellor.

One of Merkel's priorities was strengthening transatlantic economic relations. She signed the agreement for the Transatlantic Economic Council on 30 April 2007 at the White House. Merkel enjoyed good relations with U.S. Presidents George W. Bush, and Barack Obama. Obama described her in 2016 as his "closest international partner" throughout his tenure as President.

On 25 September 2007, Merkel met the 14th Dalai Lama for "private and informal talks" in the Chancellery in Berlin amid protest from China. China afterwards cancelled separate talks with German officials, including talks with Justice Minister Brigitte Zypries

In 2006 Merkel expressed concern about overreliance on Russian energy, but she received little support from others in Berlin.

Merkel favors the Association Agreement between Ukraine and the European Union; but stated in December 2012 that its implementation depends on reforms in Ukraine.

In recognition of the importance of China to the German economy, by 2014 Merkel had led seven trade delegations to China since assuming office in 2005. The same year, in March, China's President Xi Jinping visited Germany.

In 2015, with the absence of Stephen Harper, Merkel became the only leader to have attended every G20 meeting since the very first in 2008, having been present at a record thirteen summits as of 2018. She hosted the twelfth meeting at the 2017 G20 Hamburg summit.

In June 2017, Merkel criticized the draft of new U.S. sanctions against Russia that target EU–Russia energy projects, including Nord Stream 2 gas pipeline.

In June 2018, Merkel said that there had been "no moral or political justification" for the post-war expulsion of ethnic Germans from Central and Eastern European countries.

EUROZONE CRISIS

Following major falls in worldwide stock markets in September 2008, the German government stepped in to assist the mortgage company Hypo Real Estate with a bailout, which was agreed on 6 October, with German banks to contribute €30 billion and the Bundesbank €20 billion to a credit line.

On 4 October 2008 following the Irish Government's decision to guarantee all deposits in private savings accounts, a move she strongly criticised, Merkel said there were no plans for the German Government to do the same. The following day, Merkel stated that the government would guarantee private savings account deposits, after all. However, two days later, on 6 October 2008, it emerged that the pledge was simply a political move that would not be backed by legislation. Other European governments eventually either raised the limits or promised to guarantee savings in full.

SOCIAL EXPENDITURE

At the World Economic Forum in Davos, 2013, she said that Europe had only 7% of the global population and produced only 25% of the global GDP, but that it accounted for almost 50% of global social expenditure. She went on to say that Europe could only maintain its prosperity by being innovative and measuring itself against the best. Since then, this comparison has become a central element in major speeches.

APPROVAL RATINGS

Midway through her second term, Merkel's approval plummeted in Germany, resulting in heavy losses in state elections for her party. An August 2011 poll found her coalition had only 36% support compared to a rival potential coalition's 51%.However, she scored well on her handling of the recent euro crisis (69% rated her performance as good rather than poor), and her approval rating reached an all-time high of 77% in February 2012 and again in July 2014. Merkel's approval rating dropped to 54% in October 2015, during the European migrant crisis, the lowest since 2011. According to a poll conducted after terror attacks in Germany Merkel's approval rating dropped to 47% (August 2016). Half of Germans did not want her to serve a fourth term in office compared to 42% in favor. However, according to a poll taken in October 2016, her approval rating had been found to have risen again, 54% of Germans were found to be satisfied with work of Merkel as Chancellor. According to another poll taken in November 2016, 59% were to found to be in favour of a renewed Chancellor candidature of Merkel in 2017.

According to a poll carried out just days after the 2016 Berlin attack, in which it was asked which political leader(s) Germans trust to solve their country's problems; 56% named Merkel, 39% Seehofer (CSU), 35% Gabriel (SPD), 32% Schulz (SPD), 25% Özdemir (Greens), 20% Wagenknecht (Left party), 15% Lindner (FDP), and just 10% for Petry (AfD). A YouGov survey published in late December 2017 found that just 36 percent of all respondents want Merkel to stay at the helm until 2021, while half of those surveyed voters called for a change at the top before the end of the legislature.

INTERNATIONAL STATUS

Merkel has been widely described as the *de facto* leader of the European Union throughout her tenure as Chancellor. Merkel has twice been named the world's second most powerful person following Vladimir Putin by *Forbes* magazine, the highest ranking ever achieved by a woman. On 26 March 2014, Merkel became the longest-serving incumbent head of government in the European Union. In December 2015, Merkel was named as *Time* magazine's Person of the Year, with the magazine's cover declaring her to be the "Chancellor of the Free World".

In May 2016, Merkel was named the most powerful woman in the world for a record twelve time by *Forbes*. Following the election of Donald Trump to the U.S. presidency in November 2016, Merkel was described by *The New York Times* as "the Liberal West's Last Defender".Since 2016 she has been described by many commentators as the "leader of the free world". Former US Secretary of State Hillary Clinton described Merkel in 2017 as "the most important leader in the free world." She is currently the senior G7 leader.

FEDERAL CABINET

The **Cabinet of Germany** (German: ***Bundeskabinett*** *or* ***Bundesregierung***) is the chief executive body of the Federal Republic of Germany. It consists of the Chancellor and the cabinet ministers. The fundamentals of the cabinet's organization as well as the method of its election and appointment as well as the procedure for its dismissal are set down in articles 62 through 69 of the *Grundgesetz* (the Basic Law).

In contrast to the system under the pre-Hitler Weimar republic, the Bundestag may both only move a constructive vote of no-confidence (by electing a new Chancellor if it has lost trust in the existing) and can also only choose to dismiss the entire cabinet and not simply individual ministers. These procedures and mechanisms were put in place by the authors of the Basic Law to both prevent another dictatorship and to ensure that there will not be a political vacuum left by the removal of Chancellor through a vote of confidence and the failure to elect a new one in their place, as had happened during the Weimar period with the Reichstag removing Chancellors but failing to agree on the election of a new one. There is a grace period in-between the dismissal of a Chancellor by the Bundestag and until the Bundestag can elect a new Chancellor, so as to allow the federal government, if it so wishes, to advise the Federal President to dissolve the Bundestag so that elections may be held.

The Chancellor is elected by the federal parliament (*Bundestag*) after being proposed by the President. Following the election, the Chancellor is appointed by the President. The ministers are appointed (and dismissed) by the President upon proposal of the Chancellor. Eventually, before taking office, the Chancellor and ministers swear an oath in front of the parliament.

FUNCTIONING

The Chancellor is responsible for guiding the cabinet and deciding its political direction. According to the principle of departmentalization (*Ressortprinzip*), the cabinet ministers are free to carry out their duties independently within the boundaries set by the Chancellor's political directives. The Chancellor also decides the scope of each minister's duties. If two ministers disagree on a particular point, the cabinet resolves the conflict by a majority vote (*Kollegialprinzip* or principle of deference).

The Chancellor is in charge of the government's administrative affairs, which are usually delegated to the head of the Chancellery. Details are laid down in the government's rules for internal procedures (*Geschäftsordnung*). These state, e.g., that the cabinet is quorate only if at least half of the ministers including the chair are present. The cabinet regularly convenes Wednesday mornings in the Chancellery.

STRUCTURE AND TASKS

1. Government mandate issued by the people

Democracy means rule of the people by the people. The people exercise government power in elections and have the last word in monitoring the activities of key government institutions. These are the five "constitutional bodies", i.e. the Bundestag and Bundesrat with responsibility for legislation (constituting the legislative branch of government), the Federal Constitutional Court with responsibility for supreme court decisions (constituting the judicial branch of government), and finally the Federal President and the Federal Cabinet with responsibility for executive tasks (constituting the executive branch of government). The Cabinet is responsible for the conduct of government business.

2. Cabinet

It is made up of the Chancellor and the Federal Ministers.

3. Role of the Chancellor

The Chancellor has a prominent position in the government. He or she is, as it were, the "captain" of the ship of state. The Chancellor determines who will be in the government, since he or she alone has the right to form the Cabinet. The Chancellor chooses his ministers and makes a proposal that is binding for the Federal President with regard to their appointment (or dismissal). He or she determines the number of Ministers and defines their terms of reference. The Chancellor determines the general guidelines of government policy ("principle of Chancellor policy guidelines").

4. Role of the Ministers

Although the Chancellor has the right to issue orders to his ministers, the constitution emphasises the right of Ministers to conduct their affairs autonomously and on their own responsibility within the limits set by the Chancellor's guidelines ("principle of ministerial autonomy"). Many Ministers have been able to create a strong position for themselves on the basis of professional competence, skilful handling of public relations, and strong parliamentary or extra-parliamentary backing.

5. Interplay of government powers: the Chancellor and the Cabinet

The fifty-year history of the Federal Republic has shown that despite the Chancellor's strong position the ability of the government to act cannot be guaranteed by him or her alone. Even though the Chancellery makes it possible to impose central management and coordination, a non-hierarchical relationship between the Chancellor and her or his Ministers plays an important role in government practice. In this context the Cabinet deals with important interministerial issues such as the federal budget or tax reform and takes joint decisions on them ("principle of joint Cabinet decision-making"). In a government coalition the Chancellor is also bound by the terms of the coalition agreement and has to adhere to these terms to avoid straining the coalition.

6. Three important principles of government

The "principle of Chancellor policy guidelines" means that the Chancellor lays down general policy guidelines and bears responsibility for them. Stated more precisely, she or he conducts the business of government. The basis for this is provided by the Federal Government Rules of Procedure as adopted by the Federal Cabinet and approved by the Federal President.

7. "Principle of Chancellor policy guidelines"

The Basic Law distinguishes three important principles of government. These are the "principle of Chancellor policy guidelines", the "principle of joint Cabinet decision-making", and the "principle of ministerial autonomy". They regulate interaction and division of labour in the government.

8. "Principle of joint Cabinet decision-making"

The "principle of joint Cabinet decision-making" means that the Chancellor and the Ministers decide jointly on matters of general political importance. When there are differences of opinion between Ministers the Chancellor mediates (as a "primus inter pares"). Cabinet decisions are based on majority rule.

9. "Principle of ministerial autonomy"

The "principle of ministerial autonomy" means that each Minister conducts the affairs of his or her ministry independently and on his own responsibility. This means that the Chancellor cannot automatically intervene in his or her Ministers' areas of responsibility. At the same time Ministers must see to it that the decisions they take remain within the limits.

CARRENT CABINET

The fourth cabinet of Chancellor Angela Merkel is the current government of Germany, sworn in on 14 March 2018 after Merkel was proposed as Chancellor by President of Germany Frank-Walter Steinmeier and elected on the first ballot. It is the 24th cabinet of Germany (Federal Republic).

This government is supported by a coalition of the Christian Democratic Union (CDU), the Christian Social Union of Bavaria (CSU), and the Social Democrats (SPD), as was its immediate predecessor.

Protocol order	Office	Portrait	Incumbent	Party	In office	Secretaries of State scope of work (where applicable)
1	Chancellor of Germany		Angela Merkel	CDU	22 November 2005 – present	Annette Widmann-Mauz (StMin) Migrants, Refugees and Integration Monika Grütters (StMin) Culture and Media Hendrik Hoppenstedt (StMin) Cooperation between federation and states Dorothee Bär (StMin) Digitalization
2	Vice Chancellor of Germany Federal Minister of Finance		Olaf Scholz	SPD	14 March 2018 – present	Bettina Hagedorn Christine Lambrecht
3	Federal Minister of the Interior, Building and Community		Horst Seehofer	CSU	14 March 2018 – present	Günter Krings Stephan Mayer Marco Wanderwitz

Protocol order	Office	Portrait	Incumbent	Party	In office	Secretaries of State scope of work (where applicable)
4	**Federal Minister for Foreign Affairs**		Heiko Maas	SPD	14 March 2018 – present	Niels Annen (StMin) Michelle Müntefering (StMin) Culture Michael Roth (StMin) European affairs
5	**Federal Minister of Economics and Energy**		Peter Altmaier	CDU	14 March 2018 – present	Thomas Bareiß Christian Hirte Affairs of the Eastern Länder Oliver Wittke
6	**Federal Minister of Justice and Consumer Protection**		Katarina Barley	SPD	14 March 2018 – present	Rita Hagl-Kehl Christian Lange
7	**Federal Minister of Labour and Social Affairs**		Hubertus Heil	SPD	14 March 2018 – present	Annette Kramme Kerstin Griese
8	**Federal Minister of Defence**	Error! Unknown switch argument.	Ursula von der Leyen	CDU	17 December 2013 – present	Thomas Silberhorn Peter Tauber General Eberhard Zorn Inspector General of the Bundeswehr

Protocol order	Office	Portrait	Incumbent	Party	In office	Secretaries of State scope of work (where applicable)
9	**Federal Minister of Food and Agriculture**		Julia Klöckner	CDU	14 March 2018 – present	Hans-Joachim Fuchtel Michael Stübgen
10	**Federal Minister for Family Affairs, Senior Citizens, Women and Youth**		Franziska Giffey	SPD	14 March 2018 – present	Caren Marks Stefan Zierke
11	**Federal Minister of Health**		Jens Spahn	CDU	14 March 2018 – present	Thomas Gebhardt Sabine Weiss [de]
12	**Federal Minister of Transport and Digital Infrastructure**		Andreas Scheuer	CSU	14 March 2018 – present	Steffen Bilger Enak Ferlemann
13	**Federal Minister for the Environment, Nature Conservation and Nuclear Safety**		Svenja Schulze	SPD	14 March 2018 – present	Florian Pronold Rita Schwarzelühr-Sutter

Protocol order	Office	Portrait	Incumbent	Party	In office	Secretaries of State scope of work (where applicable)
14	**Federal Minister of Education and Research**		Anja Karliczek	CDU	14 March 2018 – present	Michael Meister Thomas Rachel
15	**Federal Minister for Economic Cooperation and Development**		Gerd Müller	CSU	17 December 2013 – present	Norbert Barthle Maria Flachsbarth
16	**Federal Minister for Special AffairsHead of the Chancellery**		Helge Braun	CDU	14 March 2018 – present	

Some Parliamentary Secretaries of State get awarded the honorary title *Staatsminister* (*StMin*, English: Minister of State) in order to underline the importance of their scope of work. Nevertheless, this does not give them any additional powers.

MAJOR FEDERAL MINISTRIES

FEDERAL MINISTRY OF FINANCE

Agency overview	
Formed	14 July 1879 (Reichsschatzamt)
Jurisdiction	Cabinet of Germany
Headquarters	Detlev-Rohwedder-Haus Wilhelmstraße 97, 10117 Berlin 52°30′31″N 13°23′3″ECoordinates: 52°30′31″N 13°23′3″E
Employees	1,900
Annual budget	€6.55 billion (2018)
Minister responsible	af Scholz, Federal Minister of Finance
Agency executives	Christine Lambrecht, Parliamentary State Secretary

	Bettina Hagedorn, Parliamentary State Secretary
	Werner Gatzer, State Secretary
	Wolfgang Schmidt, State Secretary
	Rolf Bösinger, State Secretary
	Jörg Kukies, State Secretary
Website	http://www.bundesfinanzministerium.de

The **Federal Ministry of Finance** (German: *Bundesministerium der Finanzen*), abbreviated **BMF**, is the cabinet-level finance ministry of Germany, with its seat at the Detlev-Rohwedder-Haus in Berlin and a secondary office in Bonn. The current Federal Minister of Finance is Olaf Scholz (SPD).

	Assumed office 14 March 2018
Chancellor	Angela Merkel
Preceded by	Sigmar Gabriel
	Minister of Finance
	Incumbent
	Assumed office 14 March 2018
Chancellor	Angela Merkel
Preceded by	Peter Altmaier (Acting)
	Deputy Leader of the Social Democratic Party
	Incumbent
	Assumed office 13 November 2009
	Serving with Manuela Schwesig, Natascha Kohnen, Malu Dreyer, Thorsten Schäfer-Gümbel and Ralf Stegner
Leader	Sigmar Gabriel Martin Schulz Himself (Acting) Andrea Nahles

Preceded by	Frank-Walter Steinmeier
	Leader of the Social Democratic Party Acting
	In office 13 February 2018 – 22 April 2018
General Secretary	Lars Klingbeil
Preceded by	Martin Schulz
Succeeded by	Andrea Nahles
	First Mayor of Hamburg
	In office 7 March 2011 – 13 March 2018
Preceded by	Christoph Ahlhaus
Succeeded by	Peter Tschentscher
	Leader of the Social Democratic Party in Hamburg
	In office 6 November 2009 – 24 March 2018
Preceded by	Ingo Egloff
Succeeded by	Melanie Leonhard
	In office 2000–2004
Preceded by	Jörg Kuhbier
Succeeded by	Mathias Peterson
	Minister of Labour and Social Affairs
	In office 21 November 2007 – 27 October 2009
Chancellor	Angela Merkel
Preceded by	Franz Müntefering
Succeeded by	Franz Josef Jung
	First Chief Whip of the Social Democratic Party in the Bundestag
	In office 22 October 2009 – 10 March 2011
Leader	Peter Struck
Preceded by	Wilhelm Schmidt
Succeeded by	Thomas Oppermann
	Secretary General of the Social Democratic Party
	In office 20 October 2002 – 21 March 2004
Leader	Gerhard Schröder
Preceded by	Franz Müntefering
Succeeded by	Klaus Uwe Benneter
	Senator for the Interior of Hamburg
	In office 30 May 2001 – 31 October 2001
First Mayor	Ortwin Runde
Preceded by	Hartmuth Wrocklage
Succeeded by	Ronald Schill

Member of the Bundestag	
In office 22 September 2002 – 10 March 2011	
In office 27 September 1998 – 30 May 2001	
Personal details	
Born	14 June 1958 (age 60) Osnabrück, Germany
Political party	Social Democratic Party
Alma mater	University of Hamburg

Olaf Scholz born 14 June 1958) is a German politician, serving as Federal Minister of Finance and Vice Chancellor alongside Chancellor Angela Merkel from the CDU since 14 March 2018. He had been First Mayor of Hamburg from 7 March 2011 to 13 March 2018 and Acting Chairman of the Social Democratic Party (SPD) from 13 February to 22 April 2018.

A member of the Bundestag from 1998 to 2001 and again from 2002 to 2011, Scholz was Minister of the Interior of Hamburg under First Mayor Ortwin Runde from May to October 2001 and General Secretary of his party under Chairman and Chancellor Gerhard Schröder from 2002 to 2004. He served as Federal Minister of Labour and Social Affairs in Merkel's first Grand Coalition from 2007 to 2009 and Leader of the SPD in Hamburg from 2000 to 2004 and again from 2009 to 2018.

2019 FEDERAL BUDGET AND THE FINANCIAL PLAN TO 2022.

The economy is humming, employment is at record highs, and public finances are in good shape. Nevertheless, we still face urgent problems. The draft 2019 budget tackles key challenges – in Germany, in Europe and in the world. My plans include record investment levels, which means more money for well-built roads, high-quality rail transport, and high-speed internet, and more resources for education and research. We are boosting spending to enhance social cohesion. We are taking steps to provide more housing that people can afford. We are strengthening families by expanding child care facilities, raising child benefit, and making it easier to buy a home. In addition, I have significantly increased the budget allocations for security and order. Forward-looking, fair and responsible: this trio of principles guides our fiscal policy, including my draft budget and our financial plan to 2022. *Federal Minister of Finance, Olaf Scholz*

To lay the foundations for tomorrow's prosperity, **the German government is significantly raising its investment in the country's future**. A total of €151.6 billion in investment spending is planned for the four years from 2019 to 2022. This is a record high that adds €8.4 billion to the benchmark figure adopted in May 2018 and nearly €16 billion to the amount projected in last year's financial plan. This means that investment levels will remain consistently high for the entire period covered by the new financial plan, at €37.9 billion per year. A particular focus will be placed on infrastructure, education, housing and digital technology.

Key benchmark figures:

	Target* 2018	Draft Budget 2019	Financial plan		
			2020	2021	2022
	– in €bn –				
Expenditure	343.6	356.8	363.2	369.3	375.5

year-on-year change in %	+3.9	+3.8	+1.8	+1.7	+1.7
Revenue	343.6	356.8	363.2	369.3	375.5
of this amount: tax revenue	321.3	333.0	333.8	346.8	359.7
Net borrowing					
Investment** (2018: excluding €2.4bn allocation to digital infrastructure fund)	37.4	37.9	37.9	37.9	37.9

Discrepancies may occur due to rounding.
* 2018: figures at the time of the Bundestag Budget Committee's settlement session.
** No "unbundling" funds after 2019 (federal allocations to the Länder following the discontinuation of co-funding programmes in the areas of university construction, education, local transport and subsidised housing).

The German government also operates several special funds that will serve to stimulate further investment on top of the record-high investment levels contained in the budget and financial plan. These funds include the Energy and Climate Fund, a fund to promote investment by local authorities, a special relief fund established to remedy the damage caused by the June 2013 floods in Germany, and a special fund for digital infrastructure. In 2018, €2.4 billion will be paid into this digital infrastructure fund, which has been set up to finance billions of euros in investment in the coming years for the purpose of expanding and upgrading the broadband network and implementing the "digital compact for schools".

In addition, a number of measures will be taken that are not categorised as investments in the budget but will play a crucial role in preparing Germany for the future and safeguarding the efficiency and viability of the German economy. This includes, in particular, expenditures on education, science and research, all of which comprise priority areas in the budget. In the years from 2019 to 2022, total spending on education and research will amount to €95 billion, including €23.7 billion in 2019. This is over €4 billion more in the coming four years than what was projected in last year's financial plan.

The German government is taking steps to enhance social equity. A planned package of measures will help to ensure that everyone benefits from the current economic upswing:

More net pay for individual taxpayers: The government is giving a boost to disposable income, especially for low- and middle-income families. Both child benefit and the tax allowance for children will be increased starting in 2019. The income tax schedule is being adjusted to offset the effects of "bracket creep". In addition, a total of €5.5 billion is being earmarked for the years from 2019 to 2022 to improve the quality of care in child care facilities and to create more cost-free care options. All-day schools will also be expanded, with a total of €2 billion being targeted toward this sector in the years up to 2022.

Socially responsible and active labour market policies: In 2019, roughly €1 billion in additional funds will be made available for training, job placement and labour market integration measures targeting the long-term unemployed. The Federation is also sending out an important signal by reducing the number of public service positions that are subject to fixed-term contracts for no substantive reason. In the future, no more than 2.5% of the people who work at authorities belonging directly to the federal administration are to be employed under contracts that have fixed terms for no substantive reason. At the same time, the Federation is adding a total of 1,760.5 new public service positions in 2018 and 2019.

More housing that people can afford: The German government plans to spend €1 billion per year in 2020 and 2021 on the construction of social housing, and an extra €500 million are being added to the roughly €1 billion already budgeted for 2019. In addition, a new grant is being introduced that aims to help families with children buy or build owner-occupied housing.

Good, future-proof pensions: The German government is improving benefits for pensioners while also taking steps to prepare the pension system's finances for future challenges. Demographic trends will make it necessary for the Federation to increase its grants to the pension system. To prepare for this increase, starting in 2021, budgets will include an annual allocation of €2 billion to a reserve fund that will be set up to safeguard the pension system against demographic effects.

A fair fiscal policy must also ensure internal security and a well-ordered labour market while also upholding Germany's commitment to fulfil its international responsibilities. This is precisely what the new draft budget and financial plan do.

Greater internal security, less undeclared work, strict minimum wage controls: Compared with last year's financial plan, roughly €3 billion have been added to the Interior Ministry's budget for internal security in 2019. Staffing will also be expanded substantially again in 2019 with the addition of about 3,100 new positions. The bulk of these new positions will go to the Federal Police and the Federal Criminal Police Office, and staffing at the customs administration will be increased again as well. The customs administration is responsible for combating undeclared work and monitoring compliance with minimum wage laws, and in this way it ensures equity and order on the German labour market. The customs administration will add 754.5 new positions in 2019 and take on over 3,000 newly trained customs officers starting in 2021.

Boosting development assistance and defence: The German government is also significantly increasing its funding for development cooperation and humanitarian aid. In 2019, the budget for the Federal Ministry for Economic Cooperation and Development will grow to approximately €9.7 billion. This is over €1 billion more than the amount projected in last year's financial plan. The Foreign Office's budget for humanitarian aid and crisis prevention is also being increased by €500 million over the amount slated in last year's financial plan. In addition, Germany is raising its defence budget by €4 billion in 2019.

The German government is pursuing responsible fiscal policies and keeping its eye on longer-term trends. This means that periods of strong growth and high tax revenue will be used to finance expenditures without adding new debt and to reduce the debt ratio. The draft budget submitted by the federal government will make a major contribution to the reduction of Germany's general government debt, which is expected to fall below 60% of GDP in 2019 for the first time in 17 years. This is responsible and intelligent budget policy that will create the fiscal space to meet future challenges and that will ease the burden on future generations.

With its draft federal budget for 2019 and its financial plan to 2022, the German government is improving the outlook for Germany's future and enhancing social cohesion. These goals will be achieved without adding new debt.

FEDERAL MINISTRY OF THE INTERIOR, BUILDING AND COMMUNITY

Agency overview	
Formed	24 December 1879 (138 years ago) as the Reichsamt des Inneren
Jurisdiction	Government of Germany
Headquarters	Alt-Moabit 140 10557 Berlin 52°31′17″N 13°21′44″ECoordinates: 52°31′17″N 13°21′44″E
Employees	1,500

Annual budget	€14.13 billion (2018)
Minister responsible	›rst Seehofer, Federal Minister of the Interior, Building and Community
Agency executive	Ole Schröder, Parliamentary State Secretary
Website	http://www.bmi.bund.de

The **Federal Ministry of the Interior, Building and Community** (German: *Bundesministerium des Innern, für Bau und Heimat*; *Heimat* also translates to "homeland"), abbreviated ***BMI***, is cabinet-level ministry of the Federal Republic of Germany. Its main office is in Berlin, with a secondary seat in Bonn. The current minister of the Interior, Building and Community is Horst Seehofer. It is comparable to the British Home Office or a combination of the US Department of Homeland Security and the US Department of Justice, because both manage several law enforcement agencies.

The BMI is tasked with the internal security of Germany. To fulfill this responsibility it maintains, among other agencies, the two biggest federal law enforcement agencies in Germany, the Federal Police and the Federal Criminal Police Office. It is also responsible for the federal domestic intelligence agency, the Federal Office for the Protection of the Constitution.

Minister of the Interior, Building and Community	
Incumbent	
Assumed office 14 March 2018	
Chancellor	Angela Merkel
Preceded by	Thomas de Maizière (Interior)
Leader of the Christian Social Union	
Incumbent	
Assumed office 25 October 2008	
General Secretary	Karl-Theodor zu Guttenberg Alexander Dobrindt Andreas Scheuer Markus Blume
Preceded by	Erwin Huber
President of Germany Acting	
In office	

	17 February 2012 – 18 March 2012
Chancellor	Angela Merkel
Preceded by	Christian Wulff
Succeeded by	Joachim Gauck
	President of the Bundesrat
	In office 1 November 2011 – 31 October 2012
Preceded by	Hannelore Kraft
Succeeded by	Winfried Kretschmann
	Minister President of Bavaria
	In office 27 October 2008 – 13 March 2018
Deputy	Martin Zeil Ilse Aigner
Preceded by	Günther Beckstein
Succeeded by	Ilse Aigner (Acting)
	Minister of Food, Agriculture and Consumer Protection
	In office 22 November 2005 – 27 October 2008
Chancellor	Angela Merkel
Preceded by	Renate Künast
Succeeded by	Ilse Aigner
	Minister of Health
	In office 6 May 1992 – 26 October 1998
Chancellor	Helmut Kohl
Preceded by	Gerda Hasselfeldt
Succeeded by	Andrea Fischer
	Member of the Bundestag for Ingolstadt
	In office 5 October 1980 – 27 October 2008
Preceded by	Karl Heinz Gierenstein
Succeeded by	Reinhard Brandl
	Member of the Landtag of Bavaria for Neuburg-Schrobenhausen
	In office 7 October 2013 – 30 April 2018
Preceded by	None
Succeeded by	Matthias Enghuber
	Personal details
	Horst Lorenz Seehofer
Born	4 July 1949 (age 69) Ingolstadt, Germany
Political party	Christian Social Union

Horst Lorenz Seehofer (born 4 July 1949) is a German politician serving as Leader of the Christian Social Union (CSU) since 2008 and Minister of the Interior, Building and Community since 2018 under Chancellor Angela Merkel. From 2008 to 2018, he was Minister President of Bavaria; he also served as President of the Bundesrat between 2011 and 2012.

First elected to the Bundestag in 1980, he served as Federal Minister for Health and Social Security from 1992 to 1998 and as Federal Minister of Food, Agriculture and Consumer Protection in the cabinet of Angela Merkel from 2005 to 2008. In October 2008 he became Leader of the CSU and the 18th Minister President of Bavaria. From 1 November 2011 until 31 October 2012 he served as President of the Bundesrat and *ex officio* deputy to the President of Germany. Because of that he was Acting President of Germany after the resignation of President Christian Wulff on 17 February 2012 and before the election of Joachim Gauck as Wulff's successor on 18 March 2012.

A staunch opponent of Chancellor Angela Merkel's refugee policy, Seehofer has threatened to file a formal complaint against the Merkel government's refugee policy with Germany's Constitutional Court and is a proponent of a federal cap on the number of refugees the German government is to take in

FEDERAL FOREIGN OFFICE

Agency overview	
Formed	1870; 148 years ago
Jurisdiction	Government of Germany
Headquarters	Werderscher Markt 1 10117 Berlin
Employees	11,602 Foreign Service staff 5,627 local employees
Annual budget	€5.45 billion (2018)
Minister responsible	›iko Maas, Federal Minister for Foreign Affairs
Agency executives	Maria Böhmer, Minister of State at the Foreign Office Michael Roth, Minister of State at the Foreign Office
Website	www.auswaertiges-amt.de

The **Federal Foreign Office** abbreviated **AA**, is the foreign ministry of the Federal Republic of Germany, a federal agency responsible for both the country's foreign policy and its relationship with the European Union. It is a cabinet-level ministry. Since March 2018, Heiko Maas has served as Foreign Minister, succeeding Sigmar Gabriel. The primary seat of the ministry is at the *Werderscher Markt* square in the Mitte district, the historic centre of Berlin.

The term ***Auswärtiges Amt*** was the name of the Foreign Office established in 1870 by the North German Confederation, which then became the German Empire's Foreign Office in 1871. It is still the name of the German foreign ministry today. From 1871 to 1919, the Foreign Office was led by a Foreign Secretary, and since 1919, it has been led by the Foreign Minister of Germany.

MINISTER FOR FOREIGN AFFAIRS

Heiko Maas

since 14 March 2018

Federal Foreign Office	
Formation	21 March 1871
First holder	Hermann von Thile
Website	auswärtiges-amt.de

FOREIGN AND EUROPEAN POLICY PRINCIPLES

Europe, the transatlantic partnership, fostering peace and security around the world, the promotion of democracy and human rights, and commitment to fair and sustainable globalisation and a rules-based international order - these are the guiding principles of German foreign policy.

European integration and the European Union

A stronger Europe is the most important response to the challenges of globalisation

A stronger Europe is the most important response to the challenges of globalisation

European integration and the European Union (EU) are the cornerstones of German foreign policy and set its course. Strengthening the EU's cohesion and close cooperation with all EU member states are thus long-term priorities for Germany.

The numerous foreign policy challenges in a constantly changing world can only be addressed by a strong Europe and by working with our European partners. Also as regards shaping globalisation and a new international order, Germany will only remain capable of effective action in a European framework in light of the shifting global balance of power. A stronger Europe is therefore the most important response to the challenges of globalisation. The German Government is thus committed to closer European cooperation, especially on the EU's common foreign and security policy, as well as to joint efforts to safeguard Europe's external borders, foster internal security and strengthen economic policy.

Following the the UK's decision to leave the EU, Germany remains committed to a good relationship with the UK in a spirit of partnership.

The transatlantic partnership

The US is one of Germany's most important partners

Alongside European integration, the transatlantic partnership is the most important pillar of German foreign policy. The US is Germany's closest ally outside Europe.

Transatlantic relations are based on historical experiences and shared values such as democracy, freedom and the rule of law. These relations are rooted in common interests and objectives, as well as the two countries' long-standing close social, political and economic ties.

At all times, German foreign policy is committed to a close transatlantic relationship in a spirit of partnership and mutual trust, as well as to a an open dialogue and respectful cooperation with the US, especially when there are differences of viewpoint or opinion.

Commitment to peace and security

German foreign policy is committed to peace and security around the world. Germany primarily defines its peace and security policy in multilateral terms, that is, within the framework of international institutions and structures such as the EU, NATO, the United Nations, the OSCE, the G7 and the G20.

In the first instance, peace policy means diplomatic efforts to reach political settlements to crises and conflicts such as those in Ukraine, Syria and Libya. Germany also takes on security responsibility, including military action when absolutely necessary, for example in combating so-called Islamic State (IS) and stabilising Afghanistan and Mali.

Endeavours in the fields of disarmament, arms control and non-proliferation of weapons and armaments are an important component of German peace policy. Along with conventional arms control, a world without nuclear weapons remains a long-term goal of German foreign policy.

Germany's work in the fields of crisis prevention, stabilisation, post-conflict peacebuilding and humanitarian aid is also part of its peace and security policy. Germany is now one of the largest donors of humanitarian aid worldwide and a pioneer in civil crisis prevention, mediation and stabilisation.

Democracy, the rule of law and human rights

German foreign policy promotes the strengthening of human rights worldwide

German foreign policy promotes the strengthening of democracy, the rule of law and human rights worldwide. Germany works to foster these principles not only out of conviction or because they are universal values, but also because this is in its foreign policy interests. Peace, security, stability and sustainable development can only prevail in the long term where democratic and rule of law principles apply and human rights are respected.

Confidently promoting democracy, the rule of law and human rights is thus an important component of German peace and security policy.

Globalisation and international order

Global justice is a prerequisite for international peace and security

German foreign policy aims to ensure that globalisation is fair and sustainable. Global justice is a key prerequisite for international peace and security. German foreign policy therefore also addresses topics such as displacement and migration, the 2030 Agenda for Sustainable Development, energy and resource security, climate protection, environmental and water issues, the spread of digital technology, internet freedom, cyber security and urbanisation.

Germany promotes binding rules and effective multilateral institutions that facilitate orderly and close cooperation in an increasingly interconnected world. As Germany is more interconnected with the world than almost any other country, a resilient, rules-based international order is in its own fundamental foreign policy interests. German foreign policy thus works to enhance long-standing and essential institutions and structures such as the EU, NATO, the UN, the OSCE and the G7, as well as new elements of order, partnerships and international formats, for example the G20, the agreement between the E3+3 countries and Iran on the dispute over Iran's nuclear programme and the Normandy format aimed at resolving the Ukraine crisis. Put briefly, Germany regards multilateralism as the most important principle for international order, and will remain committed to this principle in the future.

As the world's leading exporter, Germany has a particular interest in an effective external economic policy that helps companies to tap into international markets and to improve the conditions for doing business.

Cultural relations and education policy forms the third pillar of German foreign policy. Its instruments include academic exchange, international German schools and the promotion of German as a foreign language. By fostering intercultural dialogue, this policy creates a solid foundation for international relations and global trust in Germany – a particularly important function for a country that has such close international ties.

FEDERAL MINISTRY OF LABOUR AND SOCIAL AFFAIRS

The **Federal Ministry for Labour and Social Affairs** (**BMAS**) is a federal ministry of the Federal Republic of Germany headed by the Federal Minister of Labour and Social Affairs as a member of the Cabinet of Germany (*Bundesregierung*). Its first location is on Wilhelmstrasse in Berlin, the second in Bonn.

Agency overview	
Formed	1919 (Weimar Republic), 1949 (West Germany)
Jurisdiction	Government of Germany
Headquarters	Wilhelmstraße 49 10117 Berlin 52°30′45″N 13°23′01″ECoordinates: 52°30′45″N 13°23′01″E
Annual budget	€139.18 billion (2018)
Minister responsible	ıbertus Heil, Federal Minister for Labour and Social Affairs
Website	http://www.bmas.de

Hubertus Heil

Minister of Labour and Social Affairs	
Incumbent Assumed office 14 March 2018	
Chancellor	Angela Merkel
Preceded by	Katarina Barley (Acting)
General Secretary of the Social Democratic Party	
In office 2 June 2017 – 8 December 2017	
Leader	Martin Schulz
Preceded by	Katarina Barley
Succeeded by	Lars Klingbeil
In office 15 November 2005 – 13 November 2009	
Leader	Franz Müntefering

	Matthias Platzeck Kurt Beck Frank-Walter Steinmeier (Acting)
Preceded by	Klaus Uwe Benneter
Succeeded by	Andrea Nahles
	Member of the Bundestag for Gifhorn – Peine
	Incumbent
	Assumed office 27 September 1998
Preceded by	Engelbert Nelle
	Personal details
	Wolfgang-Hubertus Heil
Born	3 November 1972 (age 46) Hildesheim, Lower Saxony, West Germany (now Germany)
Political party	Social Democratic Party
Children	2
Alma mater	University of Potsdam University of Hagen

Hubertus Heil (born 3 November 1972) is a German politician. In 2005 he became general secretary of the Social Democratic Party of Germany (SPD). In September 2009, after immense losses for the SPD during the German federal election, Heil announced his resignation from this position for November. Andrea Nahles succeeded him as general secretary in November 2009. After Katarina Barley's appoinment as Federal Minister of Family Affairs, Senior Citizens, Women and Youth, he briefly returned to the office from 2 June to 8 December 2017. On 14 March 2018 Heil was appointed Federal Minister of Labour and Social Affairs in the fourth Merkel cabinet.

After receiving his Abitur in 1992 Heil first served his Zivildienst, then began studying sociology and political science at the University of Potsdam and the FernUniversität Hagen in 1995.

FEDERAL MINISTRY OF DEFENCE

The **Federal Ministry of Defence** (German: *Bundesministerium der Verteidigung*), abbreviated **BMVg**, is a top-level federal agency, headed by the Federal Minister of Defence as a member of the Cabinet of Germany. The ministry is headquartered at the *Hardthöhe* district in Bonn and has a second office in the *Bendlerblock* building in Berlin.

According to Article 65a of the German Constitution (*Grundgesetz)*, the Federal Minister of Defence is Commander-in-chief of the *Bundeswehr*, the German armed forces, with around 253,430 active personnel. Article 115b decrees that in the state of defence, declared by the Bundestag with consent of the Bundesrat, the command in chief passes to the Chancellor.

The ministry currently has approximately 3,730 employees. Of these, 3,230 work in Bonn while around 500 work in the *Bendlerblock* building in Berlin.

FEDERAL AGENCIES AND OFFICES

FEDERAL OFFICE FOR BUILDING AND ZONING

What would it be like if the city consisted of nothing but office buildings and no one lived there anymore? If there was no space available for a park, or if all downtown areas looked identical thanks to redevelopment? The Federal Office for Building and Zoning (Bundesamt für Bauwesen und Raumordnung, BBR) looks into these kinds of questions, develops scenarios and advises the Federation to ensure that a well-balanced mixture of region types emerges. Federal building projects in Berlin, Bonn and abroad are looked after by this authority.
www.bbr.bund.de

FEDERAL OFFICE FOR CIVIL PROTECTION AND DISASTER ASSISTANCE

Floods, chemical spills or leaks or terrorist attacks: in the event of national crises, the fire department, the army, the German Agency for Technical Relief and doctors work hand in hand. The Federal Office for Civil Protection and Disaster Assistance (BBK) draws up the emergency plans and guides and controls the rescue operations. The BBK has coordinated cooperation on the national, state and local levels since 2004.
www.bbk.bund.de

FEDERAL AGENCY FOR CARTOGRAPHY AND GEODESY

What is your exact position on the planet? Fortunately, we have topographical maps and satellite positioning services. The employees at the Federal Agency for Cartography and Geodesy provide all the basic geo-information required for the Federal Republic of Germany (BKG – Bundesamt für Kartographie und Geodäsie). They also advise the Federal Government in all matters concerning geodesy and geo-information.
www.bkg.bund.de

FEDERAL GOVERNMENT COMMISSIONER FOR MIGRATION, REFUGEES AND INTEGRATION

The Commissioner for Migration, Refugees and Integration supports the Federal Government in developing its policy of integration and promoting the co-existence of foreign residents and Germans.
www.bamf.de

FEDERAL AGENCY FOR NATURE CONSERVATION

In Germany Blattfusskrebse (a species of crab) and Apollofalter (Apollo moths) are in danger of extinction, which is why they are put on a "Red List". The Federal Agency for Nature Conservation (Bundesamt für Naturschutz, BfN) publishes the Red Lists of endangered biotopes and plant and animal species, and advises the Federal Ministry for the Environment, Nature Conservation, Construction and Atomic Safety (Bundesministerium für Umwelt, Naturschutz, Bau und Reaktorsicherheit, BMUB). It also sponsors nature conservation projects, oversees research and regulates the import and export of protected plant and animal species.

www.bfn.de

THE FEDERAL MARITIME AND HYDROGRAPHIC AGENCY

Under full sail with Germany's maritime service provider. The Federal Maritime and Hydrographic Agency (Bundesamt für Seeschifffahrt und Hydrographie, BSH) is not only the flag authority, it also publishes nautical charts, offers oceanographic services and provides information on the use and protection of the seas. It is responsible for tonnage measurements and for laying pipes and cables.

www.bsh.de

FEDERAL OFFICE FOR PROTECTION AGAINST RADIATION

Whether you want to know how long you can spend in the sun or about the effects of using mobile communications – the Federal Office for Protection against Radiation (BfS - Bundesamt für Strahlenschutz) provides you with the recommendations given by the experts. Its responsibilities also include nuclear waste disposal and transport, nuclear reactor safety and how to deal with and protect against exposure to radiation.
www.bfs.de

FEDERAL OFFICE OF CONSUMER PROTECTION AND FOOD SAFETY

The Federal Office of Consumer Protection and Food Safety (BVL) has been working to promote healthy meals in German households since 2002. This office coordinates food monitoring and approves plant protection products and veterinary drugs. The BVL also works as the German liaison office for early-warning systems in the European Union.
www.bvl.bund.de

FEDERAL OFFICE FOR THE PROTECTION OF THE CONSTITUTION

Protecting the free democratic system: to do this, the Federal Office for the Protection of the Constitution (Bundesamt für Verfassungsschutz, BfV) keeps extremist and dangerous activities under surveillance. It answers to the Federal Ministry of the Interior (Bundesinnenministerium).
www.verfassungsschutz.de

THE FEDERAL OFFICE OF ECONOMICS AND EXPORT CONTROL

Foreign trade, the promotion of economic development and energy are the key areas with which the Federal Office of Economics and Export Control (Bundesamt für Wirtschaft und Ausfuhrkontrolle, BAFA) is entrusted. As its contribution to international peacekeeping, for example, the BAFA keeps a close check on the export of arms and munitions. In European trade policy, it ensures that import regulations are carefully observed.
www.bafa.de

FEDERAL OFFICE FOR CENTRAL SERVICES AND UNRESOLVED PROPERTY ISSUES

The era of National Socialism, the division of the two German states and their reunification have led to a number of property issues. The place to go for anyone affected and their families is the Federal Office for Central Services and Unresolved Property Issues (BADV). This office is also a service provider for the federal financial administration and calculates the earnings, allowances and travel expenses of civil servants.
www.badv.bund.de

FEDERAL INSTITUTE OF OCCUPATIONAL SAFETY AND HEALTH

Do you have to sit in a draft at work? Is there mobbing going on at your office? Find the information you need at the Federal Institute of Occupational Safety and Health (BAuA – Bundesanstalt für Arbeitsschutz und Arbeitsmedizin) on topics dealing with safety and health at work. No matter whether it's about how to design call centers or about safety in process engineering plants: the BauA does the research, drafts solutions to problems and develops job training and continued training programs.
www.baua.de

GERMAN FINANCIAL SUPERVISORY AUTHORITY

More and more companies are offering comprehensive product ranges in the credit field, insurance and securities. For this reason, since May 2002 what was once three Federal monitoring agencies have now been united under the umbrella of the German Financial Supervisory Authority (Bundesanstalt für Finanzdienstleistungsaufsicht, BAFin).
www.bafin.de

FEDERAL INSTITUTE FOR GEO-SCIENCES AND RAW MATERIALS

Using raw materials economically: the staff at the Federal Institute for Geo-Sciences and Raw Materials (BGR – Bundesanstalt für Geowissenschaften und Rohstoffe) advise the ministries on questions concerning applied geo-sciences and geo-scientific issues in environmental and resources conservation. The BGR employees are commissioned by the Federal Government to carry out projects in developing countries in particular and to undertake assignments in research and development.
www.bgr.bund.de

FEDERAL INSTITUTE FOR HYDROGRAPHY

How clean are the German waterways? When does it make sense to straighten the course of a river? The Federal Institute for Hydrography (BfG - Bundesanstalt für Gewässerkunde) works in the fields of hydrography, water management and waterways protection. It supports the authorities for Water and Shipping Management (WSV - Wasser- und Schifffahrtsverwaltung) in planning, building and expanding, operating and maintaining the national waterways.
www.bafg.de

FEDERAL AGENCY FOR REAL ESTATE

Germany's real-estate and forestry assets are managed by the Federal Agency for Real Estate. Its services include the use and management of the real estate that belong to the federal government. The agency is located with its main headquarters in Bonn and acts as the property investor when federal government departments invest in new buildings.
www.bundesimmobilien.de

FEDERAL OFFICE FOR AGRICULTURE AND FOOD

The Federal Office for Agriculture and Food (BLE – Bundesanstalt für Landwirtschaft und Ernährung) has a wide range of tasks in the agricultural, food and consumer protection sector. As a market regulatory authority, it supports the enforcement of European agricultural policy and is responsible for the admission and inspection of border-crossing goods. It also monitors fishing and the use of renewable raw materials.
www.ble.de

FEDERAL INSTITUTE FOR MATERIAL RESEARCH AND TESTING

The Federal Institute for Material Research and Testing (BAM – Bundesanstalt für Materialforschung und -prüfung) aims to improve safety and reliability in chemical and material technology, while promoting the development of German industry at the same time. As the highest federal authority, BAM is also in charge of approving packaging or containers, for hazardous materials in particular.
www.bam.de

THE GERMAN FEDERAL CARTEL OFFICE

The central task of the German Federal Cartel Office (Bundeskartellamt) is to monitor competition in the free market economy. This includes such things as enforcing the prohibition of cartels and supervising mergers. It can apply European legislation on competition when the European Commission does not take action itself.
www.bundeskartellamt.de

GERMAN FEDERAL BUREAU OF INVESTIGATION

Everything comes together here: in the German Federal Bureau of Investigation (Bundeskriminalamt, BKA), the central Federal agency for police information and intelligence. The BKA coordinates the cooperation of the Federal States and is responsible for international cooperation, when such crimes as drug dealing, money laundering or trafficking in human beings cross international borders.
www.bka.de

FEDERAL NETWORK AGENCY

The Federal Network Agency for Electricity, Gas, Telecommunications, the Post Office and the Railway ensures equal opportunity for rival companies on the "network markets". In addition to overseeing fair competition, this supreme federal office also tests technical devices on their electromagnetic compatibility and draws up the frequency utilization plan for Germany.
www.bundesnetzagentur.de

FEDERAL ADMINISTRATION OFFICE

The central service provider for the Federal Republic of Germany: the Federal Administration Office (BVA – Bundesverwaltungsamt) provides more than one hundred different services for the ministries in Berlin and Bonn as well as for their divisions. This includes schools abroad, the modernization of administration and staff recruitment for government offices. The BVA, with its main offices located in Cologne, also maintains the central register for foreigners and processes applications for education loans.
www.bva.bund.de

GERMAN CENTRAL REVENUE OFFICE

The German Federal Revenue Office (BZSt), which is located in Bonn, Berlin, Saarlouis and Schwedt, is responsible for national and international tax issues on the national level and also supports the state tax authorities in auditing large companies and corporations. The BZSt is part of the Federal Ministry of Finance (BMF).
www.bzst.bund.de

GERMAN FINANCE AGENCY

The Federal Republic of Germany – Finanzagentur GmbH, or the German Finance Agency for short, keeps a watchful eye on the country's bank balance. Its tasks include taking out loans and managing the national debt. The Frankfurt-based agency also issues stocks and bonds, such as Treasury bonds or federal savings bonds.
www.deutsche-finanzagentur.de

GERMAN ARCHAEOLOGICAL INSTITUTE

Set out to discover ancient cultures: if you'd like to take a virtual trip to the Coliseum in Rome or to an oasis settlement in Oman, on this site the German Archaeological Institute (Deutsches Archäologisches Institut, DAI) will take you along with it. You can learn about the organization of

the federal institution and take a glimpse into the research on monuments, finds and written sources.
www.dainst.org

GERMAN PATENT AND TRADE MARK OFFICE

The German Patent and Trade Mark Office (Deutsches Patent- und Markenamt, DPMA), with headquarters in Munich, is a federal superior authority subordinated to the Federal Ministry of Justice. It is the central authority in the field of industrial property law in Germany.
www.dpma.de

GERMAN FEDERAL FILM BOARD

Cinema as a cultural asset: In the 1960s, the German film industry was confronted with a crisis – the state reacted by forming the German Federal Film Board (FFA). The Federal Film Board under public law receives fees from cinema operators, video program vendors and TV stations. It supports filmmakers and the quality of German productions and is also involved in marketing these films abroad.
www.ffa.de

FEDERAL OFFICE FOR MOTOR TRAFFIC

Which driver doesn't know the "files" in Flensburg? In the Central Register of Traffic Offenders at the Federal Office for Motor Traffic (Kraftfahrt-Bundesamt, KBA) traffic offenders collect "points". Records are kept on driver's licenses and vehicles as well as drivers.
www.kba.de

FEDERAL OFFICE FOR CIVIL AVIATION

The employees at the Federal Office for Civil Aviation (LBA – Luftfahrt-Bundesamt) are responsible for making sure that any flight you take is always a safe one. Whether you're flying in a plane, using a parachute or traveling with an airline – all these modes of air transportation are tested, approved and monitored here. Violations of the legal regulations in civil aviation are pursued and punished by this office.
www.lba.de

MAX RUBNER-INSTITUTE

What's for dinner today? The Max-Rubner Institute (MRI) focuses on consumer protection for everything that has to do with healthy food. The Federal Research Institute of Nutrition and Food tests fish, meat and vegetables for harmful substances. Areas of research also include careful and nutrient-preserving food processing and quality assurance for plant and animal products.
www.mri.bund.de

PAUL-EHRLICH-INSTITUTE

Who knows whether medications really help? Before a drug comes onto the German market, its quality and effectiveness must be tested, and it goes through tests for safety and environmental acceptability. Biological preparations such as vaccines and serums for humans and animals are tested by the Paul Ehrlich Institute, PEI.
www.pei.de

FEDERAL PHYSICAL-TECHNICAL INSTITUTE

What time, how long, how heavy? Everything starts with time, length and weight – babies are already measured just after they take their first breath. Measuring everything there is to measure as exactly as possible is exactly what the Federal Physical-Technical Institute (PTB - Physikalisch-Technische Bundesanstalt) does.
www.ptb.de

ROBERT-KOCH-INSTITUTE

How can infections be avoided? Are allergies on the rise? What dangers are posed by the cultivation of gene-manipulated plants? Since its foundation more than 100 years ago, the Robert Koch Institute, RKI, has been working to protect people against infectious diseases. Today its researchers also study health trends in Germany and test the safety of procedures and products using gene technology.
www.rki.de

FEDERAL STATISTICAL OFFICE GERMANY

How much does the average German earn? How many unemployed people are there in Germany? How many schools, single households or conservation areas are there in the country? The Federal Statistical Office, with its main offices located in Wiesbaden, collects all kinds of official data about Germany. Although many of these official analyses deliver facts on which important political decisions are based, they are also readily available to anyone interested.
www.destatis.de

ORGANIZATION FOR TECHNICAL SUPPORT

„T as in Technical, H as in Help, W as in worldwide“ – another way of spelling the German acronym THW of the Organization for Technical Support (Technisches Hilfswerk). The blue vehicles always turn up when people, animals or material assets are in danger, because one of the tasks of the THW is to provide technical support for civil defence, at the site of major accidents and catastrophes, within the country and abroad.
www.thw.de

THE FEDERAL ENVIRONMENTAL AGENCY

For humanity and the environment: to preserve nature as the foundation of life, for future generations as well, and to promote environmental thinking and action as a matter of course – that is the goal of the Federal Environmental Agency (Umweltbundesamt, UBA) in Dessau-Roßlau.

CUSTOMS

Illegal employment, cigarette smuggling and product piracy: the customs authorities pursue criminals and guarantee that international goods traffic runs smoothly. On behalf of the state, the customs officers also levy duties. And to protect endangered animals and plants, they check travelers with suspicious souvenirs.
www.zoll.de

GERMANY INTELLIGENCE AGENCIES

Federal Chancellor's Office
Federal Intelligence Service [BND]
Bundesnachrichtendienst

DEFENSE MINISTRY
Office of Intelligence of the Federal Armed Forces [ANBw]
Amt für Nachrichtenwesen der Bundeswehr
Office for Radio Monitoring of the Federal Armed Forces [AFMBw]
Amt für Fernmeldwesen Bundeswehr
Military Security Service [MAD]
Militaerischer Abschirmdienst

INTERIOR MINISTRY
Federal Office for the Protection of the Constitution [BfV]
Bundesamt für Verfassungsschutz
State Office for the Protection of the Constitution [LfV]
Landesamt für Verfassungsschutz
Federal Office for Information Technology Security [BSI]
Bundesamt für Sicherheit in der Informationstechnik

FEDERAL OFFICE FOR THE PROTECTION OF THE CONSTITUTION (BFV)

Federal Office for the Protection of the Constitution (BfV) Merianstrasse 100 50765 Cologne Phone: +49 (221)-792-0 oder 03018-792-0 Fax: +49 (221)-792-2915 oder 03018-10-792-2915 E-mail: poststelle@bfv.bund.de

Federal funding for the BfV was € 155,238,306 in 2008 (2007: € 144,555,652). The Federal Office for the Protection of the Constitution had a total of 2,529 staff members (2007: 2,503).

MILITARY COUNTERINTELLIGENCE SERVICE (MAD)

Federal funding for the MAD was € 70,325,121.22 in 2008 (2007: € 69,188,992). The Military Counterintelligence Service had 1,230 staff members (2007: 1,242).

OTHER ORGANISATIONAL DATA

At the beginning of the year 2009, the data holdings of the Federal Administration (*Bund*) and the *Länder* (federal states) in the Nachrichtendienstliches Informationssystem (NADIS -Intelligence Information System) totalled 1,349,258 entries of personal data (beginning of 2008: 1,172,797), of which 924,667 entries (68.5 %) were obtained in connection with security checks or background checks under the provisions of the Act on Aviation Security (*Luftsicherheitsgesetz*).

PROTECTION OF THE CONSTITUTION AND DEMOCRACY

I. PROTECTION OF THE CONSTITUTION UNDER THE BASIC LAW

The Constitution of the Federal Republic of Germany, known as the Basic Law (*Grundgesetz*, GG), guarantees German citizens a variety of basic rights. People who reject our free and democratic order also enjoy the same basic rights. But limits to these rights must be clearly set wherever it becomes obvious that they are being misused in order to undermine the free and democratic order and thereby destroy the foundation on which these same rights are based.

Drawing on the painful lessons learnt from the failure of the Weimar Republic, the principle of a strong democracy prepared to defend its values has been anchored in the Basic Law.[1]

This principle is characterised by three essential features:

– commitment to values, i.e. the state recognises its attachment to certain values it considers especially important and which are therefore not negotiable;
– the readiness to defend values, i.e. the state is willing to uphold these most important values against extremist positions; and
– preventive action to protect the Constitution, i.e. the state does not wait to react until extremists have violated the law. In other words, the protection of the Constitution functions as an early warning system for our democracy.

The principle of a strong democracy prepared to defend its values is clearly expressed in a number of the Basic Law's provisions:
– Article 79 (3) provides that fundamental principles of the Constitution – including the inviolability of human dignity under Article 1 (1) and the principles determining the fundamental order of the state (democracy, federalism, rule of law, the welfare

Thiel, Markus, *Die „wehrhafte Demokratie" als verfassungsrechtliche Grundentscheidung*, in: Thiel, Markus, ed., *Wehrhafte Demokratie* (2003), p. 1 et seqq.

system) as set out in Art. 20 -are unalterable and thus may not be modified by legislative process.

– Under Article 21 (2), political parties that seek to undermine or abolish the free and democratic basic order or to endanger the existence of the Federal Republic of Germany may be declared unconstitutional by the Federal Constitutional Court (BVerfG).
– Article 9 (2) provides that associations whose aim or activities violate criminal laws or oppose the constitutional order or the idea of international understanding shall be prohibited (see Section VI).
– Under Article 18, the Federal Constitutional Court (BVerfG) may declare certain basic rights to be forfeited if these rights are abused to attack the free and democratic basic order.

-Articles 73 No. 10 *litt.* b and 87 (1) 2nd sentence provide the basis for the establishment and operation of the Federal and *Land* Offices for the Protection of the Constitution.

II. Offices for the Protection of the Constitution: Tasks and powers

Functions Pursuant to the Federal Act on the Protection of the Constitution (*Bundesverfassungsschutzgesetz,* BVerfSchG), a main task of the federal and *Land* authorities responsible for the protection of the Constitution is gathering and analysing information on the following:

– activities directed against the free and democratic order or against the existence or security of the Federal Republic or of one of the federal states *(Länder)*, or intended to unlawfully hinder federal or *Land* constitutional bodies or their members from carrying out their official duties;
– intelligence activities or those that endanger state security, carried out on behalf of a foreign power within the area of the territorial application of the Federal Act on the Protection of the Constitution (BVerfSchG);

– activities in the area covered by the Federal Act on the Protection of the Constitution which – by actual, or preparations for intended, use of force – threaten the foreign interests of the Federal Republic of Germany;
– activities within the area covered by the Federal Act on the Protection of the Constitution which are directed against the idea of international understanding, in particular peaceful co-existence.

Information-The agencies responsible for the protection of the Constitution gathering gather most of the information needed for fulfilling their tasks from publicly accessible sources. Where this is not possible or effective, they may, within the limits of defined legal powers and in accordance with the principle of proportionality, use intelligence methods for covert information-gathering. These resources include, in particular, confidential sources, surveillance, video and audio recordings, and interception of correspondence, mail and telecommunications in accordance with the Act (adopted by virtue of Article 10 of the Basic Law) to Restrict the Privacy of Correspondence, Posts and Telecommunications (*Gesetz zur Beschränkung des Brief-, Post-und Fernmeldegeheimnisses* -short title: *Artikel 10-Gesetz*, abbr. G 10).

The powers of the Federal Office for the Protection of the Constitution (BfV) were extended under the Act to Fight International Terrorism (*Terrorismusbekämpfungsgesetz)* of 9 January 2002.2

Among other things, the Act gives the BfV the right, under narrowly defined conditions, to gather information from financial enterprises, airlines, postal services, telecommunications services, and teleservices providers.

No police powers In carrying out their duties, the agencies for the protection of the Constitution have no police powers, i.e. they may not perform arrests or searches or seize any property.

Security vetting An additional task of the agencies responsible for the protection of the Constitution is to help with security clearance checks of people entrusted in the public interest with classified information, or who are to be granted access or can access such information and who hold, or are recruited for, a security-sensitive post within a facility vital to civil and military needs. The BfV's powers in this context are governed in detail by the Security Clearance Check Act (*Sicherheitsüberprüfungsgesetz*, SÜG).

Co-operation with Within their area of responsibility, the authorities for the protection of

German security the Constitution help to ensure the internal security of the Federal authorities

Republic of Germany. As provided by law, they work closely, on a basis of trust, with other security authorities, in particular the other federal intelligence services: the Military Counterintelligence Service (MAD), responsible for the Federal Armed Forces (Bundeswehr); and the Federal Intelligence Service (BND), responsible for foreign intelligence; and with police and criminal prosecution authorities. The creation of a joint anti-terrorist database of federal and state police authorities and intelligence services, and the possibility of maintaining joint incident-related project files, has helped improve information sharing by simplifying the existing procedural regulations for data exchange. The anti-terrorist database went into operation on 31 March 2007.

International In view of the increasingly international nature of threat phenomena, cooperation the BfV also maintains active contacts with its partner services abroad.

Above all, the BfV cooperates closely with EU states, the USA and Canada. Given the need for information in the field of international

2 Originally, the regulations were set to expire on 10 January 2007, but were extended for another five years by the Act amending the Counter-Terrorism Act, which entered into force on 5 January 2007. As to substance, they correspond largely with the results of a prior evaluation.

terrorism (e.g. on countries of origin, terrorists' travel movements), this cooperation also extends to other states outside the EU. In terms of quantity and quality, the character of contacts with foreign intelligence services often varies greatly.

In view of an integrated and strategic approach to fighting international terrorism, multilateral cooperation in international bodies has become increasingly important. The priority of such cooperation lies in the analysis of the causes and origins of a terrorist threat, a forecast of developments and the development of counter-measures.

Among others, the BfV is represented in the Counter-Terrorist Group (CTG), a cooperation forum of European national intelligence services. The CTG maintains contacts with the European Joint Situation Center (SitCen) und supports the EU in fighting terrorism.

Federal Government

Parliamentary Control Panel

G-10 Commission

Monitoring by the Federal Commissioner for Data Protection and Freedom of Information (BfDI)

Right to demand information

Supervision by the courts

SUPERVISION OF THE AUTHORITIES RESPONSIBLE FOR THE PROTECTION OF THE CONSTITUTION

The activities of the Federal Office for the Protection of the Constitution (BfV) are subject to supervision by the Federal Government and control by the German Bundestag. The Parliamentary Control Panel established for this purpose is to be regularly provided with comprehensive information on the general activities of the BfV, MAD and BND and on incidents of special significance, and about other incidents at its request (Section 2 of the Parliamentary Control Panel Act (*Parlamentarisches Kontrollgremiumsgesetz,* PKGrG)). This panel must be permitted by the Federal Government to inspect records and files, and to conduct staff hearings. The Parliamentary Control Panel appoints the independent G-10 Commission which, always in advance of any such operations, will consider the permissibility and necessity of restrictions of the privacy of correspondence, posts and telecommunications in accordance with Article 10 of the Basic Law. Similar provisions apply to the rights under the new Counter-Terrorism Act to demand information from postal services, telecommunications services, and teleservices providers (see Section II).

The Federal Act on the Protection of the Constitution (BVerfSchG) as well as other special legal regulations affecting the tasks of the BfV,

e.g. the Act on Setting up a Counter-Terrorism Database (ATDG) or the Act on the Central Aliens Register (AZRG), contain a large number of provisions pertaining to data protection. On this basis, the BfDI continuously checks the BfV's compliance with data protection rules and regulations.

The BfV is legally obligated to provide data subjects, upon request, with information about their personal data files free of charge, if such persons provide reference to specific information and can demonstrate a particular interest in such information (Section 15 (1) of the Federal Act on the Protection of the Constitution). Disclosure of information will be denied only if any of the reasons for refusal as listed in sub-section 2 of Section 15 of the BVerfSchG applies.

Germany maintains a strict separation between intelligence and law enforcement/police agencies. Intelligence agencies are therefore prohibited from using police powers to gather information. There are three intelligence agencies at the federal level, two of which focus on domestic intelligence, whereas the third one, the Federal Intelligence Service, focuses on foreign intelligence. Intelligence gathering in Germany is regulated by the acts establishing the three federal intelligence agencies and the Act to Restrict the Privacy of Correspondence, Mail, and Telecommunications. The expanded powers of the law enforcement and police agencies to maintain national security are contained in the Act on the Federal Criminal Police Office, the Act on the Federal Police, the Act on the Customs Investigation Bureau and the Customs Investigation Offices, and the Code of Criminal Procedure. The intelligence and law enforcement agencies may access, intercept, and request stored communications data, subject to limits specified in applicable laws. The intelligence agencies are subject to extensive administrative as well as parliamentary oversight, which includes several specialized parliamentary control panels but also general parliamentary oversight.

In Germany, the task of maintaining national security is divided between the intelligence and the law enforcement and police agencies. Because Germany is a federation, there are federal as well as state agencies. In addition, there is a strict separation between intelligence and police agencies, although their areas of responsibility might overlap nonetheless.

The strict separation was established after the Second World War in order to prevent an accumulation of police and intelligence powers in an agency like the Nazi's Secret State Police (Gestapo). The Allied Occupation Forces made the separation a precondition of approval of the German Basic Law, the country's constitution, which provides for the establishment of police and law enforcement agencies as well as an intelligence agency. The law therefore states that the intelligence agencies are not authorized to use force or other types of police powers to gather information.

The three existing federal intelligence agencies are the Federal Office for the Protection of the Constitution (Bundesamt für Verfassungsschutz, BfV), the Military Counter-Intelligence Service (Militärischer Abschirmdienst, MAD), and the Federal Intelligence Service (Bundesnachrichtendienst, BND). The BfV and the MAD gather domestic intelligence, whereas the BND focuses on foreign intelligence.

In addition, following the September 11 terrorist attacks and the subsequent terrorist attacks in Madrid and London, federal law enforcement/police agencies were also given preventive powers to protect against "homegrown terrorists," including, among other things, the authority to intercept communications. Agencies granted such powers include the Federal Criminal Police Office, the Federal Police, and the Customs Investigation Bureau and Customs Investigation Offices.

On April 20, 2016, however, the German Federal Constitutional Court ruled that the Act on the Federal Criminal Police Office was partially unconstitutional, because various provisions that deal with the investigative powers of the Federal Criminal Police Office for fighting international terrorism were not proportional. The Court criticized the legal requirements for carrying out covert surveillance measures as too broad and unspecific and held that the norms allowing the transfer of data to third-party authorities and to authorities in third countries lacked sufficient legal restrictions. The provisions that were declared unconstitutional will mainly remain in force, subject to restrictions, up to and including June 30, 2018.

In June 2016, in reaction to terrorist attacks in Paris and Istanbul, the Federal Government published a draft act which would amend several laws in order to improve information sharing between national and foreign agencies fighting international terrorism. Among other things, the act would establish a common database for the BfV and foreign intelligence agencies and expand the powers of the BND and of the Federal Police.

INTELLIGENCES AGENCIES

A. FEDERAL OFFICE FOR THE PROTECTION OF THE CONSTITUTION (BFV)

The BfV is an executive agency that falls under the authority of the Federal Ministry of the Interior. Its purpose is to protect the free democratic order and the existence and the security of the Federation and the German states. The law provides that the BfV is required to cooperate with its counterparts at the state level to ensure the protection of the constitution.

The agency focuses its work on fighting and collecting information on politically motivated crimes (left- and right-wing extremism); Islamist terrorism and other extremist efforts of foreigners posing a threat to national security; espionage, including cyber espionage and industrial espionage; and the Scientology Organization.

According to section 3 of the Act on the Federal Office for the Protection of the Constitution, the agencies for the protection of the constitution are tasked with the collection and analysis of information, intelligence, and documents relating to individuals or subject matter, concerning

efforts

directed against the free democratic order; or

threatening the existence or the security of the federation or one of its states; or

aimed at unlawfully hampering constitutional bodies of the federation or one of its states or their members in the performance of their duties; or

jeopardizing external relations of Germany through the use of violence or preparation thereof; or

directed against the idea of international understanding (art. 9, para. 2 of the German Basic Law), in particular against the peaceful coexistence of nations (art. 26, para. 1 of the German Basic Law); or concerning

activities threatening national security or intelligence activities carried out on behalf of a foreign power (counterintelligence).

In addition, the agencies for the protection of the constitution participate in security vetting procedures for persons working in sensitive areas.

When the requirements of section 3 of the Act on the Federal Office for the Protection of the Constitution are fulfilled, the agency may use confidential informants, surveillance, telecommunications surveillance, image and sound recordings, false documents, and false vehicle license plates in order to gather intelligence. It may also request information from postal or telecommunication services, financial institutions, airlines, and Internet service providers.

B. Military Counter-Intelligence Service (MAD)

The MAD forms part of the Federal Ministry of Defense. Its purpose and tasks are similar to the BfV, but with the difference that it focuses on efforts and activities that target personnel, departments, or facilities of the Federal Ministry of Defense and are carried out by individuals who are members of, or are employed by the ministry of defense and its agencies. Section 3 of the Military Counter-Intelligence Service Act provides that the BfV and the MAD are required to cooperate closely and to provide mutual support and assistance.

Even though the MAD generally focuses on gathering domestic intelligence, as an exception, it is also authorized to collect and analyze information during the course of special foreign assignments of the German Federal Armed Forces or during the course of humanitarian missions. Other foreign intelligence gathering is prohibited.

C. Federal Intelligence Service (BND)

The BND reports directly to the federal chancellery and is generally the only intelligence agency authorized to gather foreign intelligence. For this purpose, it collects and analyzes information that is of importance for German foreign and security policy. It is also authorized to request information from postal or telecommunication services, financial institutions, airlines, and Internet service providers, as well as information required for the performance of its functions, including personal data, from every authority, and to inspect official registers.

The intelligence objectives of the BND are defined by the mission statement of the federal government. The mission statement currently focuses on proliferation, international terrorism, failing states, and conflicts over natural resources. Regions that it currently prioritizes are the Near and Middle East, North Africa, and West and Central Asia.

LEGISLATIVE FRAMEWORK

The work of the intelligence agencies is undertaken in accordance with the legislative framework of the Act on the Federal Office for the Protection of the Constitution, the Act on the Military Counter-Intelligence Service, the Act on the Federal Intelligence Service, and the Act to Restrict the Privacy of Correspondence, Mail, and Telecommunications (Article 10 Act).

For law enforcement and police agencies, authorizations are contained in the Act on the Federal Criminal Police Office, the Act on the Federal Police, the Act on the Customs Investigation Bureau and the Customs Investigation Offices, and the Code of Criminal Procedure.

INTERCEPTION AND TRANSMISSION OF COMMUNICATIONS

Article 10 of the German Basic Law provides that the privacy of correspondence, mail, and telecommunications is inviolable. Restrictions may only be imposed pursuant to law. If the restriction serves to protect the free, democratic order or the existence or security of the German federation or of a German state, the law may provide that the affected person will not be informed of the measure.

The abovementioned German intelligence and law enforcement agencies have been authorized to access, intercept, and request stored communications data. This authority and its limits are delineated in article 10 of the Basic Law as noted above, in the specific acts establishing the agencies, in the Article 10 Act, and in the Telecommunications Act.

The German Federal Constitutional Court has held that the transmission of subscriber data by telecommunications providers to a requesting agency is only permissible if there is a legal norm authorizing the agency to request the data and an additional legal norm obligating the telecommunications provider to transfer the data ("double door model"). If the agency is authorized by law to request communications data, the Telecommunications Act requires telecommunications providers to immediately comply with such a request. "Telecommunications providers" are defined as anyone who exclusively or occasionally provides telecommunications services or who contributes to the provision of such services.

Anyone who operates a telecommunications network that provides publicly available telecommunications services to more than ten thousand participants is obligated to install a surveillance system that complies with the technical requirements set out in the Telecommunications Surveillance Directive and the technical guideline adopted by the German Federal Network Agency. Telecommunications providers must ensure that they are at all times capable of being informed by telephone of incoming requests and their urgency, and that they are able to accept and process such requests during regular business hours.

V. OVERSIGHT

The intelligence agencies are subject to administrative as well as parliamentary oversight. There are several specialized parliamentary control panels that were set up to scrutinize the work of the intelligence agencies, but they are also subject to the general framework of parliamentary oversight.

A. Parliamentary Oversight

1. Parliamentary Control Panel (PKGr)

Article 45d of the German Basic Law provides that the German Parliament must appoint a panel to scrutinize the federal intelligence activities. Based on this constitutional provision, the Parliament enacted the Act on the Parliamentary Control of the Intelligence Activities of the Federation, which established the Parliamentary Control Panel (PKGr). The PKGr oversees the Federal Office for the Protection of the Constitution, the Military Counter-Intelligence Service, and the Federal Intelligence Service.

The members of the PKGr are appointed by the Parliament from among their members; the Parliament also decides the number of members, the composition, and the PKGr's working methods. The Parliamentary Control Panel currently has nine members. The deliberations of the PKGr are conducted in secret.

The federal government is required to disclose comprehensive information on the general activities of the federal intelligence services and of activities of particular importance to the Panel, as well as on other procedures if requested by the PKGr. Furthermore, the PKGr may require the federal government and the federal intelligence agencies to release files and other documents in official safekeeping and to transmit data stored in data files. It may also obtain access to all official premises and interview members of the intelligence services and the federal government. The courts and public authorities are required to provide legal and administrative assistance.

In addition, the Act on the Federal Office for the Protection of the Constitution, the Act on the Military Counter-Intelligence Service, and the Article 10 Act also contain special notification requirements.

The PKGr reports to the German Parliament on its oversight activities halfway through and at the end of each electoral term. The reports are publicly available in the Parliamentary Material Information System (DIP).

2. Article 10 Commission

Restrictions on the privacy of mail and telecommunications undertaken by the federal intelligence agencies pursuant to article 10 of the German Basic Law are monitored by the Article 10 Commission. The Article 10 Commission is appointed by the Parliamentary Control Panel and is composed of four members. The chairperson must be qualified to hold judicial office. In addition, there are four alternate members who may take part in the meetings with the right to speak and to ask questions.

The G10 Commission decides ex officio or on the basis of complaints whether restrictions on the privacy of mail and telecommunications are permissible and necessary. The oversight extends to the entire scope of collecting, processing, and using the personal data obtained pursuant to the Article 10 Act by the federal intelligence agencies.

Before a restriction on the privacy of mail and telecommunications can be enforced, the federal ministry in charge has the obligation to report every month to the Article 10 Commission and to request approval. In cases of imminent danger, a restriction may be enforced without prior approval. Approval must be obtained without undue delay.

3. Confidential Committee of the Budget Committee

The operating budgets of the federal intelligence agencies are not submitted to the general budget committee, but approved by a special committee called the Confidential Committee of the Budget Committee, which works under conditions of secrecy. The members are elected by the German Parliament according to the process used for the election of the members of the PKGr. The Federal Budget Code provides that the Confidential Committee of the Budget Committee has the same control rights as the PKGr laid down in sections 5, 6, 7, 8, 12, and 13 of the Parliamentary Control Panel Act.

These rights include access to files and data stored in data files, access to all official premises, and the right to interview members of the intelligence services and the federal government.

The PKGr and the Confidential Committee are obligated to consult with and advise each other in order to avoid oversight gaps.

4. General Parliamentary Oversight

In addition, the work of the federal intelligence agencies is subject to general parliamentary oversight. This includes responding to requests from committees of inquiry and other specialized committees, answering questions in general debates and in debates on matters of topical interest, and answering formalized requests (interpellations) from minority groupings and individual members of Parliament. The Federal Constitutional Court has held that communications concerning contacts with foreign intelligence services cannot be withheld from a committee of inquiry by generally invoking the interests of the state; instead, specific reasons must be given.

B. Administrative Oversight

1. Administrative and Technical Supervision by Competent Federal Ministry

The Federal Chancellery as well as the Federal Ministry of the Interior and the Federal Ministry of Defense are authorized to request statements and issue instructions for the respective intelligence agency under their supervision.

2. Federal Commissioner for Data Protection and Freedom of Information

The Federal Commissioner for Data Protection and Freedom of Information monitors compliance of the federal intelligent agencies with data protection laws, in particular the Federal Data Protection Act, but also with the special data provisions contained in the acts establishing the federal intelligence agencies. The Commissioner has no powers with regard to data collected through mail and telecommunications surveillance. In these cases, responsibility lies solely with the Article 10 Commission.

The Commissioner is appointed by the German Parliament on a proposal from the federal government for a five-year term. He or she is independent in the discharge of his or her duties and subject only to the law.

3. Federal Court of Audit

The Federal Court of Audit determines if public finances have been properly spent and efficiently administered. A body called the "College of Three" composed of the president or vice president of the Court of Audit, the head of the unit, and the responsible audit director is in charge of the audit of the federal intelligence agencies' budgets. The College of Three informs the Confidential Committee of the Budget Committee, the PKGr, the federal ministry supervising the intelligence agency, and the Federal Ministry of Finance about the results of the audit of the annual account and the budgetary and economic management of the respective federal intelligence agency.

GERMANY FOREIGN AND DOMESTIC POLICY STRATEGY - SELECTED SPEECHED AND STATEMENTS

PRESIDENT OF GERMANY

SPEECH AT THE CEREMONY IN THE GERMAN BUNDESTAG ON 9 NOVEMBER

Long live the German Republic!"

What a tremendous transformation Philipp Scheidemann proclaimed to the people on the streets of Berlin on 9 November 1918, here at this spot, from a window of the Reichstag: the collapse of the German Empire, the end of a centuries-old monarchical order, and the dawn of a democratic future for Germany.

What a proclamation in the dying days of the Great War. What a message for tired, emaciated men and women, for a war-torn country, for the cities, barracks and companies where mutinies and mass strikes spread like wildfire, in this explosive atmosphere of protest, hunger and uncertainty.

Peace at last, political self-determination at last, and social justice – that was the promise of these words. A ray of hope on a gloomy November day.

The revolution, as unplanned and improvised as it was, stands for a profound caesura in German history, for the beginning of the modern age.

Many of its accomplishments continue to shape our country today, even if we are not aware of this in our daily lives. The revolution brought all German parliaments the same, universal right of suffrage –including, at long last, for women for the very first time. It paved the way to the Weimar National Assembly, to a republican constitution, to parliamentary democracy – the first in the history of our country. This revolution also laid the foundation stones of the modern welfare state, with the eight-hour day, collective bargaining, co-determination with works councils – all of this stands for social progress, which began back then amidst the post-war turmoil.

However, in spite of all this, the revolution barely even features in our nation's consciousness to this day. While 9 November 1918 is listed on the map of German places of remembrance, it has never been accorded the importance it actually deserves. It is the poor relation of our democratic history – and also because 9 November is actually an ambivalent day, because it stands for light and darkness, because we almost never consider the democracy that started back then from its beginning, but usually from its end.

Sometimes it seems to me as if this turning point is doomed to be overshadowed for eternity by the failure of the republic and discredited and debased by 30 January 1933. Indeed, the end of the Weimar Republic marked the beginning of the descent into the most terrible chapter in German history. However, it was not democracy that was on the wrong side of history – it was the enemies of democracy that were on the wrong side of history. Ultra-nationalism, the dictatorship, the inhumane ideology of the National Socialists brought war and heinous crimes to Europe and ruined this country politically and morally. It was to the great fortune of us all that we were given a second chance to enjoy self-determination in unity and freedom – and this chance became reality. It, the republic, proved that it was on the right side of history. We should remind ourselves of this fact one hundred years later on and, I might add, also celebrate this fact.

Of course, there is no denying that this was a paradoxical, contradictory revolution from the outset. Its story cannot be told in a clear-cut way. But, then again, can that be said of any chapter of Germany's history?

The contradictory nature of the revolution was in evidence that very same day, 9 November, when Karl Liebknecht, the leader of the Spartacus League, proclaimed the republic for the second time – just two hours after Philipp Scheidemann. Friedrich Ebert wanted first and foremost to prevent chaos, civil war and military intervention on the part of the victorious powers; he was driven by the desire to give the people employment and livelihoods. The Council of People's Representatives had limited room for manoeuvre in these uncertain months, in the maelstrom of more radical forces to both the left and right.

And yet the People's Representatives probably should have have dared to bring about greater change than they considered to be justifiable from their point of view at the time. Too many avowed opponents of the nascent republic retained their posts in the military, judiciary and administrative apparatus. Of course, Friedrich Ebert's People's Representatives were forced to defend themselves against the radical left's attempt to prevent the elections of the National Assembly by force. However, there was no justification whatsoever for giving the brutality of nationalist Freikorps de facto free reign. Many people were murdered back then, including Rosa Luxemburg and Karl Liebknecht. We also want to remember the many victims of those days today.

Indeed, this revolution was also one characterised by wrong turns and dashed hopes. Nevertheless, it remains the great achievement of the moderate workers' movement that they, in a climate of violence, in the midst of suffering and hunger, sought compromise with the moderate forces of the middle classes and that they gave precedence to parliamentary democracy.

This day, 9 November 1918, is a milestone in the history of German democracy. It stands for the birth of the republic in Germany. It stands for the breakthrough of parliamentary democracy. And this is why it deserves pride of place in our country's culture of remembrance. After all, those who believe today that our democracy is something that we can now take for granted and that this parliament is an everyday object, very much like a piece of old furniture, should take a look at this chapter of history. No, this parliament is not something to be taken for granted, and it is certainly not a footnote. It is a historic achievement, and one that we must fight for – everywhere, but first and foremost in this House.

In the Weimar Republic, 9 November was never able to assume the symbolic power of a founding myth. Even staunch republicans were not prepared to wholeheartedly throw their weight behind a revolution whose prospects were so dim from the outset, as Theodor Wolff wrote in the "Berliner Tageblatt" on the first anniversary of the proclamation of the republic. Instead of promoting unity, the memory of 9 November even exacerbated ideological divisions in society. For parts of the radical left, this date was synonymous with the supposed betrayal of the working class, while for the enemies of the republic on the right it came to symbolise the lie that was the "stab in the back", the alleged betrayal of the soldiers at the front. It was no coincidence that Hitler made his first attempt to overthrow the republic in Munich on 9 November 1923 of all days, that "un-German system" whose representatives were subjected to the murderous hatred of extreme right-wing nationalists.

In particular, it was the flag of the republic that was the subject of its enemies' ire, and which they dragged through the mud time and again. Black-red-gold, the colours of the German freedom movement since the Hambach Festival of 1832. That alone is reason enough to bring 9 November 1918 out of the shadows of political history. Anyone who despises human rights and democracy today, who rekindles old nationalist hatred, certainly has no historical right to the colours black, red and gold.

The revolution of 1918/19 was the dawn of democracy, of a political experiment whose outcome was uncertain. We now know what a heavy burden the contemporaries who attempted democracy in the Reich and Länder had to bear back then.

The lost war and its bloody legacy of violence, the impact of the Treaty of Versailles, the turbulence of the economic crisis and inflation, of hunger and mass suffering – all of this put the Weimar Republic under strain and overwhelmed it from time to time.

And it was above all the long tradition of anti-liberal thought that poisoned the political culture of the republic. Intellectuals such as Carl Schmitt railed against the plurality of interests of the "modern mass society" and vilified the "tactical compromises and coalitions" of a so-called political "class". Members of the radical left berated parliaments and governments as instruments of the "bourgeoisie".

When we consider these challenges today, we realise just how impressive the achievements of those who shouldered political responsibility at the time were – who brought about a democratic constitution, modernised the judicial and education systems, provided housing and unemployment insurance, helped the arts and sciences to flourish, and – throughout all these years – steered highly fragile coalitions through the storms of domestic and foreign policy crises. Reich Chancellors and Ministers such as Hermann Müller, Gustav Stresemann and Matthias Erzberger, as well as parliamentarians such as Marianne Weber and Helene Weber, Ernst Heilmann, Marie Elisabeth Lüders and Marie Juchacz. Too many of them have been forgotten today.

Stalwart democrats supported the constitutional state in the judiciary and administration. Teachers of constitutional law such as Hugo Preuß, the father of the Weimar Constitution, Gerhard Anschütz, Richard Thoma, Hermann Heller and Hans Kelsen developed ideas that continue to inspire people today. Academics such as the economist Moritz Julius Bonn and the theologian Ernst Troeltsch advanced liberal thinking. Many who devoted themselves to the republic were derided, ostracised and attacked by the enemies of democracy. Leading politicians such as Matthias Erzberger and Walter Rathenau fell victim to right-wing extremist, predominantly anti-Semitically motivated murders.

Let us stop claiming that the Weimar Republic was a democracy without democrats. These courageous women and men have languished in the shadows of the history of the failure of the Weimar democracy for far too long. I believe that we owe them respect, esteem and gratitude.

The thoughts and actions of the Weimar democrats continued to reverberate above and beyond the first republic. After 1945, the founding mothers and fathers of the Federal Republic, many of whom had been deeply influenced by their experiences of the Weimar era, were able to build on their knowledge and also learn from their mistakes. To quote Heinrich August Winkler: "The fact that Bonn did not become Weimar is also due to the fact that Weimar existed."

I would like to draw on his sentiment with respect to our Berlin of today. It is true that we are living at a time in which democracy is coming under pressure once again, when its opponents are becoming more vocal and self-confident. But when whispers of the spectre of "Weimar-like conditions" are to be heard from time to time, then I reject these in the strongest possible terms. Such statements will make our democracy smaller and its enemies bigger than they actually are. And there is no reason to do either.

Especially when we recall the courageous women and men of the past, when we consider their experiences to be our foundations, then this gives me cause for hope. Not only are our institutions stronger and more robust, but, above all, we as democrats can learn from those who went before us. Freedom, the rule of law and democracy are our inheritance from these mothers and fathers – let us stake our claim to this legacy with self-confidence, and let us preserve it wisely and watchfully.

On 9 November, we Germans remember both things – the light and the shadows of our history. 9 November is a day of contradictions, a day of light and darkness, a day that demands us to consider what will always be part of looking at Germany's past, namely the ambivalence of remembering.

Exactly 80 years ago, during the night of 9 to 10 November 1938, synagogues burned in Germany. Jewish shops were looted and destroyed. Hundreds of women and men were killed by the Nazis, took their own lives, or died after being mistreated in concentration camps. These pogroms, which everyone could see at the time, were the harbinger of the persecution and annihilation of Europe's Jews. The pogroms stand for an unparalleled rupture with civilisation and for Germany's rapid descent into barbarism. Today we remember the victims of National Socialism. We are aware of our responsibility – a responsibility under which no line can ever be drawn.

This one date, 9 November, poses what is arguably the most difficult and painful question of German history: How was it possible that the same people that had the courage to embark on the path of democratic self-determination on 9 November 1918; that achieved so much in so many areas of human endeavour in the following years; that listened intently to symphonies in its concert halls and danced to swing in its nightclubs; whose scientists won Nobel Prizes; whose workers built housing cooperatives; whose artists merrily broke with tradition; and whose films packed cinemas worldwide – how was it possible that, in just a few years, this very same people brought the enemies of democracy to power in democratic elections; unleashed war and destruction on its neighbours in Europe; looked the other way – or perhaps even gawked or cheered – when in their own streets in Germany Jewish neighbours, homosexuals and people suffering from mental illnesses were dragged out of their homes by the henchmen of a criminal regime – a regime that crammed Jewish families into cattle wagons and sent parents and their children to the gas chambers?

That remains the most difficult and painful question of German history.

No historians' congress can answer this question for us. Nor can it be explained by putting it into historical context, thus putting our minds at rest. The answer can certainly not be provided by words alone. Instead, we can only provide it through our actions.

Remembrance that we only dutifully mouth at commemoration events, but which does not define our actions – such remembrance ossifies into a ritual. In the worst case, it even leads to resentments, to a sense of alienation between official remembrance and daily life and to how people feel, especially young people, who ask "what does this have to do with me?"

Esteemed Members of this House, honoured guests, in our actions we must prove that we Germans have truly learned from the past and truly become more vigilant because of our history. We need to take action any time another person's dignity is violated. We need to take a stand when a language of hatred spreads its tentacles. We cannot allow a situation where some people claim once again to be the sole voice of the "true people" and marginalise others. We need to speak up when certain groups are defined as scapegoats and when people are automatically regarded with suspicion simply because of their religion or skin colour. And we will not let up in our fight against anti-Semitism. We need to prevent groups from becoming ever more entrenched. We need to go out of our way and reach out to each other. We need to ensure that people keep talking with one another.

And we also need to fight once more for cohesion in Europe and for an international order, which is currently being called into question, even by our partners, because it is thanks to this European integration and this international order that we Germans are a people once again that has regained economic and political strength; overwhelmingly wants to live in an open-minded and pro-European way; is respected, indeed even valued, by many people in the world; still listens intently to symphonies in its concert halls and still dances in its nightclubs, albeit more likely to electro beats than to swing these days; whose scientists win Nobel Prizes once again; whose athletes break records; and whose firms and universities attract young people from all over the world, including even, and in particular, large numbers from Israel – a fact that I personally find to be most gratifying.

Living up to this great fortune through our actions is the true mandate of 9 November. It is a task for all Germans that goes far beyond commemoration events. Let us take on this task!

Berlin is not Weimar and nor will it become Weimar. The dangers of the past are not the dangers of the present. Those who only ever warn of a resurgence of the past are at risk of losing sight of new challenges. However, remembrance can focus one's sight on them. And they certainly exist.

Just as democracy on 9 November 1918 was not predestined to fail, its success, 100 years later, is not guaranteed. We are witnessing growing dissatisfaction with party democracy, right into the mainstream in our society. We are experiencing how some people no longer want to accept parliaments as places for political solutions. Not all of these people oppose democracy – but democracy is lost upon them. After all, the history of the Weimar Republic in particular shows how much we need people who are willing to take on responsibility and who put in the hard work of democratic politics because they believe in its value.

My wish today, on our parliamentary democracy's centenary, is that as many people as possible do not only sense its value, but also draw the strength and courage from it to play a part in and for this democracy. After all, courage is also needed for this today. But having courage is, fortunately, far easier than in the first German democracy after 1918.

But individual courage will not be enough. We need this uniting moment because we can feel that new forces are tearing at the fabric of our society and that the rifts are becoming deeper – not only the economic, but also the cultural rifts.

We all have a profound need for a place to call home, a profound need for cohesion and orientation. And how we see our own history plays a crucial role in this. All peoples seek meaning and a sense of belonging in their own history – why should that not hold true for us Germans?

We need remembrance. And that is also why today is an important day. Yes, 9 November can provide orientation – but no absolute clarity.

One cannot explain this Federal Republic without the catastrophe of the two World Wars and the crime against humanity of the Shoah. They are immutable parts of our identity.

But equally, the Federal Republic cannot merely be explained ex negativo, on the basis of "never again" alone. One cannot explain our country without the widespread roots of the quest for democracy and freedom, which existed for centuries and from which the Federal Republic was able to grow after 1945.

I know that it is difficult to carry both notions in one's heart, but we can certainly try. We can be proud of the traditions of freedom and democracy, without averting our eyes from the abyss of the Shoah. And we can be aware of our historic responsibility for the rupture with civilisation, without denying the pleasure in what we have achieved in our country.

Yes, we can allow ourselves to trust this country, even if – or indeed because – these two things form part of it, as we take both of them to heart. That is the core of an enlightened patriotism. It does not strive either for wreaths of laurel leaves or crowns of thorns. It is never loud or boastful – it is a soft-spoken patriotism, a patriotism that has mixed feelings.

Some may consider this to be a weakness – in particular those who are fanning the flames of a new, aggressive nationalism. I think it is the exact opposite. Nationalism gilds one's own past and wallows in the triumph over others. Nationalism, including in its new form, invokes the golden era that never existed.

However, democratic patriotism is not a comfort zone, but rather a constant incentive. An incentive for all those who do not say that the best days are behind us, but rather those who are willing and able to make the future better. That is the optimism of democrats – and that should be the attitude that we adopt.

The women and men who went before us on the long path to unity and justice and freedom in our country showed a spirit of optimism. There were pioneers at the time of the French Revolution, during the very short-lived Republic of Mainz, in the liberal Vormärz period, during the 1848 Revolution and in St. Paul's Church in Frankfurt, whose spirit not only permeates the Weimar constitution, but also our Basic Law today.

And if we look carefully, we discover even earlier beginnings of emancipation and the separation of powers, beginnings that date back as far as the Middle Ages, to the pride of the free imperial cities or Hanseatic towns, to the German peasants' demands for freedom and the old constitution of the German Empire, which even – and this will come as a surprise to you – served as an inspiration for the founding fathers of the US Constitution.

We also remember those who fought for freedom and democracy during the German Reich, the Weimar Republic, in exile and in the anti-Nazi resistance, many of whom lost their lives.

And above all, we are thinking today about the women and men who poured into the streets in the autumn of 1989 – in Leipzig, Dresden, Plauen and Chemnitz, in Berlin, Potsdam, Halle and Magdeburg, in Arnstadt, Rostock and Schwerin. They paved the path to the reunification of our country. Without their Peaceful Revolution, courage and great desire for freedom, we would not have experienced the fall of the Berlin Wall, the happiest 9 November in our history. We also remember that today with gratitude.

All of these women and men gradually achieved what Germans could only dream about for a long time – a free, united and democratic Germany. Too many of them have been forgotten today. I would like us to devote more attention, more lifeblood and yes, also more financial resources, to the places and protagonists of the history of our democracy. On behalf of our Republic's identity, we should invest in more than merely royal crypts and princes' palaces!

All of us who believe in democracy, the millions of people who work every day to make this country a better place, are part of this tradition. In the example they provide every day, they show that democratic patriotism is not something abstract or intellectual. Their commitment does not come from cold reason or calculation alone, but in almost all cases from passionately held convictions. So let us be brave! Let us dare to demonstrate the hope and the republican passion of those days in November 1918 in our own era. Let us dare to say once again with conviction – long live the German Republic! Long live our democracy!

SPEECH AT THE STATE BANQUET IN HONOUR OF THE TURKISH PRESIDENT

Welcome to Berlin!

It is good to see you again. It is good to talk. And, yes, it is also good to argue – if, at any rate, we do this "in a way that is best", as the Koran tells us. Mr President, I am glad that our countries are seeking dialogue with one another after far too much verbal sparring in the recent past.

Exactly 70 years ago this month, just a stone's throw away from here, Ernst Reuter, who later went on to be Mayor of Berlin, gave a speech that we remember to this day: "People of this world [...], look upon this city!" – it was a famous ode to Berlin, a speech rooted in the first hand experience of war and dictatorship, and an impassioned plea for freedom.

By calling to mind Reuter's speech – and the values that it invokes – I am also calling to mind the close relations between Germany and Turkey. That he was able to give this speech in the first place, after all, was thanks also to your country that was so open and bighearted to take in displaced Jews and politically persecuted Germans in the years of the National Socialist dictatorship – including hundreds of persecuted scientists such as Friedrich Dessauer and Ernst Eduard Hirsch, and artists such as Bruno Taut and Paul Hindemith.

Turkey became a second home for many of these people. Ernst Reuter himself spent 12 years of his life in Istanbul and Ankara, and he and his family came to love and cherish Turkey.

While German emigration to Turkey is not a terribly well known phenomenon, it is an equally remarkable chapter of our long and eventful relationship. It stretches back for many centuries, has been through highs and lows, and has evolved into a particularly special relationship thanks to the people who came to us from Turkey later on. This German Turkish relationship is certainly unique – and certainly not easy.

Germany has been enriched by the almost three million people with Turkish roots who have since made Germany their home. And, by the way, I also mean "enriched" in quite a literal sense. The economic progress and prosperity enjoyed by my country would have been simply inconceivable were it not for the many people from Turkey whom we asked to come here and work for us in decades past – and inconceivable without their families who joined them later on, or without their children and grandchildren. And I mean "enriched" also in a social, cultural and real world sense. I am proud and grateful to be the Federal President of a diverse and cosmopolitan Germany where generations of Turkish migrants have left their mark, which they have helped to shape, and where people with very different backgrounds have made their home – a home of freedom and the rule of law.

It goes without saying that our free and open society is full of contradictions and conflicts. There are neither magic formulas for, nor a happy end to, the oft debated issue of integration. Integration is a process that entails obligations for everyone involved – both for those who have been Germans for generations and for those who have come to live in our country. Integration begins with a commitment to which all of us – regardless of our origins – are entitled, a commitment which says "I want to live here; I want to help shape the future here". Integration is about learning together not only how to share in, but also to shoulder responsibility for this democratic community. Integration is also about respecting rules, tolerating diversity and a plurality of voices, but also standing up together to oppose attempts by others – be they in our own country or from outside – to sow the seeds of mistrust or discord. And, without a shadow of a doubt, these common obligations include countering each and every form of discrimination, racism and xenophobia. We stared into the darkest abyss of hatred only recently in the trial of the series of murders committed by the National Socialist Underground (NSU). We have not forgotten these terrible crimes, and especially not their victims. They make us ashamed to this day.

When travelling throughout our country, my wife and I have been delighted time and again to find that, more than ever before in the history of the Federal Republic of Germany, members of parliament, journalists, authors, actors, sportspeople, entrepreneurs and many others with Turkish roots are part and parcel of everyday life in Germany. Such individuals include people like Mevlüde Genç, whose perseverance and will to achieve reconciliation after the terrible arson attack in Solingen 25 years ago impressed me deeply. We would have liked to welcome her here this evening, and she would have liked to come – unfortunately, however, she is unable to muster the strength for this, and so we send her our warmest regards.

All of these people are leaving their mark on our common Germany, and I am delighted that a number of them are with us here this evening. They are the most important part, the very centre, of our relations. They are able to testify to the fact that many, many people in Germany care about the state of relations between our countries – and about the situation in our respective nations. The interest we have in each other is great and emotions run just as deep. What happens in Turkey is important to these people, and it is important to Germany, just as a close eye is kept in Turkey on the goings on in Germany. To put it in a nutshell, and above and beyond our present differences, we are, and will remain, important to one another. We should shape our future relationship with this in mind.

Remembering Ernst Reuter, whom I mentioned at the beginning of my speech, is about two things to my mind. Firstly, gratitude – for the openness and humanity that Turkey showed him and many others. And secondly, hope. Eighty years ago, Germans found refuge in Turkey – today, a worryingly large number of people from Turkey are seeking refuge here in Germany from the growing pressure on civil society. Ernst Reuter's example should be a source of encouragement for us. His entire biography embodies the struggle to overcome coercion and lack of freedom; it embodies the hope for freedom and the rule of law.

He expressed this hope for the coexistence of nations – and in particular for our two countries, Germany and Turkey, of course.

And I too share this hope, along with many other Germans. We hope that Turkey will return to the path of reconciliation, to peace on the domestic stage, two years after the trauma of the attempted coup. We hope that it will be possible to reconcile its stark social differences on the basis of human rights and the rule of law.

And we do more than hope. Germany has a most concrete and pronounced interest in a stable Turkey rooted in democracy, as well as an economically successful Turkey with a European outlook.

I therefore expressly welcome all efforts being made to help us to return to our long standing good relations after recent months ridden with conflict. Such efforts include engaging in open dialogue on the things that divide us, which were greater in number than we should have liked of late. As President of this country, I am of course – and you are aware of this, Mr President – concerned about German citizens who have been imprisoned in Turkey for political reasons. And I am also concerned about Turkish journalists, trade unionists, lawyers, intellectuals and politicians who remain behind bars. We discussed a series of individual cases in detail this morning. Mr President, I trust that you will understand that we cannot simply gloss over this issue and pretend that nothing has happened.

Mr President, Germany and Turkey need each other – also in Europe. We need each other in the bid for peace in the Middle East, in the fight against terrorism and for the efforts to alleviate the situation of the refugees from war zones in the region. Mr President, we pay tribute to your country's towering efforts to help people who have fled Syria. Just under one million school age refugee children are set to be integrated into Turkey's regular school system by the end of the next school year. And that is just one example of the major tasks that migration and integration pose – in your country, and, of course, also here in Germany. I believe that we should talk about how we can tackle these tasks together.

Ladies and gentlemen, these challenges call for us to make haste. And yet understanding takes time; it requires patience and perseverance. And it requires trust. Mr President, you have felt the strong emotions that your visit to my country has aroused. These emotions are both a reflection of the special relations between our countries and also, of course, a reflection of the tensions of past months that have yet to be overcome. A single visit is not enough to restore normality. However, it could be a start, the start of a path that leads, via many tangible steps, to new trust. Mr President, Ms Erdoğan, I would now like to propose a toast: may the trust between our two countries grow once again. May the special relationship between the Republic of Turkey and the Federal Republic of Germany and between the people of our countries give rise to amicable and fruitful relations for both sides.

SPEECH AT THE CONFERENCE "THE STRUGGLE FOR DEMOCRACY"

Today, I would like to talk about democracy. It is time to do so – also on an occasion like this. It is time to ask ourselves once again the fundamental question of what unites us at heart on both sides of the Atlantic.

In this quest, I would like to talk about a prominent German figure who stands for our democratic ties in a special and indeed ambivalent way.

Thomas Mann was one of the greatest writers in the German language. And yet he was not a born democrat. During his lifetime, he underwent more than one political change of heart. He sought, found, and lost certainties. Commenting in 1958 on Thomas Mann as a political writer, a mere three years after the author's death, Kurt Sontheimer wrote: "Hardly any other German author was as paradoxical."

Thomas Mann's meandering and contradictory path to democracy is in some respects symbolic of our own path to democracy in Germany. "Where I am, there is Germany." Without making Mann's self-confident words of defiance from exile our own, we could nevertheless say that Germany ultimately arrived at the place he set out for.

Where did this meandering path start? During the late years of the German Empire, we encounter Thomas Mann as an enlightened monarchist with liberal left-wing leanings. He celebrated freedom of expression; he railed against censorship; he vehemently opposed the bans on performances of Wedekind's plays; he defended the anarchist Erich Mühsam; he published works in Eduard Bernstein's social-democratic anthologies; and in his often overlooked second novel "Royal Highness", he drafted a first vision of a welfare state, albeit a vision that was still monarchistic, romantic and reminiscent of a fairy tale.

The year 1914 marked a watershed both in Europe and in Mann's political views. The war broke out – and nationalist, authoritarian, and openly racist sentiments broke out in Thomas Mann. "Away, then, with the alien and repulsive slogan, 'democratic'! Never will the mechanical-democratic state of the West be naturalised with us." In later years, these words would cause Thomas Mann to be appalled at himself and to struggle publicly with these earlier views.

During the early years of the Weimar Republic, Thomas Mann awakened from his intoxication with nationalism. In "The Magic Mountain", the enlightened, rational views of Settembrini engage in an imaginary clash with the nationalist, irrational views of Naphta over Hans Castorp's "German soul". But in the reality of the vulnerable Weimar Republic, Mann increasingly recognised the importance of political reason over the appeal of totalitarianism to Germans, who he said "maliciously idolise the irrational". And it was this phase of his political path that led him to the United States. He researched the founding fathers; he read intellectual greats from Emerson to Whitman; and he recognised in the United States a new type of nation in which belonging is defined by commitment to a shared constitution rather than by ethnicity.

The very title of his 1922 lecture, "The German Republic", was an affront to his former followers. The nationalist conservative journal "Das Gewissen" ("The Conscience") commented with the resigned headline, "Mann Overboard". The German right had lost its spokesperson. Thomas Mann became an admirer of the master saddler and German President Friedrich Ebert – a thorn in the flesh of those who viewed democracy with contempt. Looking back, Kurt Sontheimer wrote: "[In the early 1920s,] the German Weimar Republic was a very fragile state. It was much easier and more convenient to criticise it than to defend it." Ladies and gentlemen, in light of current events, I want to say that it is now up to us to make sure it does not become easier once again to defame democracy than to defend it!

But while Mann firmly placed himself on the side of democracy, Germany's road to disaster took its course. "O Germany, thou art undone! And I am mindful of thy hopes." This is how he brought the epic "Doctor Faustus" to a close, writing under the Californian sun. Extensive research has been conducted and much has been written about the Nazi seizure of power, Mann's despair at Germans' susceptibility to fascism, his fury at the Nazis, his hatred of Hitler, and his own and his family's suffering along the road leading to exile, first to Switzerland and eventually to the United States. Many people in this room could lecture on these topics with far greater authority than I can.

However, I would like to draw attention to one point. It seems to have been only in the United States that Thomas Mann changed from being a democrat motivated by reason to a democrat by conviction. And all his enthusiasm was focused on a single person: Franklin D. Roosevelt. Frido Mann, you gave us such a wonderfully vivid description of some of your childhood memories – how, at the breakfast table in San Remo Drive, your grandfather spoke with flashing eyes and great, dramatic gestures of the charismatic yet physically depleted President. Thomas Mann, for whom "real democracy [...] can never dispense with aristocratic attributes", found in F.D.R. the embodiment of democratic authority. He even paid him a literary tribute in the political wisdom and zeal for social reform shown by Joseph the Provider. These sentiments were not lost on the "New York Times", which entitled its review of this work "A New Deal Man in Egypt".

Thomas Mann devoted himself to the war effort with Roosevelt and for Roosevelt and gave impassioned speeches denouncing Hitler's Germany and advocating a vigilant democracy. During lecture tours across the country, he attempted to shake Americans out of their isolationism. He also broadcast a total of 55 now-famous radio addresses from San Remo Drive across the airwaves to his homeland. While Hitler's war was still raging at its fiercest, he said: "The longer the war lasts, the more desperately the people become enmeshed in a web of guilt." And yet at the same time, he hoped Germans would enjoy freedom in the future.

To sum up, here in the United States, Thomas Mann experienced the strength and mobilising force of democracy.

However, this was also where he was confronted with threats to democracy and its greatest vulnerabilities.

And this occurred within a short period of time in a way that is perhaps not entirely unfamiliar to us today. Only a few years lay between Roosevelt's shining example and the descent into a toxic political climate of intolerance and polarisation, prejudices and conspiracy theories, and the state-led erosion of fundamental rights and an independent judiciary. While the Marshall Plan was enabling the ruined Germany to start afresh, economically and morally, in California Thomas Mann found that friends, exiles, artists, intellectuals, his own children Erika, Klaus and Golo, and eventually he himself had become the target of McCarthy's zealous Communist hunters. Under the heading "Dupes and Fellow Travelers", "Life Magazine" counted him among the illustrious ranks of suspects ranging from Charlie Chaplin and Leonard Bernstein to Arthur Miller and Albert Einstein. Reporting from Washington, the "Daily News" described Mann as a "literary giant", but also an unwavering Stalinist whose loyalty had to be called into question. This pressure drove the Mann family to go into exile in Switzerland for a second time. In early 1953, he noted in his diary: "What is happening is not exactly the Machtergreifung, but something very similar." We know how wrong he was in that respect, but it shows the depth of his bitterness and fears for his United States.

Never again would Thomas Mann see San Remo Drive, "that home which I have come to love", as he described it. But even in Switzerland he followed the Congressional elections, which overturned the Republican majority in November 1954. He witnessed the beginning of the end of the hated witch-hunt committee, as he called it, and saw McCarthy's star wane. As Federal President, I am not inclined to speculate. But from what you write in your memoires, Frido Mann, it is not unrealistic to assume that after all the turbulence in his America, Thomas Mann would undoubtedly have been delighted by the young, electrifying renewal of US democracy that was soon to follow – the election of the 35th President, John F. Kennedy.

He did not live to see it. Thomas Mann died in 1955. Just a few weeks ago I was privileged to visit his grave in Kilchberg with the Swiss Federal President.

When I pay tribute to Thomas Mann today in my role as President of the Federal Republic of Germany, what I primarily learn from his experiences with democracy is humility. I said at the start of my speech that Germany ultimately arrived at the place Thomas Mann set out for. I would add the following. He owed that, and we owe that, to this country, the United States, more than to any other!

We Germans did not inherit democracy. After Germany allowed its first democracy to fail, with such fatal consequences, we relearned it from and with the United States.

The Americans were the first to entrust us with democracy again after 1945. We Germans should be the last to condescendingly give them lessons in democracy today.

I would like to remind all those in Germany who are currently shaking their heads in disgust every day over the end of US democracy, and even doing so with a certain cultural arrogance, of Thomas Mann's crystal clear words: "No, America needs no instruction in the things that concern democracy."

No other democracy in the world has proved to be as resilient and renewable as that of the United States. And that has been the case for 240 years. The democratic turbulence experienced by Thomas Mann was followed by new highs and lows. The proclamation of "the end of history" as the final victory of democracy a good 25 years ago was just as premature as the swan songs to democracy we are hearing today.

No, I am less concerned about the future of US democracy than I am about the future of our transatlantic partnership.

We have not always seen eye to eye. We are not the same and we have different interests. But the damage caused by the current upheavals could be deeper seated and longer lasting – and most importantly, it could be irreparable.

The forces driving us apart do not only have to do with a President Trump. They existed before the current US Administration and they will continue to exist after it.

First of all, Europe, unlike in Mann's day, is no longer the central geopolitical arena. The shift in focus towards Asia, and China in particular, is especially tangible here in California. Demographic changes also play a role. The percentage of Americans who greet us Germans with shining eyes and tell us their great-grandparents came from Palatinate, East Frisia or the Lower Rhine will decline. The dynamics of the global economy are also shifting the economic focus from Europe to other world regions. Isolationism is experiencing a renaissance in the United States – Andrew Jackson's portrait is hanging in the Oval Office again. And the European Union is still mainly preoccupied with itself as a result of its many internal crises.

In Thomas Mann's day, the transatlantic relationship was, so to speak, predestined. But many people no longer see it that way.

At this point in most every speech by an incumbent of high office in Germany, a commitment to transatlantic relations should be made. Despite all the differences of opinion and against all the trends, "we have to revitalise our friendship."

Yes, we do. But I am afraid that this commitment to transatlantic relations is no longer quite so straightforward. It would fall on deaf ears. The transatlantic reflex does not work anymore – incidentally, not just in the White House, or because of the shift in US interests, but also among many Germans.

The debate on how to proceed is thus marked by a wide range of opinions in Germany, too. There are those who say: "Europe must finally stand on its own two feet. America doesn't want to protect us any more and it cannot protect us any longer for the foreseeable future." Others say: "Let's look for new partners. We can protect free trade and the environment better with China than we can with the US Administration." And then there are those who say: "Germany needs to reach out to Russia again."

Dyed-in-the-wool transatlanticists will argue vehemently against all these views. And they may have good reasons. However, their good reasons cannot disguise the fact that this relationship, a constant in the past, cannot be taken for granted in the future, even if we will continue to need it, not least for our security. When the transatlantic reflex no longer works, then reflex responses no longer suffice. We have to find a new basis – one that holds on both sides. Neither economic interests nor political necessity nor demographic links alone will hold us together in the future. So what will?

Let's forget for one minute everything that has traditionally connected us, everything that welds us together in social or economic terms. Even if we were not linked by necessity we, Germans and Americans, would still be democrats. That is what connects us, undoubtedly more than with any other region in the world, certainly more than with Russia or China. And that is what gives us more of a joint mission than we believed in the last few years.

After all, "throughout the world it has become precarious to take democracy for granted." This statement by – yes, you've guessed it – Thomas Mann is topical again today, 80 years later. It means two things for us in the West. While in the last few years we were overly self-confident in our belief that we had achieved liberal democracy in our own societies once and for all and that this model would gain ground in the rest of the world, we see today that even in our own countries this liberal democracy does not go unchallenged and is certainly not considered to be the measure of all things in the rest of the world.

The future of democracy thus starts with our defending and renewing it in our own countries, and not with our explaining it to others.

Three years ago, while serving as German Foreign Minister, I had the privilege of visiting Martin Luther King's grave in Atlanta with the great John Lewis. We spoke there about King's unfinished work and I asked John where he found the strength to continue it and how he reconciled his dissatisfaction, indeed his anger, with the deeply ingrained injustices in US society with his unshakeable belief in the goodness of the country, in its people and future. John Lewis replied that the constitutional mandate "to form a more perfect union" contains the admission that this democracy is always imperfect. It will always have shortcomings. What matters is movement towards this ideal, not the actual state of affairs. As Thomas Mann wrote in 1938, the crisis in liberal democracy is thus an opportunity for it to "put aside the habit of taking itself for granted, of self-forgetfulness. It should use [...] the fact that it has again become problematical to renew and rejuvenate itself by again becoming aware of itself."

I believe this awareness also means we should define democracy broadly and widen our outlook beyond the day-to-day spectacle of the capitals and the news-feed stories and news-agency reports flooding in every minute. We Germans in particular take an oversimplified view of transatlantic relations when our irritation with tweets from the White House leads us to ignore the deeper social divisions that also exist in our own country – the conflicts in our society of immigration, the downsides of globalisation, the divide between town and country, and the gap between rich and poor. When we look at that, then we see that the current Administration is not only a root cause, but also a symptom of centrifugal forces in society. And such forces are at play on both sides of the Atlantic.

However, when we widen our view of society, we do not only see things that irritate us – we also perceive the forces of renewal. And they are found in many parts of this country – the students no longer prepared to accept rampant gun violence, the dedicated people breathing new life into Martin Luther King's Poor People's Campaign, the countless women standing for political office around the country in greater numbers than ever before. These forces of renewal are the transatlantic future – not mutual outrage.

That is what my visit is about – renewal, not nostalgia. The future of democracy cannot be won without an idea about the democracy of the future. This applies in particular to the technological developments we will be discussing in Silicon Valley. Technological developments test not only the regulatory power of the state, but also human thinking and action.

In the age of robots, algorithms, and artificial intelligence, questions about human autonomy, and thus the foundation of democracy, are raised in a completely new way. To very loosely paraphrase a maxim put forward by Kant during the Enlightenment, technological progress should make it easier for humankind to escape from its self-imposed nonage and not to enter freely into a new nonage. However, new technology can do both – enable and incapacitate. That is why I would like to talk in Silicon Valley about the ethics of digital transformation. These ethics are not primarily about the future of technology, but rather about our own future – as people and as a human society.

All of these issues affecting our future are taking us into uncharted territory and the great unknown. However, I believe there is an irreplaceable human quality that must be preserved, namely reason. Without reason, democracy will not be possible in the future.

"It is a terrible spectacle when irrationalism becomes popular," Thomas Mann stated in the Library of Congress in 1943. I fear that we are currently witnessing new episodes of this spectacle in the political debate on both sides, in the United States and Europe.

Yes, we can complain about the brutalisation of language, especially on the internet and in social media; we can complain about the longing for absolutes, the temptation of enemy stereotypes and scapegoats, the contempt for objective facts, even for scientific expertise. Such laments were not unknown to Thomas Mann.

But the question is what conclusions we should draw from them. I personally believe that the battle cry against "the Establishment" is the most dangerous enticement of populism. It is a battle cry that can be used against anyone at will – apart from the self-appointed opponents of the so-called "elites", of course. It is thus all the more important that those who shoulder responsibility in society, the media, academia and the cultural sphere – all of those who feel vilified as "the Establishment" – stand their ground! The response of intellectuals and cultural professionals to irrationalism must not be a retreat from politics, and certainly not contempt. What Mann wrote about this during the Weimar Republic is of extraordinary relevance today: "Refusal on the part of the intellect to engage with politics is an error and a self-deception. One does not get clear of politics in that way. One only ends up on wrong side. A-political simply means anti-democratic!"

This is all the more reason why the house on San Remo Drive should not be a place of retreat. When it was still a place of exile, it was home to thinking, writing and discussion that would point the way forward when it came to developing our societies in Germany and the United States. I would ask the Thomas Mann Fellows to foster an intellectual climate in which democracy can thrive once more. Put briefly, I would ask them to give democracy a future. You can work on this intellectual change, regardless of how great the political differences may be between the administrations at the moment. May this house, the new Fellows and their US counterparts, the Deutschlandjahr USA, and the many good transatlantic initiatives constantly – and on both sides – find the will and the willingness to invest in this partnership! I for one will continue to do so.

In 1921, long before Pacific Palisades, Thomas Mann read Walt Whitman's "Democratic Vistas". He enthusiastically underlined the following sentence twice: "I shall use the words America and Democracy as convertible terms." America and democracy are synonyms. Thus, when Thomas Mann became an American citizen in 1944, he never saw it as incompatible with being German. Rather, he simply regarded it as the culmination of being a democrat.

What his closest friends would not have believed possible is that even in the bitterness of his second exile, amidst his fear for the demise of American democracy, Thomas Mann never renounced his citizenship. He remained a US citizen for the rest of his life.

America and democracy as synonyms – it was not only Thomas Mann and other exiles who felt that way, but also generations from around the world who yearn for democracy. Just a few weeks ago, in a speech at Harvard University, the author Chimamanda Ngozi Adichie described how she felt as a young woman in Nigeria by saying "America always felt aspirational."

In the current crisis in the West, should we not look at this aspiration, this ideal bond, the other way round? Not only will democrats around the world always look to America, but America can also look to democrats around the world as its partners!

I believe that the United States needs partners, too. And it needs these partners. However, America can only recognise such a partnership if it regards the "West" as more than a geographical term – and the world as more than a boxing ring in which everyone fights against everyone else.

The "great task" to which Abraham Lincoln committed his nation in the hour of its deepest division is one that goes far beyond the frontiers of this country. This task was "[…] that government of the people, by the people, for the people shall not perish from the earth."

You will note that he did not say "from this country" but "from the earth". That is indeed a "great task". And I believe it is a task for which one needs partners.

SPEECH AT THE CONFERENCE "POLAND AND GERMANY IN EUROPE"

I am delighted to have the opportunity to share a few thoughts with you at the opening of this conference.

The fact that we, in this year, on this occasion and as representatives of our countries, are discussing the role of Poland and Germany in a united Europe, the fact that we are not only doing this as neighbours, but as part of this European Union, is far more than many of our predecessors could possibly have imagined.

Indeed, that we would one day work together was so unimaginable for so long that many are apt to call this a miracle. As understandable as this expression may be, it ignores the fact that this miracle required pretty mundane preconditions. It would have been unthinkable were it not for Poland's active readiness for reconciliation.

Looking back on German Polish history, there was little cause for Poland to place its trust in its German neighbours. Prussia played a major role in the disappearance of the Polish state over the course of centuries. And, Mr President, you mentioned the fact that the National Socialist regime ultimately sought to destroy Poland, its statehood and its society. We will not forget the crime against humanity perpetrated against the Jews of Europe during the German occupation of Poland. And we will not forget the suffering that Germans brought upon the whole of Poland.

It is for this reason, Mr President, Andrzej Duda, and I say this as the German head of state, that Germany is and continues to be thankful that we encounter each other today in a spirit of trust and that this partnership that we now take for granted became possible in the first place. And we are thankful also for the fact that Poland and Germany are able today to discuss – and also disagree about – the political shape that the European Union is to take. But particularly when we disagree about something, we must remember that this partnership cannot be taken for granted even today; it is only possible with an enduring awareness of and responsibility for the history that unites us.

When Poland regained its independence as a nation state one hundred years ago, Polish German togetherness was conceivable at best in a private context, through personal friendships, and not in a political sense. But even friendships left their mark, such as the one between the German author, art collector and occasional diplomat Count Harry Kessler and Marshall Józef Piłsudski.

It was in 1915 at a time of war that they made each other's acquaintance on the Eastern Front near Czartorysk, where Kessler was serving as a liaison officer to the Austrians. Their friendship is part of German Polish and also European history. More precisely, this connection between them itself made history.

You can read about this in Kessler's diary from the time immediately after the end of the First World War. It recounts three days in November 1918, three days that would come to dominate the course of Poland's history and the emergence of the Second Republic, and which would play a decisive role in the downfall of the German Empire and the proclamation of the republic in Germany.

It was Count Harry Kessler who was tasked with freeing Piłsudski and his close confidant General Sosnkowski from German imprisonment in Magdeburg on 8 November and bringing them to Warsaw. And so it was that, following this successful coup, four men, Piłsudski, Sosnkowski, Kessler and the commander of the Prussian motor unit (Kraftfahrtruppe), Rittmeister von Gülpen, sat in an automobile en route from Magdeburg to Berlin, passing through a pretty unspectacular landscape in which, nevertheless, each of the four spotted something familiar.

"It was a warm springlike day with a perfect blue sky", Kessler writes, [...] "and out of doors and surrounded by woods and fields, thoughts of enmity, war and revolution were far from the minds of all four of us. Piłsudski [...] gave me a nudge and said that this was what his home region looked like, very homely, this poor soil, the pines and woodlands, only that it was hillier where he had grown up."

And so, in the end, they all got into conversation with each other during their journey. What seems remarkable to me about this is the fact that this moment of freedom, the absence of war and revolution, that this moment causes all four of them, almost immediately, to discover something familiar amidst the unfamiliar. As men of their age through and through and soldiers on opposing sides, they are far from being on the same page. And yet they acknowledge each other; they notice that they have something in common and that this is potentially even more than they might have suspected up until then.

In the next few, eventful days, the German Kaiser would abdicate, the social democrat Philipp Scheidemann would proclaim the republic and Józef Piłsudski would board a train to Warsaw. He was to lead Poland to independence and pave the way to the Second Republic. It spelled the end, for the time being, to the division of Poland and was the dawn of a new era.

Józef Płisudski and Count Harry Kessler were to encounter each other on a few more occasions after that. Shortly afterwards, Kessler followed as the first Envoy of the new German Republic in Warsaw. The two continued to meet and respect one another. They held each other's candour in high regard and were united by the intention to guide their two peoples "out of their old enmity into new amity", as Piłsudski put it when Kessler handed him his letter of credence.

The year 1918 was a landmark year not only for Poland and Germany – it was a period of change and new beginnings. At the end of this Great War, monarchies had fallen and empires collapsed while nation states had newly or, as in the case of Poland in 1918, re emerged. For both Poland and Germany, this period of transformation was bound up with the attempt to bring about a democratic fresh start. Both Piłsudski and Kessler played an active role in this period of political upheaval, despite the fact that the latter rarely occupied a prominent position and neither of them, on closer inspection, were born democrats.

We know today that these efforts to bring about a democratic fresh start also failed because there were too few democrats who gave this endeavour their wholehearted blessing. And we know that this fresh start in Poland was made even more difficult at a time when it was necessary to bring together different administrative, legal and economic systems. For all of Piłsudski's hopes, no "new amity" was yet to emerge from old enmity in the inter war years.

What he, Piłsudski, told Kessler back then, the need to leave old enmities behind them and "work together like neighbours who have, at long last, come to their senses" took, as we know now, a very long time, to become reality.

It is thus all the more important for us today to preserve what has been achieved. The fact that Poland and Germany are closer now than at any time in their common history has much to do with us heeding this call to come to our senses and to work together, that we have learned this lesson today.

Poland and Germany are strong and independent nations in Europe and are economic and political partners within the European Union. Neither threatens the other's sovereignty, and neither country takes orders from others.

We are free because we have come together in the European Union of our own free will – and not only for economic reasons. No, because we knew that we would be out of our depth as individual nation states in our efforts to respond to new global challenges. On the basis of this realisation, the member states of the EU have relinquished part of their sovereignty in order to gain additional, common – European – sovereignty. European sovereignty interpreted in such a way is not incompatible with national sovereignty but complements and even expands it.

A Europe, a common and genuinely self confident Europe, that speaks with one voice is what is needed if each of our individual nations is to be able to make itself heard in this world at all. Separate from each other, we would not only have less economic strength, but, and I am certain of this, we would also be less able to act politically – particularly in a world in which, looking to the East, we are exposed to new and dangerous tensions. Of course, I agree that Europe should invest in transatlantic relations. However, I cannot ignore the disconcertion that we have experienced in recent times in which we can no longer be so sure about the political direction that the leading power in the West is taking, at least as far as international trade policy is concerned. This is the world in which we pursue our policies today.

But we must also not forget that sovereignty on the international stage requires certain conditions to be met at home, namely democracy and the rule of law. Indeed, we Europeans are not sovereign because we somehow pull together at random where we see fit, but because we act on the basis of values and rules that we have accorded ourselves. Within the framework of these basic rules, each nation is free to shape its democracy and constitutional order itself. Whenever basic rules are challenged, however, everyone else is also affected. And that makes no one stronger – and especially not in the eyes of those who would prefer us Europeans to be divided rather than stand together as one.

In a nutshell, we have a great deal to lose. If the European Union's cohesion crumbles, then none of us will be any more able to assert our interests as nation states. On the contrary, we will all lose out.

Let us therefore continue to venture down the path that others have cleared for us, a path to a Europe in which we stand up together for our security, our prosperity, our freedom and, yes, also for our national idiosyncrasies.

SPEECH AT THE PANEL DISCUSSION AT THE UNIVERSITY OF FRIBOURG

Thank you very much for the warm welcome, Vice-Chancellor, and for inviting me to the University of Fribourg. Federal President, as you know, I love visiting your beautiful country and frequently come here. I was here particularly often during my term as Foreign Minister because Switzerland is an essential player in diplomacy and international affairs. And now I am here for the first time as President of the Federal Republic of Germany. My state visit stands for the close ties and friendship between our two countries. Thank you very much for inviting me, my dear Alain Berset!

I have been particularly looking forward to today's discussion. No, I am not just saying that to be polite. After all, when it comes to manners, we Germans will never be in the same league as the Swiss. I say it because today's topic is one that is very close to my heart as Federal President, not because that is what I want, but rather because I see a need for discussion. The question we are addressing today is "can democracy survive in the 21st century?" Imagine someone had suggested a panel discussion on this topic ten or twenty years ago or asked this question during the 1990s when, after the fall of the Wall, some people announced the end of history. Imagine this question being asked in 2011 when the first buds of the Arab Spring were enthusiastically welcomed by all and sundry on Facebook and Twitter. I suspect that most of you would have been rather perplexed and thought the person asking the question was overreacting. And then you would have turned your thoughts to more pressing issues.

But what about today? An event like today's now attracts a large audience and great interest. I believe this is justified. Everyone can see the challenges facing democracy. Some people openly ask whether democracy is viable. And these people are not only far away, in Russia or China, where the motto is "yes to growth and security, no to freedom and democracy". On the contrary, the truth is that a new fascination with authoritarianism has already penetrated deep into the transatlantic West and Europe, where some people have now proudly declared the dawning of the age of "illiberal democracy". In a nutshell, we are in the midst of very challenging years for democracy.

As briefly as possible, I would like to suggest three topics for our discussion.

The first is the polarisation in society that is occupying us in similar ways in Germany and Switzerland. After the shock waves from the Brexit vote and the US presidential election in 2016, we Germans felt the cracks running through our society the following year, firstly in a general election campaign marked by some acrimonious outbreaks of rage and aggression, the likes of which I had never seen before, and then by the election results on 24 September.

I think it is important that as democrats we do not simply deplore polarisation, but instead take a close look at what causes it, at where life has become more difficult for many people, and at the day-to-day conflicts in our country, far away from grand global politics.

For example, we need to look at how big cities are booming and rents keep rising, but opportunities are disappearing in many rural areas and young people in particular are moving away. We need to look at how bonuses and salaries in the international financial markets are reaching dizzying heights, but many people, especially those who are not well educated, primarily see globalisation and technical advances as a threat to their jobs and fear the loss of status and income. And we need to look at how populists then use all of these fears against the so-called establishment, be it in politics, business or even academia, be it in Bern, Berlin or – a big favourite – Brussels. In such cases, opposing social forces increasingly undermine trust in the democratic system and in its representatives and institutions.

Polarisation brings me to my second topic – the spread of digital technology, which I do not think should be seen as the source of political evil. On the contrary, the Digital Revolution has brought untold liberties, allowed new business models to develop and connected people all around the world. But this revolution certainly has the potential to heighten the opposing forces in our societies even further, for example when the tone in social media becomes ever more abrupt and intransigent thanks to the cloak of anonymity, when the boundaries between what can and cannot be said are becoming increasingly blurred, when algorithms on YouTube and other sites are not programmed to provide responsible editing or objective information, but rather to obtain the greatest number of clicks and ensure user loyalty, or when a radical video is followed by an even more radical one in order to keep people on a site for as long as possible. Social media can even be used as a tool to manipulate voters during election campaigns. Since Cambridge Analytica at the latest, we all know what that means. We definitely need rules for all of this. But what should these rules be and who should make them? That is also something I would like to discuss with you.

The Israeli academic Yuval Noah Harari recently said: "The greatest danger that now faces liberal democracy is that the revolution in information technology will make dictatorships more efficient than democracies." Now, this line of attack against democracy is not new. In the 1920s and 1930s, that was precisely where the fatal appeal of radical forces lay. And there is no doubt that democracy is a tiring system of government, as it is based on compromise and not all power is held by a "strong man". Democracy guarantees every citizen liberties, but also demands that they take on a certain amount of responsibility. That is why I call it a system of government for the brave-hearted.

However, what is new – and that is what Harari means – is how autocratic regimes can make "better" decisions for the system by using digital technologies. These decisions are "better" as regards the output they generate, be it in terms of prosperity, security, the environment or infrastructure. If autocracies that don't care about privacy or civil liberties make use of all available data and feed it into ever more powerful algorithms, won't they soon be able to control even the smallest social units and people's private lives? Won't they be able to counteract the dissatisfaction and revolt often found at the start of democratic movements at an even earlier stage? By the way, all of this has been reality for a long time. It is not just dystopian science fiction. A Social Credit System is currently being set up in China. Based on big data, it will reward good conduct and punish misconduct, with both naturally being defined by the state. And if we imagine how in the future – according to reports – 600 million cameras will monitor public spaces in China and artificial intelligence will make it possible to pick out a single face in a huge crowd, then we get an idea of the enormity of Harari's words of warning.

My third and final topic follows as a sort of mirror image of all this. As a reaction to the restlessness of our time, the spread of digital technology, artificial intelligence and other, ever faster waves of technological disruption, I sense something increasingly strongly in our societies, namely a new need for identity, orientation, deceleration, clear answers and something to hold on to.

Perhaps we shouldn't be at all surprised that the political forces who know how to exploit the digital future for their own benefit are those who hark back to a golden past. Populists are using the new channels to provide old answers to the question of identity and orientation. And these answers are isolation, marginalisation and nationalism.

In my opinion, we cannot and should not accept this! Our societies need a positive model for the digital future, one that takes the need for social and financial security seriously or, as I described it earlier, the need for functioning output. At the same time, this model must uphold freedom, diversity and openness. In short, we need something that makes people look forward to the future.

I know that there are many exciting approaches to this in Switzerland and I would like to learn about them. For example, I am interested in finding out how you have repeatedly managed to use digital communication tools in recent times to promote democracy, counter populism and clearly distinguish between facts and opinion. I am excited to hear about your experiences with these fields, so I look forward to listening to four clever and dedicated Swiss people here on the panel and to hearing the questions and comments from the audience. Merci beaucoup! Thank you very much!

SPEECH AT THE FEDERAL COUNCIL OF THE SWISS CONFEDERATION

Let me tell you: these are two very special days for my wife and me! Like so many Germans, I have been to Switzerland quite often, and have always enjoyed it. However, today is the first time

I have visited as Federal President, and I would like to start by expressing my deepest gratitude for the warm reception you have accorded my wife and me.

If I were asked to sum up the political core of my visit in one sentence, it would be this:

"Throughout the world it has become precarious to take democracy for granted".

That is a clever comment. It comes not from me, but from Thomas Mann, who was looking back at democracy in the Weimar Republic. But do not we today also feel "that democracy is not an assured possession, that it has enemies, that it is threatened from within and from without"? Do we not sense that different models – whether in China, Russia or elsewhere – are becoming more and more assertive on the world stage? And do we not feel that great irritation is spreading even within our democratic societies, and that some people, including in Europe, may be preaching democracy but in truth are inflaming the mood through marginalisation and authoritarian siren songs?

If we agree that Thomas Mann's analysis is still so topical, then I would also like to repeat his appeal from back then: namely that "the time has come for democracy to take stock of itself, [...], for its renewal in thought and feeling". My wish is that our self-contemplation as democrats, the self-confidence of our democracies in a world of new challenges – alongside all the close personal, economic and political ties – will renew the bond between Switzerland and Germany in particular.

And, if I may add one more thing, then my wish holds not just for our two countries, but for all the states of Europe. I am well aware that Switzerland has never found the European Union or the combination of the individual with the shared entirely unproblematic.

But, no matter how complex Europe may be, no matter how cumbersome the process of coordination – you here in Switzerland are familiar with that – ultimately we are all linked by a deeper bond which is our heritage and which must remain our standard. And it is this: the realisation that without democracy, Europe has no shining future. Without democracy, Europe has no core and no credibility in a world where it is us, the Europeans, who are standing up again and again for the rule of law and human rights, for international law, for a global order with rules that apply to businesses as well as to states and governments.

I would like to see the EU Member States and Switzerland side by side in this endeavour. And in this context to my mind Switzerland belongs at the heart of Europe – not just geographically.

There is another reason why I recalled Thomas Mann. I am thinking of the attitudes of a German who, while undoubtedly a gifted writer, was most definitely not a born democrat. This great German not only found a haven and a home here in Switzerland at a time when his own country was neither; it was also here in Switzerland that, later in life, he was converted, becoming a democrat of reason. Tomorrow, Alain, we will be visiting his grave by Lake Zürich. And a month from now, I will have the honour of officially opening the centre for intellectuals driven out of Nazi Germany, Thomas Mann's house in California.

What I have said about Thomas Mann's life applies equally to my country as a whole. We Germans truly did not inherit democracy. Democracy was something we achieved after the most terrible aberrations; it was made possible by the Allied Powers, and it was consolidated in our partnership and growing friendship with other strong democracies. One of those was most certainly Switzerland. And that is why we Germans would never dream of claiming to be omniscient or to have ready solutions to everything. Rather, we always come ready to learn. And

I, too, have come to Switzerland as a curious President of Germany, seeking to learn, and conscious that Switzerland succeeded in becoming a republic and introducing parliamentarianism in 1848, when Prussia and Hapsburg were still failing to overcome the tension between nationhood and democracy.

And there is a great deal to learn on this trip. After all, democracy's ability to assert itself is decided not by fancy speeches, but by how we solve the pressing tasks facing our two countries: booming cities where rents are rocketing, contrasting with rural areas which are becoming more and more deserted, losing their young people; migration and the integration of migrants on the labour market and in schools; and the spread of digital technology, which of course offers many opportunities, but also needs rules so that it does not exacerbate the growing polarisation in our societies.

For my biggest worry is that if society drifts apart, if the tone becomes ever harsher, particularly on the internet, if those of differing persuasions regard themselves as enemies rather than just opponents, then we are losing something that is vital for the survival of democracy – namely the willingness to let reason prevail.

This is something that all those who are opening the doors for all forms of irrationality in the fight against the alleged power of political correctness are completely forgetting.

Goodness knows reason is not the be all and end all in politics. But it is the only way to compromise, to balance differing interests. And democracy is impossible without a willingness to compromise.

You probably saw that compromises have become more difficult in Germany, too. It took longer than ever before for three parties to agree on the formation of a government.

So I am filled with even more respect when I see – and after all the Federal Council is sitting directly in front of me – how the readiness to reach understanding and the need to compromise are, as it were, "built in" to the Swiss political system.

Of course, your constitution is unique, and there are good reasons why there are differences between us, for example as regards the balance between direct democratic and parliamentary elements.

But one thing remains the same, in every democracy: democracy is dependent on the people nurturing it.

Just recently, we saw how many people in Switzerland care about and are committed to democracy – in the amazing level of participation in the public broadcasting initiative. And when I was still Germany's Foreign Minister, I saw them for myself all over the world, in the United Nations, the OSCE and countless NGOs, even in the most dangerous crisis regions: courageous Swiss women and men, shouldering responsibility, taking off the blinkers and looking beyond their borders.

Switzerland boasts an especially high number of such people. That is a tremendous gift for your country and a stroke of good fortune for the world.

Today I would like to extend special greetings to all these people, people who think about more than just themselves. With people like you around, I am not fearful for democracy.

SPEECH AT THE UNIVERSITY OF DELHI

What a wonderful, what an impressive place! I can see why some call this building the crown of Delhi University, this esteemed place of learning now approaching its 100th anniversary. A place of learning with 200,000 students, one of India's most prestigious universities. A place of learning with global connections, not least – as I hope some of you have been able to experience at first hand – to our German universities in the cities of Potsdam, Würzburg, and Heidelberg. What a pleasure to be here!

This is certainly a highlight of my first visit to India as President of Germany. And let me say thanks to the Vice Chancellor and everyone in this room today. It is a great honour to speak to you. Thank you for having me!

Since my arrival in India, I have been to Varanasi, to the Ganga River, in Sarnath, and to the Jama Masjid here in Delhi. Seeing these highly symbolic places has reminded me of this country's many historical and cultural layers. India truly is a treasure trove of impressions and inspirations. To my German eyes, every visit to India so far has been a remarkable experience.

Take this Viceregal Lodge, for example, a colonial building. Many of you may know this story: in the basement, just a few metres from here, there once was a prison cell. A cell for a man, a Sikh, called Bhagat Singh. In 1931, aged only 23, Bhagat Singh was executed as a criminal for his violent resistance to British rule. Today, his statue can be seen in the Sansad Bhawan, the Parliament House here in Delhi. How extraordinary: a man, once labelled a criminal, now a national hero. An underground room, once a prison cell, now at the heart of a place of debate and research. What I want to say: Coming to India, I have learned to look twice.

I have also learned to broaden my own perspective, to question my own assumptions, and to be respectful of what I see. In many ways, I am deeply impressed whenever I'm here. Impressed by India's cultural heritage and its incredible diversity in daily life – but impressed also by your country's complex, vibrant and resilient democracy. I have the greatest respect for India's unique path.

I know that this path has not always been easy, with conflict and strife along the way. Who would know better about the recurring frustrations of pluralism than the exceptionally diverse people of India? Who would know better about the painful imperfections of democratic governance than those who live in the largest democracy on Earth? I am acutely aware of the suffering caused by conflicts past and present, of the many rifts, scars and divisions that run deep in Indian society to this day. And I understand that in many ways, India's democracy is different from the one we know in Germany.

But India's choices matter in today's world. They will carry even more weight tomorrow. If our two countries succeed in pooling our strengths, in realising our common potential, we will have much to learn from each other and much to give each other. That is why I have come to India: to encourage and to challenge all of us – Indians and Germans alike – to take a fresh look at each other. And I hope that our discussion today will be one of many occasions to do just that.

A few weeks ago, I saw a cartoon in a magazine. Imagine the lobby of a tall building, perhaps an office block. There are three elevators, side by side. Normally, these elevator doors all look the same. Not in this case, where each elevator had a different sign. One door said "For People Who Like Music". The second door said "For People Who Prefer Silence". And finally, the third door had a sign saying "For People Who Want To Talk". But unfortunately, only one person was waiting in that particular line. There was nobody he could to talk to.

My worry is that there are more and more people in the world who do not want to talk, who want to ride their own private little elevators. Looking out from both Berlin and Delhi, we can see many recent examples of countries behaving this way and turning their backs on multilateral co-operation. We see countries that question the value of rules and agreements, that seek strength and prosperity in isolation and confrontation.

On the one hand, there are those who claim that nations can simply do better by themselves, who say that nothing gets done in multilateral systems. We can see this when the country that brought Germany back into the free world, back to openness and democracy in 1945, is now withdrawing from established international institutions and has started imposing new tariffs on steel and aluminium. We can also see it when the European Union, the most successful project of peace and prosperity my continent has ever seen, loses one of its largest member states.

But there are also those who reap without sowing, those who destroy without building, and those who intimidate and violate with no thought for the cost to others. For example, we see powers violating the territorial integrity of their immediate neighbours. We see an arc of violence in the Middle East, or in West Asia, as it is called here, – with a terrible civil war that has cost hundreds of thousands of lives, and a deadlocked international community unable to put an end to the suffering.

These are tough challenges indeed. It would be easy to raise barriers and to look only to our own well-being. But what do you think would happen if every country, if India and Germany started acting that way? What would happen if we all retreated to our own private little elevators, with no one to talk to? What would happen to commerce, to innovation, to culture, to global stability, and to our own security, if everyone were to fight only for themselves? Would we continue to prosper, to live in peace, to develop our potential, and to shape the future of humankind in the same way we have over these remarkable past decades? … No, I think not. Without a doubt, we would all fare much worse than before.

On the European continent, we have experienced centuries of conflict and bloodshed. We saw what happens when it's a game of all against all, of pure power politics. Over the past 70 years, however, Europeans have learned to live with their diversity in an unparalleled period of peace and prosperity. Stronger together than alone, and peaceful only when bound by common rules – these are the lessons we've learned the hard way. European integration is Germany's convincing and successful response to our history and to our geographical position. That's why we need the hard work and heartfelt devotion of ever new generations of young Europeans – but I am optimistic, not least because the new German Government has put European integration at the heart of its political agenda. Germany will do everything in its power to make sure that Europe continues to prosper and to shape the world of the 21st century as part of a rules-based international order, together with India as one of our strong and close partners.

My friends, Indias neibourhood is certainly not the easiest place for international cooperation. Over the past few years, there have been many– perhaps too many – setbacks for those who believe in an open and co-operative world. Co-operation requires dedication and a lot of stamina. Common solutions hardly ever come in the shape of simple answers. But that's no reason to stop working together – on the contrary!

Take one example that is important to both India and Germany: the freedom of navigation in the Indian Ocean. Through the UN Convention on the Law of the Sea and the International Tribunal in Hamburg, we have built a solid foundation to protect our international waters. But we could make this legal framework even stronger – and it is encouraging to see how the idea of undisturbed navigation has recently gained additional traction especially in this region. The proposal for a Code of Conduct for the Indian Ocean, built on the foundation of the UN

Convention, is an encouraging sign that deserves further consideration. Germany is offering both its legal expertise and its political support, not least because this region's stability is important to our own prosperity and stability

Especially in times of setbacks, I believe that we should emphasise such examples and continue sending our message of co-operation and openness! Both India and Germany are defenders of co-operation, of joint solutions to common problems. India in particular has a long and proud tradition of multilateralism. In an increasingly multi-polar world, we both understand that no single nation will be able to manage global and regional challenges alone. And especially in a new climate marked by a resurgence of international competition, we understand that it is important to emphasise what unites us rather than focusing on our disagreements.

This is the foundation of the strategic partnership that Germany and India launched 18 years ago, providing an agenda for common action. But we must grow even closer. We should build a better understanding of what we can achieve together – because our interests are linked. From investment and technology transfer to trade in goods and services, and from infrastructure to vocational training, Germany has much to offer in areas that are important to India's development. We are also strongly engaged in cultural exchange, with a vibrant community of Max Müller Bhavans in six Indian cities, in the tradition of this great German researcher of ancient Indian scriptures. Last but not least, Germany is India's most important trading partner in the European Union – and together with our friends from France, we can be India's new strategic anchor on the European continent and in the European Single Market.

At the same time, Germany would like to build on India's growing role and responsibility in the international system – as a like-minded partner for constructive and multilateral co-operation, and as a champion of stability in the wider Indo-Pacific region. We should set ourselves the task of finding joint answers to the new challenges of globalisation – challenges that both our countries face:

For example, India and Germany both depend on international trade and investment. Free and fair trade cannot guarantee peace and prosperity, but it can bring people together across borders, drive economic development and – at the same time – make us understand how much we need each other. Since the year 2000, German companies have invested almost 10 billion US dollars in India and have contributed to the creation of around 400,000 jobs. More than 1,800 German companies are currently active in this country – and Indian investments in Germany are also increasing every day. We should continue to reduce barriers to trade, thereby increasing bilateral commerce and investments. And the European Union and India should work hard and fast to conclude their negotiations on a free trade agreement. I am certain that such an agreement can lend new momentum to bilateral economic relations. Of course, trade often causes disruption: it drives rapid change and creates pressure to adapt. We all know this is a very fine balance, so we may indeed require new answers for the trade agreements of tomorrow. But ultimately, both our countries want to trade more with each other, not less. That's why we should work together to prevent an erosion of the existing global trading system, with the World Trade Organization at its core – an erosion with negative effects for all sides.

A second challenge that unites India and Germany is the need to innovate constantly, and to stay on top in research and development, in science and technology. For you, the younger generation, Industry 4.0, artificial intelligence, and robotics will be the norm. India will be – at the same time! – a rural country and a 21st century data-driven economy. Your world will be vastly different from the one your parents inherited. ... And international competition will fuel the innovation agendas in many countries around the world. In some ways, this is a very pragmatic challenge: because the answer is - we need to invest in research and we need to create conditions for ground-breaking innovation. The Indian-German science and research partnership is now 60 years old and very much alive, covering fields ranging from basic research and scientific infrastructures to co-operation between our research organisations and universities – with more than 430 bilateral agreements so far. The German House for Research and Innovation in Delhi is the focal point for many of these partnerships.

But beyond such pragmatic answers, the challenge of innovation also leads to more fundamental questions – questions on our future prosperity. It's not just about technology itself, but also about its effects on our economies and societies.

For example, if innovation radically changes the way we produce and consume, what will happen to our jobs and to our labour markets? Will traditional occupations in agriculture and industry still exist in 20, 30, 40, 50 years' time? And will our economies be able to ensure employment for future generations?

We may also ask: Are our education and training systems equipped to keep up with technology? And what will happen to health care, to taxation, or to consumer protection– in other words, to an entire system that was designed for a very different economy?

Let me add one last question: what about economic development? Are traditional approaches still valid in a digital age? To me, it seems plausible that we need new answers and new strategies. Perhaps less developed regions can indeed leapfrog traditional industrialisation and jump straight into the digital age, as some regions in Africa are showing us.

These are difficult questions. But we need to find convincing answers if we want our societies to prosper and if we want to aim for a "happy and harmonious human existence", as Prime Minister Modi put it in his recent Davos speech. I am confident that India's and Germany's strong democratic systems will rise to this task – because they are built to adapt to changing conditions. Democracy's greatest strength, to my mind, is its ability to uncover and to correct its own weaknesses. Democracy has a unique power to self-correct and to deal with new challenges!

I believe it's worth our hard work to preserve that power, to maintain this freedom and openness. We need these qualities to overcome the challenges of our time.

For example, we should strengthen our universities, defend the freedom of research, and make sure that the arts and sciences can continue flourishing freely – rather than restricting the space for debate and politicising these institutions to our narrow advantage. When academic freedom is constrained by ideology, when students and researchers are threatened and harassed on the basis of their political beliefs, then soon democracy will dry out.

We should also continue to defend the free and critical press, and the freedom of speech – rather than discrediting uncomfortable truths as "fake news" and blurring the boundaries between facts and opinion. When reporters in many countries around the world refrain from reporting for fear of reprisals, when public debate is discouraged to the extent that criticism becomes dangerous, then it's time to speak up.

And we should continue to engage in rigorous but respectful debates, in political parties and with our political opponents. We should defend the autonomy of women and the rights of minorities. We should stand up for religious tolerance – rather than excluding those we perceive as different. We are all entitled to our own opinions and our religious beliefs. That's why religious communities deserve special protection. I know these issues from our debates back home in Germany, where public discourse has become rougher and where old certainties are increasingly being called into question. I have made it my objective as President to encourage all those who work for the cause of democracy. That's why I'm here today: I want to listen to your views, and I want to embolden you to think about the future!

Because, my friends, the future is not set in stone – we all need to shape it. As students and researchers, you have the great privilege to take the long view. Dare to look far ahead, with an open mind and with an open heart! We need you in the political debates of our time, as a strong voice for an open and peaceful world, and for the future of our democracies.

My own wish for the future would be: let's continue to ride in the same elevator, let's keep talking to each other – and let's all go up, together!

So, that's it, my friends. Now, it's your turn. I am very much looking forward to hearing your thoughts. Thank you for listening!

SPEECH AT THE ASAN INSTITUTE

My visit to Korea is taking place at a very special time. The XXIII Winter Olympic Games will be opened in Pyeongchang this evening. In keeping with the ancient Greek tradition, the Games have always been linked with the idea of the Olympic Truce. This idea is particularly pertinent here on the Korean Peninsula, which is facing very real threats, and it is particularly pertinent these days, following a very tense year for the entire East Asian region. Even if it does not significantly change the immediate situation, the Olympic spirit will enable us to see things from another perspective, at least for a few weeks. And perhaps it will even leave behind a new legacy of hope.

The Olympic Truce is not a new experience for the Republic of Korea. Your country hosted the world's athletes at the Summer Olympic Games in Seoul in 1988. At that time, Solidarity in Poland and glasnost and perestroika in the Soviet Union, which still existed back then, were big topics in my still divided country. In East Germany in particular, people were profoundly moved by these ideas, which gave them courage and fuelled their hopes for reform and change. In my part of the country, in what was then the West, hardly anyone suspected that the division of Germany would soon come to an end.

Here in Korea, the Olympic Truce of Seoul in 1988 swept across a country that had undergone dramatic development in just a few decades, rising from the devastation of the war and an authoritarian form of government to an incredible level of freedom and prosperity. Your country established democratic rule under its own steam. To this day, it is one of the world's leading industrialised countries, although the older generation still has vivid memories of hunger and displacement. South Korea's success story is a textbook example of thriving democratic development. Your country can rightfully be proud of these great achievements and I would like to take this opportunity to sincerely congratulate you on them.

My country underwent an historic transformation far sooner than most people had expected. While two German teams competed in the Olympic Games in Seoul and Calgary in 1988, it was once more united German teams which travelled to Barcelona and Albertville in 1992. Between these two years, the people of East Germany had demanded in a peaceful revolution what some today may regard as a matter of course, namely their inalienable right to freedom, democracy and opportunities for prosperity.

And they achieved this. Following unrelenting pressure from protests, the Berlin Wall fell on 9 November 1989 – peacefully and without bloodshed. Just 11 months later, German reunification had become a political reality, in part because the former Allied Powers of the Second World War put new faith in my country. Berlin, the German capital, no longer symbolised the divided Europe, but instead became a shining beacon of our continent's peaceful unification.

The deadly Wall that bisected Berlin stood for over 28 years, more precisely for 10,316 days. These more than 10,000 days tore families apart and seared deep into people's lives on both sides. It was difficult to imagine our country without this Wall, without the death strips and automatic weapons systems. For those who grew up with all of this, it had become part of normal life.

But since then, another 28 years have passed. For four days now, since 5 February, the Wall has been gone for longer than it divided our country. The fall of the Wall was followed by days of joy and relief for us Germans. However, we soon saw that years of hard work lay ahead of us as we strove to establish cohesion in our country. For many East Germans, this period went hand in hand with profound and abrupt changes. Certainly, they gained new freedoms, but they also experienced losses and disappointments – especially the loss of jobs. Reunification did not spell the end of history for Germany at any rate, but rather the start of a new, exciting and, for most Germans, very successful chapter in our history.

In speaking to you today about these two periods of 10,000 days, my main aim is to tell you that nothing is set in stone. And that is why it is worth remaining hopeful.

It is not naive or unrealistic to feel hope. On the contrary, hope is where one finds the will to change reality. At least, that is what my East German compatriots stand for – the people who proved their courage to bring about change both before and after the fall of the Wall.

Naturally, I am aware that the situation in Korea is very different. Our shared experience of division should not cause us to lose sight of another fundamentally different dimension of the challenges facing Korea today, particularly you here in the South. This other dimension is characterised by two factors. Firstly, the fact that you have already been divided for over 70 years and, secondly, that the military, and now also nuclear threat, is not abstract but immediate and omnipresent.

I firmly believe that maintaining political and economic pressure is vital. I firmly believe that this pressure is necessary to create a genuine readiness to engage in dialogue. That is what I learned from the negotiations with Iran, in which I was involved for eight years. But we must also remember that dialogue is the only possible way to achieve détente, and ultimately peace and unity. Those who are serious about finding solutions in this dialogue must, on the one hand, maintain the political pressure, but also constantly suggest ideas and make proposals for a better future. They must want to overcome the status quo. In short, they always need both – hope and courage.

The situation in East Asia is both tenser and more complex than almost ever before. Old certainties are being called into question – we in Germany and you in Korea only need to look at the new discussion with the US on the future of free trade. At the same time, rising powers such as China and Russia are promising prosperity and security – but without freedom and without democratic self-determination. China in particular is taking an increasingly self-confident stance and confronting the international community – especially the Republic of Korea – with fundamental questions on regional security structure. Nor have relations between the democratic neighbouring countries of South Korea and Japan been free from discord and conflicts in recent years, as we have observed from Germany, irrespective of the fundamental common ground that certainly exists between these two countries. And, indeed, I hope that the intensive efforts to find and cultivate this common ground will continue. Above all, nuclear armament in North Korea makes any thought of reunification or even merely meaningful and sustained dialogue seem like a flight of fancy at the moment.

But that is precisely why I am reminding you today that, in principal, nothing is written in stone. That is why I am talking about the willingness to draw up a blueprint for a better future. If this willingness does not exist here in Korea, then it is even less prevalent in other parts of the world. I know that any scenario for a peaceful and reunited Korea only has a hope of succeeding if it safeguards the region's foreign policy stability. That is why I set up an advisory group during my visit in 2014 which focuses on these foreign policy aspects of reunification. And if I may convey just one message here today, then it is that the Koreans themselves will always have the greatest and most sincere interest in peaceful reunification. Particularly here, hope must be nurtured.

I would be happy to discuss these topics with you. I cannot think of any better time for these discussions than today – the day when Korean athletes will enter the stadium under one flag during the opening of the Olympic Games.

Thank you for listening. I look forward to our discussion.

SPEECH AT THE DIPLOMATS

"Concordia domi foris pax" – "harmony within, peace without". Three years ago, while still Foreign Minister, I stood with my G7 counterparts and gazed at this inscription on the famous Holsten Gate in the Hanseatic city of Lübeck.

You are all aware that one important issue I have chosen to focus on during my term of office is the future of democracy. Ensuring "harmony within" is a challenge not only in virtually every democracy. On my travels both in Germany and abroad, I have seen again and again the polarisation of many societies, growing irreconcilability between political opponents and increasing distance between social groups. The pressures of globalisation and the changed culture of debate in the digital age are putting our societies' internal cohesion to the test.

Germany is not exempt from this. If we lose sight of all that we have in common, of all that links us, and if the tone of political debate becomes rougher, perhaps even hostile, then society is bound to be affected. In many cases, such attitudes are born of fear of what the future might bring, and the worry caused by uncertainty. Some people in our country believe the best response to this is withdrawal and isolation, a return to an allegedly golden past – though on closer inspection it wasn't really all that golden. In some countries – including in Europe – this withdrawal has become the prevailing policy: it is a matter of circling up the wagons, shutting out a hostile outside world.

Withdrawing like this to secure "harmony within" was something that never entered the minds of the citizens of the proud Hanseatic cities like Lübeck back then. They thrived on openness, on exchange, on the curiosity and confidence of their merchants and seamen, who dared to venture even into the unknown.

Particularly in this day and age, withdrawal and isolation cannot be on the agenda for a country like Germany either, a country that owes its peace and prosperity to the trust placed in it by countless partners around the world.

We are grateful for this trust and for this cooperation. Germany will continue to endeavour to formulate its interests in an enlightened and far sighted manner, attaching crucial importance to the wellbeing of our European neighbours. And, in collaboration with the global community, we want to work to protect our common heritage, to champion climate protection, clean seas, education, health and sustainable development. One thing is clear: we will not regard the world as an arena in which everyone pursues merely his own interests, on a national basis, thinking only in the short term and with no consideration for others.

"Harmony within, peace without": the phrase also points to the close link between domestic and foreign policy. Today the two appear more interwoven than ever before. This is the result of technological developments which penetrate right to the very heart of our societies while at the same time effecting sweeping changes in the world. It is therefore all the more important not to play domestic and foreign policy off against one another. Rather, we must try to reconcile them in a responsible manner.

As diplomats, ladies and gentlemen, you have the task of making such reconciliation possible. In order to read the mood correctly, to assess what room there is for manoeuvre, to understand how a country thinks, how it defines its role in the world, you have to be in that country. It does not work merely in virtual space. It does not even work if you never venture outside the capital.

That is one reason why we travelled together last September to Saxony-Anhalt, and to the Garden Kingdom of Dessau-Wörlitz. In the final chapter of 'Candide', Voltaire has his protagonist say "We must cultivate our garden" – and then withdraw from the world. Of course, in reality Voltaire meant exactly the opposite: what is happening in the other "gardens" of this world concerns us all, particularly if we want to preserve harmony within and peace without.

I am looking forward to visiting some of your countries this year in order to strengthen and develop our ties. I am also looking forward to visiting Bremen with you in the summer. Like Lübeck, it is a Hanseatic city and one of Germany's gateways to the world.

We are aware of the expectations being directed at Germany at the start of this new year. Following the Bundestag elections in September, it is taking longer to form a government than it ever has before in the Federal Republic. But just because it is happening for the first time does not mean that it falls outside the realm of the rules. The Basic Law, our constitution, gives us clear rules and clear orientation for a situation like this. The past few weeks have shown that the interplay between our country's various institutions works. Those who bear responsibility in the institutions and parties are taking it seriously. And they know that they have this responsibility not only towards the members of their own party and their own political future. Rather, it is always also a responsibility for Europe, and for reliability, partnership and engagement in international politics.

I look forward to working with you in the year ahead. I wish you, your families and all your staff harmony, peace and good health in 2018!

SPEECH AT THE UN CLIMATE CHANGE CONFERENCE IN BONN

It is just a week since I came back from a trip to the South Pacific. One image is firmly lodged in my memory: during the flight home, I took a long look out of the aircraft window, gazing down on the turquoise archipelago, on hundreds of little islands. That picture left more of an impression than any sober statistics. It was a picture of beauty, home to countless families and the heart of millennia-old traditions and cultures. But it was also a picture of vulnerability, of filigree isles surrounded by the expanse of Oceania.

Sitting there in the plane high above the Pacific, I found myself thinking back to my years as Foreign Minister, to the many talks I had on the fringes of the UN General Assembly with representatives of the Small Island Developing States, talks which, I admit, really opened my eyes to those regions most endangered by climate change. And so I am especially delighted to see many familiar faces from the Small Island Developing States here today. As President of the Federal Republic of Germany, I am very pleased to extend to them and to each and every one of you a very warm welcome to the United Nations Climate Change Conference here in Bonn. Welcome!

During the trip I mentioned just a moment ago, in New Zealand, I was shown what I regarded as a quite extraordinary newspaper article. It came from the Rodney & Otamatea Times and was dated 14 August. Very concisely, it said that burning billions of tons of coal added billions of tons of carbon dioxide to the atmosphere every year. This tended to make the air a more effective blanket for the earth and to raise its temperature. The effect, the article said, would be considerable in a few centuries. You have probably already guessed that this report was not dated 14 August 2017, and not even 2007. No, this warning appeared in the paper on 14 August 1912.

I am sure you will agree with me that back then, 105 years ago, that was a remarkably shrewd prognosis. And at a time, indeed, when mankind's terrible contribution to climate change had not really got underway. The report only got one thing wrong: the effects of climate change are not going to be felt first "in a few centuries".

On the contrary: we can already see how dramatic the situation is and we are already feeling the effects.

We can feel the effects here in Europe when we drive in winter through empty Alpine valleys – valleys which just fifty years ago were packed full of glacial ice.

We feel them in other parts of the world, where the sea floods the land more and more often, while elsewhere, far away, whole towns are disappearing in the desert sand.

And we feel them when the Gulf Stream slows in the Atlantic and at the same time ever larger icebergs calve off from the shelf of the polar ice caps.

But we are most immediately moved by the effects of climate change when, every year, environmental changes and extreme weather events destroy the homes of thousands of people; when terrible droughts and famines force the population of whole swathes of land to leave their homes; and when this all causes crises and bloody conflicts, as is happening ever more frequently.

I certainly am in no doubt that the dramatic nature of these developments, this urgency, means it is incumbent upon each and every one of us to act quickly and resolutely.

I am therefore all the more pleased that there are so many people here who wish to play a constructive part in the negotiations. They include many well-known pioneers, but also some who until recently were rather reticent with regard to climate protection. The rapidly growing economies – including, for example, the Republic of China – are particularly important in this context, as they are now among the bigger emitters. Yes, the starting positions may be very different, and in many areas China does indeed have a long way to go. However, the most recent messages from Beijing regarding decoupling economic growth from environmental impact have been clear and unambiguous, and that is a good sign. My hope is that precisely this energy, this impetus, flow into the international negotiations now too.

And when, on the other hand, we experience individual setbacks, then what I would say is this: who knows? International politics – like the climate – is a cumbersome tanker, particularly when it has really got going. And perhaps some who are leaving the command bridge for the dinghy today might decide in a few years to dock on to our common ship again. Perhaps those in positions of responsibility in state capitols and in the municipalities, in companies and in civil society, might even succeed in doing something amazing: sticking, despite opposition from their own capital and thanks merely to their own strong commitment, to the course embarked upon in Paris.

For it is clear that the historic climate accord of 2015 must remain irreversible, and we are all jointly called upon to take concrete action now. Paris will only truly have been a breakthrough if we follow the agreement with action.

I firmly believe that we have already developed a difficult but functioning model for our joint action – constructive, multilateral cooperation within the United Nations. Yes, there are repeated setbacks and disappointments. If we think back to the negotiations in Copenhagen, then many of us will also remember bitter moments of doubt. But now, when individual voices are very deliberately badmouthing multilateral cooperation, this is exactly the time for the rest of us to speak out clearly – for our rules-based international order, for its institutions and thus above all for the United Nations.

The major milestones of the past few years confirm us in this. Look at the Paris accord. Look at the Sustainable Development Goals in the 2030 Agenda. And look at the many thousands of little successes, all the measures and projects in towns and cities which really got underway in the wake of the trailblazing decisions – from the photovoltaic system replacing a village's diesel generators and kerosene stoves to all-electric public transport in a smog-ridden city.

My feeling is that we must not ignore or dismiss such successes, despite the odd disappointment along the way. After all, far beyond the bounds of individual agreements and treaties, this multilateral order is indispensable for a peaceful and prosperous future. International cooperation is a bulwark against all visions of the world in which nothing but the law of the strong or arbitrary political action or unregulated global markets determine the fate of humanity.

This is particularly important for economically weaker countries and for the world's small island states because they have contributed least to climate change and yet even now are fearing for the very existence of their country.

They are the ones who are not yet sharing in the prosperity of the industrialised countries and so suffer particularly hard in the event of natural disasters, droughts and failed harvests.

And they are the ones whose voice is often ignored in the global concert, even though they are the ones in most urgent need of our solidarity.

We owe it to the smaller and weaker states above all to make this conference a success. Climate protection is also a question of global fairness. And for some people here today, the question is not one that will arise at some point in the future, but is pressing right now. We can see this from the fate of Barbuda and Dominica, two island states which were rendered uninhabitable by this year's hurricanes. Island states like them have no time to lose. It is not enough to be talking about their situation; we must do something practical, we must help them to protect themselves. We need to take action.

It is good that the interests of these states are being clearly represented with the Republic of Fiji in the chair at this conference. Fiji itself is threatened by the effect of climate change in a very direct way. I would therefore like to express my particular gratitude and my respect to the Government of Fiji and also to thank you, Prime Minister Bainimarama, for your engagement. Thank you very much!

Allow me to conclude with a few remarks from the German viewpoint. With the negotiations here in Bonn, you are preparing what experts call a "transformative shift" in the global economy. Here in Germany we have been tackling this transformative shift for some years now. We call it the "Energiewende", the shift to green energy.

I am telling you this for two reasons.

On the one hand, we are seeing more and more instances in Germany where entrepreneurship and smart technology are helping us to combine economy and ecology in a positive way, rather than to see them as irreconcilables.

On the other, I get the impression that despite much controversy in our social debate there is increasingly a broad consensus in favour of sustainable business, the preservation of creation and effective environment and climate policy.

Happily, we are not alone in this. No, many other states are already taking the same approach and others are coming on board.

I hope that by mentioning this example from the German and European context I have at least been able to give you a bit of courage, both for the negotiations here in Bonn and for the challenges facing you at home.

We all bear responsibility for the future of our planet, especially you during the final round of negotiations. In our common interest I wish you and the conference every possible success.

GERMANY POLITICAL AND ECONOMIC STRATEGY[1]

SPEECH BY FEDERAL CHANCELLOR ANGELA MERKEL AT THE WORLD ECONOMIC FORUM ANNUAL MEETING IN DAVOS ON 24 JANUARY 2018

I am pleased to be back in Davos – in a very special situation this year, but I will get back to that later.

Today, when Europe is very much the focus of the discussions at this Davos Forum, I would like to recall that the First World War ended 100 years ago, in 1918. It is described as the seminal catastrophe of the 20th century. Worse catastrophes followed it. Like sleepwalkers, the politicians of the time blundered into a terrible situation. Today, 100 years later, when there are fewer and fewer surviving eyewitnesses to the Second World War, we need to ask ourselves if we have really learned from history or not. I think the generations of people born after the Second World War will need to prove whether they have really learned something.

The lessons of the Second World War led to the foundation of the United Nations. This was a multilateral response, a response founded on cooperation. Over 25 years ago, we experienced the end of the Cold War and of the division of the world into two blocs. This meant that for the first time, multilateralism and cooperation had an opportunity to thrive.

There was a multilateral response aimed at resolving the great challenge of 2007 and 2008, the international financial crisis. This response took the form of meetings between the Heads of State and Government of the G20, whose Presidency is held by Argentina this year. Germany held the Presidency last year and the motto of our Presidency was "shaping an interconnected world". We tried to foster global cooperation in what is not a particularly easy time. We made progress in global cooperation in the health sector, the partnership with Africa and the global steel forum, which addresses dumping and fair trade. We tried to strengthen the role of multilateral organisations and sought to promote an open global trade system. As regards the great challenge to humankind, climate change, we had to draw our conclusions without the United States of America, unfortunately. Nevertheless, climate change remains a huge threat.

We see that national egoism exists. We see that populism exists. We see that a polarising atmosphere prevails in many countries. Perhaps there is also widespread concern about whether multilateral cooperation is really capable of solving people's problems honestly and fairly and whether everyone can be included given the great technological challenges of the Digital Revolution and disruptive changes. There are doubts about this everywhere. And that, Professor Schwab, is why I think "creating a shared future in a fractured world" is exactly the right motto for 2018.

To be honest, the country I come from and where I am Federal Chancellor also has difficulties. We are experiencing a level of polarisation not seen for decades. Germany is challenged by two events, which are also a result of globalisation – the euro crisis, which we have now largely overcome, and the migration of recent years. But let me tell you that Germany – as repeatedly shown in my earlier and current talks on forming a government – wants to be a country that continues to play its part in the future in order to solve tomorrow's problems by working together in the world. We believe that isolation is not constructive. We believe that we need to cooperate and that protectionism is not the right answer. And we believe that if we think things are not being run fairly and mechanisms are not reciprocal, then we should seek multilateral solutions, and not unilateral responses, which ultimately only serve to further isolation and protectionism.

[1] Selected Speeches of Federal Chancellor Angela Merkel

That is why it is so important that Germany forms a government quickly. I hope we will achieve this. Two key ideas are important in the talks we are currently conducting. The first is how we can safeguard prosperity for our country and its people. At the moment, we have a situation in Germany in which we can say that we are doing well – we are doing very well. All signs indicate that in 2020 we will have enjoyed eleven consecutive years of growth. The last time we experienced that was in the 1950s. More people than ever before are in employment. We have a solid financial situation. We have made good progress as regards adopting digital technology in our business sector and with Industrie 4.0. However – and I want to state this very frankly – we are not leaders in other areas of digital technology such as society and the state.

For the next four years, our job will therefore be to bring digital technology to our education system and bureaucracy, to give the public the option of communicating with their state via digital technology in the digital age and to create a better ecosystem for start-ups so that we remain a good place for innovation. I take this challenge very seriously indeed. We have no time to lose, as we know that other parts of the world are developing very rapidly in this regard. We also see that countries such as Estonia, which just held the Presidency of the Council of the European Union, are far more developed than a country like Germany, which is not at the top of the European league as regards digitisation.

We know that the spread of digital technology means we need to deal with lifelong learning and find completely new solutions for our social systems. That means the lesson is, and must be, that disruptive technological changes alter our societies. In an ageing country like Germany, the willingness to respond to this and to adopt new technology is, to put it mildly, not exactly widespread. This means that the question of what resources we can allocate and how to invest in the future are major topics in our talks.

We know that if we want to keep our promise of prosperity for all in the digital age, including for everyone in Germany, we need a smart social market economy and not merely smart industry. This means we also need to deal with the question of how we can include everyone. I think this is one of the most urgent questions because countries that are divided are far less able to take multilateral action and to cooperate with others. Instead, there is a very great danger that they will withdraw.

None of these questions can be solved at national level. That is why the question of what happens next in Germany is inextricably linked with the question of what happens next in Europe. With a view to large countries such as China and India, many problems can only be solved through cooperation at European level in the European Union. Interestingly, regrettable as the decision by the people of the United Kingdom to leave the EU was, the more it has given us the courage to concentrate on the big picture. I would like to say expressly that the election of French President Emmanuel Macron has brought new impetus to the European Union – and that will make us stronger.

What do we need to do? At a time when not all EU Member States say that an ever closer union is just what they have in mind, we need to learn to find answers to the major questions in Europe and to allow issues that can be solved locally to be solved by local people. Otherwise, there will not be a good atmosphere in Europe. Our priority must be to foster our economic strength. That means that after having overcome the euro crisis relatively well, with all Member States in the euro area now experiencing growth and higher employment once again, we need to look towards the future. In my opinion, that is mainly why we need to expand the digital single market. In this regard, I believe there are two reasons why we are under pressure in the European Union.

Firstly, large US companies have access to data – and data is the raw material of the 21st century. The answer to the question of who owns this data will ultimately decide whether democracy, participation, sovereignty in the digital age and economic success can go together. On the other hand, there are countries, such as China, where you have very close cooperation between the state authorities and those who gather data, where they are virtually one and the same thing. Europeans have not yet made a real decision on how they want to deal with data. There is a great danger that we are too slow and will find ourselves overturned by events, so to speak, while we hold our philosophical debates about data sovereignty. That means we need to take action. I believe that our European social market economy gives us a chance to foster a fair digital age in which the privatisation of all personal data is not simply accepted as the normal state of affairs, but it is accepted that, in order to make the best of this era for the public, data is the raw material of the 21st century.

Secondly, we need to make our euro area stronger. That means we need a capital market union – the capital market is still fragmented. We need to complete the banking union. We need to think about how we can defend ourselves against future crises that hit us from outside so that risk is not simply communitarised and we all become liable, although everyone actually needs to manage their own risks. At the same time, we need to ensure that we are an interesting location for investment. That is why we cannot afford to isolate ourselves. Instead, we need to keep up with the world's best and promote our multilateral approach.

If we want to be taken seriously as Europeans, we face another great task, namely to work together in the field of foreign policy. Common European foreign policy remains underdeveloped. If Europe, with its future 27 Member States, is not in a position to send a coherent message to large countries such as China, India, the United States or Russia in the future, but instead conducts foreign policy at national level while trying to be a global player, this will result in failure. We still have plenty of work ahead of us in this regard because we are not yet able to feel certain that we can truly rely on each other.

At the same time, there has been great progress in one area, and I am pleased that Germany's Defence Minister is here with us. Following years of discussion in Europe, we have succeeded in establishing European defence cooperation in light of the challenges we see. That is very important for two reasons. Firstly, this cooperation does not seek to undermine NATO. We are very glad that the NATO Secretary General was involved in the foundation of our common defence policy and explicitly said that he sees it as complementary. Secondly, we are in a position to take a united stance towards third countries, something that is very important to us. This means we now have a common policy on security, development cooperation and economic development issues. We can show that we have a coherent model, particularly as regards Africa. This is very important.

Why are common foreign policy, common defence policy and common development policy of such great interest? If you look at the regions around Europe, you will see that most global conflicts are taking place on our doorstep. We experienced this in 2015 when one might say globalisation arrived in Europe in the form of people, refugees, when we did not in fact deal with the civil war in Syria or with IS in Iraq. I am sure that my Italian counterpart just reported here on the challenges regarding migration from Africa. We basically have the Sunni-Shi'ite conflicts on our doorstep. We have IS on our doorstep. Our neighbour is Africa, just a few kilometres from the southern part of Europe. Syria is a neighbour of Cyprus.

The fact that Europe was not the most active continent as regards foreign policy, but instead often relied on the United States of America, which is now focusing more on itself, must therefore lead us to say that we need to take on more responsibility and to take our fate into our own hands to a greater extent. We are doing so by establishing a common defence policy and working together to tackle the challenge of migration, although there is still a great lack of unity on this topic within the European Union.

We now agree that we need to protect our external borders. But what does that mean? Europe is an interesting continent or entity. We created a common currency, but we never thought about what would happen if it were to be hit by crisis. Now we are making up for lost time and basically building the foundation that we should have created from the outset. We were incredibly proud to have freedom of movement. When you travel around the Schengen area, you do not need to show your passport anywhere. But we did not think about how to protect our external borders and whether we know who enters or leaves Europe. In hindsight, we have to ask ourselves how we could have done something like that without thinking about these issues. But we simply felt too safe.

Now we are working on an entry and exit system. We have set up a common border protection agency. However, one thing is true – since the Roman Empire and the construction of the Great Wall of China, history has taught us that isolation alone does not help to protect borders. Instead, what we need are good relations with our neighbours, agreements and international treaties in order to know how we can cope with the challenge of illegal migration. That is exactly what we have learned. This is shown in the EU's agreement with Turkey and our migration partnerships with Africa. But naturally, we still have a great deal to do.

If you think about it, you will realise that we share responsibility. If wealth inequality becomes ever greater, we will not be able to sign treaties with one another in an open world. We share responsibility for Africa's development. We share responsibility for what happens next in Iraq. We share responsibility for what happens next in Libya. We are hesitant to get involved, but we have in fact been successful in many areas in recent years. However, there is still a huge amount of work ahead of us. There is great consensus in the European Union on this – far more consensus, in fact, than on the question of how we allocate the refugees who arrive in Europe among the various Member States. Unfortunately, there is still no agreement on that. However, we are in a better position as regards the other issues.

Naturally, we also have the challenge of working with Africa. We will only have the strength to do so if our own economy is strong. It is of great importance to me personally that we work with Africa, firstly because we Europeans owe a great debt to the continent of Africa from the time of colonisation and secondly because we have a profound interest in positive development in Africa. We say "Africa", but it actually has over 50 different countries with very different levels of development. What is now important is that we work with Africa on ensuring it shares in greater wealth. That is why we named our initiative "Compact with Africa" and not "Compact for Africa". It is not a paternalistic partnership, but rather a partnership among equals. This means investing in education so that economic growth is not lower than population growth. Above all, it means using a completely new model of development aid, one based on wide-ranging development, including economic development. We will continue working in this way.

With regard to Europe, we have a problem that I would now like to address. Naturally, we all very much regret that the United Kingdom will no longer be part of the European Union. Our colleague Theresa May will be here tomorrow. On behalf of Germany, but also other countries, I would like to say that we want to continue having a good partnership with the United Kingdom in the future. However, we will also make clear that access to the single market is tied to Europe's four freedoms. We can make no compromises on that. But we know that we are closely linked to the United Kingdom through values, convictions and foreign policy interests. It is up to the United Kingdom to say how close it wants this partnership to be. We are open to all forms of partnerships.

Ladies and gentlemen, I have tried to make clear to you what I believe can be done in a "fractured world". I think this always begins at home. The more we succeed in overcoming divisions in our own countries, the more freedom we will have to focus on solidarity, cooperation and multilateralism. Fundamentally, the solutions are always similar – we can leave no one behind. Perhaps one of the greatest tasks facing us in an age of hugely disruptive challenges arising from the spread of digital technology is to prevent division.

Professor Schwab, we spoke earlier about this and I am delighted that you are supporting networks to foster discussion between policymakers and business people on what is an ethical way to manage disruptive developments. If we do not succeed in finding an answer, the same thing will happen as in the early days of capitalism – we will be confronted with something like Luddites, as was the case back then. The task now – and in conclusion, I call on the business people here, who live in an investment environment with conditions from another era that they did not create themselves – is to please work with us on transferring these conditions to a new era.

We are wrong to think it is enough for 20 or 30 percent of a country's population to be enthusiastic about disruptive changes to ensure the entire country is on board. It is not enough. It requires lifelong learning and many other things. I believe many people will be happy to go along with this. But many others will need to be invited to do so because they are not able to keep up at once with this crazy tempo.

My hope is that this Davos forum will offer space for these questions because it brings together many people from the spheres of business, politics and society. Then we can achieve this and prevent the mistakes of the 20th century being repeated in any way. We know that the ways of causing great harm using disruptive digital developments and of confounding societies are of a very different nature to what we experienced in the 20th century. However, they are at least as harmful. That is why we need to achieve a genuine social market economy in this area, as we would say in Germany. Then global cooperation will also work. Germany would like to continue working on this in the future. If you could kindly keep your fingers crossed for me that we manage to form a government, this will work even better.

SPEECH BY FEDERAL CHANCELLOR MERKEL AT THE GERMAN EMPLOYERS' DAY[2]

I am very happy to be with you again today. You're basically celebrating two anniversaries. The German Employers' Day will be held for the 20th time. It has become one of the most important economic and socio-political events in this country. We can all congratulate each other on the other anniversary - as you have already suggested -: 100 years ago not only the Republic was proclaimed; Soon afterwards social partnership emerged - a few days after the end of the First World War in a very uncertain economic situation - when, on 15 November 1918, employers and unions agreed on the Stinnes Legislative Agreement.

That was a milestone; and I agree with you: a milestone on the way to the social market economy. At that time it prevented the socialization of private means of production; The November Revolution was, after all, comparatively left-leaning. That's why it was important to recognize unions as equal employers' contractors. Conciliation procedures have been introduced to resolve wage disputes. The collective bargaining autonomy was agreed. It was then anchored later in the Federal Republic of Germany in the Basic Law. It allowed the social partners to agree on working conditions independently and without state intervention. In other words, the Stinnes-Legia Agreement created a completely new, previously unknown partnership.

Personally, I am of the opinion that collective bargaining autonomy is one of the core elements of the social market economy. But of course that also means that this core element remains visible. If today only about 30 percent of the companies are directly bound by a collective agreement, then this is a declining and a, I think, threatening situation. You, Mr Kramer, have

[2] 22 November 2018 in Berlin

talked about why that is and who is contributing to it; and I can also tell a lot about it. Especially in the aftermath of the reunification of German Unity, there have been developments in the metalworking sector that have certainly accelerated this process. In any case, if this proportion does not rise again, but further sinks - and if collective autonomy would be guaranteed a hundred times in the Basic Law; and even if we say so many times that is a core element of the social market economy, in real life this will increase the pressure on politics. This is basically a pressure, which is no longer bundled by associations, but an individual pressure, in which there is the danger that then only the stronger will prevail and that the social wellbeing as a whole can not be kept in mind.

That's why I'm pleased that you said: We want to start discussions to discuss together with the unions how we can achieve it - by whatever means - to make collective bargaining more attractive again. Both of us, Mr Kramer and myself, have spoken a lot about this. I believe that in view of the challenges of digitization, which I will come back to later on, and also many start-ups with partly completely new structures, it will not be trivial to increase collective bargaining coverage again.

Of course, what is also important is that one keeps an eye on all aspects of trade union existence, so to speak. For classical German industry has partly maintained its collective bargaining agreement, so to speak, by outsourcing everything that was not directly related to the industrial value creation process and leaving it to other areas. If you have to answer as a union leader services, then you see that there are very different life situations in Germany - on the one hand in the automotive industry, mechanical engineering or chemical companies of the classic kind and on the other hand, if you look at, like the canteen operation, the cleaning service and many other services are valued.

That, dear Mr Kramer, is also one of the reasons why there is a tendency to spend more and more social well-being than economic growth, which I consider to be of fundamental concern if it is too long because, as I see it, the gap between the service sector and the area of industrial added value tends to get bigger and in distribution struggles some people always say "we catch up" and the others say "we have to share our wealth with our employees". Then what is available is basically distributed twice. That's the problem I ask you to bring back together, to think holistically in your business and not to think "Yes, if I have to deal only with a works council dedicated to the core business, I do not need to worry about everything around it ", but also to see the trappings around. Otherwise this leads to a deep feeling of injustice, becomes a political issue and ends up with us.

Ladies and gentlemen, it is nevertheless the case that for the ninth year in a row we have achieved economic success. This is the longest growth period since the fifties. But as it is with the success: He drives fantasies, so to speak, what else could one do. That's the hard part. Theoretically, these good times should be used to set the course for the future. Politically practical, so to speak, is the temptation to redistribute something from the existing one, of course, greater. Almost in times of economic decline, reforms improve, although the price to pay is greater. That's what we have to deal with. But we can be proud of having as many employees today as never before.

We also have the development - and this is said too rarely in my opinion - that poverty and social exclusion have declined and that the fact that as many people as ever have social insurance contributions is, of course, a factor contributing to the fight against poverty hopes to educate children who are growing up in families where people are not unemployed. I mean, when I became Chancellor, we had five million unemployed. I still remember how, in March 2006, the newspaper, which always headlines particularly large, headlined: "Mrs. Merkel, these are now your unemployed". There had been more than five million. We can already be satisfied today that we have 2.4 million or 2.3 million unemployed people.

We also agreed that we keep the additional wage costs below 40 percent. Dear Mr. Kramer, I remember my first years in the German Bundestag. At that time, they were often over 40 percent. That was the top topic. But I also understand that you are looking at certain developments with some concern. Also there - I should talk here today also a little about the cohesion in society - of course there are certain things for politicians who are worried. The whole area of nursing - which, of course, will become even more important in a society that is changing demographically like ours - is linked to questions that unbelievably disturb people. If you look at the employment situations, you see, that the working hours are sometimes dramatically uncertain. Often there are long, long distances without a day off. The collective bargaining agreement is not very good. The trainees are still paying tuition today - a fact that has not been noticed at the federal level for many years, because that is actually a country thing; a paradox. If you want to inspire young people in these professions today in an environment where you are looking for skilled workers everywhere, then it is clear that you have to make a difference in this education.

We have to take care of these things. And there, in the design of the German social system, we are faced with the question: how do we do this in order to offer better care services on the one hand and to make such occupations more attractive and, on the other hand, to keep the additional wage costs below 40 percent? As an alternative then always only control means in question; and it flows very, very much, for example, in the pension. Therefore, we are already under pressure, which will certainly not be lower in the next few years.

When we talk about the cohesion in society: As the federal government, we have one of the most complicated commissions - the Equal Living Commissions Commission. Take a look at how different the living conditions and worries of people in Germany have become. In Munich, for example, there are not enough apartments or the rents are so high that skilled workers can hardly afford them anymore. Actually, companies and the state have to build apartments for themselves and their employees. On the one hand, we are missing well over a million apartments, and on the other hand, more than one million apartments are empty. There are people in rural areas, where I too have my constituency, who have worked, done, done, all their lives for their little house. who then have to experience that their children move to Stuttgart, to Munich or elsewhere, that they stay on their property, which really is not like their children mobile, and that the life's work loses value. If you go into a nursing home today as an elderly person and own a property in Freiburg and a property in Höxter, then what you have saved from the property of your old house in Höxter - even though you have done the same thing in your life - is enough , maybe only one-fifth of what's going on in Freiburg. People find this unfair. That's not surprising. But we do not have a complete answer. who really do not like their kids is mobile, sit down and that the life's work loses value. If you go into a nursing home today as an elderly person and own a property in Freiburg and a property in Höxter, then what you have saved from the property of your old house in Höxter - even though you have done the same thing in your life - is enough , maybe only one-fifth of what's going on in Freiburg. People find this unfair. That's not surprising. But we do not have a complete answer. who really do not like their kids is mobile, sit down and that the life's work loses value. If you go into a nursing home today as an elderly person and own a property in Freiburg and a property in Höxter, then what you have saved from the property of your old house in Höxter - even though you have done the same thing in your life - is enough , maybe only one-fifth of what's going on in Freiburg. People find this unfair. That's not surprising. But we do not have a complete answer. What you are saving from the property of your old house in Höxter - although you have done the same in your life, have spent - have made, perhaps only for a fifth of what in Freiburg value. People find this unfair. That's not surprising. But we do not have a complete answer. What you are saving from the property of your old house in Höxter - although you have done the same in your life, have spent - have made, perhaps only for a fifth of what in Freiburg value. People find this unfair. That's not surprising. But we do not have a complete answer.

That is why it is very important for us to work together to make economic development in all parts of Germany reasonable. For example in Bavaria, that's because you have a good core. But in all new federal states, not a single DAX company has its headquarters. In the process of convincing the DAX companies that they should now also engage in the new countries, which are deindustrializing, so to speak, even super-traffic connections do not help. That means that then just the young people go away. And the moment the young people leave, the older ones are totally insecure. For the fact that they do not see their grandchildren growing up, that the children live far away in Munich and live in a tiny apartment, in which they turn their eyes three times, if grandma is still visiting on the second day - yes, the guest room is not included in the rental price - that is killing people. All this has nothing to do with the fact that 45 million people have a job, but it's just killing them. And we have to deal with that.

In addition, we also have to find reasonable regulatory answers. I am not one of those who believe that the fifth rent-price brake will result in more apartments, but I believe that housing shortages are only tackled by housing; that is part of it too. However, I must say at this point, even if I do not want to address personally here: If you live in a district in which there is still a piece of green space, the interest in the fact that also there new apartments are to be built, before Location also very limited. It is easier to win constituencies in Munich today if you say "no new development". I think the Secretary General of the CSU will come later. He won in Trudering because he said "No new development". I understand that, because, so to speak, the packing density in the city is already big. But we are also faced with the question: where do we get building land? How do we build more systemically to make things faster and not everyone reinvents everything? These are also questions that we face.

By the way, as far as the question of DAX companies and their involvement in the new federal states is concerned, I would also like to say thank you, because, for example, I see Mr Kaeser sitting in the front row here. Because Görlitz is such a case in which people ask what will become of them. Then hopeful answers have been found.

Now there is also uncertainty in the face of barely tangible challenges of digitization. I think it's great that you invited today the chairperson of the Digital Council, Ms. Suder. Thank you for that. This digital advice really does make us legs as a federal government, if I may say so, because it brings us in a very condensed way to the challenges of digitization. That's the first thing, and we talk a lot about that in Germany, the infrastructure. Okay, their expansion would have to go faster. But I think we're on the right track now. By the end of 2019, we will have 98 percent of households connected to broadband. By the end of 2021, we will have 99 percent connected. We'll have to do the rest with state aid, so to speak.

Incidentally, we have the following situation: Now we are expanding broadband extensively, but we have a bottleneck in civil engineering companies that are still available. The prices increase naturally. Now the connections are there. Now you go once in a Vorpommersches village or a village in the Eifel and go to the question: who really wants to benefit from this beautiful fiber optic cable? People are sitting at home with DSL; many are happy with it, the older ones anyway. Then the big question arises: how do we get the refinancing of the investments? Because there is no obligation to connect as with water and sewage. If you asked people if they wanted to have a sewer connection, many would say no. We are by the private organization of this future general interest in a situation in which perhaps only 50 percent or 60 percent in the rural areas make use of the great new offers - of course in the business parks, of course, the SMEs, of course, the schools and hospitals; all right. But there are many others. And how we handle it will one day become another very exciting question.

Second, we are talking about blanket internet. This is also one of the tasks of the commission "Equivalent living conditions". After all, humans do not only want to have Internet access at home, but maybe they also want to be able to exchange short videos with their family when he is sitting in the meadow and resting. That means we need a nationwide coverage. This causes a slightly bigger problem. For this we still need at least 10,000 new radio masts. The supply does not necessarily have to be at the level of 5G, but everyone knows that, but you would be glad if you had permanent 3G. This will be a big challenge again.

But then it's also about 5G applications - I see Mr. Lutz - along the railway lines, along the main roads, along the highways, along the country roads. Since then we will have the possibility of data transfer in real time, at least almost. So there will be least latency. The 5G applications are still coming. Of course, they are not yet fully available today. That means we do not need to expand the whole country immediately with 5G, but we have a bit more time for that. That means that five years is no drama. But those who need real-time applications need to get to these ports. And we want to bring that in the same direction.

But there is also a part of digitization that will change our lives so profoundly that I do not know if we all already know what to expect, or that I know we do not know it. How do you deal with such a situation if you want to give people security? Of course you can not promise them anything wrong, but you have to try to take them along the way. You do that in the company. I have visited companies where opportunities for digitization through permanent education are really well used. But that does not happen in all areas. I believe that the disruptiveness of our work process has not yet been fully grasped.

Therefore, my request is also to you: Let yourself be inspired by a completely new way of thinking - even less thinking in hierarchical systems. Ms. Suder can explain that to you better than me. Suppose, for example, that our major public challenge is to create the so-called Citizen Portal based on the Online Access Act. That means we need to open more than 500 functions that the citizen handles with his state - apply for parental leave, apply for child support, report relocation, register motor vehicle, etc. - with a single access for the citizen and give him the opportunity to do all these things digitally. This leads to the fact that we have to think completely differently. First of all, we have to empathize with the citizen and not build up the whole system and then look whether the whole thing is appropriate. We think today when we are planning something, not necessarily from the citizen. Rather, we think: 575 functions - you have to plan all of them somehow now; and when you've finished, you'll see how the citizen claims it. But the new work should be such that I take on a function and work on it first and try out whether it is expedient in the sense of the citizen. Then I'll take a second function. And so I build that up piece by piece. Maybe you'll do it all in your business. But the Berlin airport would have been better if you had applied this form of processing the same; that's for sure. 575 functions - you have to plan all this somehow now; and when you've finished, you'll see how the citizen claims it. But the new work should be such that I take on a function and work on it first and try out whether it is expedient in the sense of the citizen. Then I'll take a second function. And so I build that up piece by piece. Maybe you'll do it all in your business. But the Berlin airport would have been better if you had applied this form of processing the same; that's for sure. 575 functions - you have to plan all this somehow now; and when you've finished, you'll see how the citizen claims it. But the new work should be such that I take on a function and work on it first and try out whether it is expedient in the sense of the citizen. Then I'll take a second function. And so I build that up piece by piece. Maybe you'll do it all in your business. But the Berlin airport would have been better if you had applied this form of processing the same; that's for sure. whether it is expedient in the sense of the citizen. Then I'll take a second function. And so I build that up piece by piece. Maybe you'll do it all in your business. But the Berlin airport would have been better if you had applied this form of processing the same; that's for sure. whether it is expedient in the sense of the citizen. Then I'll take a second function. And so I build that up piece by piece. Maybe you'll do it all in your business. But the Berlin airport would have been better if you had applied this form of processing the same; that's for sure.

Then I come to the subject of Artificial Intelligence - a point where we are clearly not ahead. We have, so to speak, islands that can make good contributions, but the entire breadth is not sufficiently reflected. Our advantage is that we have a strong industrial pillar. With Industry 4.0 we will succeed in getting good applications.

But we have an incredible fight for the best professionals in the world with very flexible payment options everywhere. In this respect, one certainly still has to think a lot about Max Planck Institutes and non-university research institutions in Germany.

We want to set up 100 new professorships. We have identified twelve centers that are networked with each other and that are also networked with France. We will have our Agency for Disruptive Innovations, which we have both on the German and European level, also heavily involved in the AI sector. We will say to our Federal Court of Auditors: Be very calm, because we will inevitably sink more money before a major innovation comes out. All this calls for a complete rethinking.

At the moment we are experiencing in our administration - I do not know how it is with you - that if we want to put digital projects on the rails, it will take us a very long time to get it through. On the other hand, if we get 50 young people from some university and ask them to work on two topics, then we have an answer after two months. In other words, we will also have to outsource more and more young people will need to work. But of course these are also people who do not think of a collective agreement first - to come back to our starting point. Bringing it together is, of course, difficult.

On the subject of skilled workers: Yes, we now have a skilled labor immigration law. Please, now that we take the word "immigration" as members of the CDU, to call the law "immigration law" again. It is an immigration law. I do not know if you can accurately follow the depth and subtleties of such discussions; but no matter. Anyway, we have set important course and also try to make this as unbureaucratic. In the implementation, we will not be able to do this alone in the foreign missions, but we need the support of the economy. I thank you for having this willingness. We will also have to rely on the comparability of financial statements to work with you in the form of a clearing house or similar in order to try to proceed unbureaucratically. After all, it's all about the skills and abilities and not the formal qualifications.

From your point of view, in some places we are too hesitant, because we say: the worker used today is after one year, at the latest after one and a half years, someone who in the long term in Germany is entitled to social benefits; at least that is true for many of them. That's our problem; and that's why we are so careful. Because we know: we are facing disruptive upheavals. Nobody can predict exactly how the needs will develop over the next few years. This year, we have 1.24 million vacancies that we need to fill. We need specialists for that. But once we are completely honest, we need very different professionals. We need digitization and AI specialists in one place, and elsewhere - once I visit my constituency - we also need a hundred bakers and a hundred chefs in the hotels. The question is: how will this develop and what does that mean? We can not cope with this challenge so that if someone becomes unemployed, they will then give you critical remarks as to why the additional labor costs are constantly rising. That's why we just keep an eye on it.

Above all else, we must make sure that our own workforce is properly trained. This is also one of the big topics that the Federal Government has committed itself to. Here we depend on you. We must not make too much of a theoretical training, which is selected solely by the Federal Agency, but we must, wherever possible, carry out further training in the company. However, I believe that the possibility of receiving subsidies from the Federal Agency if in-service training is offered for digitization could be very effective, especially for medium-sized companies. We do not interfere with the content, we subsidize it. I think that's a sensible thing.

Then of course we have the point of flexibility of labor law. Here I would personally go on in some places. My fight for this - even though I am in office today for 13 years - has been to implement the European Working Hours Act one-to-one in Germany and at least to exploit the flexibilities that exist in it, has so far been largely unsuccessful. Wherever there are collective agreements and agreements with the works council, we have opening possibilities within the experimental clauses. Use that, so that we can gain good experiences there. But we have a working time law that is very poor for start-ups and young companies living in the digitization sector. We therefore need flexibility instruments such as temporary work; this is very important. I know, that we will expect you a lot, if we first approach the non-essential time limit. Mrs. Nahles is still here today; she may be able to talk about it.

But I have to tell you: there are also incredible things. If one reads that the public service is sometimes limited to 17 times and then people are terminated, then one wonders. This is also the case in the service sector; Do not make any illusions about that. In this respect, I can only ask again and again: the more responsible you deal with your freedom, the less we have to interfere as a state in the things.

Finally, something about Europe. Thank you for your clear commitment to Europe. Europe is a source of our prosperity; that is perfectly clear. Anyone who wants to preserve such a source must also bring something into it. However, we can not assume that the perspective of looking at the world is the same in all Member States of the European Union. That's why we need a certain amount of rules; that, too, is perfectly clear. But we also have to get involved with the wishes and ideas of others. For us, a strong France is constitutive for advancing Europe. That is why I and the whole of the Federal Government have a maximum interest in the success of French President Emmanuel Macron with his reforms, some of which are very courageous and partly for example in the area of vocational training, also benefit greatly from German experience. We really want to support this success.

We know about the challenges, especially in trade matters. Let me just say: If you imagine that Germany is exposed to the United States of America's trade-related and especially customs-related issues, we would have much worse maps. Of course, the fact that Jean-Claude Juncker and the Commission are working on trade issues for all of us in the European Union is, of course, sometimes laborious because you always need a mandate from 28 countries, 27 in the future. But it also means that we are more protected because it is always about the whole European Union. At any rate, in recent months this has been a very important matter in holding talks with the United States on trade issues.

Of course, as we are a big economy and an economy with a high trade surplus, we want to talk bilaterally with the United States of America and make it clear that we, especially for mid-sized American companies, are open country markets are. No-one rejects us if he wants to export to us. Maybe some things are not sufficiently known. In this respect, we endeavor to show maximum transparency and to make it clear, as we have an interest in the fact that there is no uncertainty. We feel that the trade conflicts between America and China create much uncertainty for German companies as well. Everything we can do to protect an open order and make it workable again,

Another source of uncertainty is of course the issue of Britain's exit from the European Union. Britain should remain a partner, should remain a friend, Britain should have close economic relations with us. Britain itself determines it. In essence, we agree that there will be a very comprehensive free-trade agreement at the end of the road, although we do not have much experience with international agreements in the services sector. But we want to see that as a future relationship.

Britain's exit is more difficult than a fictitious exit from any other member state because of the domestic situation with Ireland in mind. The fact that the "Good Friday Agreement" Northern Ireland and the Republic of Ireland are basically linked together like a single market, and that these two entities are now being separated, but that no limit is yet to be set, makes us feel great - let's say mental - challenges, because it is about the question: How to achieve that, where there is no limit, the internal market ends anyway? That's why the entire discussion that we are conducting basically gets involved. If such a problem did not exist, we would have already accomplished the exit agreement.

May I tell you: I will do everything we can to reach an agreement. A disorderly exit is the worst possible way for both the economy and the mental situation of our future relationship. We have made some progress, but there is certainly a lot of discussion going on, especially in the UK. As 27 Member States, we can only do two things: Firstly, to treat Britain in a friendly and friendly way, and secondly, to hold Britain together as 27 Member States, and not to stir up trouble among us. Both have succeeded so far. And so we will continue.

SPEECH BY FEDERAL CHANCELLOR MERKEL AT THE ECONOMIC SUMMIT OF THE "SÜDDEUTSCHE ZEITUNG"

on 13 November 2018 in Berlin

With five percent of women having leading political functions in the world, it is a rare coincidence that the Croatian President, the Icelandic Prime Minister, the Serbian Prime Minister and I are assembled here as four individuals tonight. I believe that is, so to speak, the tribute of the "Süddeutsche Zeitung" to yesterday's event here in the hall, which commemorated the introduction of women's suffrage 100 years ago.

Now I'm in a rather difficult position tonight, because you have considered that after at least one and a half days of permanent lectures, you need a dinner speech and then a discussion, and then cheerfully continue tomorrow with further lectures. Therefore, I do not want to go now absolutely into the basics and in Zahlendetails, but only a little consider what you are discussing.

I was glad that a newspaper chose the motto "Trust!". Because sometimes one thinks when reading the newspaper that more is observed with suspicion; but that does not have to be mutually exclusive. At any rate, I find this motto very correct and important - if I may say so - for our time today. Why? Because I believe that we are still a bit stuck in the happiness of the 90s, when we united in the European Union, the Cold War came to an end and a democratic European Union was created. Change had meant something good at the time. And we thought there were fewer problems than before.

But this confidence which we had at that time - now spoken from the German perspective and also from the perspective of German reunification - has then given way; Trust has been lost. That is why it is right to want to build trust again. We have gone through some things that have broken into our relatively healthy world: the financial crisis, the euro crisis, the events of flight and migration, Islamist terrorism, the challenges of a multipolar rather than a very clear - cut world, and more recently of the Cold War but very vehement attacks on multilateralism - an order that was created after the end of the Second World War and that we trusted, about which there was not much debate, even if it was imperfect,

That's why the motto "Creating trust!" Is so important. As a politician, it reminds me that we have a constructive design mandate - at least when we are in government - and have no mandate to live on the existence of a space in which mistrust can spread. I understand very well that lost trust has created more spaces in which mistrust thrives. But now we have to refill it constructively.

There we have the topic "What can we do nationally?" And that raises the big question: What does the successful model of Germany, namely the social market economy, look like in the 21st century? Can we continue to live up to the promise of prosperity, which is closely related - I would say, very narrowly - to the order of democracy? And what challenges us?

Since we have just come in the conversation at the table on the digitization, which was certainly a topic for you here today. Everyone lives a bit in a digital world - if only with their smartphone and their communication behavior. But what that means for our societies, what that means for working, for education, for the press, for all processes in our society, we have all, I believe, not yet permeated. Anyway, I have not fully penetrated it yet.

Therefore we have to work on it - I speak now as a politician - to come back into a situation in which we can grasp the processes, since we have to create the guard rails for our order. But if I do not understand what's going on, then I can not create guardrails. So now we have a time of close collaboration between people who are developing technology, people who are younger, but are not yet politically or economically responsible, and people who are observing societies and social processes.

From the experience of social market economy I would say: Our basic approach must be that even with new technologies, the human being must be the standard of what we develop. Article 1 of our Basic Law states: "The dignity of man is inviolable." The state must protect it. This means that we have to think from the individual human being, which is what made up the great success story of the social market economy. One did not think in groups, one did not think in classes, one did not put one group against the other, but one thought of the individual.

This brings me to the topic: what are the people looking for? The citizens feel that something is happening. First, they want security in the disruption. There are disruptive innovations; and in this situation, they want security. How do you as a politician provide security when one is expected to have an answer to every question but suddenly lives in a time when one can honestly not always say that you have answers to questions? Because I am also a learner myself.

I believe that the best way of communicating between the politically powerful, the decision-makers, and the citizens is that we trust them again - that we trust them to endure when we tell them: we have these and those principles for the benefit of man, but we do not already know the implications of each new technical detail; we will always have to take steps forward and steps backwards. What we are used to, namely, to make a law for 10, 20, 30 years, may not be right for the next 10 or 20 years. We have to try something and then try to learn the lessons from it. We listen to you, the citizens, and to what you tell us, and we are ready to

This is a completely new approach that we have to work with in politics - but just as everyone, whether in the factory, in the administration or wherever, has to work anew. So it's actually a great time for a democracy because you suddenly have to be interested in each and every one of their experiences. In reality, we were apart from each other. One writes newspapers, the other works in a company that makes third party politics. We had organized the division of labor well. The one is a lobbyist and tries so long to persuade the policy until the law looks as he wants it. The citizen also knows how he can defend himself. And that's what he does in elections. So we had completely clear structures. These are now completely mixed up.

Therefore, this task of regaining trust in a new time requires us politicians to make it clear that we also need to re-think that we probably have to work in much flatter hierarchies, that we need groups to which we have contact, and that we also admit that we need counselors; and we do not always find them in our administration. Let me just say a little: every time we get consultants from somewhere, they say: The government has outsourced again and somehow made itself dependent on the economy. I'll tell you quite honestly: we will not be able to do it any differently. Otherwise we are ignorant. We need further education by people who work in digitization and who have new insights. For in our own administration we find no one with these insights; and that's natural, too. So we have to make a merger, as it were with Bosch. Every senior executive gets a young nerd to learn what's going on. If you do not have that openness, you will not survive in the new age. - Now I do not want to get too detailed here.

The bad news for us in Germany and in Europe is: we are no longer what we were pretty common 100 years ago: the technology drivers. Rather, technologies are reaching us today. We can not produce a battery cell. We still make the machines that produce chips, but the chip factories are largely outside Europe. We certainly are not in the forefront of quantum computing. But we have been awake in artificial intelligence. Tomorrow we will have a digitization meeting of our government. This is the first time that we will be focusing on digitalization issues for two days.

Digital inventions currently come mainly from Asia and the United States of America. But that must not make us pessimistic right now. Sometimes we live digitally, so to speak, in the way that we live dual - that is, zero or one, sad or euphoric, but nothing in between. Rather, we just have to do a realistic analysis and ask ourselves: where do we stand? In our opinion, with our industrial base and our industrial strength, we have at least a very good starting position for what is called B2B platforms. At B2C but now takes place the actual battle. If the person holding the customer wins or wins, who has the industrial production in his hand? For example, there is currently a sharp debate in the automotive industry around the world. We will not win these challenges alone - Germany or any other European country - against countries like China or the United States of America. That means we have to gather in Europe.

In doing so, a cultural component will play a role, which again has to do with the social market economy. In the United States, technical progress is proceeding very quickly, but with the tendency that the data that is aggregated is basically in private hands and only then regulated, if at all, or decided: what happens in order to? In China - we've been talking openly about everything here - it's the data that seemingly belongs to the state in a natural way. With neither model will Europe be happy, just because we come from the tradition of a social market economy. That's why we have to find our own way.

I say: The General Data Protection Regulation was a good decision, even if it can drive us insane in some cases. If I can no longer invite my own CDU members, because they first have to agree that they want to be invited back by me, then of course one wonders if we still have all the cups in the closet. But we can then re-regulate this in a learning process.

That we have a level playing field, an equal level in all European countries, and that there is sovereignty for citizens to know what happens to their data can be a model for the future. The battle is not over yet. After the end of the Cold War, we also thought that democracy had triumphed and nothing would happen again. That is not the case; and there we are challenged. Therefore, without the European dimension, each one of us in the territory of the

European Union will be lost if he thinks he can do it alone. That is why we need to gather together - and not only because I gave a speech today in Strasbourg.

My last point: Now something starts to waver, about which I am amazed and I wonder how this can happen. We have recently commemorated the 100th anniversary of the end of the First World War. A few years later, the Second World War arose. After all, we know why that happened, because after the First World War peoples did not respect each other, but continued to humiliate each other, and because what the then American President Wilson initiated - the formation of a community of peoples, then was created within the framework of the League of Nations - failed. Together with great economic difficulties, this resulted in a war that the Germans have to answer for. - I do not want to relativize anything; so that does not arrive wrong. - But the teaching,

That just in the present time, in which the eyewitnesses are becoming fewer and fewer, who have experienced the horrors of the Second World War, strong currents arise with the message "People, let that be all; our own country is the most important to us ", makes me very restless. That challenges us. Because from my point of view - that's what I'm saying now to Germany - now and in the next few years the hour is here to show if we have learned something from history or if we did not learn anything from history again.

Now, when I sometimes see how scornfully written about the United Nations, I have to say: I can tell you many things that are completely imperfect, but the question is not "how imperfect are they?" But the question is: Why was it possible in 1948 to reconcile the Charter of Human Rights; and could something like this happen again today, or do we feel no need to get into it? That's why I say: Destroyed is fast, build up is slow. Therefore, "creating trust!" Means to me: not destroying what we created after the horrors of world history, but patiently developing it - but never forget what happened to the world when you did not have all of that. Then we will succeed again.

SPEECH IN FRONT OF THE EUROPEAN PARLIAMENT THE HEART-BEAT OF EUROPEAN DEMOCRACY"

Almost 50 years ago, former German Commission President Walter Hallstein called European unification an "unprecedented audacity". That was in 1969, ten years before the first direct election to the European Parliament. At that time, the European Community was still in its infancy. Many of our greatest achievements - Schengen, the single market, a common currency - were still visionary projects. But the foundation was laid. And with him after centuries of wars and dictatorships for the citizens of Europe for the first time was the prospect of a lasting, peaceful and stable future.

Today I stand with joy and with gratitude before the largest democratic parliament in the world. They, the 751 deputies from 28 states, together represent more than 500 million people. That's nearly seven percent of the world's population. We feel in your house the heartbeat of European democracy. This is shown by the debates conducted in 24 languages. And that also shows something that makes Europe, diversity. It is one of the great strengths of us Europeans that we have repeatedly, in spite of all diversity, the will to unite, the will to compromise have led and that despite our different origins and different attitudes, we have always been to a result for the good of Community came.

It's been over eleven years since I spoke in front of this house for the first time. At the time, Germany had taken over the EU Presidency in 2007. At that time, I spoke of the diversity that unites us and does not share, and of freedom, which must always be defended anew, and which requires both Europe and man to breathe. At that time, I spoke of a fundamental value that distinguishes Europe - a value that unites freedom and diversity in Europe. I spoke of tolerance. I have said that tolerance is the soul of Europe and thus an indispensable basic value of the European idea.

In the past eleven years, however, we have also experienced how much the world has changed and how, along with it, the soul of Europe, if you will, has been strained. Global political, economic and technological challenges have become ever faster and more profound. We have gone through a major sovereign debt crisis. International terrorism has not stopped at the European Union. Wars and armed conflicts take place just a few hours away on our doorstep. Worldwide flight and migration movements affect us Europeans in a very concrete way. Digital advances are changing our way of life at a breathtaking pace. We feel the consequences of climate change. Old allies challenge proven alliances. For the first time a country will leave the European Union with Great Britain. How deep this cut will be, we feel more than ever in these days of intense negotiations. - I would like to thank Michel Barnier for his work.

Dear Members of this House, why am I saying that? We all feel that it has become harder to predict developments. But we still feel something else. It is less and less promising to assert interests on the global stage alone. Conversely, this means that it is becoming increasingly important for us Europeans to stand together. For this, more than ever within the European Union, we need the respect of others and their interests. More than ever, we need the understanding that tolerance is the soul of Europe, that it is an integral part of what makes us Europeans, and that only with it can we develop the willingness and interests of others as well as our own To understand needs. That brings us to the core of European solidarity, without which successful action is unthinkable. This solidarity is based on tolerance. It makes our strength, which is nowhere else, European, for three reasons.

First, solidarity is a universal value. Committing oneself to one another is a basic requirement for every functioning community. This applies to the family, to the village community, to the sports club and equally to a community like the European Union. Solidarity is an integral part of the European Treaties. It is a central part of our value channel. Solidarity is part of European DNA. We support countries and regions in their economic development or in the fight against youth unemployment. We help each other in natural disasters. We are at each other's side in case of terrorist attacks or reactor accidents. In the European sovereign debt crisis, we have set up so-called bailouts to help affected countries

Even these few examples show that the individual member states of the European Union and, with them, the citizens of the European Union, are not alone in difficult times and emergencies. Conversely, these few examples also show that individual national decisions always have an impact on the whole community.

Therefore, secondly, solidarity always goes hand in hand with responsibility for the community of all. Specifically, this means that erosion of rule of law principles in his country, curtailing the rights of the opposition and civil society, limiting freedom of the press not only jeopardizes the rule of law in his own country, but endangers the rule of law of all of us throughout Europe. Of course, as a legal community, Europe can only function if the law is universally respected and respected everywhere.

Those who rely on solving problems solely through new debt and disregard commitments they have made, are questioning the foundations for the strength and stability of the euro area. Because our common currency can only work if every single member fulfills its responsibility for sustainable finances at home. Anyone questioning Europe's unity with third parties - for example, with agreed sanctions or human rights issues - undermines the credibility of all European foreign policy. For Europe can only make its voice heard in the world when it is united. This means that solidarity always means overcoming national egoisms.

I know very well that Germany has not always behaved impeccably or behave in the eyes of some not always perfectly. For example, in the years before 2015 we took far too long to accept the refugee issue in Germany as a question for all the Member States of the European Union and to understand that it is a pan-European task.

Thirdly, it follows that solidarity for the benefit of all also means acting in the well-understood own interest. Respect and support for others and the representation of their own interests are not contradictory - quite the contrary. An example of this is our cooperation with African countries of origin on the subject of flight and migration. - The President has just pointed that out. - This cooperation helps Europe because it organizes, controls and reduces flight and migration to Europe. It also serves local people by improving their lives and preventing them from undertaking an often life-threatening journey to Europe.

Another example is the European commitment to global climate protection, which is ecologically, economically and socially essential for the protection of natural resources and thus for us. It benefits Europe when industrialized and emerging economies produce less greenhouse gases and our economies become greener overall.

It will also benefit all Europeans if the Eurozone is free of dislocation and becomes a haven of strength and stability. It benefits all Europeans if everyone participates in European Civil Protection. It benefits all Europeans if we help those who are particularly affected by flight and migration. Tolerance requires respect for the fact that the issue of reception of refugees in different Member States causes different reactions due to their own history or their demographic evolution. At the same time, solidarity demands that we make every effort to find a common way in which we master these as well as all other challenges as a community.

That is what Europe is all about: solidarity as a universal basic value, solidarity as a responsibility to the community and solidarity as a well-understood self-interest.

Ladies and gentlemen, unity and unity are indispensable to Europe's success. I would therefore like to highlight three areas that I think will be particularly important.

First, foreign and security policy. We are already aware that as Europeans, we can better defend our interests wherever we act together. Only closed is Europe strong enough to be heard on the global stage and defend its values and interests. The times when we could rely unconditionally on others are over. This means that we Europeans have to take our fate more into our own hands if we want to survive as a community. This means that in the long term Europe must become more capable of acting in foreign policy. Therefore, we must be prepared to rethink our decision-making processes and to increasingly renounce unanimity where the treaties make this possible and wherever possible.

I have proposed that we establish a European Security Council with rotating, rotating memberships of the Member States, in which important decisions can be prepared more quickly. We need to create a European intervention force with which Europe can act locally. We have made great progress in the area of permanent structured cooperation in the military field. This is good and is also supported here as far as possible.

But we should - and I am very aware of this from recent years' developments - work on the vision of someday creating a true European army. Yes it is. Four years ago Jean-Claude Juncker said: "A common European army would show the world that there will never again be war between European countries." That is not an army against NATO - I ask you - but that can be a good addition to NATO. No one wants to question classic connections. But, ladies and gentlemen, it would be much easier to work with us. If today we have more than 160 defense systems or weapons systems and the United States of America only 50 or 60, if we need a separate administration, support and training for everything, then we are not an efficient partner. If we want to use our money efficiently and yet fight for much the same, then we can at NATO together with a European army to act together. I do not see any contradiction in that.

That, of course, includes - - - (heckling from the plenum) - Oh, I'm glad about it. I'm not getting irritated. I am also from the Parliament. -

Incidentally, this includes the joint development of weapons systems within Europe. And that includes - this is a difficult task; also for the Federal Republic of Germany - that we develop a common arms export policy, because otherwise we can not act uniformly in the world.

Secondly, ladies and gentlemen, Europe's economic success depends on it. It is the foundation of our strength and the prerequisite for being heard in the world at all. If we are not strong economically, then we will not be politically influential either. I am very pleased that the program of Jean-Claude Juncker, the investment fund, has had a significant impact in recent years, and we have already raised € 340 billion or € 350 billion of the investment of € 500 billion by 2020 have brought the way. This is a good program for more investment. I know how often your home has demanded more investment. That's on the way now. But then we should also talk about it.

Of course, stable economic and monetary union is part of a stable prosperity Europe. We want to further develop the European Stability Mechanism. We are working on the Banking Union. We are working on a Eurozone budget; Germany and France have spoken out in favor. I believe that this should be closely linked to the medium-term financial perspective. We also advocate that liability and control belong together. In other words, a banking union and later also a European deposit insurance system require that risks in the nation states have previously been reduced. That goes together. European solidarity and personal responsibility are always two sides of the same coin.

We will also be making progress on a topic that is being discussed very intensively these days, and in which you are also very much involved, namely digital taxation. Germany does not have the question of whether we have to carry out digital taxation - in the age of digitization that goes without saying - but we have the question of how we do it. It is, I think, part of the democratic practice that you take note of the Commission's proposals, but you can also add something. We believe that the best thing would be to find an international solution in an international context. We rely on minimum taxation. But if that does not work, then we can not wait until the day of the dead, but then we have to act European.

If we are honest, looking to the future and worrying about our prosperity, then we have to accept that today it is no longer the case that the great innovations, as they did 100 years ago and 130 years ago, always or Mostly come from Europe, but it is today that many of the fundamental innovations come from Asia and the United States of America. So, of course, the question is: will we, on the continent where the car was once invented, determine the mobility of the future? It makes me restless that we can not manufacture battery cells, for example. That Chinese companies are now investing in Germany is okay. But I think we should make a big effort to be able to to master a drive technology of the future, and to make battery cell production possible here as well. We have the European tools for that. We have it all in our hands - as we already do with the chips today.

We have to be at the forefront of quantum computers. We need to develop a common strategy for artificial intelligence. All this is still possible because we have a strong industrial base in Europe. We can build on that; and we have to use that too now. In that sense, research and innovation are central to our future prosperity.

The third area, ladies and gentlemen, whom I would like to recall is the issue of flight and migration. We had many obstacles to overcome in the euro crisis to reach a common solution, but we succeeded. But on the issue of flight and migration, Europe is not as united as I would wish. Since this is a central issue that concerns our relationship with our neighborhood, we must find common ways here.

We have made progress. We all agree that we need a common European border guard. In retrospect, it was certainly somewhat reckless, I say once, that you have created a Schengen area of free movement, but only now working to get an entry and exit register to know who is with us and who leaves us again , Nevertheless, it is right that we do it now. It is right that we develop Frontex. The Commission proposals are good in my opinion. Once again, if everyone wants to keep their national competence and none of the European border patrols wants to give any responsibilities, then no matter how big and good, they will not be able to carry out their work.

We also need to think: how can we share well the work of Africa's development aid, development cooperation and economic development? There are now excellent results - that would not have been possible two or three years ago - when it comes to individual Member States working with the Commission in individual African states, adding value compared to having them all appear individually would. But we can learn much more here. But I think we are on a good way.

It is also about developing a common European asylum procedure. If everyone makes their decisions differently then people know that too, and then you need not be surprised that secondary movement occurs in the area of free movement. We must go to great lengths to develop common standards, such as developing a common "level playing field" for the internal market, on common issues, such as those on asylum and humanitarian responsibility. Otherwise we will not manage to cope with the task of fleeing and migrating.

Ladies and gentlemen, these were three examples of many. The fact that I met the core is shown by the protest. That is beautiful and honorable. I believe that people want Europe to tackle precisely these problems that are on their nails. People want a Europe that gives answers to the questions that oppress them. That does not mean Europe has to be everywhere, so to speak. It remains unchanged that not every problem in Europe is a problem for Europe. Solidarity does not mean omnipresence. But solidarity means that Europe acts where it is needed, and that it can then act strong, decisive and effective.

I am convinced that Europe is our best chance for lasting peace, lasting prosperity and a secure future. Our meeting in Paris at the invitation of the French President, to commemorate the horror of the First World War 100 years ago, should have made us realize again what happens when nations do not respect each other, and what happens when communities like the League of Nations , which was founded as a result of the First World War, fail. It came the even greater horror. Therefore, we must not lose this European opportunity. We owe it to ourselves, we owe it to the past generation and we owe it to future generations. This means that nationalism and selfishness must never again have a chance in Europe, but tolerance and solidarity are our common future. Dear Colleagues, It is always worthwhile to strive for it.

SPEECH BY FEDERAL CHANCELLOR MERKEL AT THE "G20 INVESTMENT SUMMIT - GERMAN BUSINESS AND THE COMPACT WITH AFRICA COUNTRIES"

on October 30, 2018

I am pleased to welcome you all here today as members of the Compact with Africa initiative. I say a warm welcome to you all in Berlin. And I say a big thank you to the organizers of this conference: the African Association of German Business and the Sub-Saharan Africa Initiative of German Business.

Today, we want to send a strong signal together that we are looking for a good and profitable neighborhood between Africa and Europe. We are neighbors, we are partners - we as Europeans have a great interest in African states having good economic prospects. This requires public investment, but above all private investment. How we get from government aid to private investment - that is the big task - that is also modern development policy, as developed by our minister Gerd Müller.

Of course, entrepreneurial opportunities and risks are always weighed against each other. To make the decision easier, you need better investment conditions - for African companies as well as for European ones. In addition to strengthening Africa as an investment location, fair trade relations between Europe and Africa are also at stake. Improving the conditions for investment and trade together is the core idea of the Compact with Africa and the reform partnerships that we signed in 2017 during the German G20 presidency. We were not just talking about Africa, but talking to Africa. This is also a central lesson that we draw from the classic development aid, which often did not bring the success that we desired.

The Compact Initiative is taking a different, new approach. It is about new forms of equal and lasting partnership that benefits all parties equally. Of course, every country in Europe as well as every country in Africa has its peculiarities and its own location characteristics. Therefore, it is important that on the one hand each Compact country improves its investment climate through autonomous reform measures. On the other hand, every participating country should also express its expectations on how it wants to be supported, what concrete support it needs on the way to reforms.

The IMF, the World Bank and the African Development Bank are involved in this process - whether it is to put together appropriate reform measures or to review the implementation of the obligations of the Compact and partner countries.

Germany is also involved in reform partnerships with various countries. Thanks to this collaboration, I was recently able to inform myself on my trip to Africa and get an idea of it. I can say that already show first effects. Although foreign direct investment in Africa as a whole has declined in recent years, it has increased in the Compact-with-Africa countries. I know that time is very important to you all. You have to do something fast, because your population expects quick answers and quick results; we know this. That's why we try to get faster ourselves.

Investor confidence is to be expected just where Compact-with-Africa countries have implemented reforms. This is already evident, as I said, in the level of direct investment. I would therefore like to extend a sincere thank you to the companies and investors who will present their investment projects today. They contribute to the economic development of Africa. And you are an example for others, maybe a little closer to this continent with its 54 countries and its huge growth potentials. For many years we have been very focused on Asia. I think, in the future, the view has to turn more to Africa.

We as the Federal Government want to provide support. As regards, for example, trade with Ghana and Senegal, there were three basic cover commitments for export credits totaling 160 million euro.

As the federal government, we have considered how we can initiate further measures.

We will set up a development investment fund for small and medium-sized enterprises; for European and African companies. This should be used to finance equity investments and loans, for example to enable new market entries.

We want to make it easier to hedge exports and investments by German companies in the Compact-with-Africa countries against political risks or against payment risks. Of course, our measures are always dependent on the reform progress and debt sustainability of the respective country. A complete assumption of risk - I say that too - the state will not be able to do. But we want to make more offers than we had in the past.

For example, we can avoid companies or investors being taxed twice. That is why we attach great importance to the double taxation agreements that we already have with five Compact with Africa countries. We negotiate with three others. I wish there would be more. And I also agree that we will do our utmost to ensure that these negotiations take place quickly.

In addition, we want to enter into new employment and training partnerships with companies and institutions in Africa. We are concerned with the development of specific sectors in suitable locations, for example by promoting the establishment of regional commercial and industrial parks.

Last but not least, we are aiming for new bilateral reform partnerships with Senegal, Morocco and Ethiopia.

So these are central elements of our package of measures that we are launching. We see this as complementary to the continuation and development of the Compact with Africa initiative. This conference is an expression of the fact that we want to live and revive partnership cooperation. Part of this is the improvement of investment conditions. That is our common interest.

Once again I thank you all for coming here, and I am now looking forward to what I can see and experience at this business forum.

SPEECH BY FEDERAL CHANCELLOR MERKEL IN THE GERMAN BUNDESTAG

SPEECH BY FEDERAL CHANCELLOR MERKEL IN THE GERMAN BUNDESTAG

The majority of people in Germany live and work for a good and tolerant togetherness; I am deeply convinced of that. I see it as my task and the duty of all political leaders to support all those who are advancing our country every day through their work and their lives. Incidentally, the numbers also prove that Germany is one of the safest countries in the world, and Germany is one of the wealthiest countries in the world.

And yet, many people in our country worry these days about the cohesion of us all. I am also quite sure that the citizens are watching closely in which way we conduct the political dialogue - both in the country and here in the German Bundestag.

We all have a big responsibility.

In recent weeks, we have been particularly troubled by serious crimes in which the alleged perpetrators were asylum seekers who came to Germany. Such acts affect me and affect us all.

We mourn with the relatives, we are outraged by the crimes. Such acts must be cleared up, the perpetrators brought to justice and punished with the severity of the law.

That's exactly how our constitutional state looks like.

Many citizens who have demonstrated through demonstrations how agitated they are have exercised their constitutionally enforced rights and as politicians we are obliged to take their concerns seriously and to remedy grievances.

I can understand anyone who is outraged when it turns out after homicides once again that they are offenders who already have multiple criminal records, or people who are enforceable. Here we have a task to solve.

We are working resolutely on this task together with the federal states and the federal government. The Federal Minister of the Interior has put forward further measures to this end and we are aware of our responsibility, ladies and gentlemen.

As much as I understand and share the outrage and lack of understanding, I do not let it hold that this is an excuse for inhumane demonstrations.

No, there is no excuse and justification for incitement, some use of force, Nazi hatred, hostility from people who look different, who own a Jewish restaurant, attacks on police officers. And conceptual arguments about whether it's hounding or hunt, really help us, ladies and gentlemen.

That can only mean one thing: we are resolutely opposed to that, in the spirit of Article 1 of our Basic Law:

Human dignity is inviolable. To respect and protect them is a duty of all state authority.

Article 1 applies to every human being, and anyone who violates it lays the ax at the root of our coexistence.

Anyone who violates it opposes our values of unity, justice and freedom. But these are our luck pledge.

Therefore, respect for human dignity should not be discounted - for anyone - and therefore relativizations are misleading.

That is why the rule of law is required here at its core - with the security forces, with independent courts, with all the institutions of a vibrant democracy and a strong civil society.

I thank all those who work for it: the police and all the security forces, the judges, the prosecutors and the employees of the courts, as well as those who serve in our detention centers, which is far from easy, ladies and gentlemen Men's.
I thank the main and voluntary workers in our democratic institutions and associations. Fortunately, there are many everywhere, everywhere in our country. Therefore, all-inclusive judgments about entire groups or areas such as Saxony or the new federal states are wrong and completely inappropriate.

This also applies to the many refugees who live here peacefully with us. On such a day, I particularly thank the many volunteers and helpers in the refugee work, who are anything but easy in these social discussions.
We will not allow whole groups to be marginalized in our society: Jews, Muslims, as well as Christians and atheists, belong to our society, to our schools, to our parties, to our social life. I am grateful for anyone who is committed to our democracy, ladies and gentlemen.

The question of whether we have consensus on it determines our social cohesion.

Then, when we have a common foundation, we can talk about all the other important issues that move people in our country.

There are rules with us. And these rules can not be replaced by emotions. That is the essence of the constitutional state.

Because we are aware that this constitutional state is challenged, we have agreed a pact for the rule of law in our coalition agreement. This federal budget shows first measures. Another 3,000 new posts for security authorities, just under 50 million euros more for the equipment and equipment of the Federal Police, 85 million euros for the digitization of police work, investments in cybersecurity. These are important, right signals. And we will continue to talk intensively with the federal states about the equipment of courts and other judicial authorities. Citizens have a right to a functioning constitutional state, including in day-to-day practice, ladies and gentlemen.

We are currently discussing the budget for the year 2019. Of course, the underlying tasks go well beyond the next year. Part of these discussions is medium-term financial planning. We got used to it, but I'll say it again: it's the fifth budget in a row without new debt. That's a hint and good news for the young generation.

We have a rising gross domestic product for over 13 quarters. Corporate insolvencies are at their lowest level since the introduction of the new insolvency code. For the first time in the autumn of this year, more than 45 million people will be gainfully employed. We can all be proud of this record together.

Our fundamental goals remain. Since the foundation of the Federal Republic, we have been working for peace, for freedom and for prosperity; and this already in the 70th year of the social market economy. Today we know that our prosperity no longer decides on our own and through our work in Germany, but that we are connected within the framework of the European Union's internal market. We are connected with other countries. That is, caring for others, working with others, relying on a multinational functioning system is in our very own interest. If we look back on ten years of the global economic crisis and the financial crisis, as the Federal Minister of Finance did yesterday, we will realize this once more.

Because this is the case, the question arises: how much do we invest in our own country and how much do we use for development cooperation? These are two sides of the same coin, which is about prosperity for our country.

Freedom also has to be worked out again and again, and it is challenged by digitization. In a digital society, it's about big data, about data security, about privacy - completely new requests for our freedom. That's why the data ethics committee we set up is exactly the right answer.

To secure peace, we need completely new instruments. We ourselves must work harder. But with the attitude that we stay out everywhere, it will not work. Our maxim for securing peace is always: the political efforts are the first priority.
That's why we are committed to Syria, of course, in the Small Group with the Astana Group under the auspices of the United Nations. But simply saying we could look away, if chemical weapons are used anywhere and an international convention is not respected, can not be the answer. All the answers we give will always be at the level of the Basic Law and within the framework of our parliamentary commitment. That's perfectly clear. But from the outset simply saying no, no matter what happens in the world, can not be the German attitude, dear friends.

Prosperity, freedom, peace - that is what people expect of us, and they all have a very special point of view. That's why this household has so many facets. First, there is the desire for stability, for comparable living conditions and for relief, wherever possible, so that people can shape their lives independently.

We have good news in this budget: Relieving families and working people. We increase the child benefit, we increase the corresponding tax allowances, we clean up the income tax by the cold progression. In 2019 and 2020, this will be a total relief of 10 billion euros. Parity is reintroduced for all members of the statutory health insurance. That is a relief of 8.3 billion euros for the contributors per year. As stated in the medium-term financial plan, we will abolish the solidarity surcharge from 2021 onwards for 90 per cent of the payer of the solidarity surcharge. This is another relief of 10 billion euros.

Of course, some say: You also create additional burdens, for example in nursing. - But we have good news here: the very good employment situation allows us to reduce the unemployment insurance contribution by 0.5 percentage points as of 1 January 2019, which then compensates for the additional expenses in the care sector. These additional expenses are important expenses for the citizens; because the questions "How are I aged?" and "How do we treat those who care?" are some of the key issues regarding justice in our country.

Next week, we have a very important event, which is about living conditions: the residential summit. There we will present a package for living and living that is second to none. We know that housing is a huge challenge for millions of people, especially in urban areas. Affordable rents - that is the legitimate expectation, because that also has something to do with security in life.

On the one hand, we want to protect tenants and give them rights, but on the other hand, it's all about creating affordable housing. We have good news: First, social housing is being strengthened. The federal government is taking more part than it had originally intended. Secondly, a special depreciation is introduced, which ensures that those who want to invest can also invest. Thirdly, the news for the families that we introduce the building allowance is a very important means of giving them home ownership. These are all contributions that we can say: In this legislative period, we will create the conditions for 1.5 million new homes to be built. This also includes procedural simplifications, faster building site provision and the like. That is exactly what we will discuss on the 21st of September. This is good news for many, many people in our country.

We know that securing old age is one of the big challenges, both in the face of demographic changes and people's expectations about their life after work. We have set up a commission to deal with the post-2025 pension. We have introduced a bill that will be discussed here shortly, with a constant pension level until 2025, with an improved incapacity pension and with an improved maternal pension. These are three messages of great importance to millions of people. Here we have kept our word, and in the household is exactly this picture.

Dear Colleagues, The subject of care - we all feel that - employs almost every family in the country. I myself have visited nursing homes in recent months, and I know what outstanding work is being done there. Much is still in trouble, and we work on it. But one message that those who work in nursing have told me over and over again is: Please also say that our job is a nice job, a demanding job, a job where the older ones are People give us something too! You always just talk about it as if it were a job that you can hardly do. Do something for the job description of those who care! - I think there is every reason for that, and that's exactly what we want to do.

Now, of course, comes the question of payment; but let me tell you, my discussions have shown that pay is an important issue, working time is at least as important, the question of whether to get a training allowance is such a point - we have tackled it now - but so too important is the respect and observance of this profession. Incidentally, this is what happened to me recently in a conversation with teachers; this applies to nurses in the hospitals. These are people who do a great job, but also have a great job, and we should perhaps emphasize that, ladies and gentlemen.

Of course, we also take the perspective of those who are affected by the effects of digitization. Here we will adopt a training strategy shortly. We will ask ourselves: what does this turnaround mean for those who are workers today? We have to take care of the infrastructure. We have to deal with the dangers and the topic of cybersecurity. But above all, we sometimes have to dare to look beyond our own nose. Today, there is a statistic that states that we are in 21st place in digital public administration services in Europe according to the Commission's Communication. That can not satisfy us. Therefore, the creation of a citizen portal by the federal government, Countries and municipalities is one of the central tasks of this legislature. It is not enough just to expand the infrastructure - we will do that - but that is exactly where work has to continue.

When you are in China, you see that we do not want what happens there: total surveillance, social observation - I certainly do not want that. Digitalization also knows values. But, ladies and gentlemen, the form in which platforms are used there, in which form there start-ups, in which speed they arise, that can not leave us cold, because that determines our competitiveness of the future. That's why we need to accelerate digitization, and that's exactly what the federal government is doing with the Digital Council, with its new structures, with federal IT. And yes, when you look at things, you realize that at first it gets more complicated and the task may get bigger; but we are tackling this task

Incidentally, we will only be successful here if we do this together in Europe. That is why we invest together in research and development. That's why Germany and France have said: we need an agency that also deals with completely unusual inventions and disruptive innovations. - We did that at the federal level too. There are also many discussions: What should that be? We have to be open to all possibilities to go new ways, because that is the prerequisite for our current industrial strength tomorrow being our strength, which creates jobs for the people in our country.

In this context, we will continue to rely on international specialists.

Ladies and gentlemen, that is of central importance, and I am therefore pleased that we will soon adopt the cornerstones for a law on the transfer of skilled workers and will present such a bill by the end of the year; because in some cases the discussions of our entrepreneurs in the country are more geared to whether we get skilled workers rather than tax relief. It must not be that companies leave our country because they can no longer find any employees. We have to do something here, and the coalition has decided to do it, ladies and gentlemen.

And then we have a lot of problems to solve. We are dealing with the future of Germany in the European Union. At the moment, Jean-Claude Juncker, President of the European Commission, is giving his speech to the European Union in the European Parliament, as the saying goes, to the European Union. Ladies and gentlemen, I am deeply convinced that Germany's future will only be a good one, even if Europe is on the right track.
That sounds so trivial, but that's not it.

Yesterday, Olaf Scholz explained what we were doing in the international financial crisis and later in the euro crisis. That was a path that was quite controversial: Shall we save banks? We did it to keep payments for the citizens and to keep financing for our companies. Should we help other euro states? Is this something for us? After hard discussions we decided again and again: Yes, we do it because the euro area is an added value for us and because cooperation in Europe makes us stronger, also in an international context.

On the allegations against Germany over our trade surplus and many other things I have to say: I am grateful that we are part of Europe and that trade talks are brought together by the European Commission for all European countries, that we have a single currency and that we in the euro area can not speculate against a single currency. That makes us stronger, and that is also for the benefit of Germany. On the thesis that we would constantly give something to others: It is in our interest to ensure a strong Europe, ladies and gentlemen.

The question of the euro is about money, about principles - important! - but even more intense is the question: how do we want to solve the problems of migration, illegal migration and refugees? For the cohesion of the European Union, this seems to me to be a far greater challenge than what we experienced in the euro crisis.

It is basically - Wolfgang Schäuble said it yesterday - again a "rendezvous with globalization". Even the euro crisis was a rendezvous with globalization. Now the challenges are even bigger, and the question is: how do we respond? Is it possible to destroy Europe in such a situation, to fragment it, to let everyone fall back on themselves, or is it not possible?

In May 2019, the European elections will be held, in which exactly this question will be discussed.

This European election will be about the question: where and how do we solve the problems, and do we do it together? It is quite clear that if Europe simply says, "We are holding off and we are not taking care of what is happening in our neighborhood," then that will go awry. That has already gone wrong in the context of Syria and Iraq and the many refugees who came to us. Because it has also shown there: If you do not care about the situation on the ground that people are fine, then they are on their way.

This also applies to Africa, our neighboring continent. It is about a lasting and long-term approach. And then it is good news that we spend more on development cooperation. I would like to thank the Minister for Development expressly for the many activities.
I was in Africa recently and one thing is palpable: development cooperation is the number one step, but it is not done at work if the young people get a great training but then have no job. They are then super trained in agriculture, but unfortunately there is no economic backbone of these

countries. That is why we will be intensified - and the German Federal Government does - in order to deal with this: How do we make classical development cooperation economic development?

Unfortunately, one has to say that others go a very clear path. At the last China-Africa Summit, $ 60 billion was agreed over the next three years for investment in Africa's infrastructure. This is a house number. Every African country tells us: You do not need to come with an interested company at all, if you do not bring us a financing concept. - We have to work out these financing concepts. We have to consider: where can we give interest subsidies, where can we possibly provide credit facilities, how can we combine that with development cooperation? We also have KfW, which has the appropriate development bank. We will strengthen all this. To this end, the Federal Government works together with all ministries. This is really urgent

End of October - Wolfgang Schäuble started it during our G20 presidency; We will continue that, even though we are no longer solely responsible, but we do it with the World Bank and the International Monetary Fund - we will be the countries that have entered into a Compact with Africa, or about ten African countries Invite us to a big business forum to promote investment. We will call on the German economy to invest; because some companies still have the impression that this should not be a blanket verdict - Africa today is like Africa 30 years ago. - That's not it anymore. Africa is a great continent, a young continent, a continent with future markets. I can only invite the German economy, to be more interested in Africa. We will try to give it a boost in October.

Of course, combating illegal migration also means strengthening external border protection.

Jean-Claude Juncker will make suggestions. He has already made suggestions: reinforcing Frontex.

But that also implies - at least that is what I am saying - that the states that are located at the external border have national competencies to really give Frontex comprehensive powers. And that also means a degree of solidarity when it comes to people coming to us, or when we have commitments, for example, to allow legal migration or to help countries that are really in need. That, ladies and gentlemen, remains the sore point of the European Union. We have not found a solution yet. Germany is ready to join this solidarity. That too will be another topic during the Austrian Presidency.

So one can say that we face huge challenges in general, but also that we consciously tackle these challenges with regard to pension, care and health insurance, in terms of relief, in terms of investment in research, in terms of infrastructure investment , The Federal Minister of Transport yesterday with all your help founded the infrastructure company for the German motorways. Ladies and gentlemen, this is a big project that will enable us to spend the money we have faster. This is a step that absolutely needs to be appreciated.

We must, and I deeply believe so, sometimes also talk about what we succeed in doing.

We can always be critical when it comes to what we do not succeed; but if we do not tell people what works, then they will not understand where we are getting better. Therefore, it will be a common task - at least for those who fight together for this country - to say: yes, we know that much has not yet been achieved, we know that there are still many shortcomings; but we face the challenges and we are progressing step by step. - That is our mission, our claim, and we will redeem it.

SPEECH BY FEDERAL CHANCELLOR MERKEL ON THE OCCASION OF THE CELEBRATORY EVENT "70 YEARS OF THE SOCIAL MARKET ECONOMY"[3]

70 years of social market economy - this is a significant anniversary. I was very happy to come to this historic house, which has been home to state institutions since the time of the Kaiser, during the Weimar Republic and in the days of the GDR. But today it is no longer about planned economy, but about market economy thought. It is good that this hall is called "Ludwig-Erhard-Saal" from today. The presidium room of the CDU has been called this way for a long time. So it was time that this happens in the Ministry of Economics.

As much as we have become accustomed to the successes of the social market economy, this was hardly to be expected. Because Ludwig Erhard had to fight against considerable resistance. Shortly after the end of the Second World War, there was still no consensus on the future economic policy orientation. All that was clear was that very existential problems had to be solved. Apartments, food and much else that you need to live were scarce. So it was natural to speak the state steering. Who, if not the state, should fairly distribute the goods that are too scarce? - Many thought so.

The precursors of the social market economy, however, relied on competition, the will to achieve and a state that protects freedom while at the same time providing social compensation. I consider this basic decision as before a very, very courageous, if I imagine the situation of Germany at that time. Even the Allies did not like it at the beginning, because they could not really imagine it all. More than nine million workers in the then American and British zones participated in the general strike in November 1948 against the market economy, against price increases, and for the reintroduction of the price regulations, which Erhard daringly abolished. I think, given what was going on back then, even the DGB is jealous today. The industry associations and large companies did not save with criticism, albeit for other reasons. Because they were the vehement commitment Erhard for competition and against cartels a thorn in the eye. But today we know that was the basis for having many medium-sized companies that enrich our market economy.

The then Minister of Economic Affairs was confirmed in his directional decision in view of the economic boom, which he did not consider to be miracles, by the way, but rather as a result of rational economic policy. The word "economic miracle" actually reflects the astonishment of even those who opposed it, about what came out. Cars, washing machines, holidays in Italy and much more meant that "prosperity for all" was not a theoretical concept, but practically experienced. It also went from year to year better. Therefore one can say today: The social market economy is the foundation of the economic success of our country.

I think we should keep reminding ourselves, which are the constitutive principles that are an immediate and integral part of our democratic order. When discussing democracy in Europe today, it sometimes seems as though simply winning majorities already meant democracy. But much more belongs to a democratic society in a comprehensive sense.

The principles were essentially designed by Walter Eucken. They basically served to create and maintain a competitive order. A functioning competition is the central element of the social market economy. He releases his energies to enable steady growth. In this sense social market economy requires freedom. But it does not mean a laissez-faire principle and unconditional competition without state intervention. Because competition always tends to limit itself. That's why we also

[3] Friday, June 15, 2018

have a cartel office, although I want to make it clear that we also have new challenges today. I'll talk to you again.

Freedom, competition and the recognition of personal achievements - but also always include solidarity and social justice. In this sense, justice demands equal treatment of equal and unequal unequal things, that is, something other than egalitarianism. It is about equity, which is aimed at the individual and not at the collective. It should give everyone the opportunity to unfold in the same freedom according to their respective inclinations and abilities - responsible, but always always responsible to others. The orientation towards these values - of freedom, solidarity and justice - in sum makes us strong as a community and a country. But since we can not assume that everyone is always guided by these values, do we need a constitutional state for a functioning social market economy - a constitutional state that guarantees reliable framework conditions; a state as guardian of order.

But we also know that the state really is not the better entrepreneur. We are also aware that the social partners - which is why I think it is absolutely necessary that a round table discussion has taken place here - can find more suitable answers in business and working life than is possible for the legislature with flat-rate regulations. That is why I want to expressly say that we can not accept that, as it were, a whole sector of the economy that is growing out of digitization may never become part of this social partnership. I can still live with the fact that it is not the first thought after starting a business to deal with the issue of social partnership. But I'm not sure if it still works that way automatically, Mr Kramer, that after a while, when it gets too much for you, you can leave the tasks of care to the BDA. You must also pay attention to this. In this respect, it might then also be one of the fine cooperations between BDI and BDA that they suggest the business associations in the field of digital economy, that there are in addition to the BDI and the Federal Association of German Employers' Associations. We would have to talk about that at one of the social partner talks. In any case, I thank you for the work you are doing in the context of social partnership and thus also for the functioning of the social market economy. In this respect, it might then also be one of the fine cooperations between BDI and BDA that they suggest the business associations in the field of digital economy, that there are in addition to the BDI and the Federal Association of German Employers' Associations. We would have to talk about that at one of the social partner talks. In any case, I thank you for the work you are doing in the context of social partnership and thus also for the functioning of the social market economy. In this respect, it might then also be one of the fine cooperations between BDI and BDA that they suggest the business associations in the field of digital economy, that there are in addition to the BDI and the Federal Association of German Employers' Associations. We would have to talk about that at one of the social partner talks. In any case, I thank you for the work you are doing in the context of social partnership and thus also for the functioning of the social market economy.

Now there is - it has already been said today - no automatic, that the social market economy in the future just so works. Because the topic "prosperity for all" is no longer so obvious today. The gradient has become smaller if it still points in the right direction. People are living very strongly on something changing in a positive direction. However, this can no longer be promised to everyone today, in line with the classic, narrow concept of growth. In that sense, as we saw in the film, it is true and important that education, for example, also contributes to prosperity and perhaps also to increasing importance.

If we look at how job opportunities are changing today through digitization, when we see how much competition is changing as a result of globalization, then we know that we need to act, that we are open on the one hand, but on the other On the other hand, the balance that has prevailed over many periods of the classic industrial society has to be maintained even during the time of Industry 4.0.

It is not a given that in times of digitization we are always among the leaders in innovation. This of course has repercussions on the prosperity promise of the social market economy. As we spoke recently with representatives of the industry in the Federal Government about the strategy for artificial intelligence, it has become quite clear that right now, God knows, we are not at the head of the movement and that we have to be careful that talents from Germany are not move away.

We also have to see - that is not a criticism of the Federal Constitutional Court; I do not agree with that - in times of big data, the principle of data economy, which has been elevated to a constitutional rank, must at least be intelligently spelled out. Now that we're struggling with the General Data Protection Regulation, the question of how to handle data and how to create a level playing field on the one hand, and not to exaggerate bureaucracy on the other hand, is one of the big ones. exciting questions of the social market economy. I do not want to go any further now, but I think there is still a lot of work ahead of us in terms of the role of data in the social market economy and its evaluation, with scientists invited as well. to think about it further. For, somewhat simplistically speaking, neither the Chinese answer that the state has access to all the data, nor the more American that everything is privately owned can be a response from the social market economy. The social market economy must give other answers.

Ladies and Gentlemen, That's why we see ourselves facing great challenges, also with regard to the competitive order. In addition to talking with representatives of the artificial intelligence industry, we recently had a talk about the platform economy - also a huge problem that challenges both our and the European competition authorities. Basically, the concentration of the large platforms from the United States of America also raises the question of whether the social market economy really ought to be dealt with here in the sense of the competitive order. The timing of the European Union's procedures in this regard is so slow that you simply have to be afraid that the speed of factual development is dulling our sword of competition law in Europe.

The European economic system also contains elements of the social market economy. The independence of the European Central Bank, with its focus on price stability, is one such element, including the European competition authority, as outlined above, and the European Union's commitment to free and fair trade.

As with the social market economy, ownership and solidarity are inseparable in the European Economic and Monetary Union. This question is also preoccupying us these days when we prepare the Franco-German Council of Ministers. We want the ESM to evolve towards a European Monetary Fund. But the question of how much joint liability and how much personal responsibility we need of course drives politicians into their discussions. We think that personal responsibility is very important, but that we also need elements of overall responsibility for the maintenance of the common whole.

Ladies and gentlemen, as I have already said, we will continue to develop the ESM - a symbol of solidarity intergovernmentally in a currency crisis - into a long-term instrument. This brings with it a multitude of negotiating tasks both for the Federal Minister of Finance and for me as Federal Chancellor. But I hope that we can move a little bit ahead on Tuesday and thus be able to further develop the Eurozone as a whole.

Ladies and gentlemen, Ludwig Erhard has always looked beyond Germany and Europe to the world. I would like to quote him: "The world is already too integrated, too intertwined, that any country can shape its own destiny for itself." - That is a very smart sentence for the present time, because we have something every day to hear about how multilateralism will evolve or not. - Ludwig Erhard said that in 1963; at a time when not much has been said about globalization. But today we feel and see that we do that more and more. We need multilateral cooperation; and basically, I am deeply convinced, we need a global governance. Their design, however, is progressing very slowly. But we need guarantees of fair competition. The World Trade Organization is the institution for it. However, it is not developing as well as we would like it at the moment. We need ways to enforce the law. And we also need ways of taking account of social and environmental concerns.

Difficulties have been apparent for some time. We could see that again at the last G7 summit in Canada. Unilateral measures seem to be faster. They then require counter reactions again. Of course, one can say that in times of disruptive change, we simply proceed with a completely new methodology. I just think that the outcome of this approach is too uncertain and that too much is at stake to avoid being bothered by multilateral arrangements.

Ladies and gentlemen, that is why the Federal Minister for Economic Affairs will have to deal very concretely not only with tariffs on steel and aluminum and the corresponding countermeasures of the European Union, but also with the questions that are now in the room, what the strategic importance of the automotive industry for the security of the United States of America. I suggest that we also think about the strategic importance of the automotive industry for the European Union in the same way, so that we can prepare for an exchange with the United States of America.

The social market economy is therefore anything but a static thing, anything but a birthday child, which we can sit in the chair and we congratulate, but it is an assignment for the daily work. All those who are here, I think, feel like participating in it. Therefore, congratulations and all the best for the future of the social market economy.

SPEECH BY FEDERAL CHANCELLOR MERKEL IN THE GERMAN BUNDESTAG[4]

Mister President! Dear Colleagues, Good morning!

Ladies and gentlemen! I think it is clear to everyone that the 2018 budget and the associated medium-term financial planning again show very good data.

That is extremely pleasing. It is now sometimes taken for granted. But that we have the highest employment since reunification, that since 2014 we do not make any new debts, that is anything but obvious.

Next year, for the first time since 2002, we will be back with total debt where the European Stability Pact refers us to, namely below 60 per cent of gross domestic product. In 2012, after the international financial and economic crisis, the total debt was just under 80 percent. That we can do this is nothing other than generational justice and thinking about the people who will live after us. That's why it's good.

The International Monetary Fund, in its recently concluded Article IV consultations with Germany, has described the development of the German economy as - I quote - "impressive". Fiscal margins should be used to increase growth potential, government investment in infrastructure should be made, investment in education should be strengthened and procedures should be speeded up. That is exactly what we have laid down in our coalition agreement and what is reflected in this budget. So there is also quite support internationally.

[4] May 16, 2018

But, ladies and gentlemen, regardless of these good numbers and values, we get daily disturbing news from all parts of the world, unfortunately also from parts that are very close to the European Union: the horrible images from Syria including pictures of poison gas attacks in the recent termination of the US nuclear deal with Iran, the bombing of positions on the Golan Heights by Iran, a threatened US-EU trade dispute, daily truce on the line of contact in Ukraine, terror victims, again in Paris and Indonesia last weekend; 70 years of Israel, that was a day to celebrate, and yet 59 dead Palestinians and many, many wounded.

We follow these headlines on a daily basis, showing us in what troubled and confusing world we live. We now know that we can not disconnect from these events.

After the Arab Spring, which is also referred to by many as the Arabian quake, the region on our doorstep has become restless: the civil war in Syria since 2011, the overthrow of Gaddafi in Libya with the collapse of state order, 2014 the annexation of Crimea, the problems in eastern Ukraine, the ISIS in Syria and Iraq in 2014, the genocide against the Yazidis in Iraq and the attacks planned in Rakka that so shattered Paris - "Charlie Hebdo". The security situation in our neighborhood has changed dramatically. This has profound implications, also for us. They show us once more: A country alone can not guarantee safety. That is why we have become aware of what we have often said almost stereotypically: Our security is inextricably linked with that of our neighborhood; For its own security, Germany needs to be integrated into alliances as a member of the European Union and as a member of NATO. Despite all the difficulties we have these days, transatlantic relations are and remain of paramount importance. That remains a constant.

But these transatlantic relations have to withstand differences of opinion, especially in these days. This is particularly evident in the termination of the nuclear agreement with Iran by the United States of America. We have been negotiating for over a decade to bring this agreement to fruition. This agreement is far from ideal; but, according to all the findings of the International Atomic Energy Agency, Iran adheres to the obligations of this agreement. This agreement was unanimously endorsed by the UN Security Council. That is why we, Britain, France, Germany, but also the other member states of the European Union, believe that it is not right to terminate this agreement now, in this situation.

That does not mean that we can be satisfied with what Iran is otherwise doing. We need to talk more about the ballistic missile program, the influence of Iran and Hezbollah in Syria, and other issues. The question that we have to answer, and which we have answered so differently from the United States of America, is: can we speak better if we terminate this agreement or can we speak better if we stay in this agreement? We believe that one can and must continue to talk to each other better - I say that explicitly because the ballistic missile program is also and precisely a threat to the security of Israel - if one stays in this agreement. Exactly in this sense, the Federal Foreign Minister has just held talks again yesterday evening.

We also know - and this is becoming more and more urgent every day - that, of course, we need a political solution in Syria, that the lives of the people of Syria are terribly frightening. Half of the citizens of Syria are now on the run: a large part of Syria, another part outside Syria.

We have progressed in the fight against the IS. Germany has participated in the anti-IS coalition and operations against Daesh, by training the Peshmerga in Iraq and air surveillance. But now the civil war in Syria, the fight against Islamist terrorism, has become a regional conflict of gigantic proportions that can not be solved without Russia, without Turkey, without Iran, without Saudi Arabia, without Jordan and basically without Europe is.

But true is also - the writer Mathias Énard, who has just received the literary prize of the Konrad-Adenauer-Stiftung, has put the oppressive on paper -: Europe is immanently affected and at the same time has not sufficiently contributed to the political solution of this conflict; I say that self-critically. Therefore, we are glad that we now belong to the so-called Small Group, in which France, Great Britain, Germany, Jordan, Saudi Arabia and the USA are looking for solutions together. Of course, the so-called Astana Group - Turkey, Iran and Russia - must also be included in the talks. This may mean that we can finally better support the work of UN mediator de Mistura. I think, it is worth while - although I have no illusions about the complexity of this conflict - that we are more involved politically. That's what the federal government will do.

There is also only one political solution to another conflict in our environment, which we have already dealt with a lot, that between Russia and Ukraine. he can not be solved militarily. We do that in Normandy format. We are trying to revive the Minsk Agreement, although it is depressing to see ceasefire violations on the line every night, and there are always obstructions to OSCE observers, whom I would like to sincerely thank from that point of view.

Years of doing this work there for years, these are really peacekeeping measures.

Germany has always supported the networked approach. The new federal government will do this step up. We know that we can solve such problems only by pursuing development by seeking political solutions and by using military force as a last resort. But military force alone will not solve the problem. In our coalition agreement, we have agreed, as it were symptomatic, that we will increase development spending and defense spending one to one, to make it clear that this networked approach is not one of our concerns, but a central one.

But we have to keep commitments on all sides; that is, the ODA quota that we have not yet reached, on the one hand, and the goals of Wales and NATO on the other. We feel committed to these goals. We have also laid this down in the coalition agreement. The Federal Finance Minister said yesterday - with his permission I may quote him -: "A defense policy concept is not good because it is expensive."

That's true; that is undisputed. But the question is different. The question is: What do we need for a Bundeswehr to meet today's requirements?

I would like to refer here to the 2006 White Paper, which we also adopted in a Grand Coalition. In this White Paper, we have focused fully on foreign missions. At that time Peter Struck's sentence, which he rightly said: "The security of Germany is also defended in the Hindu Kush" - "Hindu Kush" is pars pro toto - "defended." That was absolutely correct.

Due to the events in 2014 and because of what is happening on our doorstep - for example in the Syria area - NATO decided in 2014 - as we have seen in the White Paper 2016 - that in addition to foreign missions, the state and regional governments are also involved Alliance defense are again of greater importance.

It is precisely at this point that we are confronted with the challenges facing the Bundeswehr and, of course, the Federal Government. Not only do we have to equip and equip our soldiers in foreign missions so that they can perform their missions well, but because of the national and alliance defense, they must also be provided at home with much greater material and equipment to carry out the additional tasks that we have today: airspace surveillance in the Baltics, reinsurance for Poland and the three Baltic States - for which we operate as a framework nation in Lithuania - strengthening the corps in Szczecin and engagements in Romania and Bulgaria.

For this you have to be able to move troops faster and not just equip every hundredth soldier reasonable - I just picked out this number; I'm not an expert - while everyone else has to do with little exercise equipment. In order to be able to shoulder these tasks, corresponding equipment has to be made available on a large scale. That's a job that the Bundeswehr is facing.

The second task is to tackle the big challenge of digitization. On the one hand, this involves the digitization of Bundeswehr structures and, on the other hand, completely new skills, such as the ability to cyber. It was right to set up a cybercommando; For example, hybrid warfare is part of the military doctrine of Russia - officially described. They are good in that; and of course we have to be able to fight back. Otherwise we will not have a chance.

It's not about upgrading, it's just about equipment. I think we should have a quiet dialogue about that, for example with the Wehrbeauftragten, who can express that wonderfully, especially in his reports. We should just help the inspector-general write positive reports again.

Ladies and gentlemen, this shows that we naturally gear our foreign policy towards multilateralism. Multilateralism is under great pressure right now. We know that because multilateralism is under such great pressure, Europe needs to take its own fate more into its own hands than was previously the case. That's why we need European answers.

It was good news that in a very short time, following the shock we had when Britain decided to leave the European Union, we were the first to launch a decade-long project, a European Defense Union, a structured one Collaboration. As part of this structured cooperation, there are now the first projects. Incidentally, Germany also assumes responsibility for some of these projects.

However, the important message is quite different: if you look at the number of weapon systems of the Member States of the European Union, you will see that we are proud. If you look at the number of weapons systems in the United States of America you will see that they are at 30. The United States spends around 3.5 percent of its gross domestic product on defense, with the European Union averaging less than 2 percent. With 178 weapon systems you can not be efficient at all. In other words, a big job will be to get there to be much more efficient with common systems and much easier to interact with each other in training. From this we will be able to benefit greatly in the long term. That is always right and a huge progress,

The third big task that Europe has to shoulder is to answer the question of how we regulate and control migration. This will be a topic that will occupy us for years - I will say: decades - with the neighborhood of Syria, but above all with the neighborhood of Africa.

That is why it is right for us to work on a common European asylum system. That's why it was right to introduce Frontex. But with just under 1,400 police officers at Frontex, you will certainly be unable to protect the external borders of the European Union. Therefore, one of the great tasks of the future is to strengthen and properly equip Frontex, and Germany will do its part, ladies and gentlemen.

We also know that isolation alone will not help if we do not fight causes of flight and displacement. I talked about the political solution in Syria and the fight against IS in Iraq. And the big task - Gerd Müller would now call the Marshall Plan with Africa, which I support - means here, again in a common European effort - because our European development policy is not always efficient - really contribute to the development of Africa.

This has two components. One component is humanitarian aid. We experienced that. When the refugees in Jordan and Lebanon no longer had any money to buy groceries and feed their children, the pressure to escape had grown immensely.

But if you look at the budgets of the UN relief agencies today, the truth is that although we do many more things, not so much has been done internationally as it should have been done. All budgets, whether UNHCR or World Food Program, are dramatically deficient, and we need to raise our voices wherever possible, and of course make our contribution to these humanitarian issues.

Of course, it should not be the case that we redirect the entire development budget for humanitarian aid, so to speak. Because development does not take place sufficiently. Then it is also right that we ask ourselves: are our means and methods of development aid really sufficient? I say no. The classic development aid alone is not enough. We need to think about how we can bring economic momentum into things, how we can make even more investments in Africa possible with credit instruments, with Hermes and many more, but of course also through what Wolfgang Schäuble did in the G-20 presidency better environment - Compact with Africa - creating a good investment environment. Otherwise, economic development will not get going there. It will not work with state funds, ladies and gentlemen. Fourth, of course, we need in Europe a strengthening of Economic and Monetary Union. We came through the crises.

Today we have a situation where all the European Member States that have the euro are growing again. Employment is rising. But that does not satisfy us, because we know, of course, that at the moment the European Central Bank is pursuing a policy that will not go on forever. Therefore, the task of sustainably strengthening and crisis-proofing the Eurozone is that there is intense discussion about it and that we are talking about what national responsibility is.

Many of the policies in Europe are not communitized. We can not conclude a trade agreement on our own, but of course we can do our own labor market policy. Everyone has this responsibility. Budget sovereignty is a national responsibility. The issue of competitiveness and / or permits is in many areas - not all; Much is also regulated in Europe - in national responsibility. Therefore, the primary task at home, in each Member State, is to help make competitiveness better, not better than our European average, but better than what is needed globally.

The global view of a common monetary union is such that one says: You must also have ultimate responsibility somewhere. We want to know if you all stand together for the euro.

That is why it is right and proper to develop the ESM and to give it tasks in the direction of an international monetary fund. We can do it alone. And that's why I agree that if risk reduction is well advanced nationally, then we have a common backstop and this common backstop could also be located at the ESM, as the Federal Finance Minister said yesterday.

Then we have the task of considering: how can we ensure the convergence of the euro area and the stability of the euro area?

There are discussions going on right now. We have two projects right now. One project is the euro zone, also the financial resources, for my part an investment budget or similar, as we have written in our coalition agreement. But at the same time we have the discussions on the medium-term financial perspectives in Europe. Now let me say: The Minister of Finance is generous, but somehow the basic maths apply to him as well. In other words, spending significantly more on the European budget and even more on the Eurozone budget, while still meeting the stability criteria, is not easy, of course. That's why we're going to talk to France about the interactions: What do we have to pack in the household? After the United Kingdom's exit, 85 percent of the gross domestic product of the European Union is in the euro zone. Further question: What do we have to do as a hedge, possibly in the euro-budget? These talks will take place and we will reach agreement by the June Council. By the way, that's the only question that's still really open -

among all the suggestions that have been made. I believe that we have already made good progress. that were made. I believe that we have already made good progress. that were made. I believe that we have already made good progress.

Then, ladies and gentlemen, of course, it is also about enlargement. This is essentially about the question: what will happen to the Western Balkans? I will fly to Sofia today. We will meet tomorrow with representatives from the Western Balkan countries. That they have the European perspective is undisputed. Now the question is: how and under what conditions can we do that? But I can only say that the Western Balkans and the situation there decide on war and peace in our absolute neighborhood. Just look how quickly there the sparks blow up between Serbia and Kosovo, within Bosnia and Herzegovina, how difficult it is to clarify the name issue of Macedonia, how to fight for border agreements. Kosovo has finally concluded a border agreement with Montenegro - a huge success, considering that even today there is no clarity between Slovenia and Croatia on lake access, even though Croatia and Slovenia are members of the European Union. Incidentally, this is another reason to say: before border issues are not resolved, never join a country! I have to say that in retrospect.

It is immensely important that we take care of these issues and contribute to economic empowerment.

This is important for Europe. In order to fulfill our prosperity promise in Europe, it is now also about creating a digital single market. We have a myriad of regulations that we need to implement or negotiate. This is very much about the competitiveness of Europe, and that is why it is also very much about the competitiveness of Germany.

Ladies and gentlemen, as I have said many times and say this again today, perhaps the most ambitious project - because we have to think in some new ways - is the question: how do we shape this comprehensive social change, which is linked to digitization? It's not just about building infrastructure; we have to do that too. And we can get better as well.

One day it must be possible to abolish the app again, with which one notifies the dead spots of the Federal Network Agency. However, to believe that it is enough to tell the telecommunications providers, is not very promising because so the dead spots are not gone. The providers sometimes need pressure. Of course, after focusing on the 50 megabit per second expansion, in the future we will only have to promote broadband connections, fiber or cable; that is clear. For this we have the appropriate programs, we have the projects. The Federal Finance Minister has said that additional funds will be invested in a digital fund, so that we can start and not have to wait another two years before it finally starts.

The tenders must be such that local people can use the funds and not suffocate in bureaucracy; we have learned that, too. We will work on that.

But that will continue. It's about research and development. We are among the five countries that spend the most on research and development. But it is true that we have decided to increase the share, which today amounts to 2.94 percent of gross domestic product, to 3.5 percent in 2025, because today there are countries that already reach this 3.5 percent to have.

Of course, it is crucial that we are at the forefront of digitization in the industrial sector, especially in the area of mobility. In digitization in the consumer sector, we have lost the connection yes. Since we use all Asian or American devices; We got used to it - okay. We will not catch up so fast.

But now, when it comes to our industrial fundamentals, the Internet of Things - we are a country that still has a high industrial value added - we need to be at the forefront. Fifth place, sixth place or whatever is not enough; otherwise we will no longer be a leading industrial country.

I start with mobility. Mobility will change dramatically. Therefore, of course, it is not only criticized, but actually also unbelievable, I say, the trust that the German automotive industry has lost in connection with the diesel scandal.

It is now our job to tell the industry: you have to make up for lost trust yourself; that is not the job of politics.

But I also say that it can not be in our interest to weaken the automotive industry so much through political measures that it no longer has the strength to make any real investments in the future. That's the argument we're having now, for example hardware upgrades.

The reports are now on the table. They have to be rated. Then we will invite the communities again. Then the Forum Diesel will meet. But, ladies and gentlemen, thousands of euros - whether they are 2,000, 3,000 or 5,000 - and two to three years of employment of many engineers with the question of how to get the type approval because something has changed in the engine : Is this the right job for the automotive industry? Or do we not have to pull together all the forces and say to the automotive industry: "You must now invest in the mobility of the future, in autonomous driving, in alternative drive systems; we support you "?

There is a point for me that has been bothering me for years. I am glad that there is now a rethinking of the economy: the fact that it is claimed that we could no longer have battery cell production in Europe. Let me tell you: the battery accounts for around 40 percent of the value added of a car of the future - let's assume that electric mobility is the driving technology of the future, which is not certain - and there is still 20 to 30 percent digital value added. One part then comes from America or Asia; the other part, the battery, also comes, definitely, from Asia. What is the added value that we have here in Europe?

That's why I say: we need structured funding. The European Commission provides for such opportunities. We are already doing this with chips, where we make an effort to get into cell production as well. Of course, this can not be done without economic pressure and without economic facilitators; we can not do that as a state. That's why I'm grateful that some in the automotive industry are rethinking. We will support that.

We need the consistent digitization of administration, which should be compatible with the health card. This is what I say to birthday child Jens Spahn today. It's his birthday today.

We need an access of citizens to all administrative services. Creating that will naturally be a great effort. And we need a national education offensive, both through the Digital Pact School and in the area of employee training. Because the changes that are now taking place in the technical field, of course, have massive effects on what is needed in the future.

Today we already have a large demand for skilled workers, which we have to satisfy. That is why it is right that we will launch a Law on Special Needs Immigration; because we want to strengthen the economy. At the moment, the whole thing no longer depends on the high social security contributions or the tax question; It depends on the fact that you can not find anyone in Germany anymore. We have to help that the economy can stay in Germany and create value and that it does not have to go somewhere because it does not find any skilled workers here.

That's why that's the right answer.

Ladies and gentlemen, this will be a huge effort for us. Incidentally, I am very grateful that the coalition parties have decided to hold two Enquete commissions related to digitalisation.

One of these commissions deals with artificial intelligence. We've been doing relatively well for 20, 30 years, in terms of artificial intelligence. But now we are in a situation where we may have lost the connection a bit or are about to lose. Why? Because suddenly two developments come together: the development of artificial intelligence - algorithms and the like - as such plus the ability to process huge amounts of data.

Now it's like that with artificial intelligence: It only develops well if it can handle a lot of data. Of course, with regard to the volume of data, the question is - we are currently talking about the implementation of the General Data Protection Regulation - how do we handle the data and how do we provide many - moreover: often anonymous data? But to believe that we can be at the forefront of artificial intelligence and be as restrictive as possible in the data is just like breeding cows and giving them no food; that's just how it is. This is why the Commission Ethics of Data is important, but it must not end up turning data into a rare commodity, so to speak. Data can be used to develop new products.

- It gets a bit uneasy on a regular basis when I talk about something like that. But I'm pretty serious about that.

The fact that data becomes an important factor in the social market economy basically means that we need to rethink: from the tax system to social protection systems. Of course, it's not alright that Google, Amazon, Facebook - and whatever they're called; "GAFA", as the saying goes - do not pay taxes in Europe. But to say, "Look, now let's just invent a virtual factory, and we'll tax it as if it were a proper business" - what's this going to do? We are one of the big export nations. The companies that German companies have establishments anywhere in China or elsewhere. Then the home countries will say: Okay, these are proper establishments. Now we tax that too. - That's why we are hesitant about certain proposals that are made. We are not because we do not think you have to pay taxes.

But if we have a corporate tax law here, that we have an old corporate tax law and there the taxation of the Internet companies, and then we no longer know whether a car is a rolling Internet or if a car still belongs to the old corporate tax category: Da must we find control systems that are compatible with each other. That is why the work of the OECD is so important. And that's why we can not just hit it like this and say: "For two years we'll try something out", but we have to think it through rationally. That does not mean that we do nothing.

Similarly, it will be because data has value as much as work or otherwise. We urgently need to discuss this. Maybe we can also involve the appropriate professionals.

Ladies and gentlemen, I have talked about digitization for so long, because I believe it depends on prosperity, the redemption of prosperity. If we look at our coalition agreement - this is reflected in the budget - then we can say: we have done really well in this direction. We now have a digital cabinet; that will be before the summer break. We will set up a digital council to advise us specifically on things we do not know yet, about developments we have. We have improved the digital cooperation between the ministries of the Federal Government, also through the Minister of State for Digitization in the Chancellery.

Incidentally, with the digital cabinet, every minister today is a digital minister in a certain way. This permeates all areas of society. That's why we're working together. In the near future, I will also invite you to a hearing on artificial intelligence so that we can say, "Where are we?" And so that we can say what is missing and where we need to work better together.

Incidentally, this is a classic subject of Franco-German cooperation. This is what we agreed in our coalition agreement. France and Germany in Sofia today at dinner, where we talk about innovation, will suggest how we deal with disruptive innovations in Europe; Keyword "DARPA". That's what Europe needs, and that has to be done together.

Well, ladies and gentlemen, we have also passed our coalition agreement in a mood that tells us --

- The mood was not bad.

She was capable of it. She was due to the seriousness of the situation, let's say so.

We were also able to build on some preliminary work, although we never admitted that; no matter. - In any case, we have been driven by the fact that citizens in Germany are looking at life from the perspective of "How does this stand for me?" And not looking at it from the perspective: who is currently responsible for what? That's why we've outgrown ourselves in some places, so I'll say it as a CDU member. We now have the opportunity to promote schools not only in financially weak communities.

- We work on it and hope for active assistance. We also know that we need this help. - We have decided to do more for social housing. We have decided to do more for municipal transport finance - all of which is linked to changes in the Basic Law.

Ladies and gentlemen, this is not such a trivial decision for the federal government in combination with the federal-state financial equalization; because by the new federal-state financial equalization, which comes into force in this legislative period, namely in 2020, the federal government also weakens its financial resources. Yesterday, Olaf Scholz rightly pointed out: If we give the responsibility for social housing to the countries, if the federal government is more in the federal-state financial equalization, if the municipal transport finance law, the focus is on the countries and then the investment of the Federal government reduced by the corresponding shares, then one must not say: The federal government no longer invests. - You can not do it that way.

We said: We spend the money where it works best. But you should not forget that first 14 days later. Nevertheless, we invest more. Incidentally, we are not only investing taxpayers' money, we also have the proceeds from auctioning the 5G frequencies; we will make something out of it.

Our problem right now is not that we have too little money for investment; our problem is to find a construction company and get permits. That is why we need to accelerate the procedures in the licensing legislation and try to create more foundations so that we can move forward.

In the housing sector, it is also correct and important to introduce the AfA and the Baukindergeld. These are all incentives, as they say today, incentives to live better.

- Yes, the last few years we have done a lot, but not enough. That's life, Herr Bartsch.

Otherwise, we would eventually have to stop being MPs. Politics will always have new tasks. That's the beautiful and exciting.

Ladies and gentlemen, the huge area of safety is important to us. Again, we will enter into cooperations. The pact for the rule of law is inconceivable if you do not work with communities and countries. That is, the whole coalition is based on a very cooperative behavior of the entire federal system.

I am counting on the fact that what we spend on funds for specific purposes is actually used by the Länder and local authorities for these purposes. Since we will be very careful that this does not disappear somewhere.

Ladies and gentlemen, a huge area besides security is, of course, also the control and organization of the internal migration. That's why we opted for the AnKER centers. I think everyone should stand by now. The proposals of the Federal Minister of the Interior at this point are really very practice-oriented. With leave of absence: If on April 19th, when we were not even 100 days in office, because of maladministration in the BAMF, which are abuses says the Minister has not got the matter under control, I must honestly say: That's it a bit strange. - Among coalition friends I wanted to have noted that again.

We orient the social security systems to the future. Yesterday the pension commission was used; this is going to be a tough job. Of course, we will have to make huge efforts in care and health. We need more specialists; Again, there is a huge problem. Incidentally, I think we are all in agreement - this is largely the responsibility of the Länder - that until recently, nursing fees have been paid in nursing training occupations and no training allowance has been paid, is one of the anachronisms of the Federal Republic of Germany. I am very grateful to you for doing so, just before the Republic is turning 70, dear friends.

It is also about securing the natural foundations of life. I call the keyword "climate protection". We will set up a commission to deal with the withdrawal from lignite.

You remember: More than ten years ago we dealt with the exit from the coal. We managed to close the last pit this year, but the people who worked there were able to cope with this change and have been designed with them.

It must be the same with lignite: first ask what will become of the region, then get out, and not just determine the exit data and then think about what will become of the people. That is the only way to make a shoe out of it.

We will also pay attention to a liveable environment: more animal welfare, more rational agriculture. I just hope that the European Union is able to get the second-pillar reduction bureaucracy dedicated to this issue. Otherwise we will not make it.

I want to conclude with something that may seem a bit small to some, but that is a big topic: on May 20, next week, the World Bee Day will take place for the first time - by the way an initiative of Slovenian beekeepers. The bees now stand pars pro poto for what we mean by biodiversity, by nature, by how it has to function and should and how we need to protect it. That's why we should think about biodiversity on this day and do something good for the bees. Germany, Julia Klöckner, and the Slovenian Minister of Agriculture have concluded an agreement on how we want to work with Slovenia in this field - a small part of good, very precise and concrete use.

Ladies and Gentlemen, As you can see, we have a lot of work. We want to do that too. The Federal Government will work vigorously.

SPEECH BY FEDERAL CHANCELLOR MERKEL AT THE FEDERAL RESISTANCE MEETING ON MAY 14, 2018 IN BERLIN[5]

Dear colleagues from the German Bundestag,
Dear Parliamentary State Secretaries!
I greet all attendees very warmly, who will deal today and tomorrow with the situation of the Bundeswehr!

It is a great honor for me to be here again after 2012, when I was in Strausberg. Through my presence, I would also like to express my appreciation for the work of the Bundeswehr - in a far from simple environment and in a time of discussion in which the social debates are alive and sometimes the debates within the Bundeswehr. This shows that the Bundeswehr is part of our society; And that's right. I would also like to express my appreciation because I believe that you are making a great contribution to ensuring that our citizens in Germany can live in safety - a great contribution to our country being recognized as a reliable partner.

I would like to thank all the soldiers as well as the civilian employees of the Bundeswehr. And at this point I would also like to remind you of the soldiers who lost their lives in the ministry who fell. We will not forget her and the painful loss suffered by her families and friends. We know that being a soldier is a very special job. And that must also be reflected in the recognition of the entire society.

2012, looking at the challenges, seems like an eternity ago. The Bundeswehr, however, has been exposed to a permanent process of change ever since the end of the Cold War. Those who have been with them since then may be able to publish a multi-volume work on reform by now. There is almost a bit of history in it. At that time it was thought that now the big confrontation was over and that one had the opportunity to look at a time that is more conflict-free. Instead, it has to be said that the world became confusing pretty quickly and anything but conflict-free. In retrospect, the bipolarity of the Cold War seems to have been an extremely difficult phase, but also a relatively clear phase. Compared to this, multilateralism actually seems to be something nice - and sometimes that's not so easy for you to do. But a world with unclear balance of power is also a very complicated world. We have to adapt to this world.

At the time, after the end of the Cold War, it was properly restructured. It has also been said that we have a so-called peace dividend. It is very important today to tell people and also to discuss it in Parliament: During the Cold War one did not have to, but sat on the other side of the Iron Curtain or the Wall - without complaint in the German society 2.3 percent of gross domestic product was spent on defense spending. That was worth the safety. Therefore, the demand that we someday have to spend two percent of our gross domestic product in a very dangerous world, is not completely outside of any imagination. We've already got over 2 under very different conditions

To show how things have changed, we landed at 1.2 percent of GDP in 2015 and thought we could get along quite well. It had been preceded by many things. All in Europe have reduced their defense spending after the end of the Cold War. Then came the big international financial and

[5] May 14, 2018

economic crisis. I still remember very well the households with billions of euros in new debt. We were far away from the black zero. I also remember very well that we said: We must reduce the large increase in staff numbers after the restoration of German unity. Today we know that the Bundeswehr has made a huge contribution to this. For a decade, virtually no new civilian personnel has been hired. So there were big cuts. Added to this was the decision to suspend military service; It was a far-reaching decision that opened the door for a new approach in a modern army - which I was also recently able to discuss with leading representatives of the Bundeswehr - but which also posed completely new challenges for the Bundeswehr personnel recruitment. In the years to come, we must continue to ensure that the Bundeswehr remains an attractive employer - and that in a competition for young people, which is really tough given our demographic changes and in view of many other attractive occupational fields. That is why it was right for the Minister, when she came to office more than four years ago, to give great importance to an attractive working environment. If you know

In 2011, other things took place in the world - for example, what we call the Arab Spring, which subsequently led to massive problems when we remember the developments in Libya. On the one hand, it is good that dictator Gaddafi no longer exists in Libya. On the other hand, we also had to learn that the absence of dictators alone does not lead to a stable society. We have already experienced that in Iraq. We still experience that in Libya today.

This was followed by the civil war in Syria, which also dealt with the question of how to get rid of Assad as a tyrannical dictator. Since 2011, the war has become one of the biggest conflicts. We have only slowly realized that conflicts are not taking place anywhere in the world, but right in front of the European door and that they do not always lead immediately to more democracy. We saw that during the civil war, IS has spread to Syria and Iraq. It is now a religious conflict between Shiites and Sunnis - and a conflict over spheres of influence in a strategically important region, involving Turkey, Iran, Russia, and, of course, Saudi Arabia, the United States and, at some point, Europe.

If we thought we could disconnect from these events, then at the latest the refugee movement in 2015 taught us a better way. We did not sufficiently take care of the situation in the refugee camps. In Syria, there is an incredible disaster. Half of the country - over ten million people - is either on the run or in the surrounding countries, such as Turkey - or even to us, but not to the greatest extent. But that has given us huge tasks. At this point, let me say a heartfelt thank you to the German Armed Forces - as far as the rescue of refugees at sea is concerned, as well as what the Bundeswehr has done in the interior was an emergency for a man or a woman. That is unparalleled. Thank you very much that you helped so quickly and unbureaucratically. - I have good memories of my discussions with Ursula von der Leyen or State Secretary Hoofe. - That was a big deal; Thanks for that.

With all that not enough: In Iraq and Syria, the IS spread. In addition, in March 2014, the occupation of the Crimea and then the conflict in eastern Ukraine and their destabilization were added, so that in September 2014, when we had the NATO meeting in Wales, the world had changed. Suddenly the conflicts took place again on our doorstep. Not us in the middle of territorial Europe, but those who are geographically marginalized were suddenly faced with completely new tasks and also with completely new fears and fears. This made the situation completely different from 2006, when the penultimate White Paper was written. It was, so to speak, that there would be a lot of missions abroad, for example in Afghanistan and Kosovo.

At that time, everything seemed to focus on foreign missions. And suddenly, the second pillar, which after the end of the Cold War had actually played no outstanding role - the national and alliance defense - returned to full focus. This was also reflected in Wales' decision to move defense spending towards two percent over the next ten years. This decision was taken by all of us. And that raises the question: what about the credibility of Germany? This question is not only the Federal Minister of Defense asked, but I get lubricated on the sandwich. So we have to deal with it.

There has now been a discussion in which we all - and I now turn to all parliamentarians - have to be a bit careful that the development towards two percent is not interpreted as a militarization of Germany. Those who are familiar with the issues - and all of them are here in the room - know that these two percent are not fetters, but that fulfilling the tasks - international missions plus alliance and national defense - makes this value necessary. That means that a functioning German army, a Bundeswehr, where you do not get any bad news every day, requires more equipment. That's just the truth.

I did not know from the beginning, I say frankly, but only with the active help of people who understand defense more than I do, that for a small part of the troupe a very Very good, precise and safe equipment and equipment are required, but the issues of national and Alliance defense are much, much wider, which is why in the breadth of the troupe a much better equipment in all areas is needed. There are buzzwords from which we were quite far away: for example the so-called full equipment. As a layman, one imagines that everyone who serves has his package of equipment and equipment for what he could be used for. It was a long way from this idea. Now you need an order-oriented equipment. And that is just as it is in the national and Alliance defense. If you have to move quickly, if you have to perform all the new tasks, then you have to practice more, you have to do more things together. This also means that you need a lot more material and equipment in width. I think you can not say that often enough. I'm not telling that because I think you do not know that, but because of course my speech is also addressed to the public. if you have to do all the new tasks, then you have to practice more, you have to do more things together. This also means that you need a lot more material and equipment in width. I think you can not say that often enough. I'm not telling that because I think you do not know that, but because of course my speech is also addressed to the public. if you have to do all the new tasks, then you have to practice more, you have to do more things together. This also means that you need a lot more material and equipment in width. I think you can not say that often enough. I'm not telling that because I think you do not know that, but because of course my speech is also addressed to the public.

The decisions of Wales, in which the defense of the country and allies play a greater role again, have also found their way into our White Paper 2016, which the Federal Government has approved. Above all, they have found their way into very practical measures in which we are actively involved, namely airspace control in the Baltics, for example, in the reinsurance of Poland and the three Baltic states. We lead the increased presence and work as a framework nation in Lithuania. That's a big contribution. And we have also strengthened our involvement in the Multinational Corps Northeast in Szczecin. We are involved in Romania and Bulgaria - so also always on the borders, where it is about the Alliance defense. All this is a great effort. Thank you very much.

I want to emphasize something else, because this is already a very long commitment - it still fits into the philosophy of 2006 -: the mission in Afghanistan. It shows something that Germany can be proud of. Some say it will take forever before you decide where you are going. Yes, sometimes it may take a bit longer than others. But once we are there, we stay as long as necessary. We decided for it - I fought very politically for it; even with President Obama - that you do not make an overdue withdrawal from Afghanistan - Afghanistan has once experienced this in connection with the Soviet Union - that we do not repeat this mistake - because that would have been just from the perspective of Russia, exactly what you might have wished - but stay there.

Our work in northern Afghanistan can not take place without the United States of America; that's right. But we are also the framework nation of around 20 nations with whom we work very, very well and reliably. Also a big thank you. It clearly shows the change in philosophy, which I will talk about later, namely that we also take care of the training, so that the Afghan troops can take their fate into their own hands. But without our support, without our help, they will not succeed.

We still have soldiers in Kosovo. We have just seen it again in the last few days: you think it is quiet and nothing actually happens; and suddenly one is arrested again and the waves beat up. I recently hosted both the Kosovar President and the Serbian President in urging urgent action to promote stabilization. - Christian Schmidt is here; just now he knows how much love and attention to detail one must try again and again to minimize small conflicts, so they do not grow up and it does not come back to the outbreak of violence.

I want to give you a motive that has me very busy in the whole refugee issue. It was clear that Greece alone could not cope with many refugees. But there was also the danger that the whole Western Balkans would be destabilized if we did not tackle the problem together with Turkey. This danger was always there. And that's why the EU-Turkey agreement was absolutely necessary. It was necessary to support Turkey in the care of three million refugees.

Now, in the meantime, the situation in Syria has also worsened. We are part of the coalition in the fight against IS with all the contributions we make both there and in Iraq. Thank you very much. This was also connected with an incision in the history of the Federal Republic of Germany, because until then we have always said: we are not going directly into areas of tension. This time, however, we supported the Peshmerga in their struggle to save the Yazidis. And we are working on airspace control - first in Turkey, now in Jordan.

But it turns out that Syria in particular - we can also take Afghanistan or Libya as examples - still needs different efforts. Purely militarily, a conflict can not be resolved. They depend on us to act politically. The solution search of the conflict in Syria has meanwhile reached proportions that a comparison with the Thirty Years War in Europe is almost no longer presumptuous, because it has just become a deep regional conflict over spheres of influence. In order to find a political solution, Russia, Turkey, Iran, Saudi Arabia, the USA, Jordan, France, Great Britain and also Germany are needed. There are currently two groups - the so-called Small Group, which includes France, Great Britain, Germany, the USA, Jordan and Saudi Arabia. On the other hand, there is the so-called Astana Group, which includes Iran, Turkey and Russia. All these are actors that need to be worked with. There will be no political solution from Syria alone. And only then, when a solution is found, we will again have some stability in this region.

Since the beginning of the Thirty Years' War marks the 400th anniversary of this year, I want to point out that the Peace of Westphalia was not created in two months. It was years, long years, in which some parties never talked to each other. Even if they were in one place - in Münster - not everyone was allowed to talk to everyone. From this one can learn lessons on how to resolve conflicts. We will also need this knowledge.

In the meantime, our focus on Libya has once again focused heavily on Africa. The unity government in Libya is weak; she has no access to the entire territory. As a result, the conflict has shifted further to Africa, through a great many weapons, through the strengthening of numerous terrorist attacks. That's why we are now involved in Mali.

I remember well: Shortly after I became Federal Chancellor, President Chirac asked me if we were ready to secure the elections in Congo. - There are certainly people here who remember exactly. - At the time I was quite blumbling, I say frankly, because the Congo was not the field we knew very well about. The German Armed Forces managed the operation there wonderfully. But then we also saw that we came home after the elections were over. And that was not wrong.

We can see in our Mali mission, especially in the MINUSMA mission, but also in the training used to see how things are going. Terrorist attacks, planned by the IS in Syria, are damaging France - such as the attack on "Charlie Hebdo" and other terrorist attacks. France, for the first time in Europe, called for some kind of covenant and asked us to help. And suddenly we are in Africa and thus faced with a whole new challenge. This mission is anything but easy. He must be done with great care. The Secretary of Defense keeps reminding me that the reconnaissance drones fly there faultlessly and stably. One can also say something good with all the horror news; That's why I'm very reassured, because that certainly helps MINUSMA.

Currently, a total of 12 missions abroad, 7,100 soldiers, in addition to the same tasks with about 13,000 soldiers - so the Bundeswehr makes so permanently important in the national and Alliance Defense as well as continue in foreign missions.

I believe that in view of the events we have heard about in the last few days, such as the termination of the Iran Agreement by the United States of America, it is now important that we stay on course and dependable in our attitude and our beliefs are. What does that mean? Once, that we do not treat the resolutions of 2014 as if they were never taken. But that also means that we should politically cement our commitment to alliances and affirm that we are a reliable ally, and that we also say: yes, we are a country that politically believes that multilateralism is the best form of conflict to solve in the world. That is not so clear today. Russia felt weighed down by the interpretation of the UN Security Council resolution on Syria, which led to the combat mission in Syria. The Iran Agreement was endorsed in the UN Security Council, unanimously approved by the UN Security Council, but it is now unilaterally terminated. The United States of America has also withdrawn from the Framework Convention on Climate Change. In trade conflicts we see an increase in protectionism; that means a weakening of the World Trade Organization.

Now we are faced with the question: Should we give it all up, because it has just become more difficult or should we continue to stand by it? I plead for multilateralism, even if there are crises in multilateralism. But that means we have to be all the more reliable in what we promise. Because in the United States of America the view is that we spend 3.4 percent of gross domestic product on defense; we help you to protect you, to give you security; You have a huge trade surplus in front of us and you are on an economically good side. Is that fair from the American perspective?

We have to deal with these questions. That is why I am not averse to say - the last major trade agreement was concluded in 1994; Since then, the international community has been unable to negotiate new tariffs at all - why should we negotiate trade issues only with Canada, Singapore, Japan and South Korea? Of course we can also negotiate with the United States of America; and that is what we are talking about in the European Union. But we are under pressure and need to be consistent ourselves. That is the task we are facing right now.

Reliable alliance partnership, of course, above all concerns NATO. Germany's solid anchorage in NATO is essential. I think I do not need to convince anyone here. While there are disagreements over specific issues - those about the Iran Agreement are no small matter - we must firmly believe that transatlantic friendship is and remains one of the essential foundations of our security. That goes for military security. I can just as well say that in the field of intelligence services; This is also true in the same way. Our whole fight against terrorism would be extremely weakened if the transatlantic link did not exist. Therefore, I also thank all of you here,

The decision of the British to leave the EU is very regrettable. Nevertheless, I am very happy that - sometimes negative events are needed - there has been a certain boost and we are also tackling some things that we have not been able to do in Europe so far. Better defense cooperation in the form of permanent structured cooperation is an important, necessary, long overdue completion of the Common Security and Defense Policy of the European Union. I would like to thank Ursula von der Leyen and all those who worked on it very, very sincerely. In a short time - Germany and France have been the key players - it has been created as an open project for all member states of the European Union. And there are already significant things have been achieved. The fact that Germany is responsible for four of the seventeen projects that have been agreed so far shows that we are getting involved. Maybe our abilities are not always sufficient, but we like to share what we have with the Alliance. And that's why we're the second largest troop contributor, if I understand that correctly, and always quite active when needed, and reliable.

This European cooperation is not designed to question or weaken NATO in any way. But it is necessary. And when Ursula von der Leyen reports on how many weapons systems we bring into the Alliance on the European side, it shows that there are huge inefficiencies and that it would be better to spend the money and develop new weapons systems together. That's absolutely right and important. And if, as Chancellor, you're fighting for the Eurofighter all over the world, but there's always been someone in front of you who talked about Rafale, that's sometimes almost anachronistic. So, if it succeeds - what you almost smelled at the ILA in Schönefeld - that you will soon have a common development, then that would certainly not hurt the reputation of Europe in the world, but make us stronger. So we should also operate together.

What you sometimes do not quite understand is that the development of weapon systems is a rather long, almost intergenerational story. And just as the protective vest might need to be bought a bit quicker, so you have to have the patience and predictability of the financial resources when you embark on new projects. It really dawned on me what Ursula von der Leyen has said over and over again in the last few days: If you are committed to long-term international community projects and perhaps also take your own price development, which of course we want to prevent in the future, then - the Bundeswehr has such a nice word for it - to be downgraded. This is actually an anachronism, because then, so to speak, everything what can be left to wait for half a year, pushed back to the back; and that's not good, of course. That's why reliability has to go into the whole of planning to do both things: everyday things and long-term things.

Added to this, as everywhere else in our society, is digitization as an additional driver of changes within the Bundeswehr. Anyone who has ever worked in his ministry to standardize the data processing structure can imagine what that means for such a large organization. I say: the German Bundestag is not an unrestricted front runner in all renewals; And yet he is still a small entity compared to the Bundeswehr. Of course you have to be able to work reliably.

In addition, there is a new pillar that is reflected in a new command, cybersecurity, which we know to be very, very active in other countries that are clearly involved in hybrid warfare in their military doctrine. We can not wait there, but in order to be able to defend ourselves, we must also be involved in cybersecurity. I want to congratulate the German Armed Forces, because in the last few years they have done a lot of things, which is absolutely necessary.

So we have to be faithful allies. We are friends of the networked approach. That is one of the reasons why European security and defense policy is so important because it enables us to better combine the military component, the development component and the good governance component. We know: Mali, Afghanistan, Syria - all these countries can be kept in military security, if only in a fragile security; but lasting security is only created if development is possible. Security and development are mutually dependent. Therefore, in our coalition agreement for this government, the 1: 1 coupling of ODA and defense spending is not only a nice thing - so you know who gets how much money - but also the philosophy behind it, that security and development are intimately connected. And that's why I think that determination is very, very important.

An area that has also caused many discussions, but at the moment may not be so much in focus, but also very important to me: the empowerment of others. We have found that German soldiers in Mali are good, but best of all, if they are used to train Malian soldiers, and that we have made better progress in Afghanistan since we trained the soldiers ourselves, and that we support our commitment will not be accepted in the long term if the countries themselves are not enabled. That's why I really wish that Europe would be much more willing to accept workforce initiative initiatives - and that we should also be a little bit more honest about that. When Mali trains soldiers, gets shoes, gets a transport truck from us, but then the question also arises: Do they also get rifles from us? To train soldiers who have nothing to do with arming the opponents they have to fight - in this case very often terrorists - and then say that perhaps France will do it for us is not a very honest approach. I believe that we need to continue this discussion.

Of course, we also have to install collateral so that, for example, the Peshmerga do not resell their "Milane" or they do not fall into the hands of the enemy. This also leads back to the development aspect, because if you ensure that the soldiers receive decent pay, that they are paid so that their families can live on, that they are practically not forced to do illegal business to their own livelihood then you can insist that the weapons systems stay where they are. That is why we are now also working with France and many others to support the soldiers in the G5 Sahel states in the fight against terrorism. They say: Look, MINUSMA has a mandate that is not enough; that's Chapter 5, but it's not Chapter 7. In your opinion, you need a Chapter 7 mandate; they have not gotten that from the UN. But they want to set up an anti-terrorist force now. In this anti-terrorist force, we have to and we want to help them with what we can teach in terms of know-how.

In principle, that's right. But when you talk to the president of one of the poorest countries in the world - Niger - he says: Look, you're giving me development aid, you - the World Bank, Europe, Germany - give me everything, but nobody gives me anything for that Security of my country; I have to be able to maintain security and to be able to fight terrorism, but for which I receive very little financial support. That's why collecting financial support is also part of Europe's initiative to pay the soldiers and fund their equipment so they can fight terrorists there. And I believe them that the people of the African countries - I do not want to offend anyone now - are at least as good as the MINUSMA soldiers, by the way, they do not even have the job. So that is also a very important part, which in my opinion will gain in importance and in which Germany is indeed very, very committed.

Ladies and gentlemen, you bring the whole thing up and running permanently. We have a lot of work ahead of us. They will discuss all this. But I think you have to be careful now - and I want to do my part and the whole federal government wants to do its part - that we discuss the strengths and weaknesses of the Bundeswehr in a balanced and reasonable discourse and not, so to speak, from scare report to scare report rush. This means that there is a medium and long-term reliability.

You can assume that the Federal Government does not rely solely on the Bundeswehr. Of course, we are proud to have them, but we also seek to reduce conflicts through political contributions and thus make operations superfluous. This is also behind the candidacy for a non-permanent seat on the UN Security Council 2019/20, where we believe we have a good chance.

I want to tell you: you enjoy recognition. Of course you are required. Be good. I think the principle of inner guidance in the 21st century is also a great principle. They have young people who are very motivated. And we know that you have to be an attractive employer. With this in mind, I wish your conference every success and we wish you a good cooperation.

SPEECH BY FEDERAL CHANCELLOR MERKEL TO THE GERMAN BUNDESTAG[6]

We have always appreciated your work. If necessary, you have assigned us the place laid down in the Basic Law, and we have tried, to the best of our knowledge and belief, to comply with it.

I have been reminded of dramatic situations in the past three legislative sessions, such as the global financial crisis, the euro crisis and the refugee crisis, when many refugees came to us. In these crises, the government and parliament, despite great time constraints and despite the most pressing decisions, have always succeeded in finding solutions in a good consensus and gradually strengthening Parliament's role, which, I believe, was right and good for us as a Federal Republic of Germany. but also to find solutions that have shown us to be a reliable partner in Europe and in the world. I would like to thank you from the bottom of my heart.

For me, one of the most emotional situations was when we recently voted on federal-state fiscal equalization; in contrast to today, the Bundesrat bank was well staffed. These were really tough negotiations that dealt with the questions: what role does the Confederation play? What role do countries play? That this could be negotiated in spite of all the controversy in such a good atmosphere speaks for our country. You, dear Herr Lammert, dear Norbert, have a very important part in that. Thanks for that!

Dear Colleagues, Ladies and Gentlemen, We have achieved a lot in the last four years. Undeniably, Germany is doing well in many areas. But we can not rest on our laurels.

I am deeply convinced that we are on the threshold of a new stage of development. We now have to create the conditions for Germany to be economically successful and socially equitable even in 10 or 15 years time, and for even more people to have a good and safe job.

We just let our eyes wander back to the time of German unity. Since then 27 years have passed. At the beginning of the 1990s, Germany had the strength to master German unity well. A decade later, we were the sick man of Europe. We then succeeded - essentially with the Agenda 2010, which we have always supported by CDU / CSU - to regain the strength to catch up. We are the growth engine today. Today, we are one of the countries with the highest employment rates we have ever had and in Europe we are receiving a lot of recognition.

But I have the feeling that we are once again on the threshold of a new stage. This has a lot to do with the driver of today's development: with digital progress.

What we are currently experiencing in the automotive industry shows - as in a burning glass - the sum of the new challenges. The automotive industry is one of the pillars of German economic success. The German automotive industry is recognized worldwide. The products of the German automotive industry embody what is understood worldwide as "Made in Germany". Incidentally, 800 000 people and more work in the automobile industry. These people were guilty of nothing; they have worked well, very well or even excellently. But they are now in danger that

[6] 05. September 2017

what has been caused by loss of confidence by the leadership of automobile companies back on them.

Here we have an overall social responsibility to name mistakes, but at the same time to help secure the future of the German automotive industry.

That's why we need to make sure - through sound framework conditions, as we've done with Industry 4.0 in our Digital Agenda - that the conditions for the transition of production to a digital age are created, in which not only people through smartphones but in which all objects are networked together - that is the Internet of Things - so that the production can continue to be successful.

We will still need internal combustion engines for years and decades, and yet at the same time we will have to pave the way for a new mobility with new drives. We from the Christian Democratic Union and the CSU say:

We do not work with prohibitions, but we want to make such transitions reasonably possible, with regard to employees and to technological change.

I am convinced that this is also the approach of the entire Federal Government.

Ladies and Gentlemen, Yesterday we had a conversation with the municipalities on the part of the Federal Government, which are subject to exceedances of thresholds and which are threatened by driving bans. I say explicitly for the whole government: We will do everything in our power to prevent such prohibitions.

We must give the people, who by the way in good faith and by us also encouraged diesel cars bought, the possibility that they can use these cars also. Incidentally, it is the case that we recommended the purchase of diesel cars - of which there are about 15 million in Germany - because it saved CO 2emissions. Acting against the diesel also means acting against the CO 2 targets we set ourselves. And that must not happen.

That's why we need clean diesel cars, and we need the transition to modern mobility.

Ladies and gentlemen, that does not make up for the fact that unforgiving mistakes have occurred in the automotive industry. That's why we can not just move on to the agenda. But that does not entitle us to deprive the entire industry of their future, so to speak.

Now it's about finding the right ways with measure and middle. And this is what this Federal Government, ladies and gentlemen, stands for in terms of its employees and the economic power of Germany.

When it comes to cars, the big challenges we face are showing. I just mention the areas "autonomous driving" and "new drives", which we should promote in a way that is open to technology. At the same time, there are big challenges in terms of climate protection.

Of course, we will also have to implement all this with a view to the Paris Agreement on Climate Change of December 2015. That's why the federal government has presented a climate protection plan. It is already foreseeable that in the next legislative period, in 2018, this climate protection plan will have to be specified. Again, we do not want to do this against those affected, but in conversation with those affected. For example, talking about lignite areas and calling for an exit without giving people any perspective in any way will not encourage them to be pro-climate, but prevent them. Therefore, we are in favor of working out alternatives with the affected parties and then making decisions. I think we owe it to people.

We have made a lot of progress with the Digital Agenda. We will have to start this process in the next legislative period and we will have to accelerate and tighten some things. We are not the top global player in terms of digital advances and measures. We have achieved a great deal in the area of business, especially among large companies. The Federal Government has given much help to medium-sized companies. She promoted the start-ups during this legislative period, so we can say that we are doing much better than we did four years ago. But the world does not sleep. The world is developing at a rapid pace. Therefore, it will be necessary to continue working here. We invented the MP3 format in the past. We built the first computer. But as Germany we do not want to end up in the Technikmuseum, but we want to be at the forefront when it comes to developing new goods and new production possibilities. We have a lot to do there.

This also means that we have to go ahead on the part of the state and the administration. I am very grateful that it was possible within the framework of the negotiations on the federal-state financial relations to agree and to change the Basic Law so that the federal, state and local authorities will develop a common citizen portal. The legal requirements to implement this have been created by the Federal Government. We have set ourselves a period of five years in which we want to achieve that. If it's done by the end of the next legislature, it would be even better. Citizens need to feel that their relationship with the state is finally in line with digital progress. There we have a lot in common with us. - The legal conditions created are good; Mr. Heil,

If we want to remain a high-tech country, we have the task of further promoting research and development. Even in the time of Chancellor Schröder in 2000, the European states decided that every European country should spend 3 percent of the gross domestic product on research and development. - That does not mean that you spend nothing on education. It simply means spending 3% of GDP on research and development, and that's right. We are happy that we have achieved this 17 years later

and one of the few countries in the European Union that has done it. However, we must also note that there are Scandinavian countries that already spend 3.5% of gross domestic product on research and development, as well as South Korea and Israel. Therefore, we must not rest here, but must continue to develop.

In this context, it should be mentioned that the Federal Government - the Federal Government and the Parliament have agreed - fully accepts the BAföG payments. - Mr Heil, I respect the number of Members of your group. But against my will and the will of the Union faction you could not enforce anything in this Parliament. You just have to accept that now.

Perhaps, Mr. Heil, your arguments were so good that they convinced me. Or rather: it was the arguments of the First Mayor Olaf Scholz, who finally convinced me. By this you can see how well I can listen, how I can respond to good arguments.

So it's a good, shared success for us all.

Here, we placed great value on the fact that as many countries as possible have subsequently used the funds released for higher education again. We were not completely successful. But for the Union-led countries, I can say that's how it happened, and we're proud of that.

Ladies and gentlemen, through good economic policies, and also the fact that we have not been in debt for four years, we have been able to show that sound fiscal policies and economic growth can go hand in hand, and that sustainable economic growth can emerge. The last four years are characterized by the fact that the engine of growth in Germany is no longer exports, but domestic consumption. This can also be seen in the wage increases.

- First, it's your turn later. And second: Rejoice with us or with me.

I can not understand what you are doing here. Imagine that you did not do anything in this government. That would not have been nice.

We have put together a government. We have set a lower wage limit in the last election campaign. You have sought the uniform minimum wage. We finally agreed that we would introduce the uniform minimum wage. Millions of people have more in their pockets today, and we can all enjoy that. Even the skilled workers have more. Real wages have risen; This is also reflected in the increase in pensions.

I think many people in our country are happy about that.

Ladies and Gentlemen, The networked world, which is reflected in digital progress, is of course also reflected in foreign policy. The limits of economic, financial, trade and security policy are becoming increasingly blurred; We see that in many trouble spots in the world. Unfortunately, at the moment, of course, the situation in the Asian region, where North Korea's nuclear tests are a flagrant violation of all international conditions, is of particular concern to us. It is true that the UN Security Council has clear positions. I say expressly, also on behalf of the entire Federal Government: here there can only be a peaceful diplomatic solution, for which, however, we must work with all our might.

That's why, ladies and gentlemen, I talked to the French president on Sunday. The Federal Foreign Minister is in contact with his colleague. There will be a Foreign Ministers meeting in Gymnich this weekend, where we will discuss further sanctions from the European side towards North Korea; that is also urgently needed. I talked about it yesterday with the South Korean President and also with US President Donald Trump. Both greatly support these European efforts. The fact that North Korea has some distance from us should not prevent us from resolutely advocating a diplomatic solution. Europe has an important voice in the world and needs to use that voice in this situation.

Ladies and gentlemen, for sad reasons - twelve German citizens are in custody in Turkey for political reasons - we are dealing with developments in Turkey in a very special way. This development is more than worrying. Turkey is increasingly leaving the rule of law, in part at a very fast pace. We have the task - the Foreign Office and we all do everything - to get the German citizens freed.

I will give an example of Ms. Tolu, who is in jail with a two-year-old child; Her husband is also in custody. I can also call Deniz Yücel and Mr Steudtner and others. First, we should not forget anybody about them. Secondly, we should give everyone the best possible care. Third, at every level, we should do everything in our power - day by day - to release these people, who in our opinion are innocently in pre-trial detention. I think that is our concern.

Of course, this dealings with German citizens, as well as the overall situation in Turkey, causes us to reflect on how we are reorganizing relations with Turkey. The Federal Government has taken first steps; This was explained in detail by the Federal Foreign Minister on the occasion of the arrest of Mr Steudtner. We have asked the Estonian Presidency to put any negotiations on enlargement of the Customs Union on the agenda for the next few months, as long as the situation persists; that excludes itself. We will also discuss future relations with Turkey - I will propose that this will take place at the European Council in October - including the question of suspending or ending the negotiations. For this one needs majorities in Europe. This is a process

Relations with Turkey are strategic. A few days before I became Chancellor, on 3./4. October 2005, my predecessor Gerhard Schröder has opened accession negotiations with Turkey. This was preceded by a long discussion process; The basic decision had already been made at the end of 2004. We from the Union faction have always been skeptical or against entering into these accession negotiations.

However, in the spirit of great foreign policy continuity - pacta sunt servanda - I have always held these negotiations. We opened chapters. We have not closed chapters for a long time. Relations with Turkey are very important.

Therefore, I will work to ensure that we act decisively, but that we act and speak with our European partners; For nothing would be more astonishing than if we in Europe publicly dispute the question of the future dealings with Turkey in the eyes of President Erdogan. That would dramatically weaken Europe's position. I can only advise against that.

The same determination we have in dealing with the Turkish Government, with the President, must also be had when we look at the many who are not satisfied with the current political developments in Turkey. We also need to look at the many Turkish citizens of the Federal Republic of Germany because they are our citizens, even those who have been living here for a long time with Turkish citizenship. They contribute to the prosperity of our country. We must not offend her. We must also talk to them about the further developments; because they are part of our country and we should make that clear to them. In that sense, it is a very responsible task

Ladies and Gentlemen, Another thing that symbolically reflects the situation and the global challenges is the situation of the refugees worldwide. Here we have done a lot. I do not want to respond to this on a case-by-case basis today, but I want to say that the partnership with Africa is particularly important to me. We spoke recently with the Italian and Spanish Prime Ministers and the French President about the partnership with the Unity Government in Libya, about the partnership with Niger, about cooperation with Chad and other African countries.

- I did not say that this is a democracy on our model. Nevertheless, we have to talk to these countries.

It makes no sense to believe that simply by condemning the German Bundestag, the world is changing for the better, but we have to keep an eye on people:

People who are fleeing through the Sahara, people who go through Niger, people who come to Libya. All these countries are certainly not democracies as we imagine them, and yet we need to talk to and build relationships with these countries.

Ladies and gentlemen, we will have an EU-Africa summit by the end of the year, and this EU-Africa summit will set the course for more fair trade with Africa and more economic development in Africa,

as Wolfgang Schäuble proposed with his Compact with Africa in the G-20 presidency; This is also the aim of many initiatives by the Minister of Economic Affairs and other ministers initiated by us. In this respect, there is a very networked cooperation throughout the Federal Government to help these African countries.

Ladies and gentlemen, when it comes to security in the world, of course, the issue of defense also plays a role. We already had a remarkable discussion this morning. That's why I want to say something.

In 2002, NATO decided that new member states would only be admitted to NATO if they made a commitment to spend 2 percent of their defense budgets as part of the Membership Action Plan. Of course, this was not without consequences for the discussion on the level of defense spending by the Member States, which had been members of NATO for many years. That's why the ministers of defense repeated this decision in 2006, so it has been playing a central role ever since. And throughout the term of US President Barack Obama, there was a recurrent theme, which meant that you Germans can not assume that in the long run others will provide you with a piece of security without your efforts

As a result, in Wales - also strongly influenced by the conflict in Ukraine - it was decided to say - and this position was shared by the Federal Government -: Even the countries that still do not meet the 2% target today - the new Member States are doing so as much as possible, should consider the benchmark 2 percent, and should therefore move towards defense spending of 2 percent of the budget by 2024.

This, in turn, is reflected in the White Paper passed by the entire federal government in July 2016. These are all decisions taken before the US election, in which Donald Trump was elected President of the United States of America has been.

Ladies and gentlemen, we have then made moderate increases in the defense budget, regularly accompanied by comments from our defense experts both from the CDU / CSU faction and from the SPD faction that these are much-needed increases, but still insufficient increases,

because we alone demand the equipment of the Bundeswehr in many ways. I do not even talk about blue helmet missions and help for other countries, for example in the equipment and training of soldiers.

Then I listened to my non-joy

that this goal is no longer accepted. Then, to my delight, I heard that the Social Democratic Party chancellor candidate was seeking advice from defense experts, such as Rainer Arnold, and that he had recommended that you raise 3 to 5 billion euros more each year should use for the Bundeswehr. That's where I put my mathematical skills together

and thought to myself: If there are 3 billion, we move quickly towards 2 percent target. If it's \$ 5 billion, we probably reached the 2 percent target in 2024. - So no problem, no dissent. I am glad and hope that the word of Chancellor candidate Martin Schulz applies.

To name the source, Mr. Heil: It was at the forum of Deutschlandfunk and Phoenix. - In addition, it was claimed that I wanted to spend 30 billion euros more, which would have resulted from one year to the other, that we had met the 2-percent target, which - well, so that everything is clear.

Ladies and gentlemen, now I just want to point out that because my time is almost over, that we -

- I mean my speaking time here. My God, how far have we already come? Guys, come, there are only a few days to go! Let us, to some extent, accept this successful government work, at least today! Because we have really achieved a lot together.

We have a lot of differences; that is not a question at all. These are also reflected in the government programs; that is not a question. But what we have done, we should already tell people. And with that I conclude.

FEDERAL GOVERNMENT SYSTEM AND POLITICAL DEVELOPMENTS

BASIC INFORMATION AND CONSTITUTIONAL DEVELOPMENTS

The **Basic Law for the Federal Republic of Germany** (German: *Grundgesetz für die Bundesrepublik Deutschland*) is the constitution of the Federal Republic of Germany.

The Basic Law was approved on 8 May 1949 in Bonn, and, with the signature of the occupying western Allies of World War II on 12 May, came into effect on 23 May. Its original field of application (German: *Geltungsbereich*) — that is, the states that were initially included in the Federal Republic of Germany — consisted of the three Western Allies' zones of occupation, but at the insistence of the Western Allies, formally excluded West Berlin. In 1990, the Two Plus Four Agreement between the two parts of Germany and all four Allied Powers stipulated the implementation of a number of amendments. In the subsequent Unification Treaty of 1990, this amended Basic Law was adopted as the constitution of a united Germany.

The German word ***Grundgesetz*** may be translated as either *Basic Law* or *Fundamental Law* (*Grund-* is cognate with the English word *ground*). The term *Verfassung* (constitution) was deliberately avoided as the drafters regarded the *Grundgesetz* as an interim arrangement for a provisional West German state, expecting that an eventual reunified Germany would adopt a proper constitution, enacted under the provisions of Article 146 of the Basic Law, which stipulates that such a constitution must be "freely adopted by the German people". Nevertheless, although the amended Basic Law would finally be approved in 1990 by all four Allied Powers (who thereby relinquished their continued reserved constitutional rights), it was never submitted to a popular vote, neither in 1949 nor in 1990.

The authors of the Basic Law sought to ensure that a potential dictator would never again be able to come to power in the country. Although some of the Basic Law is based on the Weimar Republic's constitution, the authors also elevated human rights and human dignity to core values protected by the Basic Law. The principles of democracy, republicanism, social responsibility, and federalism are key components of the Basic Law; the principles and fundamental rights underlying these articles are constitutionally entrenched and; although several of these articles have since been reworded, extended or refined, they are barred from being removed or repealed by the normal amendment process.

FUNDAMENTAL RIGHTS

Main article: Fundamental rights in the German Constitution

Fundamental rights (German: *Grundrechte*) are guaranteed in Germany by the Federal Constitution and in some state constitutions. In the Basic Law, most fundamental rights are guaranteed in the first section of the same name (Articles 1 to 19). They are subjective public rights with constitutional rank which bind all authorities of the state. In case of a violation of the fundamental rights and the legal protection to be granted by the courts fails, the Basic Law provides with the constitutional complaint an extraordinary appeal to the Federal Constitutional Court (Article 93 paragraphs 1 No. 4a Basic Law). These fundamental rights cannot be removed from the constitution, and no constitutional amendment may 'affect their essence'.

According to this regulation the Federal Constitutional Court can be called not only because of a violation of fundamental rights, but also by violation "of the rights set out in Article 20 paragraph 4 and Articles 33, 38, 101, 103 and 104". Hence, these rights are called the rights identical to fundamental rights.

EXTENSIONS OF THE FIELD OF APPLICATION BY ARTICLE 23

As with the Weimar Constitution before it, the 1949 Basic Law was explicitly irredentist; maintaining that there remained separated parts of 'Germany as a whole' in the form of German peoples living outside the territory under the control of the Federal Republic of 1949, with whom the Federal Republic was constitutionally bound to pursue reunification; and in respect of whom mechanisms were provided by which such other parts of Germany might subsequently declare their accession to the Basic Law. Since initially the Basic Law did not apply for all of Germany, its legal provisions were only valid in its field of application (German: *Geltungsbereich des Grundgesetzes für die Bundesrepublik Deutschland*). This legal term was frequently used in West German legislation when West German laws did not apply to the entirety of Germany, as was usually the case.

Article 23 of the Basic Law provided other *de jure* German states, initially not included in the field of application of the Basic Law, with the right to declare their accession (*Beitritt*) at a later date. Therefore, although the Basic Law was considered provisional, it allowed more parts of Germany to join its field of application. On one side, it gave the Federal Republic of Germany – composed as it was in 1949 – no right to negotiate, reject or deny another German state's declaration of its accession to the FRG, subject to the FRG's recognising that state *de jure* and being satisfied that the declaration of accession resulted from the free self-determination of its people; while on the other side an acceding state would have to accept the Basic Law and all laws so far legislated under the institutions of the FRG as they were. As the Federal Republic could not itself declare the accession of another part of Germany under Article 23, this provision could not be applied as an instrument of annexation; nor could accession under Article 23 be achieved by international treaty with third party states, although the Federal Constitutional Court recognised that a future declared accession could be framed *de facto* as a compact between the Federal Republic and the acceding state. It remained unclear whether accession under Article 23 could be achieved by a part of Germany whose government was not recognised *de jure* by the Federal Republic, and if so how; but in practice this situation did not arise. Article 23, altered after 1990, originally read as follows:

> **Former Article 23 of the Basic Law for the Federal Republic of Germany**
>
> For the time being, this Basic Law shall apply in the territory of the Länder of Baden, Bavaria, Bremen, Greater Berlin, Hamburg, Hesse, Lower Saxony, North Rhine-Westphalia, Rhineland-Palatinate, Schleswig-Holstein, Württemberg-Baden, and Württemberg-Hohenzollern. In other parts of Germany it shall be put into force on their accession.

Whereas the West German state had gained restricted sovereignty in May 1955, the Sarrois rejected in a referendum (1955) the transformation of their protectorate into an independent state within the emerging European Economic Community. The Saar Treaty then opened the way for the government of the Saar Protectorate to declare its accession to the West German state under Article 23, including the new Saarland into the field of application of the Basic Law. The Saar held no separate referendum on its accession. With effect from 1 January 1957 the Federal Republic regarded itself as including almost all of Western Germany such that the only "other parts of Germany" to which Article 23 might be extended were now to the east; hence relinquishing all claims to those western parts of the former German Reich that had been surrendered to France and Denmark. (cf. Little Reunification with the Saar). The towns of Elten, Selfkant, and

Suderwick, which had been occupied and annexed by Netherlands in 1949, were reunited with the Federal Republic in 1963 by means of an international treaty without invoking Article 23.

Although the Basic Law, in its original form, maintained the continuing existence of a larger Germany, "Germany as a whole"; nevertheless, the extent of the associated wider German national territory is nowhere defined in the Basic Law, although it was always clearly understood that both East Germany and Berlin were included. In its judgement of 1973, confirming the constitutional validity of the Basic Treaty between East Germany and West Germany, the Federal Constitutional Court justified the recognition of East Germany as a valid German state, on the basis that this would enable the GDR in the future to declare accession to the Basic Law under Article 23. But the Court then explicitly acknowledged that this limited *de jure* recognition of the GDR also implied acceptance of the constitutional power of the GDR in the interim to enter into international treaties on its own account, naming in particular the treaty with Poland which confirmed the transfer of the "Eastern Territories" to Polish sovereignty.

The Communist regime in East Germany fell in 1990.

Following free elections the parliament of the GDR (East Germany) declared the accession of the GDR according to Article 23 to the Federal Republic of Germany to come into effect on 3 October 1990, making unification an act unilaterally initiated by the last East German parliament.

East Germany's "declaration of accession" (*Beitrittserklärung*) envisaged the East German territories being included into the field of application of the Basic Law; but subject to the Basic Law being first being amended in accordance with both the previously negotiated Unification Treaty between East and West Germany, and also the Two-Plus-Four Treaty, under which the Allied Powers had relinquished their residual German sovereignty.

So, prior to the date of accession of East Germany to the Federal Republic of Germany Article 23 was repealed, representing an explicit commitment under Two-Plus-Four Treaty that, following the unification of East Germany, West Germany and Berlin, no "other parts of Germany" remained in east or west to which the Berlin Republic might validly be extended. Rather than adopting a new constitution under Article 146 of the Basic Law, the *Bundestag* (Parliament of Germany) amended Article 146 and the Preamble of the Basic Law to state that German unification had now been fully achieved; while also adding a further clause 143(3) to entrench in the Basic Law the irreversibility of acts of expropriation undertaken by the Soviet occupying powers between 1945 and 1949. Hence when the GDR's nominal accession to the Federal Republic under Article 23 came into effect on 3 October 1990, Article 23 was no longer in place. Strictly therefore, German reunification was effected by the Unification Treaty between two sovereign states, the GDR and the Federal Republic, and not by the GDR's prior declaration of accession under Article 23; although the former Article 23 was agreed by both parties to the Treaty as setting the constitutional model by which unification would be achieved.

As part of the process, East Germany, which had been a unitary state since 1952, was re-divided into its initial five partially self-governing states (*Bundesländer*), being granted equal status as the already existing Länder, with East and West Berlin reuniting into a new city-state (like Bremen and Hamburg). After the changes of the Basic Law, mostly pertaining to the accession in 1990, additional major modifications were made in 1994 ("Verfassungsreform"), 2002 and 2006 (2006 = "Föderalismusreform").

LEGAL STATUS OF GERMANY

The **legal status of Germany** concerns the question of the extinction, or otherwise continuation, of the German nation state, (i.e., the German Reich created in the 1871 unification); following the rise and downfall of Nazi Germany, and constitutional hiatus of the military occupation of Germany by the four Allied powers from 1945 to 1949. It became current once again when the German Democratic Republic (East Germany) joined the Federal Republic of Germany (West Germany) in 1990.

After World War II, determination of legal status was relevant, for instance, to resolve the issue of whether the post-1949 Federal Republic of Germany (West Germany) would be the successor state of the pre-1945 German Reich—with all at the time uncodified implications of state succession, such as the continuation of treaties—or if, according to international law, it would be identical with the German Reich. Further, determination of authority, for instance to assert or deny territorial claims, especially with respect to the former eastern territories, was dependent upon this determination of legal status. The 1945 Potsdam Agreement had specified that a full peace treaty concluding World War II, including the exact delimitation of Germany's postwar boundaries, required to be "accepted by the Government of Germany when a government adequate for the purpose is established." The Federal Republic always maintained that no such government could be said to have been established until the peoples of East and West Germany had been reunited within a free democratic state; but a range of opinions continued within West Germany over whether a unified state consisting of the populations of West Germany, East Germany and Berlin alone could be said to represent the whole German people for this purpose. The key question being whether a Germany that remained bounded to the east by the Oder–Neisse line could act as a 'united Germany' in signing a peace treaty, without qualification.

A related question arose from the Basic Law for the Federal Republic of Germany (*Grundgesetz*). As adopted by West Germany in 1949 as an interim constitution, the preamble looked forward explicitly to a future free and united German state; "The entire German people is called upon to accomplish, by free self-determination, the unity and freedom of Germany." The Basic Law potentially provided two routes for the establishment of a reborn and unified German state; either under Article 23 whereby 'other parts of Germany' over and above the named States of the Federal Republic (*Bundesland*) could subsequently apply for admission; or under Article 146 where constituent power (*pouvoir constituant*) could be exercised by elected representatives of the entirety of the German people in creating a new permanent constitution that would replace the Basic Law. Adoption of a constitution under Article 146 would have implied that the legal validity of a unified German State would rest on "a free decision by the German people" as a whole.

No effective national government existed in Germany following the surrender of the German High Command in May 1945; all national military and civil authority and powers were therefore exercised by the four Allied Powers. The Allies then maintained that as the former German Reich no longer existed in fact; so, as the 'highest authority' for Germany, they were entitled to assume all sovereign powers without limitation of scope or duration and could legitimately impose whatever measures on the German people within German national territory as any government could legally do on its own people—including validly ceding parts of that territory and people to another country. They argued furthermore that international conventions constraining occupying powers in wartime from enforcing fundamental changes of governmental system, economic system or social institutions within the territory under their control—the Hague Regulations of Land Warfare and the Geneva Conventions—did not apply; and could not apply, as the termination of Nazi Germany and the total Denazification of German institutions and legal structures had been agreed by the Allied Powers as absolute moral imperatives. Consequently, the Potsdam Agreement envisaged that an eventual self-governing state would emerge from the wreckage of WWII covering 'Germany as a whole', reuniting Berlin and the four Allied control zones; but that this would derive its sovereignty solely from that then being assumed by the Allied Powers, and its constitution would require the approval of all the Allies through the Council of Foreign Ministers. From the 1950s onwards however, a school of German legal scholars developed the alternative view that the Allies had only taken custody of German sovereignty while the former German state had been rendered powerless to act; and that consequently, once a freely constituted German government had come into being in the form of the Federal Republic, it would resume the identity and legal status of the former German Reich without requiring any formal devolution of sovereignty from the institutions of the Occupation.

GERMANY AS 'NATIONAL PEOPLE'; VERSUS GERMANY AS 'STATE TERRITORY'

At the 1871 Unification of Germany, the Reich was established constitutionally as a federation of monarchies, each having entered the federation with a defined territory; and consequently the unitary nationalism of the 'German Reich' was initially specified (at Article 1 of the 1871 constitution) in territorial terms, as the lands within the former boundaries of this particular subset of German monarchies. This geographical understanding of the German state became steadily superseded in the period up to the first World War by an understanding of Germany as a unitary nation state identified with the German national people according to the principle of *jus sanguinis*, and drawing on the rhetoric of "the sovereignty of the nation" in the Frankfurt Constitution ; albeit that many ethnic 'Germans' (as with the German-speaking peoples of Austria) remained outside the national people constituting the German Empire of 1871; and also that the Empire of 1871 included extensive territories (such as Posen) with predominantly non-German populations. This transition became formalised in the constitution of the Weimar Republic, where Article 1 identifies the Reich as deriving its authority from the German national people; while Article 2 identifies the state territory under the Reich as the lands which, at the time of the constitution's adoption, were within the authority of the German state. The identity of the German state and German people ran both ways; not only did the institutions of the German state derive their legitimacy from the German people; so, too, the German people derived their inherent identity and patriotic duties from their being collectively constituted as an organ and institution of the German Reich. Subsequently, the term 'German Reich' continued to be applied both as identifying with the national people, and also as denoting German state territory; but increasingly the application of the term to the German national people came to be seen as primary. Following the Second World War, the term 'German Reich' fell out of use in constitutional formulations, being replaced by the term 'nation as a whole', as applied to denote the state as a totality of the German national people; and the term 'Germany as a whole', as applied to denote the state as a totality of German national territory. Nevertheless, it remains fundamental to German constitutional understanding that the legal status of Germany is a function of the unified German people, and is not constrained by the boundaries of territories falling under the jurisdiction of the German state at any one time.

WEST AND EAST GERMANY

Under the Potsdam Agreement the three Allied Powers, the United States, the United Kingdom and the Soviet Union, had agreed that a final peace agreement would have to wait on the re-establishment of a German government adequate for the purpose of agreeing to Allied peace terms. In the interim, it was intended that the Allied Control Council would act exercise all sovereign authority within Germany; while the Council of Foreign Ministers would oversee the development of new German State institutions. France was invited to membership of both bodies (although De Gaulle had not been invited to Potsdam, and refused to be bound by any agreements made there); but France from the first pursued a policy of obstructing any joint Allied actions that might lead to the re-emergence of Germany as a single unified state. Consequently, any establishment of formal institutions or agencies that might eventually restore unified German sovereignty was initially stalled by French objections. Subsequently, as Cold War antagonisms grew, the same institutions came to be largely nullified by disputes between the Western Allies and the Soviet Union. The United States and the United Kingdom therefore came round to the French view that a unified German state partially subject to Soviet authority could not be allowed to emerge while the Soviet Bloc remained in eastern Europe, and so the three Western Allies resolved upon the foundation of a West German federation consisting of the territories in their three zones of occupation. This was established on 23 May 1949 with the promulgation of the Basic Law as it had been adopted by the Parliamentary Council and approved by the Western occupation forces. The Federal Republic created by the Basic Law was empowered to act upon the federal election held on August 14, the constitutive meeting of the Bundestag parliament on September 7, the investiture of the first Federal President, Theodor Heuss on September 13, the appointment of Konrad Adenauer as the first Federal Chancellor on September 15 and the accession of the Federal Cabinet on September 20, 1949. In turn the Soviet Military Administration on October 7 implemented the People's Chamber (*Volkskammer*) parliament in the Soviet occupation zone and East Berlin, which passed the Constitution of East Germany, officially named "German Democratic Republic" (GDR). The Council of Ministers of the GDR assumed office on October 12, 1949.

On April 10, 1949, the Western Allies had drawn up the occupation statute and had it conveyed to the Parliamentary Council. Officially announced on May 12, it reserved a number of sovereign rights, such as foreign policy and external trade, to the three western Allied authorities. Any amendment to the West German Constitution was subject to (western) Allied permission, specific laws could be rejected, and the military governors could take over all governmental power in times of crisis. Those reservations were to be executed by the Allied High Commission of the three western allies, established on June 20 and claiming to exercise supreme state power within the former western zones of occupation. On November 22, 1949, Chancellor Konrad Adenauer signed the Petersberg Agreement, under which it was recognized that the sovereignty of West Germany remained limited. The Agreement, however, extended the rights of the German Government vis-à-vis the powers provided for in the original version of the Occupation Statute. By the General Treaty of 1955, the western allies recognized the full sovereignty of West Germany. However, in so far as the Allied High Commission was acting outside the authority of the dormant Allied Control Council, it was highly uncertain what, if any, sovereign authority it could claim over western Germany; or whether it could validly convey any sovereign authority to the new West German government.

From the 1950s, the claim that there was a single continuing German Reich whose legal status was wholly untouched by the institutions established by the Allied Powers, and that in some sense the Federal Republic and the Federal Republic alone could represent that Reich, was adopted both by the Federal Government itself and by the Federal Constitutional Court. Initially, the 1949 constitution of the German Democratic Republic adopted a mirror image version of this claim; in being framed in anticipation of a future all-German constitution on its own political terms; but all references to a wider national German nation were removed in constitutional amendments in 1968 and 1974, and from that date the GDR maintained that from 1949 there had existed two entirely separate sovereign German states. The Federal Republic's Cold-war Allies supported its claims in part, as they acknowledged the Federal Republic as the sole legitimate democratically organised state within former German territory (the GDR being held to be a Soviet puppet state); but they did not accept the associated arguments for the pre-1945 Reich's continuing 'metaphysical' existence *de jure* within the organs of the Federal Republic. Subsequently, under the *Ostpolitik*, the Federal Republic in the early 1970s sought to end hostile relations with the countries of the Eastern Bloc, in the course of which it negotiated in 1972 a Basic Treaty with the GDR, recognising it as one of two German states within one German nation, and relinquishing any claim to *de jure* sovereign jurisdiction over those parts of Germany within the GDR. The Treaty was challenged in the Federal Constitutional Court, as apparently contradicting the overriding aspirations of the Basic Law for a unified German state; but the Treaty's legality was upheld by the court, heavily qualified by a reassertion of the claim that the German Reich continued to exist as an 'overall state' such that the duty to strive for future German unity could not be abandoned, albeit that without any institutional organs of itself the Reich was currently not capable of action. The Federal Republic was indeed identical with the German Reich; but this was a 'partial identity' that stopped at the boundaries of the Federal Republic and did not extend retrospectively to the period 1945-1949 before the Federal Republic had come into being. The Western Allies took this as their cue to repudiate any support for the former claims of the Federal Republic to an exclusive mandate for Germany, all thereon recognising the GDR as a separate sovereign state and supporting the admission of both German states as equivalent members of the United Nations. In 1975 both German states participated in the Helsinki Final Act under which the existing post-war boundaries of Europe, including the separation of East and West Germany and the border between East Germany and Poland, were confirmed as legitimate in international law.

GOVERNMENT COMPOSITION AND BASIC RULES[7]

Conscious of their responsibility before God and man,

Inspired by the determination to promote world peace as an equal partner in a united Europe, the German people, in the exercise of their constituent power, have adopted this Basic Law.

Germans in the Länder of Baden-Württemberg, Bavaria, Berlin, Brandenburg, Bremen, Hamburg, Hesse, Lower Saxony, Mecklenburg-Western Pomerania, North Rhine-Westphalia, Rhineland-Palatinate, Saarland, Saxony, Saxony-Anhalt, Schleswig-Holstein, and Thuringia have achieved the unity and freedom of Germany in free self-determination. This Basic Law thus applies to the entire German people.

I. BASIC RIGHTS

Article 1 [Human dignity]

(1) Human dignity shall be inviolable. To respect and protect it shall be the duty of all state authority.
(2) The German people therefore acknowledge inviolable and inalienable human rights as the basis of every community, of peace and of justice in the world.
(3) The following basic rights shall bind the legislature, the executive, and the judiciary as directly applicable law.

Article 2 [Personal Freedoms]

(1) Every person shall have the right to free development of his personality insofar as he does not violate the rights of others or offend against the constitutional order or the moral law.
(2) Every person shall have the right to life and physical integrity. Freedom of the person shall be

[7] Basic Law of the Republic of Germeny

inviolable. These rights may be interfered with only pursuant to a law.

Article 3 [Equality before the law]

(1) All persons shall be equal before the law.
(2) Men and women shall have equal rights. The state shall promote the actual implementation of equal rights for women and men and take steps to eliminate disadvantages that now exist.
(3) No person shall be favored or disfavored because of sex, parentage, race, language, homeland and origin, faith, or religious or political opinions. No person shall be disfavored because of disability.

Article 4 [Freedom of faith, conscience, and creed]

(1) Freedom of faith and of conscience, and freedom to profess a religious or philosophical creed, shall be inviolable.
(2) The undisturbed practice of religion shall be guaranteed.
(3) No person shall be compelled against his conscience to render military service involving the use of arms. Details shall be regulated by a federal law.

Article 5 [Freedom of expression]

(1) Every person shall have the right freely to express and disseminate his opinions in speech, writing, and pictures and to inform himself without hindrance from generally accessible sources. Freedom of the press and freedom of reporting by means of broadcasts and films shall be guaranteed. There shall be no censorship.
(2) These rights shall find their limits in the provisions of general laws, in provisions for the protection of young persons, and in the right to personal honor.
(3) Art and scholarship, research, and teaching shall be free. The freedom of teaching shall not release any person from allegiance to the constitution.

Article 6 [Marriage and the family; children born outside of marriage]

(1) Marriage and the family shall enjoy the special protection of the state.
(2) The care and upbringing of children is the natural right of parents and a duty primarily incumbent upon them. The state shall watch over them in the performance of this duty.
(3) Children may be separated from their families against the will of their parents or guardians only pursuant to a law, and only if the parents or guardians fail in their duties or the children are otherwise in danger of serious neglect.
(4) Every mother shall be entitled to the protection and care of the community.
(5) Children born outside of marriage shall be provided by legislation with the same opportunities for physical and mental development and for their position in society as are enjoyed by those born within marriage.

Article 7 [School education]

(1) The entire school system shall be under the supervision of the state.
(2) Parents and guardians shall have the right to decide whether children shall receive religious instruction.
(3) Religious instruction shall form part of the regular curriculum in state schools, with the exception of non-denominational schools. Without prejudice to the state's right of supervision, religious instruction shall be given in accordance with the tenets of the religious community concerned. Teachers may not be obliged against their will to give religious instruction.
(4) The right to establish private schools shall be guaranteed. Private schools that serve as alternatives to state schools shall require the approval of the State and shall be subject to the

laws of the Länder. Such approval shall be given when private schools are not inferior to the state schools in terms of their educational aims, their facilities, or the professional training of their teaching staff, and when segregation of pupils according to the means of their parents will not be encouraged thereby. Approval shall be withheld if the economic and legal position of the teaching staff is not adequately assured.
(5) A private elementary school shall be approved only if the educational authority finds that it serves a special pedagogical interest or if, on the application of parents or guardians, it is to be established as a denominational or interdenominational school or as a school based on a particular philosophy and no state elementary school of that type exists in the municipality.
(6) Preparatory schools shall remain abolished.

Article 8 [Freedom of assembly]

(1) All Germans shall have the right to assemble peacefully and unarmed without prior notification or permission.
(2) In the case of outdoor assemblies, this right may be restricted by or pursuant to a law.

Article 9 [Freedom of association]

(1) All Germans shall have the right to form corporations and other associations.
(2) Associations whose aims or activities contravene the criminal laws, or that are directed against the constitutional order or the concept of international understanding, shall be prohibited.
(3) The right to form associations to safeguard and improve working and economic conditions shall be guaranteed to every individual and to every occupation or profession. Agreements that restrict or seek to impair this right shall be null and void; measures directed to this end shall be unlawful. Measures taken pursuant to Article 12a, to paragraphs (2) and (3) of Article 35, to paragraph (4) of Article 87a, or to Article 91 may not be directed against industrial disputes engaged in by associations within the meaning of the first sentence of this paragraph in order to safeguard and improve working and economic conditions.

Article 10 [Privacy of correspondence, posts and telecommunications]

(1) The privacy of correspondence, posts and telecommunications shall be inviolable.
(2) Restrictions may be ordered only pursuant to a law. If the restriction serves to protect the free democratic basic order or the existence or security of the Federation or of a Land, the law may provide that the person affected shall not be informed of the restriction and that recourse to the courts shall be replaced by a review of the case by agencies and auxiliary agencies appointed by the legislature.

Article 11 [Freedom of movement]

(1) All Germans shall have the right to move freely throughout the federal territory.
(2) This right may be restricted only by or pursuant to a law, and only in cases in which the absence of adequate means of support would result in a particular burden for the community, or in which such restriction is necessary to avert an imminent danger to the existence or the free democratic basic order of the Federation or of a Land, to combat the danger of an epidemic, to respond to a grave accident or natural disaster, to protect young persons from serious neglect, or to prevent crime.

Article 12 [Occupational freedom; prohibition of forced labor]

(1) All Germans shall have the right freely to choose their occupation or profession, their place of work, and their place of training. The practice of an occupation or profession may be regulated by or pursuant to a law.

(2) No person may be required to perform work of a particular kind except within the framework of a traditional duty of community service that applies generally and equally to all.
(3) Forced labor may be imposed only on persons deprived of their liberty by the judgment of a court.

Article 12a [Compulsory military or alternative service]

(1) Men who have attained the age of eighteen may be required to serve in the Armed Forces, in the Federal Border Police, or in a civil defense organization.
(2) Any person who, on grounds of conscience, refuses to render military service involving the use of arms may be required to perform alternative service. The duration of alternative service shall not exceed that of military service. Details shall be regulated by a law, which shall not interfere with the freedom to make a decision in accordance with the dictates of conscience, and which shall also provide for the possibility of alternative service not connected with units of the Armed Forces or of the Federal Border Police.
(3) Persons liable to compulsory military service who are not called upon to render service pursuant to paragraph (1) or (2) of this Article may, when a state of defense is in effect, be assigned by or pursuant to a law to employment involving civilian services for defense purposes, including the protection of the civilian population; they may be assigned to public employment only for the purpose of discharging police functions or such other sovereign functions of public administration as can be discharged only by persons employed in the public service. The employment contemplated by the first sentence of this paragraph may include services within the Armed Forces, in the provision of military supplies, or with public administrative authorities; assignments to employment connected with supplying and servicing the civilian population shall be permissible only to meet their basic requirements or to guarantee their safety.
(4) If, during a state of defense, the need for civilian services in the civilian health system or in stationary military hospitals cannot be met on a voluntary basis, women between the ages of eighteen and fifty-five may be called upon to render such services by or pursuant to a law. They may under no circumstances be required to bear weapons.
(5) Prior to the existence of a state of defense, assignments under paragraph (3) of this Article may be made only if the requirements of paragraph (1) of Article 80a are met. In preparation for the provision of services under paragraph (3) of this Article that demand special knowledge or skills, participation in training courses may be required by or pursuant to a law. In this case the first sentence of this paragraph shall not apply.
(6) If, during a state of defense, the need for workers in the areas specified in the second sentence of paragraph (3) of this Article cannot be met on a voluntary basis, the right of German citizens to abandon their occupation or place of employment may be restricted by or pursuant to a law in order to meet this need. Prior to the existence of a state of defense, the first sentence of paragraph (5) of this Article shall apply mutatis mutandis.

Article 13 [Inviolability of the home]

(1) The home is inviolable.
(2) Searches may be authorized only by a judge or, when time is of the essence, by other authorities designated by the laws, and may be carried out only in the manner therein prescribed.
(3) If particular facts justify the suspicion that any person has committed an especially serious crime specifically defined by a law, technical means of acoustical surveillance of any home in which the suspect is supposedly staying may be employed pursuant to judicial order for the purpose of prosecuting the offense, provided that alternative methods of investigating the matter would be disproportionately difficult or unproductive. The authorization shall be for a limited time. The order shall be issued by a panel composed of three judges. When time is of the essence, it may also be issued by a single judge.
(4) To avert acute dangers to public safety, especially dangers to life or to the public, technical means of surveillance of the home may be employed only pursuant to judicial order. When time is

of the essence, such measures may also be ordered by other authorities designated by a law; a judicial decision shall subsequently be obtained without delay.
(5) If technical means are contemplated solely for the protection of persons officially deployed in a home, the measure may be ordered by an authority designated by a law. The information thereby obtained may be otherwise used only for purposes of criminal prosecution or to avert danger and only if the legality of the measure has been previously determined by a judge; when time is of the essence, a judicial decision shall subsequently be obtained without delay.
(6) The Federal Government shall report to the Bundestag annually as to the employment of technical means pursuant to paragraph (3) and, within the jurisdiction of the Federation, pursuant to paragraph (4) and, insofar as judicial approval is required, pursuant to paragraph (5) of this Article. A panel elected by the Bundestag shall exercise parliamentary control on the basis of this report. A comparable parliamentary control shall be afforded by the Länder.
(7) Interferences and restrictions shall otherwise only be permissible to avert a danger to the public or to the life of an individual, or, pursuant to a law, to confront an acute danger to public safety and order, in particular to relieve a housing shortage, to combat the danger of an epidemic, or to protect young persons at risk.

Article 14 [Property, inheritance, expropriation]

(1) Property and the right of inheritance shall be guaranteed. Their content and limits shall be defined by the laws.
(2) Property entails obligations. Its use shall also serve the public good.
(3) Expropriation shall only be permissible for the public good. It may only be ordered by or pursuant to a law that determines the nature and extent of compensation. Such compensation shall be determined by establishing an equitable balance between the public interest and the interests of those affected. In case of dispute respecting the amount of compensation, recourse may be had to the ordinary courts.

Article 15 [Socialization]

Land, natural resources, and means of production may for the purpose of socialization be transferred to public ownership or other forms of public enterprise by a law that determines the nature and extent of compensation. With respect to such compensation the third and fourth sentences of paragraph (3) of Article 14 shall apply mutatis mutandis.

Article 16 [Citizenship; extradition]

(1) No German may be deprived of his citizenship. Citizenship may be lost only pursuant to a law, and against the will of the person affected only if he does not become stateless as a result.
(2) No German may be extradited to a foreign country. A different regulation to cover extradition to a Member State of the European Union or to an international court of law may be laid down by law, provided that constitutional principles are observed.

Article 16a [Right of asylum]

(1) Persons persecuted on political grounds shall have the right of asylum.
(2) Paragraph (1) of this Article may not be invoked by a person who enters the federal territory from a member state of the European Communities or from another third state in which application of the Convention Relating to the Status of Refugees and of the Convention for the Protection of Human Rights and Fundamental Freedoms is assured. The states outside the European Communities to which the criteria of the first sentence of this paragraph apply shall be specified by a law requiring the consent of the Bundesrat. In the cases specified in the first sentence of this paragraph, measures to terminate an applicant's stay may be implemented without regard to any legal challenge that may have been instituted against them.

(3) By a law requiring the consent of the Bundesrat, states may be specified in which, on the basis of their laws, enforcement practices, and general political conditions, it can be safely concluded that neither political persecution nor inhuman or degrading punishment or treatment exists. It shall be presumed that a foreigner from such a state is not persecuted, unless he presents evidence justifying the conclusion that, contrary to this presumption, he is persecuted on political grounds.
(4) In the cases specified by paragraph (3) of this Article and in other cases that are plainly unfounded or considered to be plainly unfounded, the implementation of measures to terminate an applicant's stay may be suspended by a court only if serious doubts exist as to their legality; the scope of review may be limited, and tardy objections may be disregarded. Details shall be determined by a law.
(5) Paragraphs (1) through (4) of this Article shall not preclude the conclusion of international agreements of member states of the European Communities with each other or with those third states which, with due regard for the obligations arising from the Convention Relating to the Status of Refugees and the Convention for the Protection of Human Rights and Fundamental Freedoms, whose enforcement must be assured in the contracting states, adopt rules conferring jurisdiction to decide on applications for asylum, including the reciprocal recognition of asylum decisions.

Article 17 [Right of petition]

Every person shall have the right individually or jointly with others to address written requests or complaints to competent authorities and to the legislature.

Article 17a [Restriction of certain basic rights by laws respecting defense and alternative service]

(1) Laws respecting military and alternative service may provide that the basic right of members of the Armed Forces and of alternative service freely to express and disseminate their opinions in speech, writing, and pictures (first clause of paragraph (1) of Article 5), the basic right of assembly (Article 8), and the right of petition (Article 17) insofar as it permits the submission of requests or complaints jointly with others, be restricted during their period of military or alternative service.
(2) Laws respecting defense, including protection of the civilian population, may provide for restriction of the basic rights of freedom of movement (Article 11) and inviolability of the home (Article 13).

Article 18 [Forfeiture of basic rights]

Whoever abuses the freedom of expression, in particular the freedom of the press (paragraph (1) of Article 5), the freedom of teaching (paragraph (3) of Article 5), the freedom of assembly (Article 8), the freedom of association (Article 9), the privacy of correspondence, posts and telecommunications (Article 10), the rights of property (Article 14), or the right of asylum (Article 16a) in order to combat the free democratic basic order shall forfeit these basic rights. This forfeiture and its extent shall be declared by the Federal Constitutional Court.

Article 19 [Restriction of basic rights]

(1) Insofar as, under this Basic Law, a basic right may be restricted by or pursuant to a law, such law must apply generally and not merely to a single case. In addition, the law must specify the basic right affected and the Article in which it appears.
(2) In no case may the essence of a basic right be affected.
(3) The basic rights shall also apply to domestic artificial persons to the extent that the nature of such rights permits.

(4) Should any person's rights be violated by public authority, he may have recourse to the courts. If no other jurisdiction has been established, recourse shall be to the ordinary courts. The second sentence of paragraph (2) of Article 10 shall not be affected by this paragraph.

II. THE FEDERATION AND THE LÄNDER

Article 20 [Basic institutional principles; defense of the constitutional order]

(1) The Federal Republic of Germany is a democratic and social federal state.
(2) All state authority is derived from the people. It shall be exercised by the people through elections and other votes and through specific legislative, executive, and judicial bodies.
(3) The legislature shall be bound by the constitutional order, the executive and the judiciary by law and justice.

(4) All Germans shall have the right to resist any person seeking to abolish this constitutional order, if no other remedy is available.

Article 20a [Protection of the natural bases of life]

(1) Every person shall have the right to free development of his personality insofar as he does not violate the rights of others or offend against the constitutional order or the moral law.
(2) Every person shall have the right to life and physical integrity. Freedom of the person shall be inviolable. These rights may be interfered with only pursuant to a law.

Mindful also of its responsibility toward future generations, the state shall protect the natural bases of life by legislation and, in accordance with law and justice, by executive and judicial action, all within the framework of the constitutional order.

Article 21 [Political parties]

(1) Political parties shall participate in the formation of the political will of the people. They may be freely established. Their internal organization must conform to democratic principles. They must publicly account for their assets and for the sources and use of their funds.
(2) Parties that, by reason of their aims or the behavior of their adherents, seek to undermine or abolish the free democratic basic order or to endanger the existence of the Federal Republic of Germany shall be unconstitutional. The Federal Constitutional Court shall rule on the question of unconstitutionality.
(3) Details shall be regulated by federal laws.

Article 22 [The flag]

The federal flag shall be black, red, and gold.

Article 23 [The European Union]

(1) With a view to establishing a united Europe, the Federal Republic of Germany shall participate in the development of the European Union that is committed to democratic, social, and federal principles, to the rule of law, and to the principle of subsidiarity, and that guarantees a level of protection of basic rights essentially comparable to that afforded by this Basic Law. To this end the Federation may transfer sovereign powers by a law with the consent of the Bundesrat. The establishment of the European Union, as well as changes in its treaty foundations and comparable regulations that amend or supplement this Basic Law, or make such amendments or supplements possible, shall be subject to paragraphs (2) and (3) of Article 79.

(2) The Bundestag and, through the Bundesrat, the Länder shall participate in matters concerning the European Union. The Federal Government shall keep the Bundestag and the Bundesrat informed, comprehensively and at the earliest possible time.
(3) Before participating in legislative acts of the European Union, the Federal Government shall provide the Bundestag with an opportunity to state its position. The Federal Government shall take the position of the Bundestag into account during the negotiations. Details shall be regulated by a law.
(4) The Bundesrat shall participate in the decision-making process of the Federation insofar as it would have been competent to do so in a comparable domestic matter, or insofar as the subject falls within the domestic competence of the Länder.
(5) Insofar as, in an area within the exclusive competence of the Federation, interests of the Länder are affected, and in other matters, insofar as the Federation has legislative power, the Federal Government shall take the position of the Bundesrat into account. To the extent that the legislative powers of the Länder, the structure of Land authorities, or Land administrative procedures are primarily affected, the position of the Bundesrat shall be given the greatest possible respect in determining the Federation's position consistent with the responsibility of the Federation for the nation as a whole. In matters that may result in increased expenditures or reduced revenues for the Federation, the consent of the Federal Government shall be required.
(6) When legislative powers exclusive to the Länder are primarily affected, the exercise of the rights belonging to the Federal Republic of Germany as a member state of the European Union shall be delegated to a representative of the Länder designated by the Bundesrat. These rights shall be exercised with the participation and concurrence of the Federal Government; their exercise shall be consistent with the responsibility of the Federation for the nation as a whole.
(7) Details respecting paragraphs (4) through (6) of this Article shall be regulated by a law requiring the consent of the Bundesrat.

Article 24 [International organizations]

(1) The Federation may by a law transfer sovereign powers to international organizations.
(1a) Insofar as the Länder are competent to exercise state powers and to perform state functions, they may, with the consent of the Federal Government, transfer sovereign powers to transfrontier institutions in neighboring regions.
(2) With a view to maintaining peace, the Federation may enter into a system of mutual collective security; in doing so it shall consent to such limitations upon its sovereign powers as will bring about and secure a lasting peace in Europe and among the nations of the world.
(3) For the settlement of disputes between states, the Federation shall accede to agreements providing for general, comprehensive, and compulsory international arbitration.

Article 25 [International law and federal law]

The general rules of international law shall be an integral part of federal law. They shall take precedence over the laws and directly create rights and duties for the inhabitants of the federal territory.

Article 26 [Ban on preparations for war of aggression]

(1) Acts tending to and undertaken with intent to disturb the peaceful relations between nations, especially to prepare for a war of aggression, shall be unconstitutional. They shall be made a criminal offense.
(2) Weapons designed for warfare may be manufactured, transported, or marketed only with the permission of the Federal Government. Details shall be regulated by a federal law.

Article 27 [Merchant fleet]

All German merchant vessels shall constitute a unitary merchant fleet.

Article 28 [Federal guarantee of Land constitutions and of local self-government]

(1) The constitutional order in the Länder must conform to the principles of a republican, democratic, and social state governed by the rule of law, within the meaning of this Basic Law. In each Land, county, and municipality the people shall be represented by a body chosen in general, direct, free, equal, and secret elections. In county and municipal elections, persons who possess citizenship in any member state of the European Community are also eligible to vote and to be elected in accord with European Community law. In municipalities a local assembly may take the place of an elected body.
(2) Municipalities must be guaranteed the right to regulate all local affairs on their own responsibility, within the limits prescribed by the laws. Within the limits of their functions designated by a law, associations of municipalities shall also have the right of self-government according to the laws. The guarantee of self-government shall extend to the bases of financial autonomy; these bases shall include the right of municipalities to a source of tax revenues based upon economic ability and the right to establish the rates at which these sources shall be taxed.
(3) The Federation shall guarantee that the constitutional order of the Länder conforms to the basic rights and to the provisions of paragraphs (1) and (2) of this Article.

Article 29 [New delimitation of the Länder]

(1) The division of the federal territory into Länder may be revised to ensure that each Land be of a size and capacity to perform its functions effectively. Due regard shall be given in this connection to regional, historical, and cultural ties, economic efficiency, and the requirements of local and regional planning.
(2) Revisions of the existing division into Länder shall be effected by a federal law, which must be confirmed by referendum. The affected Länder shall be afforded an opportunity to be heard.
(3) The referendum shall be held in the Länder from whose territories or parts of territories a new Land or a Land with redefined boundaries is to be established (affected Länder). The question to be voted on is whether the affected Länder are to remain as they are or whether the new Land or the Land with redefined boundaries should be established. The proposal to establish a new Land or a Land with redefined boundaries shall take effect if the change is approved by a majority in the future territory of such Land and by a majority in the territories or parts of territories of an affected Land taken together whose affiliation with a Land is to be changed in the same way. The proposal shall not take effect if within the territory of any of the affected Länder a majority reject the change; however, such rejection shall be of no consequence if in any part of the territory whose affiliation with the affected Land is to be changed a two-thirds majority approves the change, unless it is rejected by a two-thirds majority in the territory of the affected Land as a whole.
(4) If in any clearly defined and contiguous residential and economic area located in two or more Länder and having at least one million inhabitants one tenth of those entitled to vote in Bundestag elections petition for the inclusion of that area in a single Land, a federal law shall specify within two years whether the change shall be made in accordance with paragraph (2) of this Article or that an advisory referendum shall be held in the affected Länder.
(5) The advisory referendum shall establish whether the changes the law proposes meet with the voters' approval. The law may put forward not more than two distinct proposals for consideration by the voters. If a majority approves a proposed change of the existing division into Länder, a federal law shall specify within two years whether the change shall be made in accordance with paragraph (2) of this Article. If a proposal is approved in accordance with the third and fourth sentences of paragraph (3) of this Article, a federal law providing for establishment of the proposed Land shall be enacted within two years after the advisory ballot, and confirmation by referendum shall no longer be required.
(6) A majority in a referendum or in an advisory referendum shall consist of a majority of the votes

cast, provided that it amounts to at least one quarter of those entitled to vote in Bundestag elections. Other details respecting referenda, petitions, and advisory referenda shall be regulated by a federal law, which may also provide that the same petition may not be filed more than once within a period of five years.
(7) Other changes respecting the territory of the Länder may be effected by agreements between the Länder concerned or by a federal law with the consent of the Bundesrat, if the territory that is to be the subject of the change has no more than 50,000 inhabitants. Details shall be regulated by a federal law requiring the consent of the Bundesrat and of a majority of the Members of the Bundestag. The law must provide affected municipalities and counties with an opportunity to be heard.
(8) Länder may revise the division of their existing territory or parts of their territory by agreement without regard to the provisions of paragraphs (2) through (7) of this Article. Affected municipalities and counties shall be afforded an opportunity to be heard. The agreement shall require confirmation by referendum in each of the Länder concerned. If the revision affects only part of a Land's territory, the referendum may be confined to the areas affected; the second clause of the fifth sentence shall not apply. In a referendum under this paragraph a majority of the votes cast shall be decisive, provided it amounts to at least one quarter of those entitled to vote in Bundestag elections; details shall be regulated by a federal law. The agreement shall require the consent of the Bundestag.

Article 30 [Division of authority between the Federation and the Länder]

Except as otherwise provided or permitted by this Basic Law, the exercise of state powers and the discharge of state functions is a matter for the Länder.

Article 31 [Supremacy of federal law]

Federal law shall take precedence over Land law.

Article 32 [Foreign relations]

(1) Relations with foreign states shall be conducted by the Federation.
(2) Before the conclusion of a treaty affecting the special circumstances of a Land, that Land shall be consulted in timely fashion.
(3) Insofar as the Länder have power to legislate, they may conclude treaties with foreign states with the consent of the Federal Government.

Article 33 [Equal citizenship; professional civil service]

(1) Every German shall have in every Land the same political rights and duties.
(2) Every German shall be equally eligible for any public office according to his aptitude, qualifications, and professional achievements.
(3) Neither the enjoyment of civil and political rights, nor eligibility for public office, nor rights acquired in the public service shall be dependent upon religious affiliation. No one may be disadvantaged by reason of adherence or nonadherence to a particular religious denomination or philosophical creed.
(4) The exercise of sovereign authority on a regular basis shall, as a rule, be entrusted to members of the public service who stand in a relationship of service and loyalty defined by public law.
(5) The law governing the public service shall be regulated with due regard to the traditional principles of the professional civil service.

Article 34 [Liability for violation of official duty]

If any person, in the exercise of a public office entrusted to him, violates his official duty to a third party, liability shall rest principally with the state or public body that employs him. In the event of intentional wrongdoing or gross negligence, the right of recourse against the individual officer shall be preserved. The ordinary courts shall not be closed to claims for compensation or indemnity.

Article 35 [Legal and administrative assistance; assistance during disasters]

(1) All federal and Land authorities shall render legal and administrative assistance to one another.
(2) In order to maintain or restore public security or order, a Land in particularly serious cases may call upon personnel and facilities of the Federal Border Police to assist its police when without such assistance the police could not fulfill their responsibilities, or could do so only with great difficulty. In order to respond to a grave accident or a natural disaster, a Land may call for the assistance of police forces of other Länder or of personnel and facilities of other administrative authorities, of the Armed Forces, or of the Federal Border Police.
(3) If the natural disaster or accident endangers the territory of more than one Land, the Federal Government, insofar as is necessary to combat the danger, may instruct the Land governments to place police forces at the disposal of other Länder, and may deploy units of the Federal Border Police or the Armed Forces to support the police. Measures taken by the Federal Government pursuant to the first sentence of this paragraph shall be rescinded at any time at the demand of the Bundesrat, and in any event as soon as the danger is removed.

Article 36 [Personnel of federal authorities]

(1) Civil servants employed by the highest federal authorities shall be drawn from all Länder in appropriate proportion. Persons employed by other federal authorities shall, as a rule, be drawn from the Land in which they serve.
(2) Laws respecting military service shall also take into account both the division of the Federation into Länder and the regional loyalties of their people.

Article 37 [Federal execution]

(1) If a Land fails to comply with its obligations under this Basic Law or other federal laws, the Federal Government, with the consent of the Bundesrat, may take the necessary steps to compel the Land to comply with its duties.
(2) For the purpose of implementing such coercive measures, the Federal Government or its representative shall have the right to issue instructions to all Länder and their authorities.

III. THE BUNDESTAG

Article 38 [Elections]

(1) Members of the German Bundestag shall be elected in general, direct, free, equal, and secret elections. They shall be representatives of the whole people, not bound by orders or instructions, and responsible only to their conscience.
(2) Any person who has attained the age of eighteen shall be entitled to vote; any person who has attained the age of majority may be elected.
(3) Details shall be regulated by a federal law.

Article 39 [Convening and legislative term]

(1) Save the following provisions, the Bundestag shall be elected for four years. Its term shall end when a new Bundestag convenes. New elections shall be held no sooner than forty-six months and no later than forty-eight months after the legislative term begins. If the Bundestag is dissolved, new elections shall be held within sixty days.
(2) The Bundestag shall convene no later than the thirtieth day after the elections are held.
(3) The Bundestag shall determine when its sessions shall be adjourned and resumed. The President of the Bundestag may convene it at an earlier date. He shall be obliged to do so if one third of the Members, the Federal President or the Federal Chancellor so demand.

Article 40 [President; rules of procedure]

(1) The Bundestag shall elect its President, Vice-Presidents, and secretaries. It shall adopt rules of procedure.
(2) The President shall exercise proprietary and police powers in the Bundestag building. No search or seizure may take place on the premises of the Bundestag without his permission.

Article 41 [Scrutiny of elections]

(1) Scrutiny of elections shall be the responsibility of the Bundestag. It shall also decide whether a Member has lost his seat.
(2) Complaints against such decisions of the Bundestag may be lodged with the Federal Constitutional Court.
(3) Details shall be regulated by a federal law.

Article 42 [Proceedings; voting]

(1) Sessions of the Bundestag shall be public. On the motion of one tenth of its Members, or on the motion of the Federal Government, the public may be excluded by a two-thirds majority. The motion shall be voted upon at a session not open to the public.
(2) Decisions of the Bundestag shall require a majority of the votes cast unless this Basic Law otherwise provides. The rules of procedure may permit exceptions with respect to elections to be conducted by the Bundestag.
(3) Truthful reports of public sessions of the Bundestag and of its committees shall not give rise to any liability.

Article 43 [Attendance of members of the Federal Government and of the Bundesrat]

(1) The Bundestag and its committees may require the appearance of any member of the Federal Government.
(2) The members of the Bundesrat and of the Federal Government as well as their representatives may attend all sessions of the Bundestag and of its committees. They shall have the right to be heard at any time.

Article 44 [Investigative committees]

(1) The Bundestag shall have the right, and on the motion of one quarter of its Members the duty, to establish an investigative committee, which shall take the requisite evidence at public hearings.

The public may be excluded.
(2) The rules of criminal procedure shall apply mutatis mutandis to the taking of evidence. The privacy of correspondence, posts and telecommunications shall not be affected.
(3) Courts and administrative authorities shall be required to provide legal and administrative assistance.
(4) The decisions of investigative committees shall not be subject to judicial review. The courts shall be free to evaluate and rule upon the facts that were the subject of the investigation.

Article 45 [Committee on the European Union]

The Bundestag shall appoint a Committee on European Union Affairs. It may authorize the committee to exercise the rights of the Bundestag under Article 23 vis-à-vis the Federal Government.

Article 45a [Committees on Foreign Affairs and Defense]

(1) The Bundestag shall appoint a Committee on Foreign Affairs and a Committee on Defense.
(2) The Committee on Defense shall also have the powers of an investigative committee. On the motion of one quarter of its members it shall have the duty to make a specific matter the subject of investigation.
(3) Paragraph (1) of Article 44 shall not apply to defense matters.

Article 45b [Parliamentary Commissioner for the Armed Forces]

A Parliamentary Commissioner for the Armed Forces shall be appointed to safeguard basic rights and to assist the Bundestag in exercising parliamentary control over the Armed Forces. Details shall be regulated by a federal law.

Article 45c [Petitions Committee]

(1) The Bundestag shall appoint a Petitions Committee to deal with requests and complaints addressed to the Bundestag pursuant to Article 17.
(2) The powers of the Committee to consider complaints shall be regulated by a federal law.

Article 46 [Immunities]

(1) At no time may a Member be subjected to court proceedings or disciplinary action or otherwise called to account outside the Bundestag for a vote cast or for any speech or debate in the Bundestag or in any of its committees. This provision shall not apply to defamatory insults.
(2) A Member may not be called to account or arrested for a punishable offense without permission of the Bundestag, unless he is apprehended while committing the offense or in the course of the following day.
(3) The permission of the Bundestag shall also be required for any other restriction of a Member's freedom of the person or for the initiation of proceedings against a Member under Article 18.
(4) Any criminal proceedings or any proceedings under Article 18 against a Member and any detention or other restriction of the freedom of his person shall be suspended at the demand of the Bundestag.

Article 47 [Right not to give evidence]

Members may refuse to give evidence concerning persons who have confided information to them in their capacity as Members of the Bundestag, or to whom they have confided information in this capacity, as well as evidence concerning this information itself. To the extent that this right of refusal to give evidence applies, no seizure of documents shall be permissible.

Article 48 [Entitlements of Members]

(1) Every candidate for election to the Bundestag shall be entitled to the leave necessary for his election campaign.
(2) No one may be prevented from accepting or exercising the office of Member of the Bundestag. No one may be given notice of dismissal or discharged from employment on this ground.
(3) Members shall be entitled to remuneration adequate to ensure their independence. They shall be entitled to the free use of all publicly owned means of transport. Details shall be regulated by a federal law.

Article 49 [Repealed]

[Repealed]

IV. THE BUNDESRAT

Article 50 [Functions]

The Länder shall participate through the Bundesrat in the legislation and administration of the Federation and in matters concerning the European Union.

Article 51 [Composition]

(1) The Bundesrat shall consist of members of the Land governments, which appoint and recall them. Other members of those governments may serve as alternates.

(2) Each Land shall have at least three votes; Länder with more than two million inhabitants shall have four, Länder with more than six million inhabitants five, and Länder with more than seven million inhabitants six votes.
(3) Each Land may appoint as many members as it has votes. The votes of each Land may be cast only as a unit and only by Members present or their alternates.

Article 52 [President; rules of procedure]

(1) The Bundesrat shall elect its President for one year.
(2) The President shall convene the Bundesrat. He shall be obliged to do so if the delegates of at least two Länder or the Federal Government so demand.
(3) Decisions of the Bundesrat shall require at least a majority of its votes. It shall adopt rules of procedure. Its sessions shall be public. The public may be excluded.
(3a) For matters concerning the European Union the Bundesrat may establish a Chamber for European Affairs whose decisions shall be considered decisions of the Bundesrat; paragraph (2) and the second sentence of paragraph (3) of Article 51 shall apply mutatis mutandis.
(4) Other members or representatives of Land governments may serve on committees of the Bundesrat.

Article 53 [Attendance of members of the Federal Government]

The members of the Federal Government shall have the right, and on demand the duty, to participate in sessions of the Bundesrat and of its committees. They shall have the right to be heard at any time. The Bundesrat shall be kept informed by the Federal Government with regard to the conduct of its affairs.

IVA. THE JOINT COMMITTEE

Article 53a [Composition; rules of procedure; right to information]

(1) The Joint Committee shall consist of Members of the Bundestag and Members of the Bundesrat; the Bundestag shall provide two thirds and the Bundesrat one third of the committee members. The Bundestag shall designate Members in proportion to the relative strength of the various parliamentary groups; they may not be members of the Federal Government. Each Land shall be represented by a Bundesrat Member of its choice; these Members shall not be bound by instructions. The establishment of the Joint Committee and its proceedings shall be regulated by rules of procedure to be adopted by the Bundestag and requiring the consent of the Bundesrat.

(2) The Federal Government shall inform the Joint Committee about its plans for a state of defense. The rights of the Bundestag and its committees under paragraph (1) of Article 43 shall not be affected by the provisions of this paragraph.

V. THE FEDERAL PRESIDENT

Article 54 [Election]

(1) The Federal President shall be elected by the Federal Convention without debate. Any German who is entitled to vote in Bundestag elections and has attained the age of forty may be elected.
(2) The term of office of the Federal President shall be five years. Reelection for a consecutive term shall be permitted only once.
(3) The Federal Convention shall consist of the Members of the Bundestag and an equal number of members elected by the parliaments of the Länder on the basis of proportional representation.
(4) The Federal Convention shall meet not later than thirty days before the term of office of the Federal President expires or, in the case of premature termination, not later than thirty days after that date. It shall be convened by the President of the Bundestag.
(5) After the expiration of a legislative term, the period specified in the first sentence of paragraph (4) of this Article shall begin when the Bundestag first convenes.
(6) The person receiving the votes of a majority of the members of the Federal Convention shall be elected. If after two ballots no candidate has obtained such a majority, the person who receives the largest number of votes on the next ballot shall be elected.
(7) Details shall be regulated by a federal law.

Article 55 [Incompatibility]

(1) The Federal President may not be a member of the government or of a legislative body of the Federation or of a Land.
(2) The Federal President may not hold any other salaried office, or engage in any trade or profession, or belong to the management or supervisory board of any enterprise conducted for profit.

Article 56 [Oath of office]

On assuming his office, the Federal President shall take the following oath before the assembled Members of the Bundestag and the Bundesrat:
"I swear that I will dedicate my efforts to the well-being of the German people, promote their welfare, protect them from harm, uphold and defend the Basic Law and the laws of the Federation, perform my duties conscientiously, and do justice to all. So help me God."
The oath may also be taken without religious affirmation.

Article 57 [Disability or vacancy]

If the Federal President is unable to perform his duties, or if his office falls prematurely vacant, the President of the Bundesrat shall exercise his powers.

Article 58 [Countersignature]

Orders and directions of the Federal President shall require for their validity the countersignature of the Federal Chancellor or of the competent Federal Minister. This provision shall not apply to the appointment or dismissal of the Federal Chancellor, the dissolution of the Bundestag under Article 63, or a request made under paragraph (3) of Article 69.

Article 59 [Representation of the Federation]

(1) The Federal President shall represent the Federation in terms of international law. He shall conclude treaties with foreign states on behalf of the Federation. He shall accredit and receive envoys.
(2) Treaties that regulate the political relations of the Federation or relate to subjects of federal legislation shall require the consent or participation, in the form of a federal law, of the bodies responsible in such a case for the enactment of federal law. In the case of executive agreements the provisions concerning the federal administration shall apply mutatis mutandis.

Article 59a [Repealed]

Article 60 [Appointment and dismissal of federal judges, federal civil servants, and military officers; pardon]

(1) The Federal President shall appoint and dismiss federal judges, federal civil servants, and commissioned and noncommissioned officers of the Armed Forces, except as may otherwise be provided by a law.
(2) He shall exercise the power to pardon individual offenders on behalf of the Federation.
(3) He may delegate these powers to other authorities.
(4) Paragraphs (2) to (4) of Article 46 shall apply to the Federal President mutatis mutandis.

Article 61 [Impeachment before the Federal Constitutional Court]

(1) The Bundestag or the Bundesrat may impeach the Federal President before the Federal Constitutional Court for willful violation of this Basic Law or of any other federal law. The motion of impeachment must be supported by at least one quarter of the Members of the Bundestag or one quarter of the votes of the Bundesrat. The decision to impeach shall require a majority of two thirds of the Members of the Bundestag or of two thirds of the votes of the Bundesrat. The case for impeachment shall be presented before the Federal Constitutional Court by a person commissioned by the impeaching body.

(2) If the Federal Constitutional Court finds the Federal President guilty of a willful violation of this Basic Law or of any other federal law, it may declare that he has forfeited his office. After the Federal President has been impeached, the Court may issue an interim order preventing him from exercising his functions.

VI. THE FEDERAL GOVERNMENT

Article 62 [Composition]

The Federal Government shall consist of the Federal Chancellor and the Federal Ministers.

Article 63 [Election and appointment of the Federal Chancellor]

(1) The Federal Chancellor shall be elected by the Bundestag without debate on the proposal of the Federal President.
(2) The person who receives the votes of a majority of the Members of the Bundestag shall be elected. The person elected shall be appointed by the Federal President.
(3) If the person proposed by the Federal President is not elected, the Bundestag may elect a Federal Chancellor within fourteen days after the ballot by the votes of more than one half of its Members.
(4) If no Federal Chancellor is elected within this period, a new election shall take place without delay, in which the person who receives the largest number of votes shall be elected. If the person elected receives the votes of a majority of the Members of the Bundestag, the Federal President must appoint him within seven days after the election. If the person elected does not receive such a majority, then within seven days the Federal President shall either appoint him or dissolve the Bundestag.

Article 64 [Appointment and dismissal of Federal Ministers]

(1) Federal Ministers shall be appointed and dismissed by the Federal President upon the proposal of the Federal Chancellor.
(2) On taking office the Federal Chancellor and the Federal Ministers shall take the oath provided for in Article 56 before the Bundestag.

Article 65 [Authority within the Federal Government]

The Federal Chancellor shall determine and be responsible for the general guidelines of policy. Within these limits each Federal Minister shall conduct the affairs of his department independently and on his own responsibility. The Federal Government shall resolve differences of opinion between Federal Ministers. The Federal Chancellor shall conduct the proceedings of the Federal Government in accordance with rules of procedure adopted by the Government and approved by the Federal President.

Article 65a [Command of the Armed Forces]

Command of the Armed Forces shall be vested in the Federal Minister of Defense.

Article 66 [Incompatibility]

Neither the Federal Chancellor nor a Federal Minister may hold any other salaried office, or engage in any trade or profession, or belong to the management or, without the consent of the Bundestag, to the supervisory board of an enterprise conducted for profit.

Article 67 [Constructive vote of no confidence]

(1) The Bundestag may express its lack of confidence in the Federal Chancellor only by electing a successor by the vote of a majority of its Members and requesting the Federal President to dismiss the Federal Chancellor. The Federal President must comply with the request and appoint the person elected.
(2) Forty-eight hours shall elapse between the motion and the election.

Article 68 [Vote of confidence; dissolution of the Bundestag]

(1) If a motion of the Federal Chancellor for a vote of confidence is not supported by the majority of the Members of the Bundestag, the Federal President, upon the proposal of the Federal Chancellor, may dissolve the Bundestag within twenty-one days. The right of dissolution shall lapse as soon as the Bundestag elects another Federal Chancellor by the vote of a majority of its Members.
(2) Forty-eight hours shall elapse between the motion and the vote.

Article 69 [Deputy Federal Chancellor; tenure of members of the Federal Government]

(1) The Federal Chancellor shall appoint a Federal Minister as his deputy.
(2) The tenure of office of the Federal Chancellor or of a Federal Minister shall end in any event when a new Bundestag convenes; the tenure of office of a Federal Minister shall also end on any other occasion on which the Federal Chancellor ceases to hold office.
(3) At the request of the Federal President the Federal Chancellor, or at the request of the Federal Chancellor or of the Federal President a Federal Minister, shall be obliged to continue to manage the affairs of his office until a successor is appointed.

VII. LEGISLATIVE POWERS OF THE FEDERATION

Article 70 [Division of legislative powers between the Federation and the Länder]

(1) The Länder shall have the right to legislate insofar as this Basic Law does not confer legislative power on the Federation.
(2) The division of authority between the Federation and the Länder shall be governed by the provisions of this Basic Law respecting exclusive and concurrent legislative powers.

Article 71 [Exclusive legislative power of the Federation: definition]

On matters within the exclusive legislative power of the Federation, the Länder shall have power to legislate only when and to the extent that they are expressly authorized to do so by a federal law.

Article 72 [Concurrent legislative power of the Federation: definition]

(1) On matters within the concurrent legislative power, the Länder shall have power to legislate so long as and to the extent that the Federation has not exercised its legislative power by enacting a law.

(2) The Federation shall have the right to legislate on these matters if and to the extent that the establishment of equal living conditions throughout the federal territory or the maintenance of legal or economic unity renders federal regulation necessary in the national interest.
(3) A federal law may provide that federal legislation that is no longer necessary within the meaning of paragraph (2) of this Article may be superseded by Land law.

Article 73 [Subjects of exclusive legislative power]

The Federation shall have exclusive power to legislate with respect to

1. foreign affairs and defense, including protection of the civilian population;
2. citizenship in the Federation;
3. freedom of movement, passports, immigration, emigration, and extradition;
4. currency, money, and coinage, weights and measures, and the determination of standards of time;
5. the unity of the customs and trading area, treaties respecting commerce and navigation, the free movement of goods, and the exchange of goods and payments with foreign countries, including customs and border protection;
6. air transport;
6a. the operation of railways wholly or predominantly owned by the Federation (federal railways), the construction, maintenance, and operation of tracks belonging to federal railways as well as the imposition of charges for the use of such tracks;
7. postal and telecommunication services;
8. the legal relations of persons employed by the Federation and by federal corporations under public law;
9. industrial property rights, copyrights, and publishing;
10. cooperation between the Federation and the Länder concerning
(a) criminal police work,
(b) protection of the free democratic basic order, existence, and security of the Federation or of a Land (protection of the constitution), and
(c) protection against activities within the federal territory which, by the use of force or preparations for the use of force, endanger the external interests of the Federal Republic of Germany, as well as the establishment of a Federal Criminal Police Office and international action to combat crime;
11. statistics for federal purposes.

Article 74 [Subjects of concurrent legislation]

(1) Concurrent legislative powers shall extend to the following subjects:

1.	civil law, criminal law, and corrections, court organization and procedure, the legal profession, notaries, and the provision of legal advice;
2.	registration of births, deaths, and marriages;
3.	the law of association and assembly;

4.	the law relating to residence and establishment of aliens;
4a.	the law relating to weapons and explosives;
5.	[repealed]
6.	matters concerning refugees and expellees;
7.	public welfare;
8.	[repealed]
9.	war damage and reparations;
10.	benefits for persons disabled by war and for dependents of deceased war victims as well as assistance to former prisoners of war;
10a.	war graves and graves of other victims of war or despotism;
11.	the law relating to economic affairs (mining, industry, energy, crafts, trades, commerce, banking, stock exchanges, and private insurance);
11a.	the production and utilization of nuclear energy for peaceful purposes, the construction and operation of facilities serving such purposes, protection against hazards arising from the release of nuclear energy or from ionizing radiation, and the disposal of radioactive substances;
12.	labor law, including the organization of enterprises, occupational safety and health, and employment agencies, as well as social security, including unemployment insurance;
13.	the regulation of educational and training grants and the promotion of research;
14.	the law regarding expropriation, to the extent relevant to matters enumerated in Articles 73 and 74;
15.	the transfer of land, natural resources, and means of production to public ownership or other forms of public enterprise;

16.	prevention of the abuse of economic power;
17.	the promotion of agricultural production and forestry, ensuring the adequacy of the food supply, the importation and exportation of agricultural and forestry products, deep-sea and coastal fishing, and preservation of the coasts;
18.	real estate transactions, land law (except for laws respecting development fees), and matters concerning agricultural leases, as well as housing, settlement, and homestead matters;
19.	measures to combat dangerous and communicable human and animal diseases, admission to the medical profession and to ancillary professions or occupations, as well as trade in medicines, drugs, narcotics, and poisons;
19a.	the economic viability of hospitals and the regulation of hospital charges;
20.	protective measures in connection with the marketing of food, drink, and tobacco, essential commodities, feedstuffs, agricultural and forest seeds and seedlings, and protection of plants against diseases and pests, as well as the protection of animals;
21.	maritime and coastal shipping, as well as navigational aids, inland navigation, meteorological services, sea routes, and inland waterways used for general traffic;
22.	road traffic, motor transport, construction and maintenance of long-distance highways, as well as the collection of tolls for the use of public highways by vehicles and the allocation of the revenue;
23.	non-federal railways, except mountain railways;
24.	waste disposal, air pollution control, and noise abatement;
25.	state liability;
26.	human artificial insemination, analysis and modification of genetic information, as well as the regulation of organ and tissue transplantation.

Laws adopted pursuant to clause 25 of paragraph (1) of this Article shall require the consent of the Bundesrat.

Article 74a [Concurrent legislative power of the Federation: remuneration, pensions, and related benefits of members of the public service]

(1) Concurrent legislative power shall also extend to the remuneration, pensions, and related benefits of members of the public service who stand in a relationship of service and loyalty defined by public law, insofar as the Federation does not have exclusive legislative power pursuant to clause 8 of Article 73.
(2) Federal laws enacted pursuant to paragraph (1) of this Article shall require the consent of the Bundesrat.
(3) Federal laws enacted pursuant to clause 8 of Article 73 shall likewise require the consent of the Bundesrat, insofar as they contemplate standards for the structure or computation of remuneration, pensions, and related benefits including the classification of positions, or minimum or maximum rates, that differ from those provided for in federal laws enacted pursuant to paragraph (1) of this Article.
(4) Paragraphs (1) and (2) of this Article shall apply mutatis mutandis to the remuneration, pensions, and related benefits of judges of the Länder. Paragraph (3) of this Article shall apply mutatis mutandis to laws enacted pursuant to paragraph (1) of Article 98.

Article 75 [Areas of federal framework legislation]

(1) Subject to the conditions laid down in Article 72, the Federation shall have power to enact provisions on the following subjects as a framework for Land legislation

1.	the legal relations of persons in the public service of the Länder, municipalities, or other corporate bodies under public law, insofar as Article 74a does not otherwise provide;
1a.	general principles respecting higher education;
2.	the general legal relations of the press;
3.	hunting, nature conservation, and landscape management;
4.	land distribution, regional planning, and the management of water resources;
5.	matters relating to the registration of residence or domicile and to identity cards;
6.	measures to prevent expatriation of German cultural assets.

Paragraph (3) of Article 72 shall apply mutatis mutandis.
(2) Only in exceptional circumstances may framework legislation contain detailed or directly

applicable provisions.
(3) When the Federation enacts framework legislation, the Länder shall be obliged to adopt the necessary Land laws within a reasonable period prescribed by the law.

Article 76 [Bills]

(1) Bills may be introduced in the Bundestag by the Federal Government, by the Bundesrat, or from the floor of the Bundestag.
(2) Federal Government bills shall first be submitted to the Bundesrat. The Bundesrat shall be entitled to comment on such bills within six weeks. If for important reasons, especially with respect to the scope of the bill, the Bundesrat demands an extension, the period shall be increased to nine weeks. If in exceptional circumstances the Federal Government on submitting a bill to the Bundesrat declares it to be particularly urgent, it may submit the bill to the Bundestag after three weeks or, if the Bundesrat has demanded an extension pursuant to the third sentence of this paragraph, after six weeks, even if it has not yet received the Bundesrat's comments; upon receiving such comments, it shall transmit them to the Bundestag without delay. In the case of bills to amend this Basic Law or to transfer sovereign powers pursuant to Article 23 or 24 the comment period shall be nine weeks; the fourth sentence of this paragraph shall not apply.
(3) Bundesrat bills shall be submitted to the Bundestag by the Federal Government within six weeks. In submitting them the Federal Government shall state its own views. If for important reasons, especially with respect to the scope of the bill, the Federal Government demands an extension, the period shall be increased to nine weeks. If in exceptional circumstances the Bundesrat declares a bill to be particularly urgent, the period shall be three weeks or, if the Federal Government has demanded an extension pursuant to the third sentence of this paragraph, six weeks. In the case of bills to amend this Basic Law or to transfer sovereign powers pursuant to Article 23 or 24 the comment period shall be nine weeks; the fourth sentence of this paragraph shall not apply. The Bundestag shall consider and vote on bills within a reasonable time.

Article 77 [The legislative process]

(1) Federal laws shall be adopted by the Bundestag. After their adoption the President of the Bundestag shall submit them to the Bundesrat without delay.
(2) Within three weeks after receiving an adopted bill, the Bundesrat may demand that a committee for joint consideration of bills, composed of Members of the Bundestag and of the Bundesrat, be convened. The composition and proceedings of this committee shall be regulated by rules of procedure adopted by the Bundestag and requiring the consent of the Bundesrat. The Members of the Bundesrat on this committee shall not be bound by instructions. When the consent of the Bundesrat is required for a bill to become law, the Bundestag and the Federal Government may likewise demand that such a committee be convened. Should the committee propose any amendment to the adopted bill, the Bundestag shall vote on it a second time.
(2a) Insofar as its consent is required for a bill to become law, the Bundesrat, if no request has been made pursuant to the first sentence of paragraph (2) of this Article or if the mediation proceeding has been completed without a proposal to amend the bill, shall vote on the bill within a reasonable time.
(3) Insofar as its consent is not required for a bill to become law, the Bundesrat, once proceedings under paragraph (2) of this Article are completed, may within two weeks object to a bill adopted by the Bundestag. The time for objection shall begin, in the case described in the last sentence of paragraph (2) of this Article, upon receipt of the bill as readopted by the Bundestag, and in all other cases upon receipt of a communication from the chairman of the committee provided for in paragraph (2) of this Article to the effect that the committee's proceedings have been concluded.
(4) If the objection is adopted by the majority of the votes of the Bundesrat, it may be rejected by a decision of the majority of the Members of the Bundestag. If the Bundesrat adopted the

objection by a majority of at least two thirds of its votes, its rejection by the Bundestag shall require a two-thirds majority, including at least a majority of the Members of the Bundestag.

Article 78 [Passage of federal laws]

A bill adopted by the Bundestag shall become law if the Bundesrat consents to it, or fails to make a demand pursuant to paragraph (2) of Article 77, or fails to enter an objection within the period stipulated in paragraph (3) of Article 77, or withdraws such an objection, or if the objection is overridden by the Bundestag.

Article 79 [Amendment of the Basic Law]

(1) This Basic Law may be amended only by a law expressly amending or supplementing its text. In the case of an international treaty respecting a peace settlement, the preparation of a peace settlement, or the phasing out of an occupation regime, or designed to promote the defense of the Federal Republic, it shall be sufficient, for the purpose of making clear that the provisions of this Basic Law do not preclude the conclusion and entry into force of the treaty, to add language to the Basic Law that merely makes this clarification.
(2) Any such law shall be carried by two thirds of the Members of the Bundestag and two thirds of the votes of the Bundesrat.
(3) Amendments to this Basic Law affecting the division of the Federation into Länder, their participation on principle in the legislative process, or the principles laid down in Articles 1 and 20 shall be inadmissible.

Article 80 [Issuance of statutory instruments]

(1) The Federal Government, a Federal Minister, or the Land governments may be authorized by a law to issue statutory instruments. The content, purpose, and scope of the authority conferred shall be specified in the law. Each statutory instrument shall contain a statement of its legal basis. If the law provides that such authority may be further delegated, such subdelegation shall be effected by statutory instrument.
(2) Unless a federal law otherwise provides, the consent of the Bundesrat shall be required for statutory instruments issued by the Federal Government or a Federal Minister respecting fees or basic principles for the use of postal and telecommunication facilities, basic principles for levying of charges for the use of facilities of federal railways, or the construction and operation of railways, as well as for statutory instruments issued pursuant to federal laws that require the consent of the Bundesrat or that are executed by the Länder on federal commission or in their own right.
(3) The Bundesrat may submit to the Federal Government drafts of statutory instruments that require its consent.
(4) Insofar as Land governments are authorized by or pursuant to federal laws to issue statutory instruments, the Länder shall also be entitled to regulate the matter by a law.

Article 80a [Application of legal provisions in a state of tension]

(1) If this Basic Law or a federal law respecting defense, including protection of the civilian population, provides that legal provisions may be applied only in accordance with this Article, their application, except when a state of defense has been declared, shall be permissible only after the Bundestag has determined that a state of tension exists or has specifically approved such application. The determination of a state of tension and specific approval in the cases mentioned in the first sentence of paragraph (5) and the second sentence of paragraph (6) of Article 12a shall require a two-thirds majority of the votes cast.
(2) Any measures taken pursuant to legal provisions by virtue of paragraph (1) of this Article shall

be rescinded whenever the Bundestag so demands.
(3) Notwithstanding paragraph (1) of this Article, the application of such legal provisions shall also be permissible on the basis of and in accordance with a decision made by an international body within the framework of a treaty of alliance with the approval of the Federal Government. Any measures taken pursuant to this paragraph shall be rescinded whenever the Bundestag, by the vote of a majority of its Members, so demands.

Article 81 [Legislative emergency]

(1) If, in the circumstances described in Article 68, the Bundestag is not dissolved, the Federal President, at the request of the Federal Government and with the consent of the Bundesrat, may declare a state of legislative emergency with respect to a bill, if the Bundestag rejects the bill although the Federal Government has declared it to be urgent. The same shall apply if a bill has been rejected although the Federal Chancellor had combined it with a motion under Article 68.
(2) If, after a state of legislative emergency has been declared, the Bundestag again rejects the bill or adopts it in a version the Federal Government declares unacceptable, the bill shall be deemed to have become law to the extent that it receives the consent of the Bundesrat. The same shall apply if the Bundestag does not pass the bill within four weeks after it is reintroduced.
(3) During the term of office of a Federal Chancellor, any other bill rejected by the Bundestag may become law in accordance with paragraphs (1) and (2) of this Article within a period of six months after the first declaration of a state of legislative emergency. After the expiration of this period, no further declaration of a state of legislative emergency may be made during the term of office of the same Federal Chancellor.
(4) This Basic Law may neither be amended nor abrogated nor suspended in whole or in part by a law enacted pursuant to paragraph (2) of this Article.

Article 82 [Promulgation, publication, and entry into force]

(1) Laws enacted in accordance with the provisions of this Basic Law shall, after countersignature, be certified by the Federal President and promulgated in the Federal Law Gazette. Statutory instruments shall be certified by the agency that issues them and, unless a law otherwise provides, shall be promulgated in the Federal Law Gazette.
(2) Every law or statutory instrument shall specify the date on which it shall take effect. In the absence of such a provision, it shall take effect on the fourteenth day after the day on which the Federal Law Gazette containing it was published.

VIII. THE EXECUTION OF THE FEDERAL LAWS AND THE FEDERAL ADMISTRATION

VIIIA. JOINT TASKS

Article 91a [Participation of the Federation pursuant to federal legislation]

(1) In the following areas the Federation shall participate in the discharge of responsibilities of the Länder, provided that such responsibilities are important to society as a whole and that federal participation is necessary for the improvement of living conditions (joint tasks)

1.	extension and construction of institutions of higher learning, including university clinics;
2.	improvement of regional economic structures;

3.	improvement of the agrarian structure and of coastal preservation.

(2) Joint tasks shall be defined in detail by a federal law requiring the consent of the Bundesrat. This law shall include general principles governing the performance of such tasks.
(3) The law referred to in paragraph (2) of this Article shall provide for the procedure and institutions required for joint overall planning. The inclusion of a project in the overall plan shall require the consent of the Land in whose territory it is to be carried out.
(4) In cases to which subparagraphs 1 and 2 of paragraph (1) of this Article apply, the Federation shall finance one half of the expenditure in each Land. In cases to which subparagraph 3 of paragraph (1) of this Article applies, the Federation shall finance at least one half of the expenditure, and the proportion shall be the same for all Länder. Details shall be regulated by the law. The provision of funds shall be subject to appropriation in the budgets of the Federation and the Länder.
(5) Upon request the Federal Government and the Bundesrat shall be informed about the execution of joint tasks.

Article 91b [Cooperation between the Federation and the Länder pursuant to agreements]

Pursuant to agreements, the Federation and the Länder may cooperate in educational planning and in the promotion of research institutions and research projects of supraregional importance. The apportionment of costs shall be regulated by the relevant agreement.

IX. THE JUDICIARY

Article 92 [The courts]

The judicial power shall be vested in the judges; it shall be exercised by the Federal Constitutional Court, by the federal courts provided for in this Basic Law, and by the courts of the Länder.

Article 93 [Federal Constitutional Court: jurisdiction]

(1) The Federal Constitutional Court shall rule:

1.	on the interpretation of this Basic Law in the event of disputes concerning the extent of the rights and duties of a supreme federal body or of other parties vested with rights of their own by this Basic Law or by the rules of procedure of a supreme federal body;
2.	in the event of disagreements or doubts respecting the formal or substantive compatibility of federal law or Land law with this Basic Law, or the compatibility of Land law with other federal law, on application of the Federal Government, of a Land government, or of one third of the Members of the Bundestag;
2a.	in the event of disagreements whether a law meets the requirements of paragraph (2) of Article 72, on application of the Bundesrat or of the government or legislature of a Land;

3.	in the event of disagreements respecting the rights and duties of the Federation and the Länder, especially in the execution of federal law by the Länder and in the exercise of federal oversight;
4.	on other disputes involving public law between the Federation and the Länder, between different Länder, or within a Land, unless there is recourse to another court;
4a.	on constitutional complaints, which may be filed by any person alleging that one of his basic rights or one of his rights under paragraph (4) of Article 20 or under Article 33, 38, 101, 103, or 104 has been infringed by public authority;
4b.	on constitutional complaints filed by municipalities or associations of municipalities on the ground that their right to self-government under Article 28 has been infringed by a law; in the case of infringement by a Land law, however, only if the law cannot be challenged in the constitutional court of the Land;
5.	in the other instances provided for in this Basic Law.

(2) The Federal Constitutional Court shall also rule on such other matters as may be assigned to it by a federal law.

Article 94 [Federal Constitutional Court: composition]

(1) The Federal Constitutional Court shall consist of federal judges and other members. Half the members of the Federal Constitutional Court shall be elected by the Bundestag and half by the Bundesrat. They may not be members of the Bundestag, of the Bundesrat, of the Federal Government, or of any of the corresponding bodies of a Land.
(2) The organization and procedure of the Federal Constitutional Court shall be regulated by a federal law, which shall specify in which instances its decisions shall have the force of law. The law may require that all other legal remedies be exhausted before a constitutional complaint may be filed, and may provide for a separate proceeding to determine whether the complaint will be accepted for decision.

Article 95 [Supreme federal courts]

(1) The Federation shall establish the Federal Court of Justice, the Federal Administrative Court, the Federal Finance Court, the Federal Labor Court, and the Federal Social Court as supreme courts of ordinary, administrative, financial, labor, and social jurisdiction.
(2) The judges of each of these courts shall be chosen jointly by the competent Federal Minister and a committee for the selection of judges consisting of the competent Land ministers and an equal number of members elected by the Bundestag.
(3) A Joint Chamber of the courts specified in paragraph (1) of this Article shall be established to preserve the uniformity of decisions. Details shall be regulated by a federal law.

Article 96 [Other federal courts; exercise of federal jurisdiction by courts of the Länder]

(1) The Federation may establish a federal court for matters respecting industrial property rights.
(2) The Federation may establish federal military criminal courts for the Armed Forces. These courts may exercise criminal jurisdiction only during a state of defense or over members of the Armed Forces serving abroad or on board warships. Details shall be regulated by a federal law. These courts shall be under the aegis of the Federal Minister of Justice. Their full-time judges shall be persons qualified to hold judicial office.
(3) The supreme court of review from the courts designated in paragraphs (1) and (2) of this Article shall be the Federal Court of Justice.
(4) The Federation may establish federal courts for disciplinary proceedings against, and for proceedings on complaints by, persons in the federal public service.
(5) With the consent of the Bundesrat, a federal law may provide for the exercise of federal jurisdiction over criminal proceedings arising under paragraph (1) of Article 26 or involving national security by courts of the Länder.

Article 97 [Independence of judges]

(1) Judges shall be independent and subject only to the law.
(2) Judges appointed permanently to full-time positions may be involuntarily dismissed, permanently or temporarily suspended, transferred, or retired before the expiration of their term of office only by virtue of judicial decision and only for the reasons and in the manner specified by the laws. The legislature may set age limits for the retirement of judges appointed for life. In the event of changes in the structure of courts or in their districts, judges may be transferred to another court or removed from office, provided they retain their full salary.

Article 98 [Legal status of federal and Land judges]

(1) The legal status of federal judges shall be regulated by a special federal law.
(2) If a federal judge infringes the principles of this Basic Law or the constitutional order of a Land in his official capacity or unofficially, the Federal Constitutional Court, upon application of the Bundestag, may by a two-thirds majority order that the judge be transferred or retired. In the case of an intentional infringement it may order him dismissed.
(3) The legal status of Land judges shall be regulated by special Land laws. The Federation may enact framework provisions on this subject to the extent that paragraph (4) of Article 74a does not otherwise provide.
(4) The Länder may provide that Land judges shall be chosen jointly by the Land Minister of Justice and a committee for the selection of judges.
(5) The Länder may enact provisions respecting Land judges that correspond with those of paragraph (2) of this Article. Existing Land constitutional law shall not be affected. The decision in cases of judicial impeachment shall rest with the Federal Constitutional Court.

Article 99 [Decision by the Federal Constitutional Court and the supreme federal courts in disputes concerning Land law]

A land law may assign the decision of constitutional disputes within a Land to the Federal Constitutional Court, and the final decision in matters involving the application of Land law to the supreme courts specified in paragraph (1) of Article 95.

Article 100 [Compatibility of laws with the Basic Law]

(1) If a court concludes that a law on whose validity its decision depends is unconstitutional, the proceedings shall be stayed, and a decision shall be obtained from the Land court with jurisdiction over constitutional disputes where the constitution of a Land is held to be violated, or from the Federal Constitutional Court where this Basic Law is held to be violated. This provision

shall also apply where the Basic Law is held to be violated by Land law and where a Land law is held to be incompatible with a federal law.
(2) If, in the course of litigation, doubt exists whether a rule of international law is an integral part of federal law and whether it directly creates rights and duties for the individual (Article 25), the court shall obtain a decision from the Federal Constitutional Court.
(3) If the constitutional court of a Land, in interpreting this Basic Law, proposes to deviate from a decision of the Federal Constitutional Court or of the constitutional court of another Land, it shall obtain a decision from the Federal Constitutional Court.

Article 101 [Ban on extraordinary courts]

(1) Extraordinary courts shall not be allowed. No one may be removed from the jurisdiction of his lawful judge.
(2) Courts for particular fields of law may be established only by a law.

Article 102 [Abolition of capital punishment]

Capital punishment is abolished.

Article 103 [Hearing in accordance with law; ban on retroactive criminal laws and on multiple punishment]

(1) In the courts every person shall be entitled to a hearing in accordance with law.
(2) An act may be punished only if it was defined by a law as a criminal offense before the act was committed.
(3) No person may be punished for the same act more than once under the general criminal laws.

Article 104 [Legal guarantees in the event of detention]

(1) Freedom of the person may be restricted only pursuant to a formal law and only in compliance with the procedures prescribed therein. Persons in custody may not be subjected to mental or physical mistreatment.
(2) Only a judge may rule upon the permissibility or continuation of any deprivation of freedom. If such a deprivation is not based on a judicial order, a judicial decision shall be obtained without delay. The police may hold no one in custody on their own authority beyond the end of the day following the arrest. Details shall be regulated by a law.
(3) Any person provisionally detained on suspicion of having committed a criminal offense shall be brought before a judge no later than the day following his arrest; the judge shall inform him of the reasons for the arrest, examine him, and give him an opportunity to raise objections. The judge shall, without delay, either issue a written arrest warrant setting forth the reasons therefor or order his release.
(4) A relative or a person enjoying the confidence of the person in custody shall be notified without delay of any judicial decision imposing or continuing a deprivation of freedom.

X. FINANCE

Article 104a [Apportionment of expenditures between the Federation and the Länder]

(1) The Federation and the Länder shall separately finance the expenditures resulting from the discharge of their respective responsibilities insofar as this Basic Law does not otherwise provide.
(2) Where the Länder act on federal commission, the Federation shall finance the resulting

expenditures.
(3) Federal laws providing for money grants to be administered by the Länder may provide that the Federation shall pay for such grants wholly or in part. If any such law provides that the Federation shall finance one half or more of the expenditure, it shall be executed by the Länder on federal commission. If any such law provides that the Länder shall finance one quarter or more of the expenditure, it shall require the consent of the Bundesrat.
(4) The Federation may grant the Länder financial assistance for particularly important investments by the Länder or by municipalities (associations of municipalities), provided that such investments are necessary to avert a disturbance of the overall economic equilibrium, to equalize differing economic capacities within the federal territory, or to promote economic growth. Details, especially with respect to the kinds of investments to be promoted, shall be regulated by a federal law requiring the consent of the Bundesrat or by executive agreements under the Federal Budget Law.
(5) The Federation and the Länder shall finance the administrative expenditures incurred by their respective authorities and shall be responsible to one another for ensuring proper administration. Details shall be regulated by a federal law requiring the consent of the Bundesrat.

Article 105 [Legislative powers]

(1) The Federation shall have exclusive power to legislate with respect to customs duties and fiscal monopolies.
(2) The Federation shall have concurrent power to legislate with respect to all other taxes the revenue from which accrues to it wholly or in part or as to which the conditions provided for in paragraph (2) of Article 72 apply.
(2a) The Länder shall have power to legislate with respect to local taxes on consumption and expenditures so long and insofar as they are not substantially similar to taxes imposed by a federal law.
(3) Federal laws relating to taxes the revenue from which accrues wholly or in part to the Länder or to municipalities (associations of municipalities) shall require the consent of the Bundesrat.

Article 106 [Apportionment of tax revenue]

(1) The yield of fiscal monopolies and the revenue from the following taxes shall accrue to the Federation:

1.	customs duties;
2.	taxes on consumption insofar as they do not accrue to the Länder pursuant to paragraph (2), or jointly to the Federation and the Länder in accordance with paragraph (3), or to municipalities in accordance with paragraph (6) of this Article;
3.	the highway freight tax;
4.	the taxes on capital transactions, insurance, and bills of exchange;
5.	nonrecurring levies on property and equalization of burdens levies;

6.	income and corporation surtaxes;
7.	levies imposed within the framework of the European Communities.

(2) Revenue from the following taxes shall accrue to the Länder:

1.	the property tax;
2.	the inheritance tax;
3.	the motor vehicle tax;
4.	such taxes on transactions as do not accrue to the Federation pursuant to paragraph(1) or jointly to the Federation and the Länder pursuant to paragraph (3) of this Article;
5.	the beer tax;
6.	the tax on gambling establishments.

(3) Revenue from income taxes, corporation taxes, and turnover taxes shall accrue jointly to the Federation and the Länder (joint taxes) to the extent that the revenue from the income tax and the turnover tax is not allocated to municipalities pursuant to paragraphs (5) and (5a) of this Article. The Federation and the Länder shall share equally the revenues from income taxes and corporation taxes. The respective shares of the Federation and the Länder in the revenue from the turnover tax shall be determined by a federal law requiring the consent of the Bundesrat. Such determination shall be based on the following principles:

1.	The Federation and the Länder shall have an equal claim against current revenues to cover their necessary expenditures. The extent of such expenditures shall be determined with due regard to multi-year financial planning.
2.	The financial requirements of the Federation and of the Länder shall be coordinated in such a way as to establish a fair balance, avoid excessive burdens on taxpayers, and ensure uniformity of living standards throughout the federal territory. In determining the respective shares of the Federation and the Länder in the revenue from the

> Länder from January 1, 1996 because of the provisions made with respect to children in the income tax law shall also be taken into account. Details shall be regulated by the federal law enacted pursuant to the third sentence of this paragraph.

(4) The respective shares of the Federation and the Länder in the revenue from the turnover tax shall be apportioned anew whenever the ratio of revenues to expenditures of the Federation becomes substantially different from that of the Länder; reductions in revenue that are taken into account in determining the respective shares of revenue from the turnover tax under the fifth sentence of paragraph (3) of this Article shall not be considered in this regard. If a federal law imposes additional expenditures on or withdraws revenue from the Länder, the additional burden may be compensated for by federal grants pursuant to a federal law requiring the consent of the Bundesrat, provided the additional burden is limited to a short period of time. This law shall establish the principles for calculating such grants and distributing them among the Länder.
(5) A share of the revenue from the income tax shall accrue to the municipalities, to be passed on by the Länder to their municipalities on the basis of the income taxes paid by their inhabitants. Details shall be regulated by a federal law requiring the consent of the Bundesrat. This law may provide that municipalities may establish supplementary or reduced rates with respect to their share of the tax.
(5a) From and after January 1, 1998, a share of the revenue from the turnover tax shall accrue to the municipalities. It shall be passed on by the Länder to their municipalities on the basis of a formula reflecting geographical and economic factors. Details shall be regulated by a federal law requiring the consent of the Bundesrat.
(6) Revenue from taxes on real property and trades shall accrue to the municipalities; revenue from local taxes on consumption and expenditures shall accrue to the municipalities or, as may be provided for by Land legislation, to associations of municipalities. Municipalities shall be authorized to establish the rates at which taxes on real property and trades are levied, within the framework of the laws. If there are no municipalities in a Land, revenue from taxes on real property and trades as well as from local taxes on consumption and expenditures shall accrue to the Land. The Federation and the Länder may participate, by virtue of an apportionment, in the revenue from the tax on trades. Details regarding such apportionment shall be regulated by a federal law requiring the consent of the Bundesrat. In accordance with Land legislation, taxes on real property and trades as well as the municipalities' share of revenue from the income tax and the turnover tax may be taken as a basis for calculating the amount of apportionment.
(7) An overall percentage of the Land share of total revenue from joint taxes, to be determined by Land legislation, shall accrue to the municipalities or associations of municipalities. In all other respects Land legislation shall determine whether and to what extent revenue from Land taxes shall accrue to municipalities (associations of municipalities).
(8) If in individual Länder or municipalities (associations of municipalities) the Federation requires special facilities to be established that directly result in an increase of expenditure or in reductions in revenue (special burden) to these Länder or municipalities (associations of municipalities), the Federation shall grant the necessary compensation if and insofar as the Länder or municipalities (associations of municipalities) cannot reasonably be expected to bear the burden. In granting such compensation, due account shall be taken of indemnities paid by third parties and financial benefits accruing to these Länder or municipalities (associations of municipalities) as a result of the establishment of such facilities.
(9) For the purpose of this Article, revenues and expenditures of municipalities (associations of municipalities) shall also be deemed to be revenues and expenditures of the Länder.

Article 106a [Federal grants for local mass transit]

Beginning January 1, 1996 the Länder shall be entitled to an allocation of federal tax revenues for purposes of local mass transit. Details shall be regulated by a federal law requiring the consent of the Bundesrat. Allocations made pursuant to the first sentence of this Article shall not be taken into account in determining the financial capacity of a Land under paragraph (2) of Article 107.

Article 107 [Financial equalization]

(1) Revenue from Land taxes and the Land share of revenue from income and corporation taxes shall accrue to the individual Länder to the extent that such taxes are collected by revenue authorities within their respective territories (local revenue). Details respecting the delimitation as well as the manner and scope of allotment of local revenue from corporation and wage taxes shall be regulated by a federal law requiring the consent of the Bundesrat. This law may also provide for the delimitation and allotment of local revenue from other taxes. The Land share of revenue from the turnover tax shall accrue to the individual Länder on a per capita basis; a federal law requiring the consent of the Bundesrat may provide for the grant of supplementary shares not exceeding one quarter of a Land share to Länder whose per capita revenue from Land taxes and from income and corporation taxes is below the average of all the Länder combined.
(2) Such law shall ensure a reasonable equalization of the disparate financial capacities of the Länder, with due regard for the financial capacities and needs of municipalities (associations of municipalities). It shall specify the conditions governing the claims of Länder entitled to equalization payments and the liabilities of Länder required to make them as well as the criteria for determining the amounts of such payments. It may also provide for grants to be made by the Federation to financially weak Länder from its own funds to assist them in meeting their general financial needs (supplementary grants).

Article 108 [Financial administration]

(1) Customs duties, fiscal monopolies, taxes on consumption regulated by a federal law, including the turnover tax on imports, and levies imposed within the framework of the European Communities shall be administered by federal revenue authorities. The organization of these authorities shall be regulated by a federal law. The heads of intermediate authorities shall be appointed in consultation with the Land governments.
(2) All other taxes shall be administered by the revenue authorities of the Länder. The organization of these authorities and the uniform training of their civil servants may be regulated by a federal law requiring the consent of the Bundesrat. The heads of intermediate authorities shall be appointed in agreement with the Federal Government.
(3) To the extent that taxes accruing wholly or in part to the Federation are administered by revenue authorities of the Länder, those authorities shall act on federal commission. Paragraphs (3) and (4) of Article 85 shall apply, provided that the Federal Minister of Finance shall take the place of the Federal Government.
(4) Where and to the extent that execution of the tax laws will be substantially facilitated or improved thereby, a federal law requiring the consent of the Bundesrat may provide for collaboration between federal and Land revenue authorities in matters of tax administration, for the administration of taxes enumerated in paragraph (1) of this Article by revenue authorities of the Länder, or for the administration of other taxes by federal revenue authorities. The functions of Land revenue authorities in the administration of taxes whose revenue accrues exclusively to municipalities (associations of municipalities) may be delegated by the Länder to municipalities (associations of municipalities) wholly or in part.
(5) The procedures to be followed by federal revenue authorities shall be prescribed by a federal law. The procedures to be followed by Land revenue authorities or, as provided by the second sentence of paragraph (4) of this Article, by municipalities (associations of municipalities) may be prescribed by a federal law requiring the consent of the Bundesrat.
(6) Financial jurisdiction shall be uniformly regulated by a federal law.
(7) The Federal Government may issue general administrative rules which, to the extent that

administration is entrusted to Land revenue authorities or to municipalities (associations of municipalities), shall require the consent of the Bundesrat.

Article 109 [Budgets of the Federation and the Länder]

(1) The Federation and the Länder shall be autonomous and independent of one another in the management of their respective budgets.
(2) In managing their respective budgets the Federation and the Länder shall take due account of the requirements of the overall economic equilibrium.
(3) A federal law requiring the consent of the Bundesrat may establish principles applicable to both the Federation and the Länder governing budgetary law, the responsiveness of budgetary management to economic trends, and long-term financial planning.
(4) With a view to averting disturbances of the overall economic equilibrium, a federal law requiring the consent of the Bundesrat may

1.	prescribe the maximum amounts, terms, and timing of loans to be raised by territorial entities and special purpose associations and
2.	require the Federation and the Länder to maintain interest-free deposits at the German Federal Bank (anticyclical reserves). Only the Federal Government may be authorized to issue the relevant statutory instruments. The statutory instruments shall require the consent of the Bundesrat. They shall be rescinded insofar as the Bundestag may so demand; details shall be regulated by the federal law.

Article 110 [Federal budget and Budget Law]

(1) All revenues and expenditures of the Federation shall be included in the budget; in the case of federal enterprises and special trusts, only payments to or remittances from them need be included. The budget shall be balanced with respect to revenues and expenditures.
(2) The budget for one or more fiscal years shall be set forth in a law enacted before the beginning of the first year and making separate provision for each year. The law may provide that various parts of the budget apply to different periods of time, divided by fiscal years.
(3) Bills to comply with the first sentence of paragraph (2) of this Article as well as bills to amend the Budget Law or the budget itself shall be submitted simultaneously to the Bundesrat and to the Bundestag; the Bundesrat shall be entitled to comment on such bills within six weeks or, in the case of amending bills, within three weeks.
(4) The Budget Law may contain only such provisions as relate to federal revenues and expenditures and to the period for which it is enacted. The Budget Law may specify that its provisions shall expire only upon promulgation of the next Budget Law or, in the event of an authorization pursuant to Article 115, at a later date.

Article 111 [Interim budget management]

(1) If, by the end of a fiscal year, the budget for the following year has not been adopted by a law, the Federal Government, until such law comes into force, may make all expenditures that are necessary:

(a)	to maintain institutions established by a law and to carry out measures authorized by a law;
(b)	to meet the legal obligations of the Federation;
(c)	to continue construction projects, procurements, and the provision of other benefits or services, or to continue to make grants for these purposes, to the extent that amounts have already been appropriated in the budget of a previous year.

(2) To the extent that revenues based upon specific laws and derived from taxes, or duties, or other sources, or the working capital reserves, do not cover the expenditures referred to in paragraph (1) of this Article, the Federal Government may borrow the funds necessary to sustain current operations up to a maximum of one quarter of the total amount of the previous budget.

Article 112 [Extrabudgetary expenditures]

Expenditures in excess of budgetary appropriations or for purposes not contemplated by the budget shall require the consent of the Federal Minister of Finance. Such consent may be given only in the event of an unforeseen and unavoidable necessity. Details may be regulated by a federal law.

Article 113 [Consent of the Federal Government to increases in expenditures or decreases in revenue]

(1) Laws that increase the budget expenditures proposed by the Federal Government, or entail or will bring about new expenditures, shall require the consent of the Federal Government. This requirement shall also apply to laws that entail or will bring about decreases in revenue. The Federal Government may demand that the Bundestag postpone its vote on bills to this effect. In this event the Federal Government shall submit its comments to the Bundestag within six weeks.
(2) Within four weeks after the Bundestag has adopted such a law, the Federal Government may demand that it vote on the law a second time.
(3) If the bill has become law pursuant to Article 78, the Federal Government may withhold its consent only within six weeks and only after having initiated the procedure provided for in the third and fourth sentences of paragraph (1) or in paragraph (2) of this Article. Upon the expiration of this period such consent shall be deemed to have been given.

Article 114 [Submission and auditing of accounts]

(1) For the purpose of discharging the Federal Government, the Federal Minister of Finance shall submit annually to the Bundestag and to the Bundesrat an account of all revenues and expenditures as well as of assets and debts during the preceding fiscal year.
(2) The Federal Court of Audit, whose members shall enjoy judicial independence, shall audit the account and determine whether public finances have been properly and efficiently administered. It shall submit an annual report directly to the Bundestag and the Bundesrat as well as to the

Federal Government. In other respects the powers of the Federal Court of Audit shall be regulated by a federal law.

Article 115 [Borrowing]

(1) The borrowing of funds and the assumption of surety obligations, guarantees, or other commitments that may lead to expenditures in future fiscal years shall require authorization by a federal law specifying or permitting computation of the amounts involved. Revenue obtained by borrowing shall not exceed the total of investment expenditures provided for in the budget; exceptions shall be permissible only to avert a disturbance of the overall economic equilibrium. Details shall be regulated by a federal law.
(2) With respect to special trusts of the Federation, exceptions to the provisions of paragraph (1) of this Article may be authorized by a federal law.

XA. STATE OF DEFENSE

Article 115a [Definition and declaration of a state of defense]

(1) Any determination that the federal territory is under attack by armed force or imminently threatened with such an attack (state of defense) shall be made by the Bundestag with the consent of the Bundesrat. Such determination shall be made on application of the Federal Government and shall require a two-thirds majority of the votes cast, which shall include at least a majority of the Members of the Bundestag.
(2) If the situation imperatively calls for immediate action, and if insurmountable obstacles prevent the timely convening of the Bundestag or the Bundestag cannot muster a quorum, the Joint Committee shall make this determination by a two-thirds majority of the votes cast, which shall include at least a majority of its members.
(3) The determination shall be promulgated by the Federal President in the Federal Law Gazette pursuant to Article 82. If this cannot be done in time, promulgation shall be effected in another manner; the determination shall be printed in the Federal Law Gazette as soon as circumstances permit.
(4) If the federal territory is under attack by armed force, and if the competent federal authorities are not in a position at once to make the determination provided for in the first sentence of paragraph (1) of this Article, the determination shall be deemed to have been made and promulgated at the time the attack began. The Federal President shall announce that time as soon as circumstances permit.
(5) If the determination of a state of defense has been promulgated, and if the federal territory is under attack by armed force, the Federal President, with the consent of the Bundestag, may issue declarations under international law respecting the existence of the state of defense. Under the conditions specified in paragraph (2) of this Article, the Joint Committee shall act in place of the Bundestag.

Article 115b [Transfer of command to the Federal Chancellor]

Upon the promulgation of a state of defense the power of command over the Armed Forces shall pass to the Federal Chancellor.

Article 115c [Extension of the legislative powers of the Federation]

(1) The Federation shall have the right to legislate concurrently for a state of defense even with respect to matters within the legislative powers of the Länder. Such laws shall require the consent

of the Bundesrat.
(2) To the extent required by circumstances during a state of defense, a federal law for a state of defense may:

1.	make temporary provisions respecting compensation in the event of expropriation that deviate from the requirements of the second sentence of paragraph (3) of Article 14;
1a.	establish a time limit for deprivations of freedom different from that specified in the third sentence of paragraph (2) and the first sentence of paragraph (3) of Article 104, but not exceeding four days, for cases in which no judge has been able to act within the time limit that normally applies.

(3) To the extent necessary to repel an existing or imminently threatened attack, a federal law for a state of defense may, with the consent of the Bundesrat, regulate the administration and finances of the Federation and the Länder without regard to Titles VIII, VIIIa and X of this Basic Law, provided that the viability of the Länder, municipalities, and associations of municipalities, especially with respect to financial matters, is assured.
(4) Federal laws enacted pursuant to paragraph (1) or subparagraph 1 of paragraph (2) of this Article may, for the purpose of preparing for their enforcement, be applied even before a state of defense arises.

Article 115d [Legislative process in the case of urgent bills]

(1) During a state of defense the federal legislative process shall be governed by the provisions of paragraphs (2) and (3) of this Article without regard to the provisions of paragraph (2) of Article 76, the second sentence of paragraph (1) and paragraphs (2) to (4) of Article 77, Article 78, and paragraph (1) of Article 82.
(2) Federal Government bills that the Government designates as urgent shall be forwarded to the Bundesrat at the same time as they are submitted to the Bundestag. The Bundestag and the Bundesrat shall debate such bills in joint session without delay. Insofar as the consent of the Bundesrat is necessary for any such bill to become law, a majority of its votes shall be required. Details shall be regulated by rules of procedure adopted by the Bundestag and requiring the consent of the Bundesrat.
(3) The second sentence of paragraph (3) of Article 115a shall apply to the promulgation of such laws mutatis mutandis

Article 115e [Powers of the Joint Committee]

(1) If, during a state of defense, the Joint Committee by a two-thirds majority of the votes cast, which shall include at least a majority of its members, determines that insurmountable obstacles prevent the timely convening of the Bundestag or that the Bundestag cannot muster a quorum, the Joint Committee shall occupy the position of both the Bundestag and the Bundesrat and shall exercise their powers as a single body.
(2) This Basic Law may neither be amended nor abrogated nor suspended in whole or in part by a law enacted by the Joint Committee. The Joint Committee shall have no power to enact laws pursuant to the second sentence of paragraph (1) of Article 23, paragraph (1) of Article 24, or Article 29.

Article 115f [Powers of the Federal Government]

(1) During a state of defense the Federal Government, to the extent circumstances require, may:

1.	employ the Federal Border Police throughout the federal territory;
1a.	issue instructions not only to federal administrative authorities but also to Land governments and, if it deems the matter urgent, to Land authorities, and may delegate this power to members of Land governments designated by it.

(2) The Bundestag, the Bundesrat, and the Joint Committee shall be informed without delay of the measures taken in accordance with paragraph (1) of this Article.

Article 115g [Status of the Federal Constitutional Court]

Neither the constitutional status nor the performance of the constitutional functions of the Federal Constitutional Court or its judges may be impaired. The law governing the Federal Constitutional Court may be amended by a law enacted by the Joint Committee only insofar as the Federal Constitutional Court agrees is necessary to ensure that it can continue to perform its functions. Pending the enactment of such a law, the Federal Constitutional Court may take such measures as are necessary to this end. Determinations by the Federal Constitutional Court pursuant to the second and third sentences of this Article shall be made by a majority of the judges present.

Article 115h [Continued functioning of constitutional bodies]

(1) Any legislative terms of the Bundestag or of Land parliaments due to expire during a state of defense shall end six months after the termination of the state of defense. A term of office of the Federal President due to expire during a state of defense, and the exercise of his functions by the President of the Bundesrat in case of the premature vacancy of his office, shall end nine months after the termination of the state of defense. The term of office of a member of the Federal Constitutional Court due to expire during a state of defense shall end six months after the termination of the state of defense.
(2) Should it be necessary for the Joint Committee to elect a new Federal Chancellor, it shall do so by the votes of a majority of its members; the Federal President shall propose a candidate to the Joint Committee. The Joint Committee may express its lack of confidence in the Federal Chancellor only by electing a successor by a two-thirds majority of its members.
(3) The Bundestag shall not be dissolved while a state of defense exists.

Article 115i [Powers of the Land governments]

(1) If the competent federal bodies are incapable of taking the measures necessary to avert the danger, and if the situation imperatively calls for immediate independent action in particular areas of the federal territory, the Land governments or the authorities or representatives they designate shall be authorized, within their respective spheres of competence, to take the measures provided for in paragraph (1) of Article 115f.
(2) Any measures taken in accordance with paragraph (1) of this Article may be rescinded at any time by the Federal Government, or, with respect to Land authorities and subordinate federal authorities, by Minister-Presidents of the Länder.

Article 115k [Duration of extraordinary legal provisions]

(1) Laws enacted in accordance with Articles 115c, 115e, and 115g, as well as statutory instruments issued on the basis of such laws, shall suspend the operation of incompatible law so long as they are in effect. This provision shall not apply to earlier law enacted pursuant to Articles 115c, 115e or 115g.
(2) Laws adopted by the Joint Committee, as well as statutory instruments issued on the basis of such laws, shall cease to have effect no later than six months after the termination of a state of defense.
(3) Laws containing provisions that diverge from Articles 91a, 91b, 104a, 106, and 107 shall apply no longer than the end of the second fiscal year following the termination of a state of defense. After such termination they may, with the consent of the Bundesrat, be amended by a federal law so as to revert to the provisions of Titles VIIIa and X.

Article 115l [Repeal of extraordinary measures; termination of a state of defense; conclusion of peace]

(1) The Bundestag, with the consent of the Bundesrat, may at any time repeal laws enacted by the Joint Committee. The Bundesrat may demand that the Bundestag reach a decision on this question. Any measures taken by the Joint Committee or by the Federal Government to avert a danger shall be rescinded if the Bundestag and the Bundesrat so decide.
(2) The Bundestag, with the consent of the Bundesrat, may at any time, by a decision to be promulgated by the Federal President, declare a state of defense terminated. The Bundesrat may demand that the Bundestag reach a decision on this question. A state of defense shall be declared terminated without delay if the conditions for determining it no longer exist.
(3) The conclusion of peace shall be determined by a federal law.

XI. TRANSITIONAL AND CONCLUDING PROVISIONS

Article 116 [Definition of "German"; restoration of citizenship]

(1) Unless otherwise provided by a law, a German within the meaning of this Basic Law is a person who possesses German citizenship or who has been admitted to the territory of the German Reich within the boundaries of December 31, 1937 as a refugee or expellee of German ethnic origin or as the spouse or descendant of such person.
(2) Former German citizens who between January 30, 1933 and May 8, 1945 were deprived of their citizenship on political, racial, or religious grounds, and their descendants, shall on application have their citizenship restored. They shall be deemed never to have been deprived of their citizenship if they have established their domicile in Germany after May 8, 1945 and have not expressed a contrary intention.

Article 117 [Transitional provision respecting paragraph 2 of Article 3 and Article 11]

(1) Law which is inconsistent with paragraph (2) of Article 3 of this Basic Law shall remain in force until adapted to that provision, but not beyond March 31, 1953.
(2) Laws that restrict freedom of movement in view of the present housing shortage shall remain in force until repealed by a federal law.

Article 118 [New delimitation of Länder in the Southwest]

The division of the territory comprising Baden, Württemberg-Baden and Württemberg-Hohenzollern into Länder may be revised, without regard to the provisions of Article 29, by agreement between the Länder concerned. If no agreement is reached, the revision shall be effected by a federal law, which shall provide for an advisory referendum.

Article 118a [New delimitation of Berlin and Brandenburg]

The division of the territory comprising Berlin and Brandenburg into Länder may be revised, without regard to the provisions of Article 29, by agreement between the two Länder with the participation of their inhabitants who are entitled to vote.

Article 119 [Statutory instruments respecting refugees and expellees]

In matters relating to refugees and expellees, especially as regards their distribution among the Länder, the Federal Government, with the consent of the Bundesrat, may issue statutory instruments having the force of law, pending settlement of the matter by a federal law. In this connection the Federal Government may be authorized to issue individual instructions in particular cases. Unless time is of the essence, such instructions shall be addressed to the highest Land authorities.

Article 120 [Occupation costs and burdens resulting from the war]

(1) The Federation shall finance the expenditures for occupation costs and other internal and external burdens resulting from the war, as regulated in detail by federal laws. To the extent that these war burdens were regulated by federal laws on or before October 1, 1969, the Federation and the Länder shall finance such expenditures in the proportion established by such federal laws. Insofar as expenditures for such of these war burdens as neither have been nor will be regulated by federal laws were met on or before October 1, 1965 by Länder, municipalities (associations of municipalities), or other entities performing functions of the Länder or municipalities, the Federation shall not be obliged to finance them even after that date. The Federation shall be responsible for subsidies toward meeting the costs of social security, including unemployment insurance and public assistance to the unemployed. The distribution of war burdens between the Federation and the Länder prescribed by this paragraph shall not be construed to affect any law respecting claims for compensation for consequences of the war.
(2) Revenue shall pass to the Federation at the time it assumes responsibility for the expenditures referred to in this Article.

Article 120a [Execution of laws respecting equalization of burdens]

(1) Laws implementing the equalization of burdens may, with the consent of the Bundesrat, provide that with respect to equalization payments they shall be executed partly by the Federation and partly by the Länder acting on federal commission, and that the relevant powers vested in the Federal Government and the competent highest federal authorities by virtue of Article 85 shall be wholly or partly delegated to the Federal Equalization of Burdens Office. In exercising these powers, the Federal Equalization of Burdens Office shall not require the consent of the Bundesrat; except in urgent cases, its instructions shall be given to the highest Land authorities (Land Equalization of Burdens Offices).
(2) The second sentence of paragraph (3) of Article 87 shall not be affected by this provision.

Article 121 [Definition of "majority of the members"]

Within the meaning of this Basic Law, a majority of the Members of the Bundestag and a majority of the members of the Federal Convention shall be a majority of the number of their members specified by a law.

Article 122 [Termination of preexisting legislative powers]

(1) From the date on which the Bundestag first convenes, laws shall be enacted only by the legislative bodies recognized by this Basic Law.
(2) Legislative bodies and institutions participating in the legislative process in an advisory capacity, whose competence expires by virtue of paragraph (1) of this Article, shall be dissolved as of that date.

Article 123 [Continuing validity of preexisting law and treaties]

(1) Law in force before the Bundestag first convenes shall remain in force insofar as it does not conflict with this Basic Law.
(2) Subject to all rights and objections of interested parties, treaties concluded by the German Reich concerning matters within the legislative competence of the Länder under this Basic Law shall remain in force, provided they are and continue to be valid under general principles of law, until new treaties are concluded by the authorities competent under this Basic Law, or until they are in some other way terminated pursuant to their provisions.

Article 124 [Continuing applicability as federal law within the sphere of exclusive legislative power]

Law respecting matters subject to the exclusive legislative power of the Federation shall become federal law in the area in which it applies.

Article 125 [Same: within the sphere of concurrent legislative power]

Law respecting matters subject to the concurrent legislative power of the Federation shall become federal law in the area in which it applies:
1. insofar as it applies uniformly within one or more occupation zones;
2. insofar as it is law by which former Reich law has been amended since May 8, 1945.

Article 125a [Same: within the spheres of concurrent or framework legislation]

(1) Law that was enacted as federal law, but that by virtue of amendments to paragraph (1) of Article 74 or paragraph (1) of Article 75 could no longer be enacted as federal law, shall remain in force as federal law. It may be superseded by Land law.
(2) Law that was enacted pursuant to paragraph (2) of Article 72 as it stood until November 15, 1994 shall remain in force as federal law. A federal law may provide that it may be superseded by Land law. The same shall be true of federal law enacted before that date which could no longer be enacted by virtue of paragraph (2) of Article 75.

Article 126 [Disagreements respecting the continued applicability of law as federal law]

Disagreements respecting the continued applicability of law as federal law shall be resolved by the Federal Constitutional Court.

Article 127 [Law of the Administration of the Combined Economic Area]

Within one year after promulgation of this Basic Law the Federal Government, with the consent of the governments of the Länder concerned, may extend to the Länder of Baden, Greater Berlin, Rhineland-Palatinate and Württemberg-Hohenzollern any law of the Administration of the Combined Economic Area, insofar as it remains in force as federal law under Article 124 or 125.

Article 128 [Continuing authority to issue instructions]

Insofar as law that remains in force grants authority to issue instructions within the meaning of paragraph (5) of Article 84, this authority shall remain in existence until a law otherwise provides.

Article 129 [Continuing authority to issue statutory instruments etc.]

(1) Insofar as legal provisions that remain in force as federal law grant authority to issue statutory instruments or general administrative rules or to make administrative decisions in individual cases, such powers shall pass to the authorities that henceforth have competence over the subject matter. In cases of doubt the Federal Government shall decide in agreement with the Bundesrat; such decisions shall be published.
(2) Insofar as legal provisions that remain in force as Land law grant such authority, it shall be exercised by the authorities competent under Land law.
(3) Insofar as legal provisions within the meaning of paragraphs (1) and (2) of this Article grant authority to amend or supplement the provisions themselves or to issue legal provisions that have the force of laws, such authority shall be deemed to have expired.
(4) The provisions of paragraphs (1) and (2) of this Article shall apply mutatis mutandis to legal provisions that refer to provisions no longer in force or to institutions no longer in existence.

Article 130 [Control of existing institutions]

(1) Administrative agencies and other institutions that serve the public administration or the administration of justice and are not based on Land law or on agreements between Länder, as well as the Administrative Union of South West German Railways and the Administrative Council for Postal and Telecommunications Services for the French Occupation Zone, shall be placed under the control of the Federal Government. The Federal Government, with the consent of the Bundesrat, shall provide for their transfer, dissolution, or liquidation.
(2) The supreme disciplinary authority for the personnel of these administrative bodies and institutions shall be the competent Federal Minister.
(3) Corporations and institutions under public law not directly subordinate to a Land nor based on agreements between Länder shall be under the supervision of the competent highest federal authority.

Article 131 [Legal relations of persons formerly in the public service]

The legal relations of persons, including refugees and expellees, who on May 8, 1945 were employed in the public service, have left the service for reasons other than those recognized by civil service regulations or collective bargaining agreements, and have not yet been reinstated or are employed in positions that do not correspond to those they previously held, shall be regulated by a federal law. The same shall apply mutatis mutandis to persons, including refugees and expellees, who on May 8, 1945 were entitled to pensions and related benefits and who for reasons other than those recognized by civil service regulations or collective bargaining agreements no longer receive any such pension or related benefits. Until the pertinent federal law takes effect, no legal claims may be made, unless Land law otherwise provides.

Article 132 [Temporary suspension of rights of persons in the public service]

(1) Civil servants and judges who enjoy life tenure when this Basic Law takes effect may, within six months after the Bundestag first convenes, be retired, suspended, or transferred to lower-salaried positions if they lack the personal or professional aptitude for their present positions. This provision shall apply mutatis mutandis to salaried public employees, other than civil servants or

judges, whose employment cannot be terminated at will. In the case of salaried employees whose employment may be terminated at will, notice periods longer than those set by collective bargaining agreements may be rescinded within the same period.
(2) The preceding provision shall not apply to members of the public service who are unaffected by the provisions respecting "Liberation from National Socialism and Militarism" or who are recognized victims of National Socialism, absent important personal grounds.
(3) Persons affected may have recourse to the courts in accordance with paragraph (4) of Article 19.
(4) Details shall be specified by a statutory instrument issued by the Federal Government with the consent of the Bundesrat.

Article 133 [Succession to rights and duties of the Administration of the Combined Economic Area]

The Federation shall succeed to the rights and duties of the Administration of the Combined Economic Area.

Article 134 [Succession to Reich assets]

(1) Reich assets shall basically become federal assets.
(2) Insofar as such assets were originally intended to be used principally for administrative tasks not entrusted to the Federation under this Basic Law, they shall be transferred without compensation to the authorities now entrusted with such tasks and to the extent that such assets are now being used, not merely temporarily, for administrative tasks that under this Basic Law are now performed by the Länder, they shall be transferred to the Länder. The Federation may also transfer other assets to the Länder.
(3) Assets that were placed at the disposal of the Reich without compensation by Länder or municipalities (associations of municipalities) shall revert to those Länder or municipalities (associations of municipalities) insofar as the Federation does not require them for its own administrative purposes.
(4) Details shall be regulated by a federal law requiring the consent of the Bundesrat.

Article 135 [Succession to assets of previously existing Länder and corporations]

(1) If after May 8, 1945 and before the effective date of this Basic Law an area has passed from one Land to another, the Land to which the area now belongs shall be entitled to the assets of the Land to which it previously belonged that are located in that area.
(2) The assets of Länder or other public-law corporations or institutions that no longer exist, insofar as they were originally intended to be used principally for administrative tasks or are now being so used, not merely temporarily, shall pass to the Land, corporation, or institution that now performs those tasks.
(3) Real property of Länder that no longer exist, including appurtenances, shall pass to the Land within which it is located, insofar as it is not among the assets already referred to in paragraph (1) of this Article.
(4) Insofar as an overriding interest of the Federation or the particular interest of a region requires, a federal law may depart from the rules prescribed by paragraphs (1) to (3) of this Article.
(5) In all other respects, the succession to and disposition of assets, insofar as it has not been effected before January 1, 1952 by agreement between the affected Länder or corporations or institutions established under public law, shall be regulated by a federal law requiring the consent of the Bundesrat.
(6) Holdings of the former Land of Prussia in enterprises established under private law shall pass to the Federation. Details shall be regulated by a federal law, which may also depart from this

provision.
(7) Insofar as assets that on the effective date of this Basic Law would devolve upon a Land or a corporation or institution established under public law pursuant to paragraphs (1) to (3) of this Article have been disposed of by or pursuant to a Land law or in any other manner by the party thus entitled, the transfer of assets shall be deemed to have taken place before such disposition.

Article 135a [Old obligations]

(1) Federal legislation enacted pursuant to paragraph (4) of Article 134 or paragraph (5) of Article 135 may also provide that the following obligations shall not be performed, or that they shall be performed only in part:

1.	obligations of the Reich, of the former Land of Prussia, or of such other corporations and institutions under public law as no longer exist;
2.	such obligations of the Federation or of corporations and institutions under public law as are connected with the transfer of assets pursuant to Article 89, 90, 134, or 135, and such obligations of these bodies as arise from measures taken by the bodies designated in subparagraph 1;
3.	such obligations of the Länder or municipalities (associations of municipalities) as have arisen from measures taken by them before August 1, 1945 within the framework of administrative functions incumbent upon or delegated by the Reich to comply with orders of the occupying powers or to terminate a state of emergency resulting from the war.

(2) Paragraph (1) of this Article shall apply mutatis mutandis to obligations of the German Democratic Republic or its institutions as well as to obligations of the Federation or other corporations and institutions under public law that are connected with the transfer of assets of the German Democratic Republic to the Federation, Länder, or municipalities, and to obligations arising from measures taken by the German Democratic Republic or its institutions.

Article 136 [First convening of the Bundesrat]

(1) The Bundesrat shall convene for the first time on the day the Bundestag first convenes.
(2) Until the election of the first Federal President, his powers shall be exercised by the President of the Bundesrat. He shall not have authority to dissolve the Bundestag.

Article 137 [Right of civil servants to stand for election]

(1) The right of civil servants, other salaried public employees, professional or volunteer members of the Armed Forces, and judges to stand for election in the Federation, in the Länder, or in the municipalities may be restricted by a law.
(2) The election of the first Bundestag, of the first Federal Convention, and of the first Federal President shall be governed by an electoral law to be enacted by the Parliamentary Council.
(3) Until the Federal Constitutional Court is established, its authority under paragraph (2) of

Article 41 shall be exercised by the German High Court for the Combined Economic Area, which shall make determinations in accordance with its procedural rules.

Article 138 [South German notaries]

Changes in the rules governing the notarial profession as it now exists in the Länder of Baden, Bavaria, Württemberg-Baden, and Württemberg-Hohenzollern shall require the consent of the governments of these Länder.

Article 139 [Continuing validity of denazification provisions]

The legal provisions enacted for the "Liberation of the German People from National Socialism and Militarism" shall not be affected by the provisions of this Basic Law.

Article 140 [Provisions respecting religious societies]

The provisions of Articles 136, 137, 138, 139, and 141 of the German Constitution of August 11, 1919 shall be an integral part of this Basic Law.

Article 141 ["Bremen Clause"]

The first sentence of paragraph (3) of Article 7 shall not apply in any Land in which Land law otherwise provided on January 1, 1949.

Article 142 [Basic rights in Land constitutions]

Notwithstanding Article 31, provisions of Land constitutions shall also remain in force insofar as they guarantee basic rights in conformity with Articles 1 to 18 of this Basic Law.

Article 142a [Repealed]

Article 143 [Deviations from the Basic Law]

(1) The law in the territory specified in Article 3 of the Unification Treaty may deviate from provisions of this Basic Law for a period extending no later than December 31, 1992 insofar and so long as disparate circumstances make full compliance impossible. Deviations may not violate paragraph (2) of Article 19 and must be compatible with the principles specified in paragraph (3) of Article 79.
(2) Deviations from Titles II, VIII, VIIIa, IX, X, and XI shall be permissible for a period extending no later than December 31, 1995.
(3) Independently of paragraphs (1) and (2) of this Article, Article 41 of the Unification Treaty and the rules for its implementation shall also remain in effect insofar as they provide for the irreversibility of acts interfering with property rights in the territory specified in Article 3 of this Treaty.

Article 143a [Privatization of federal railways]

(1) The Federation shall have exclusive power to legislate with respect to all matters arising from the transformation of federal railways administered by the Federation into business enterprises. Paragraph (5) of Article 87e shall apply mutatis mutandis. Civil servants employed by federal railways may be assigned by a law to render services to federal railways established under

private law without prejudice to their legal status or the responsibility of their employer.
(2) Laws enacted pursuant to paragraph (1) of this Article shall be executed by the Federation.
(3) The Federation shall continue to be responsible for local passenger services of the former federal railways until December 31, 1995. The same shall apply to the corresponding functions of rail transport administration. Details shall be regulated by a federal law requiring the consent of the Bundesrat.

Article 143b [Privatization of the Deutsche Bundespost]

(1) The special trust Deutsche Bundespost shall be transformed into enterprises under private law in accordance with a federal law. The Federation shall have exclusive power to legislate with respect to all matters arising from this transformation.
(2) The exclusive rights of the Federation existing before the transformation may be transferred by a federal law for a transitional period to the enterprises that succeed to the Deutsche Bundespost Postdienst and to the Deutsche Bundespost Telekom. The Federation may not surrender its majority interest in the enterprise that succeeds to the Deutsche Bundespost Postdienst until at least five years after the law takes effect. To do so shall require a federal law with the consent of the Bundesrat.
(3) Federal civil servants employed by the Deutsche Bundespost shall be given positions in the private enterprises that succeed to it, without prejudice to their legal status or the responsibility of their employer. The enterprises shall exercise the employer's authority. Details shall be regulated by a federal law.

Article 144 [Ratification of the Basic Law]

(1) This Basic Law shall require ratification by the parliaments of two thirds of the German Länder in which it is initially to apply.
(2) Insofar as the application of this Basic Law is subject to restrictions in any Land listed in Article 23 [since repealed] or in any part thereof, such Land or part thereof shall have the right to send representatives to the Bundestag in accordance with Article 38 and to the Bundesrat in accordance with Article 50.

Article 145 [Promulgation of the Basic Law]

(1) The Parliamentary Council, with the participation of the members for Greater Berlin, shall confirm the ratification of this Basic Law in public session and shall certify and promulgate it.
(2) This Basic Law shall take effect at the end of the day on which it is promulgated.
(3) It shall be published in the Federal Law Gazette.

Article 146 [Duration of validity of the Basic Law]

This Basic Law, which since the achievement of the unity and freedom of Germany applies to the entire German people, shall cease to apply on the day on which a constitution freely adopted by the German people takes effect.

APPENDIX TO THE BASIC LAW

Extracts from the German Constitution of August 11, 1919 [Weimar Constitution]

Article 136 (Weimar Constitution)

(1) Civil and political rights and duties shall be neither dependent upon nor restricted by the exercise of religious freedom.
(2) Enjoyment of civil and political rights and eligibility for public office shall be independent of religious affiliation.
(3) No person shall be required to disclose his religious convictions. The authorities shall have the right to inquire into a person's membership in a religious society only to the extent that rights or duties depend upon it or that a statistical survey mandated by a law so requires.
(4) No person may be compelled to perform any religious act or ceremony, to participate in religious exercises, or to take a religious form of oath.

Article 137 (Weimar Constitution)

(1) There shall be no state church.
(2) The freedom to form religious societies shall be guaranteed. The union of religious societies within the territory of the Reich shall be subject to no restrictions.
(3) Religious societies shall regulate and administer their affairs independently within the limits of the law that applies to all. They shall confer their offices without the participation of the state or the civil community.
(4) Religious societies shall acquire legal capacity according to the general provisions of civil law.
(5) Religious societies shall remain corporations under public law insofar as they have enjoyed that status in the past. Other religious societies shall be granted the same rights upon application, if their constitution and the number of their members give assurance of their permanency. If two or more religious societies established under public law unite into a single organization, it too shall be a corporation under public law.
(6) Religious societies that are corporations under public law shall be entitled to levy taxes on the basis of the civil taxation lists in accordance with Land law.
(7) Associations whose purpose is to foster a philosophical creed shall have the same status as religious societies.
(8) Such further regulation as may be required for the implementation of these provisions shall be a matter for Land legislation.

Article 138 (Weimar Constitution)

(1) Rights of religious societies to public subsidies on the basis of a law, contract, or special grant shall be redeemed by legislation of the Länder. The principles governing such redemption shall be established by the Reich.
(2) Property rights and other rights of religious societies or associations in their institutions, foundations, and other assets intended for purposes of worship, education, or charity shall be guaranteed.

Article 139 (Weimar Constitution)

Sunday and holidays recognized by the state shall remain protected by law as days of rest from work and of spiritual improvement.

Article 141 (Weimar Constitution)

To the extent that a need exists for religious services and pastoral work in the army, in hospitals, in prisons, or in other public institutions, religious societies shall be permitted to provide them, but without compulsion of any kind.

SUPPLEMENTS

GERMAN FEDERAL MINISTRIES

Federal Ministry for Economic Affairs and Energy (BMWi)http://www.bmwi.de/

Scharnhorststraße 34 – 3710115 BerlinPhone: +49 (0) 30 18 615-0Fax: +49 (0) 30 18 615-7010

Villemombler Straße 76 53123 Bonn Phone: +49 (0) 228 99 615-0 Fax: +49 (0) 228 99 615-4436

Federal Foreign Office (AA)http://www.auswaertiges-amt.de/

Werderscher Markt 110117 BerlinPostal address: 11013 BerlinPhone: +49 (0) 30 18 17-0Fax: +49 (0) 30 18 17-3402

Adenauerallee 99 – 10353113 BonnPhone: +49 (0) 228 99 17-0Fax: +49 (0) 228 99 17-3402

Federal Ministry of the Interior (BMI)http://www.bmi.bund.de/

Alt-Moabit 14010557 BerlinPhone: +49 (0) 30 18 580-0Fax: +49 (0) 30 18 681-2926

Graurheindorfer Straße 19853117 BonnPhone: +49 (0) 228 99 681-0Fax: +49 (0) 228 99 681-2926

Federal Ministry of Justice and Consumer Protection (BMJV)http://www.bmjv.de/

Mohrenstraße 3710117 BerlinPhone: +49 (0) 30 18 580-0Fax: +49 (0) 30 18 580-9525

Adenauer Allee 99 – 10353113 BonnPhone: +49 (0) 228 99 580-0Fax: +49 (0) 228 99 580-8325

Federal Ministry of Finance (BMF)http://www.bundesfinanzministerium.de/

Wilhelmstraße 9710117 BerlinPhone: +49 (0) 30 18 682-0Fax: +49 (0) 30 18 682-3260

Am Propsthof 78a53121 BonnPhone: +49 (0) 30 18 682-0Fax: +49 (0) 30 18 682-4420

Federal Ministry of Labour and Social Affairs (BMAS)http://www.bmas.de/

Wilhelmstraße 4910117 BerlinPhone: +49 (0) 30 18 527-0Fax: +49 (0) 30 18 527-1830

Rochusstraße 153123 BonnPhone: +49 (0) 228 99 527-0Fax: +49 (0) 228 99 527-2965

Federal Ministry of Food and Agriculture (BMEL)http://www.bmel.de

Wilhelmstraße 5410117 BerlinPhone: +49 (0) 30 18 529-0Fax: +49 (0) 30 18 529-3179

Rochusstraße 153123 BonnP.O. Box 14 02 70, 53107 BonnPhone: +49 (0) 228 99 529-0Fax: +49 (0) 228 99 529-3179

Federal Ministry of Defence (BMVg)http://www.bmvg.de

Stauffenbergstraße 1810785 BerlinPhone: +49 (0) 30 18 24-000Fax: +49 (0) 30 18 24-5357

Fontainengraben 15053123 BonnPhone: +49 (0) 228 120-0Fax: +49 (0) 228 12-5357

Federal Ministry of Family Affairs,Senior Citizens, Women and Youth (BMFSFJ)http://www.bmfsfj.de/

Glinkastraße 2410117 BerlinPhone: +49 (0) 30 18 555-0Fax: +49 (0) 30 18 555-4400

Rochusstraße 8 – 1053123 BonnPhone: +49 (0) 30 18 555-0Fax: +49 (0) 30 18 555-2221

Federal Ministry of Health (BMG)http://www.bmg.bund.de/

Friedrichstraße 10810117 BerlinPostal address: 11055 BerlinPhone: +49 (0) 30 18 441-0Fax: +49 (0) 30 18 441-1921

Rochusstraße 153123 BonnPostal address: 53107 BonnPhone: +49 (0) 228 99 441-0Fax: +49 (0) 228 99 441-1921

Federal Ministry of Transport and Digital Infrastructure (BMVI)http://www.bmvi.de/

Invalidenstraße 44, 10115 BerlinKrausenstraße 17 – 20, 10117 BerlinPhone: +49 (0) 30 18 300-0Fax: +49 (0) 30 18 300-1920

Robert-Schuman-Platz 153175 BonnPhone: +49 (0) 228 99 300-0Fax: +49 (0) 228 99 300-3428

Federal Ministry for Environment, Nature Conservation, Building and Nuclear Safety (BMUB)http://www.bmub.bund.de

Stresemannstraße 12810117 BerlinPhone: +49 (0) 30 18 305-0Fax: +49 (0) 30 18 305-4375

Robert-Schuman-Platz 353175 BonnPhone: +49 (0) 228 99 305-0Fax: +49 (0) 228 99 305-3225

Federal Ministry of Education and Research (BMBF)http://www.bmbf.de/

Kapelle-Ufer 110117 BerlinPhone: +49 (0) 30 18 57-0Fax: +49 (0) 30 18 57-83601

Heinemannstraße 253175 BonnPhone: +49 (0) 228 99 57-0Fax: +49 (0) 228 99 57-83601

Federal Ministry of Economic Cooperationand Development (BMZ)http://www.bmz.de/

Stresemannstraße 9410963 BerlinPhone: +49 (0) 30 18 535-0Fax: +49 (0) 30 18 535-2595

Dahlmannstraße 453113 BonnPhone: +49 (0) 228 99 535-0Fax: +49 (0) 228 99 535-3500

GERMAN EMBASSIES BY COUNTRY - ALPHABETICAL LISTING

German Embassy in Kabul, Afghanistan
Embassy of Germany in Kabul, Afghanistan
Wazir Akbar Khan, Mena 6 , P.O. Box 83, Kabul, Afghanistan
City Kabul
Phone calls from Germany and worldwide: + 93 (0) 20 - 210 15 12, calls from Afghanistan: (020) - 210 15 12
Fax + 49 (0) 30 5000 - 7518
Website http://www.kabul.diplo.de
Office Hours Embassy: Sunday till Thursday, 9 a.m. to 12 noon (appointments only) Visa section: Sunday till Thursday, 8.30 a.m. - 12 noon; except Thursday also 2.30 p.m. to 3.30 p.m.
Details In urgent cases only (duty officer for emergencies of German nationals only!): Mobile + 93 (0) 799 883 173

German Embassy in Tirana, Albania
German Embassy in Tirana, Albania
Rruga Skenderbeu Nr. 8 Tirana, Albania
City Tirana
Phone (00355 4) 27 45 05
Fax (00355 4) 23 34 97
Website http://www.tirana.diplo.de
Email German.Embassy@icc.al.eu.org

German Embassy in Algiers, Algeria
German Embassy in Algeria
165, Chemin Sfindja (ex Laperlier) Algiers
City Algiers
Phone 213 21 74 19 41
Fax 213 21 74 05 21
Website http://www.algier.diplo.de/spr_2/home/index.html
Email info@allemagne-dz.org

German Embassy in Luanda, Angola
Embassy of Germany in Luanda, Angola
Caixa Postal 12 95 Avenida 4 de Fevreiro, 120 Luanda, Angola
City Luanda
Phone (+244) (222) 33 47 73/ 33 45 16/39 92 69
Fax (+244) (222) 37 25 51
Website http://www.luanda.diplo.de

German Consulate in St. John's, Antigua & Barbuda
Honorary Consulate Office of Germany in Antigua
Ocean View, Hodges Bay/Antigua, W.I., 1259, St. John's, Antigua W.I.
City St. John's
Phone (001268) 462 31 74
Fax (001268) 462 34 96
Email bielc@candw.ag

German Embassy in Buenos Aires, Argentina
Embassy of Germany in Buenos Aires, Argentina
Calle Villanueva 1055, C1426BMC, Buenos Aires, Argentina
City Buenos Aires
Phone 005411 4778 2500
Fax 005411 4778 2550
Website http://www.buenos-aires.diplo.de
Email administracion@embajada-alemana.org.ar

German Consulate in Cordoba, Argentina
Honorary Consulate General of Germany in Cordoba
Cónsul Honorario de la República Federal de Alemania, Elíseo Canton 1870 -, Barrio Villa Paez,X5003AHB Córdoba,
City Cordoba
Phone (0054 351) 489 09 00
Fax (0054 351) 489 08 09
Email consul@oechsle.com.ar

German Consulate in Eldorado, Argentina
Honorary Consulate General of Germany in Eldorado
Cónsul Honorario de la República Federal de Alemania, , Avda. San Martin 1666, 1° piso,N 3380ABQ Eldorado,
City Eldorado
Phone (0054 3751) 42 32 14
Fax (0054 3751) 42 40 77
Email wachnitz@ceel.com.ar

German Consulate in Mendoza, Argentina
Honorary Consulate General of Germany in Mendoza
Cónsul Honorario de la República Federal de Alemania, Montevideo 127, piso 2° , Depto. 1, M5500GGC Mendoza. Argentina.
City Mendoza
Phone (0054 261) 429 65 39
Fax (0054 261) 429 66 09
Email fhilbing@yahoo.com.ar

German Consulate in Posadas, Argentina
Honorary Consulate General of Germany in Posadas
Cónsul Honorario de la República Federal de Alemania, Junin 1811, Piso 1°, Of. 1°, N3300MRM Posadas, Misiones.
City Posadas
Phone (0054 3752) 43 55 08
Fax (0054 3752) 43 05 70
Email consulado@estudio.kegler.com.ar

German Consulate in Salta, Argentina
Honorary Consulate General of Germany in Salta
Cónsul Honorario de la República Federal de Alemania, Gral. Las Heras 3, A 4400 DUA Salta, Argentina.
City Salta
Phone (0054 387) 422 90 88
Fax (0054 387) 492 11 84
Email consusal@arnet.com.ar

German Consulate in San Carlos De Bariloche, Argentina
Honorary Consulate General of Germany in San Carlos de Bariloche, Argentina.
Cónsul Honorario de la República Federal de Alemania, Emilio Morales 460, R8400GHJ San Carlos de Bariloche, Argentina.
City San Carlos de Bariloche
Phone (0054 2944) 42 56 95
Fax (0054 2944) 42 50 17
Email consuladobariloche@gmail.com

German Consulate in San Miguel De Tucuman, Argentina
Honorary Consulate General of Germany in San Miguel de Tucuman, Argentina.
Cónsul Honorario de la República Federal de Alemania, San Martin 631, 6A, T4000 CVM San Miguel de Tucumán.
City San Miguel de Tucuman

Phone (0054 381) 421 58 11
Fax (0054 381) 421 58 11
Email consuladoalemantuc@arnet.com.ar

German Consulate in Santa Fe, Argentina
Honorary Consulate General of Germany in Santa Fe
Cónsul Honorario de la República Federal de Alemania, Juan de Garay 2957, S3000CRK Santa Fé.
City Santa Fe
Phone (0054 342) 459 75 44
Fax (0054 342) 459 97 84
Email consuladohonorariosfe@hotmail.com

German Consulate in Ushuaia, Argentina
Honorary Consulate General of Germany in Ushuaia
Cónsul Honorario de la República Federal de Alemania, Alem 966, V9410ACT Ushuaia, Argentina.
City Ushuaia
Phone (0054 2901) 43 07 63
Fax (0054 2901) 43 07 63
Email rodolfowantz@yahoo.com.ar

German Embassy in Yerevan, Armenia
German Embassy in Armenia
Charents Street 29
City Yerevan
Phone 37 41 52 32 79
Fax 37 41 52 47 81
Website http://www.eriwan.diplo.de
Email info@eriwan.diplo.de

German Embassy in Canberra, Australia
Embassy of Germany in Canberra, Australia
119 Empire Circuit, Yarralumla ACT 2600, Australia
City Canberra
Phone (02) 6270 1911
Fax (02) 6270 1951
Website http://www.canberra.diplo.de
Email info1@germanembassy.org.au
Office Hours Monday to Thursday 8 am to 5 pm Friday 8 am to 2 pm

German Consulate in Melbourne, Australia
Office of the Honorary Consul-General of the Fed.Rep.of Germany in Melbourne
Level 4, Suite 8 / 118 Queen Street, Melbourne, Victoria, 3000
City Melbourne
Phone (0061 3) 9642 8088
Fax (0061 3) 9642 8482
Website http://http://www.australia.diplo.de
Email melbourne@hk-diplo.de

German Consulate in Perth, Australia
Honorary Consulate General of Germany in Perth
16 St. George's Terrace, Perth, Western Australia 6000.
City Perth
Phone (0061 8) 93 25 88 51
Fax (0061 8) 92 21 32 00
Email germanhc@wantree.com.au

German Consulate in Adelaide, Australia
Honorary Consulate General of Germany in Adelaide
1st Floor, 23 Peel Street, Adelaide, S. A. 5000.
City Adelaide
Phone (0061 8) 82 31 63 20
Fax (0061 8) 82 31 63 20
Email germanhc@bigpond.net.au

German Consulate in Brisbane, Australia
Honorary Consulate General of Germany in Brisbane
10 Eagle Street, 32 Floor, AMP Place, Brisbane, Qld. 4000, Australia
City Brisbane
Phone (0061 7) 32 21 78 19
Fax (0061 7) 32 21 73 35
Email germancons@iprimus.com.au

German Consulate in Cairns, Australia
Honorary Consulate General of Germany in Cairns
Shop 11 The Conservatory, 12 Lake Street, Cairns, QLD 4870
City Cairns
Phone (0061 7) 40 41 53 44
Fax (0061 7) 40 41 53 66
Email iraymond@questapartments.com.au

German Consulate in Darwin, Australia
Honorary Consulate General of Germany in Darwin
Action Sheet Metal Lot, 1824 Berrimah Road, Berrimah, NT 0828., P.O Box 38995, Winnellie 0821, Darwin, N.T.
City Darwin
Phone (0061 8) 89 84 37 70 / (0061 8) 89 84 37 69
Fax (0061 8) 89 47 00 37
Email harry@actionsheetmetal.com.au

German Consulate in Tasmania, Australia
Honorary Consulate General of Germany in Tasmania
143 Hampden Road, Hobart TAS 7000
City Tasmania
Phone (0061 3) 62 23 82 39
Fax (0061 3) 62 34 61 55
Email consulhobart@bigpond.com
Office Hours Monday & Wednesday 10.30am - 1.30pm

German Consulate in Sydney, Australia
Consulate General of Germany in Sydney
13 Trelawney Street, Woollahra, N.S.W. 2025.
City Sydney
Phone (0061 2) 93 28 77 33
Fax (0061 2) 93 27 96 49
Website http://www.sydney.diplo.de
Email info@sydney.diplo.de

German Consulate in Melbourne, Australia
German Consulate-General in Melbourne
480 Punt Rd. (PO Box 76), South Yarra VIC 3141
City Melbourne
Phone +61 (0)3 9864 6888
Fax +61 (0)3 9820 2414
Website http://www.melbourne.diplo.de

Office Hours Opening hours: We are open to the public Monday to Friday from 9:00 am to 12:00 noon. If you wish to speak to a Consular officer, you can reach us by phone (++61 3 9864 6888) between 2:00 pm and 4:30 pm (Monday to Thursday) or 12:00 noon and 2:00 pm (Friday). Individual appointments may be arranged at other times.
Details Jurisdiction: Victoria, South Australia, Tasmania and Western Australia.

German Embassy in Wien, Austria
German Embassy in Austria
Metternichgasse 3, 1030
City Wien
Phone 71154 0
Fax 7138366
Website http://www.wien.diplo.de
Email info@wien.diplo.de

German Consulate in Bregenz, Austria
Honorary Consulate General of Germany in Bregenz
Mariahilfstraße 27 - 31, 6900 Bregenz, P.O Box 77, 6901 Bregenz, Österreich
City Bregenz
Phone (0043 55 74) 4 31 80
Fax (0043 5574) 4 70 83
Email deutscher.honorarkonsul.bregenz@vol.at

German Consulate in Graz, Austria
Honorary Consulate General of Germany in Graz
Statteggerstr. 18, 8045 Graz.
City Graz
Phone (0043 316) 69 49 70
Fax (0043 316) 690 24 25
Email deutscher-honorarkonsul-graz@andritz.com

German Embassy in Baku/Aserbaidschan, Azerbaijan
German Embassy in Azerbaijan
Ul. Mamedalieva 15, Baku/Aserbaidschan, 370000
City Baku/Aserbaidschan
Phone 0099412 4654100
Fax 0099 412 985 419
Website http://www.baku.diplo.de
Email postmaster@botschaftbaku.de

German Consulate in Nassau, Bahamas
Honorary Consulate General of Germany in Nassau
c/o Banque SCS Alliance Nassau) Ltd., Alliance House, East Bay Street, Nassau., P.O. Box N 1724, Nassau, Bahamas.
City Nassau
Phone (001 242) 394 61 61
Fax (001 242) 394 62 62

German Embassy in Manama, Bahrain
Embassy of Germany in Bahrain
Alhasan Building, Sh. Hamad Causeway, Building No. 668, Diplomatic Area 317,, Manama, P.O. Box 10306, Manama, Bahrain.
City Manama
Phone (00973) 17 53 02 10
Fax (00973) 17 53 62 82
Email GERMEMB@BATELCO.COM.BH

German Embassy in Dhaka, Bangladesh
German Embassy in Dhaka, Bangladesh
Embassy of the Federal Republic of Germany, 178, Gulshan Avenue, Dhaka - 1212, Bangladesh
City Dhaka
Phone 008802 - 885 35 21 - 24
Fax 008802 - 885 35 28
Website http://www.dhaka.diplo.de/Vertretung/dhaka/en/Startseite.html
Email aadhaka@optimaxbd.net
Office Hours From 1st April till 30th November:
Sundays: 8.00 - 12.30 and 13.00 - 16.30
Monday to Thursday: 8.00 - 12.30 and 13.00 - 15.15

From 1st December till 31st March:
Sunday to Thursday: 8.00 - 12.30 and 13.00 - 16.30
Office hours of the visa section:
Sunday through Thursday: 9.00 - 11.00
(registration 7.30 am)

German Consulate in Barbados, Barbados
Honorary Consulate General of Germany in Barbados
Brittons Hill, St. Michael, Barbados. W. I., P.O. Box 17 B, Brittons Hill, St. Michael. Barbados. W. I.
City Barbados
Phone (001246) 427 18 76
Fax (001246) 427 81 27
Email germancon@sunbeach.net

German Embassy in Minsk, Belarus
German Embassy in Belarus
220034 Zaharova, 26
City Minsk
Phone 375 17 2133752 and 375 17 2133357
Fax 375 17 2368552
Email germanembassy@mail.belpak.by

German Embassy in Brussels, Belgium
German Embassy in Belgium
Avenue de Tervuren 190
City Brussels
Phone 32 2 774 19 11
Fax 32 2 772 36 92
Website http://www.bruessel.diplo.de
Email info@bruessel.diplo.de
Details ---

German Consulate in Hasselt, Belgium
Honorary Consulate General of Germany in Hasselt
Mombeekdreef 18, 3500 Hasselt
City Hasselt
Phone (0032 11) 27 09 58
Fax (0032 11) 27 09 58
Email honorarkonsul.cajot@skynet.be

German Consulate in Lüttich, Belgium
Honorary Consulate General of Germany in Lüttich
Boulevard Frère Orban 18, B-4000 Lüttich.
City Lüttich
Phone (0032 4) 230 57 68
Fax (0032 4) 230 57 69
Email g.blaise@consulallemagne.be

German Consulate in Ostend, Belgium
Honorary Consulate General of Germany in Ostend
Orteliuslaan 8, 8420 De Haan
City Ostend
Phone (0032 59) 32 63 34
Fax (0032 59) 32 63 34
Email decrop@belgacom.net

German Consulate in Schilde, Belgium
Honorary Consulate General of Germany in Schilde
Gladiolenlaan 4, 2970 Schilde.
City Schilde
Phone (0032 3) 354 29 75
Fax (0032 3) 544 89 67
Email rene.loix@skynet.be

German Consulate in Belize City, Belize
Honorary Consulate General of Germany in Belize City
57 Southern Foreshore, Belize City, Belize.
City Belize City
Phone (00501 8) 22 23 50 / (00501 2) 22 43 69
Fax (00501 2) 22 43 75
Email maritza@cisco.com.bz

German Embassy in Cotonou, Benin
Embassy of Germany in Cotonou, Benin
Avenue Jean-Paul II. BP 504
City Cotonou
Phone 229 31 29 67
Fax 229 31 29 62
Website http://www.cotonou.diplo.de
Email info@cotonou.diplo.de
Office Hours -
Details -

German Consulate in Hamilton, Bermuda
Honorary Consulate General of Germany in Hamilton
Cedar House, 41 Cedar Avenue, Hamilton HM 12, Bermuda.
City Hamilton
Phone (001441) 2 95 06 14
Fax (001 441) 298 33 01
Details Consul: MR Jens Alers

German Embassy in La Paz, Bolivia
German Embassy in Bolivia
Avenida Arce 2395
City La Paz
Phone 591 2 244 00 66
Fax 591 2 244 14 41
Website http://www.la-paz.diplo.de/
Email info@embajada-alemana-bolivia.org
Details ---

German Consulate in Cochabamba, Bolivia
Honorary Consulate General of Germany in Cochabamba
Calle España Edif. La Promotora, esq. Heroinas 6°, piso, of. 602, Cochabamba.
City Cochabamba

Phone (00591 4) 425 40 23 / (00591 4) 425 40 24
Fax (00591 4) 425 40 23

German Consulate in Cruz De La Sierra, Bolivia
Honorary Consulate General of Germany in Cruz de la Sierra
Condominio Plaza Libertad, Oficina 201, Santa Cruz de la Sierra.
City Cruz de la Sierra
Phone (00591 3) 234 39 14
Fax (00591 3) 345 39 51
Email hcmibi@cotas.com.bo

German Consulate in Sucre, Bolivia
Honorary Consulate General of Germany in Sucre
Calle Avaroa Nr. 326, Sucre.
City Sucre
Phone (00591 464) 520 91
Fax (00591 464) 520 91
Email gmielke@entelnet.bo

German Consulate in Tarija, Bolivia
Honorary Consulate General of Germany in Tarija
Calle Sucre No. 665, Tarija.
City Tarija
Phone (00591 4) 664 20 62
Fax (00591 4) 663 08 26
Email gmielke@entelnet.bo

German Embassy in Gaborone, Botswana
German Embassy in Botswana
Professional House, Broadhurst, Segodithsane Way
City Gaborone
Phone 267 3 95 31 43
Fax 267 3 95 30 38
Website http://www.gaborone.diplo.de
Email germanembassy@info.bw
Details ---

German Consulate in Maun, Botswana
German Consulate in Maun, Botswana
Crocodile Safaris, Plot No.4,, Moremi Rd, Matlapaneng, P.O. Box 46
City Maun
Phone (267) 686 0265
Fax (267) 686 0793
Email khg@info.bw

German Consulate in Maun, Botswana
Honorary Consulate General of Germany in Maun
Crocodile Safaris, Plot No.: 4, Moremi Road, Matlapaneng.
City Maun
Phone (00267) 686 02 65
Fax (00267) 686 07 93
Email khg@info.bw

German Embassy in Brasilia, Brazil
Embassy of Germany in Brasilia, Brazil
SES Avenida das Nacoes, Qd. 807, Lot 25, 70415-900
City Brasilia
Phone 55-61-443-7330

Fax (55-61) 443 7508
Website http://www.brasil.diplo.de/Vertretung/brasilien/pt/Startseite.html
Email germanembassy@zaz.com.br
Office Hours 9h - 12h

German Consulate in Sao Paulo, Brazil
German Consulate in Sao Paulo
Avenida Brigadeiro Faria Lima, 2092-120 andar, Jardim Paulistano
City Sao Paulo
Phone (55-11) 3097 6644
Fax (55-11) 3815 7538
Website http://www.sao-paulo.diplo.de/pt/Startseite.html
Email info.saopaulo@alemanha.org.br

German Consulate in Recife, Brazil
Consulate of Germany in Recife
Edf. Empresarial Center III, Rua Antonio Lumack do Monte, 128, 16Â° andar Boa Viagem
City Recife
Phone (55-81) 3463 5350
Fax (55-81) 3465 4084
Website http://www.recife.diplo.de/pt/Startseite.html
Email info.recife@alemanha.org.br
Office Hours 9:00 Ã s 12:00

German Consulate in Blumenau, Brazil
Consulate of Germany in Blumenau
Rua XV. de Novembro, 759, EdifÃcio Hering, 10Â° andar, Sala 1006
City Blumenau
Phone (55-47) 322 1172
Fax (55-47) 321 3450

German Consulate in Cuiaba, Brazil
Consulate of Germany in Mato Grosso
Rua FranÃ§a 199, Bairro Santa Rosa
City Cuiaba
Phone (55-65) 626 1787, 2073
Fax (55-65) 626 1309

German Consulate in Porto Alegre, Brazil
German Consulate in Porto Alegre
Rua Prof. Annes Dias 112, 11Â° andar
City Porto Alegre
Phone (55-51) 3224 9592, 55
Fax (55-51) 3226 4909
Website http://www.porto-alegre.diplo.de/pt/Startseite.html
Email info.portoalegre@alemanha.org.br

German Consulate in Rio De Janeiro, Brazil
Consulate of Germany in Rio de Janeiro
Rua Presidente Carlos de Campos, 417
City Rio de Janeiro
Phone (55-21) 2554 0004
Fax (55-21) 2553 0184
Website http://www.rio-de-janeiro.diplo.de/pt/Startseite.html
Email dtgkrio.ntg@terra.com.br
Office Hours 8:30 Ã s 11:30 horas

German Consulate in Belem, Brazil
Consulate of Germany in Belem
Travessa ApinagÃ©s No. 944, Apt. 601, Bairro Batista Campos, Para
City Belem
Phone (55-91) 212 8366, 5634
Fax (55-91) 212 8366
Email hsteffen.bel@zaz.com.br

German Embassy in Brasilia, Brazil
German Embassy in Brasilia, Brazil
SES Avenida das Nacoes, Qd. 807, Lot 25, 70415-900
City Brasilia
Phone (55-61) 442-7000
Fax (55-61) 443 7508
Website http://brasilia.diplo.de
Email pr@embaixada-alemanha.org.br

German Consulate in Porto Alegre, Brazil
Honorary Consulate General of Germany in Porto Alegre
Rua Prof. Annes Dias 112, 11° andar, 90020-090 Porto Alegre-RS.
City Porto Alegre
Phone (0055 51) 32 24 95 92 / (0055 51) 32 24 92 55
Fax (0055 51) 32 26 49 09
Website http://www.rio-de-janeiro.diplo.de
Email info.portoalegre@alemanha.org.br

German Consulate in Cuiaba, Brazil
Honorary Consulate General of Germany in Cuiaba
Avenida França 199, Bairro Santa Rosa, 78040-170 Cuiabá-MT.
City Cuiaba
Phone (0055 65) 36 26 20 73 / (0055 65) 36 26 13 09
Fax (0055 65) 36 26 17 87
Email consulkramm@terra.com.br

German Consulate in Curitiba, Brazil
Honorary Consulate General of Germany in Curitiba
Rua Emiliano Perneta, 297, cj. 232, 80010-050 Curitiba-PR.
City Curitiba
Phone (0055 41) 32 22 69 20
Fax (0055 41) 32 22 03 22
Email hansgschorer@aol.com

German Consulate in Fortaleza, Brazil
Honorary Consulate General of Germany in Fortaleza
Rua Dr. José Lourenço, 2244, 60115-282 Fortaleza-CE.
City Fortaleza
Phone (0055 85) 32 46 28 33
Fax (0055 85) 32 46 70 99
Email dghonkonsulbrd@secrel.com.br

German Consulate in Joinville, Brazil
Honorary Consulate General of Germany in Joinville
Rua Alexandre Döhler, 78, 89201-260 Joinville-SC.
City Joinville
Phone (0055 47) 34 33 86 79
Fax (0055 47) 34 22 35 52
Email konsul@dohler.com.br

German Consulate in Manaus, Brazil
Consulate of Germany in Brazil
Martin Klenke, R.Franco de Sa, 270, S.805 - Sao Francisco, Edif. Amazon Trade Center, CEP: 69079 - 210
City Manaus
Phone (0055 92) 36 59 33 00
Fax (0055 92) 36 59 33 00
Email m.klenke@hotmail.com

German Consulate in Ribeirao Preto, Brazil
Honorary Consulate General of Germany in Ribeirao Preto
Rua Campos Salles 658, 14015-110 Ribeirao Preto-SP.
City Ribeirao Preto
Phone (0055 16) 36 35 27 25
Fax (0055 16) 36 35 23 78
Email ieba@terra.com.br

German Consulate in Rolândia, Brazil
Honorary Consulate General of Germany in Rolandia
Avenida dos Expedicion rios, 342, sala 81, Edificio Center Comercial de Rolândia, 86600-000 Rolandia-PR
City Rolândia
Phone (0055 43) 32 56 19 31
Fax (0055 43) 32 56 33 74
Website http://www.brasil.diplo.de
Email rolandia@hk-diplo.de

German Consulate in Salvador, Bahia. Brazil., Brazil
Honorary Consulate General of Germany in Salvador, Bahia. Brazil.
Rua Jogo de Carneiro, 49, Saude, 40045-040 Salvador-BA..
City Salvador, Bahia. Brazil.
Phone (0055 71) 32 42 26 70
Fax (0055 71) 32 41 50 93
Email hksalvador@yahoo.de

German Consulate in Santos, Brazil
Honorary Consulate General of Germany in Santos
Rua Frei Gaspar 22 , 10° andar, sala 104, 11010-909 Santos-SP, (Sprechstunden von 09.00 bis 12.00 Uhr
City Santos
Phone (0055 13) 32 19 50 92
Fax (0055 13) 32 13 82 44
Email consuladoalemao-sts@stocklerltda.com.br

German Consulate in Vitoria, Brazil
Honorary Consulate General of Germany in Vitoria
Av. Nossa Senhora dos Navegantes, 755 - s.906, Enseada do Sul, 29055-335 Vitoria
City Vitoria
Phone (0055 27) 21 21 68 89
Fax (0055 27) 21 21 68 90
Email petra@hk.vitoria.nom.br

German Embassy in Bandar Seri Begawan, Brunei
German Embassy in Brunei Darussalam
Block A, Second Floor, Unit 2.01, Yayasan Sultan Haji Hassanal Bolkiah Complex, Jalan Pretty, BS 8711, P.O. Box 3050, BS 8675
City Bandar Seri Begawan
Phone (+673) 2 225 547
Fax (+673) 2 225 583
Website http://www.bandar-seri-begawan.diplo.de/en/02/Botschaft.html
Email prgerman@brunet.bn

Office Hours Monday to Friday 9.oo - 12.oo hrs, Monday to Thursday 14.oo - 16.oo hrs The visa section is open Monday to Friday from 9 - 12 hrs
Details ---

German Embassy in Sofia, Bulgaria
German Embassy in Bulgaria
Ulica Frederic Joliot Curie 25
City Sofia
Phone 359 2 91 83 80
Fax 359 2 9 63 41 17
Website http://www.german-embassy.bg
Email gemb@vilmat.com
Details ---

German Consulate in Varna, Bulgaria
Consulate of Germany in Varna, Bulgaria
Ul. Dragoman Nr. 1
City Varna
Phone (359-52) 693 693~4
Fax (359-52) 601 930
Email nedyalko.nedelchev@cargoexpress.bg

German Embassy in Quagadougou, Burkina Faso
German Embassy in Burkina Faso
399, Avenue Joseph Badoua
City Quagadougou
Phone 226 5030 67 31
Fax (226) 5031 39 91
Email amb.allemagne@fasonet.bf
Details ---

German Embassy in Bujumbura, Burundi., Burundi
Embassy of Germany in Bujumbura, Burundi.
Hotel Source de Nil, Suite Nr. 301, Avenue de Stade, Bujumbura.
City Bujumbura, Burundi.
Phone (00 257) 22 64 12 / (00 257)22 64 16

German Embassy in Phnom Penh, Cambodia
German Embassy in Cambodia
No. 76-78 Rue Yougoslavie
City Phnom Penh
Phone (844) 216 193, 381
Fax (844) 23 42 77 46
Email germanembassy@everyday.com.kh
Details ---

German Embassy in Yaounde, Cameroon
German Embassy in Cameroon
Nouvelle Route Bastos, Bastos-Usine, B.P. 1160, Yaounde, Cameroon
City Yaounde
Phone (00237) 221 0056 or 220 0566
Fax (00237) 221 6211
Website http://www.jaunde.diplo.de
Email info@jaun.diplo.de
Office Hours Monday through Friday from 8 am to 11 am

German Embassy in Ottawa, Canada
Embassy of Germany in Ottawa, Canada
1 Waverley Street, Ottawa, Ontario, K2P 0T8, Canada
City Ottawa
Phone (1 613) 232 1101
Fax (1 613) 594 9330
Website http://www.ottawa.diplo.de/
Email info@ottawa.diplo.de
Office Hours Monday to Friday 09.00 a.m. to noon

German Consulate in Montreal, Canada
Consulate of the Federal Republic of Germany in Montreal
1250, Boulevard Rene-Levesque Ouest,, Suite 4315, Montreal,
City Montreal
Phone 1-514-931-2277
Fax 1-514-931-7239
Website http://www.montreal.diplo.de/
Email mail@montr.diplo.de
Office Hours The Consulate General ist open for the public from Monday to Friday from 9.00 to 12.00 and can be reached by telephone from Monday to Thursday until 16.45 and on Fridy until 13.45.
Details Area of Responsibility: Provinces of New Brunswick, Nova Scotia, Prince Edward Island, Newfoundland, Québec (except the region "Communauté Urbaine de l'Outaouais")

German Consulate in Toronto, Canada
Consulate General of the Federal Republic of Germany in Toronto, Canada
2 Bloor St. East, 25th floor, Toronto, Ontario, M4W 1A8
City Toronto
Phone 416-925-2813
Fax 416-925-2818
Website http://www.toronto.diplo.de
Email info@toronto.diplo.de
Office Hours The consular section (passport and visa applications as well as other legal matters) is open to the public Monday through Friday, 9:00 a.m. - noon.

Working hours of the Consulate are Monday through Thursday, 8:00 a.m. to 5:00 p.m., and Fridays from 8:00 a.m. to 3:30 p.m., except on holidays.
Details Area of Responsibility: Provinces of Manitoba and Ontario (except the Counties of Carleton, Lanark, Leeds and Grenville, Prescott and Russell, Renfrew and Stormont, Dundas and Glengary)

German Consulate in Edmonton, Canada
Consulate of Germany in Edmonton, Canada
8005-102 Street, Edmonton, AB, T6E 4A2
City Edmonton
Phone 780-434-0430
Fax 780-439-9950
Email edmonton@hk-diplo.de
Office Hours Tuesday to Thursday, from 9:00 a.m. to noon

German Consulate in Vancouver, Canada
Consulate General of Germany in Vancouver
Suite 704, World Trade Centre, 999 Canada Place, Vancouver, B.C. V6C 3E1, Canada
City Vancouver
Phone (1-604) 684 8377
Fax (1-604) 684 8334
Website
http://www.vancouver.diplo.de/Vertretung/vancouver/en/02/Unterbereich__Address__and__Opening.html
Email GermanConsulateVancouver@telus.net

Office Hours The consular section (passport and visa applications as well as other legal matters) is open to the public Monday through Friday, 9:00 a.m. - noon. Working hours of the Consulate are Monday through Thursday, 7:30 a.m. to 4:30 p.m., and Fridays from 7:30 a.m. to 1:30 p.m., except on holidays
Details Area of Responsibility: Provinces of New Brunswick, Nova Scotia, Prince Edward Island, Newfoundland, Québec (except the region "Communauté Urbaine de l'Outaouais")

German Consulate in Halifax, Canada
Consulate of Germany in Halifax, Canada
1100 - 1959 Upper Water Street, Halifax, Nova Scotia, B3L 3E5, Post: P.O. Box 2380, Stn. Central RPO,, Halifax, Nova Scotia, B3J 3E5, Canada
City Halifax
Phone 902-491-4106
Fax 902-421-3130
Email achapman@coxhanson.ca

German Consulate in Prince George, Canada
Consulate of Germany in Prince George, Canada
203 - 2289 Westwood Dr., Prince George, B.C., V2N 4V6, Canada
City Prince George
Phone 250-649-0202
Fax 250-563-6563
Email akoehler@telus.net

German Consulate in Saskatoon, Canada
Consulate of Germany in Saskatoon, Canada
823 Brookhurst Bay, Saskatoon, SK, S7V 1G1, Canada
City Saskatoon
Phone 306-979-4911
Fax 306-979-4912
Email hksask@shaw.ca

German Consulate in St. John's, Canada
Consulate of Germany in St. John's, Canada
3 Blackmarsh Road, St. John's, Newfoundland, A1E 1S2, Canada
City St. John's
Phone 709-579-2222
Fax 709-739-8911
Email westend@westendelectronics.com

German Embassy in Ottawa, Canada
German Embassy in Canada
1 Waverley Street, ON, K2P 0T8
City Ottawa
Phone 00-1-613-232-1101
Fax 00-1-613-594-9330
Website http://www.ottawa.diplo.de/Vertretung/ottawa/en/Startseite.html
Email germanembassyottawa@on.aibn.com
Office Hours Monday through Friday 9.00 a.m. to noon

German Consulate in Cayman Islands
Honorary Consulate of Germany in Cayman Island
81 Admiral's Avenue, George Town, P.O. Box 10557 KY1-1005
Phone (345) 924-3561
Email schuettemcfield@gmail.com
Details Mrs Christiane SCHUETTE–McFIELD, Honorary Consul (unofficial)

German Embassy in Yaounde, Central African Republic
Embassy of the Federal Republic of Germany in the Central African Republic
Nouvelle Route Bastos, Bastos-Usine
City Yaounde
Phone (00237) 22 21 00 56, 22 20 05 66, 22 21 44 34, 22 21 72 92
Fax (00237) 22 21 62 11, 22 20 73 13
Website http://www.jaunde.diplo.de/
Email info@jaunde.diplo.de

German Embassy in N'Djamena, Chad
German Embassy in Chad
Av. Felix Eboue, P.O. Box 893
City N'Djamena
Phone 235 51 62 02, 647
Fax 235 51 48 00
Email allemagne@intnet.td
Details ---

German Embassy in Santiago, Chile
Embassy of Germany in Santiago, Chile
Las Hualtatas 5677 - Vitacura, Casilla 220, Correo 30 , Santiago de Chile, Chile
City Santiago
Phone (00 56 2) 463 2500
Fax (00 56 2) 463 2525
Website http://www.santiago.diplo.de
Email info@santiago-de-chile.diplo.de
Office Hours Monday to Thursday: 7:45 AM - 5:00 PM Friday: 7:45 AM - 1:45 PM

German Consulate in Puerto Montt, Chile
Consulate of German in Puerto Montt
Antonio Varas 525, of. 306
City Puerto Montt
Phone (56-65) 252 828
Fax (56-65) 252 828
Email c.aleman_ptomontt@surnet.cl

German Consulate in Arica, Chile
Honorary Consul of the Federal Republic of Germany in Arica
Arturo Prat 391, Piso 10,, Oficina 101
City Arica
Phone (56-58) 58 37 40, 58 37 41, 58 37 42
Fax (56-58) 58 37 43
Email upribnow@gership.cl

German Consulate in Antofagasta, Chile
Honorary Consul of the Federal Republic of Germany
Avenida Edmundo Pérez Zujovic 4940, Antofagasta, Postal Address: Consul Honorario de la Republica Federal de Alemania, Casilla 454, Antofagasta, Chile
City Antofagasta
Phone 56 55 55 63 87
Fax 56 55 55 63 88
Email hans.schaefer@reptal.cl, yamile.gonazalez@reptal.cl

German Consulate in Valdivia, Chile
Consulate of Germany in Valdivia
Avenida Arauco 159, of. 201
City Valdivia
Phone (56-63) 218 821, 841, 203 791

Fax (56-63) 213 046
Email eschildcia@telsur.cl, eduardoschild@schild.cl

German Consulate in Temuco, Chile
Honorary Consul of the Federal Republic of Germany in Temuco
Andres Bello 824, Of. 204, Temuco
City Temuco
Phone (56-45) 27 26 66, 29 43 00
Fax (56-45) 214 167
Email cfingerh@entelchile.net, consulado@laolleta.cl

German Consulate in Concepcion, Chile
Honorary Consulate General of Germany in Concepcion
Diagonal Pedro Aguirre Cerda 1151, Piso 2
City Concepcion
Phone (0056 41) 318 95 32
Fax (0056 41) 273 07 44
Email cs.alemania@gmail.com, mccartes@hotmail.com

German Consulate in La Serena, Chile
Honorary Consul of the Federal Republic of Germany in La Serena
Matta 665, La Serena/IV Region
City La Serena
Phone (0056 51) 21 10 05
Fax (0056 51) 21 10 05
Email juansamacoits@hotmail.com

German Consulate in Vina Del Mar, Chile
Honorary Consul of the Federal Republic of Germany in Vina del Mar
1 Norte 525 Of. 208 (entre 1 y 2 Poniente)
City Vina del Mar
Phone (0056 32) 269 50 95
Fax (0056 32) 269 50 95
Email helga.behrend@terra.cl, emma.barends@terra.cl

German Consulate in Guangzhou, China
Consular Office of Germany in Guangzhou, China
19th floor, Guangdong International Hotel, 339 Huanshi Dong Road, Guangzhou, 510098
City Guangzhou
Phone (0086 20) 83 30 65 33
Fax (0086 20) 83 31 70 33
Website http://www.kanton.diplo.de
Email info@kanton.diplo.de

German Consulate in Shanghai, China
Consulate General of Germany in Shanghai, China
181, Yongfu Road, Shanghai 20 00 31.
City Shanghai
Phone (0086 21) 34 01 01 06
Fax (0086 21) 64 71 44 48
Website http://www.shanghai.diplo.de
Email info@gk-shanghai.org.cn

German Embassy in Beijing, China
Embassy of Germany in Beijing, China
17, Dong Zhi Men Wai Da Jie, Chaoyang District, 100600
City Beijing
Phone (0086 10) 85 32 90 00

Fax (0086 10) 65 32 53 36
Website http://www.peking.diplo.de
Email embassy@peki.diplo.de

German Embassy in Bogota, Colombia
Embassy of Germany in Bogota, Colombia
Cra. 69 No. 25B-44, piso 7, Edificio "World Business Port" (edificio El Tiempo) , Bogota, Colombia
City Bogota
Phone 0057-1-4232600
Fax 0057-1-4293145
Website http://www.bogota.diplo.de/Vertretung/bogota/de/Startseite.html
Email info@bogota.diplo.de

German Consulate in Barranquilla, Colombia
Honorary Consulate of Germany in Barranquilla, Colombia
Calle 77 B No. 57 - 141, Ofc. 309, P.O Box Apartado Aéreo 668, Barranquilla., Centro Empresarial de las Americas, Barranquilla, Colombia
City Barranquilla
Phone (57-5)3685384
Fax (57-5)3685384
Website http://www.bogota.diplo.de/Vertretung/bogota/es/seite__honorarkonsul.html
Email consulalemanbq@hotmail.com

German Consulate in Cali, Colombia
Honorary Consulate of Germany in Cali
Calle 1 B Nr. 66 B - 29, Cali, Valle del Cauca
City Cali
Phone (0057 2) 3 23 44 35 /(57-2)3234435/ (57-2)3238402/ (0057 310) 8 22 75 87 Mobile
Fax (0057 2) 3 23 37 84
Website http://www.bogota.diplo.de/Vertretung/bogota/es/seite__honorarkonsul.html
Email consuladoalemancali@lycos.com
Office Hours Monday to Friday: 8:30 to 11:00 am

German Consulate in Medellin, Colombia
Honorary Consulate of Germany in Medellin, Colombia
Cra. 48 No. 26 sur - 181, local 106, Centro Integral Las Vegas, Medellin, Colombia
City Medellin
Phone (57-4)3346474
Fax (57-4)3318716
Website http://www.bogota.diplo.de/Vertretung/bogota/es/seite__honorarkonsul.html
Email mconsulalemanmed@une.net.co

German Consulate in Cartagena, Colombia
Honorary Consulate of Germany in Cartagena, Colombia
Diagonal 21 # 53-25 Piso 2, Bosque, Avenida Principal, Cartagena, Colombia
City Cartagena
Phone +57 5 6694041
Fax +57 5 6694089
Website http://www.bogota.diplo.de/Vertretung/bogota/es/seite__honorarkonsul.html
Email fbolle@costa.net.co
Office Hours Monday to Friday: 2:30 to 4:30 pm

German Consulate in Rarotonga, Cook Islands
Honorary Consulate of Germany in Rarotonga, Cook Islands
Browne Gibson Harvey P.C., Parekura Place, Avarua, Rarotonga.
City Rarotonga
Phone (00682) 245 67 / (00682) 245 77
Fax (00682) 21 15 67, 255 67

Email law@bgh.co.ck

German Embassy in Costa Rica, Costa Rica
Embassy of Germany in Costa Rica
Edificio -Torre La Sabana , 8° piso, 300 mts oeste del ICE, Sabana Norte, P.O Box 4017-1000, San José, Costa Rica.
City Costa Rica
Phone (00506) 290 90 91
Fax (00506) 231 64 03
Website http://www.san-jose.diplo.de
Email info@embajada-alemana-costarica.org

German Embassy in San Jose, Costa Rica
Embassy of Germany in San Jose, Costa Rica
Barrio Rohrmoser, de la Residencia del ex-presidente Oscar Arias, 200 metros al Norte y 75 Metros al Este., Mail to: P.O. Box. 40 17 - 1000
City San Jose
Phone (00 506) 232 55 33/232 54 50/232 56 03
Fax (00 506) 231 64 03
Email info@embajada-alemana.org

German Embassy in Zagreb, Croatia
German Embassy in Croatia
Ulica Grada, Vukovara 64, Zagreb, 1000
City Zagreb
Phone 385 1 6158100 or 385 1 6158101
Fax 385 1 6158103
Website http://www.deutschebotschaft-zagreb.hr/de/home/index.html
Email deutsche.botschaft.zagreb@inet.hr
Details ---

German Embassy in La Habana, Cuba, Cuba
Embassy of Germany in Bahrain in La Habana, Cuba
Calle 13, No. 652, Esquina á B, Vedado, La Habana., P.O Box 6610, La Habana, Cuba.
City La Habana, Cuba
Phone (0053 7) 833 24 60 / (0053 7) 833 25 39
Fax (0053 7) 833 15 86
Website http://www.havanna.diplo.de
Email info@havanna.diplo.de

German Embassy in Nicosia, Cyprus., Cyprus
Embassy of Germany in Nicosia, Cyprus
10 Nikitaras Street, 1080 Nicosia.
City Nicosia, Cyprus.
Phone (00357 2) 2 45 11 45
Fax (00357 2) 2 66 56 94
Website http://www.nikosia.diplo.de
Email info@nikosia.diplo.de

German Consulate in Limassol, Cyprus
Honorary Consulate of Germany in Limassol, Cyprus
21 Archbishop Kyprianos Street, 3036 Limassol., P.O Box 50336, 3603 Limassol, Cyprus.
City Limassol
Phone (00357 2) 5 82 09 20
Fax (00357 2) 5 34 13 61
Email sitinal@cytanet.com.cy

German Embassy in Prague, Czech Republic
German Embassy in Czech Republuc
Vlasska 19, Mala Strana, Prague
City Prague
Phone 420 2 57 11 31 11
Fax 420 2 57 53 40 56
Website http://www.deutsche-botschaft.cz
Email ZReg@Prag.auswaertiges-amt.de
Details ---

German Embassy in Copenhagen, Denmark, Denmark
Embassy of Germany in Copenhagen, Denmark
Stockholmsgade 57, 2100 København Ø ., P.O Box 2712, 2100 København Ø, Danmark.
City Copenhagen, Denmark
Phone (0045) 35 45 99 00
Fax (0045) 35 26 71 05
Website http://www.kopenhagen.diplo.de
Email tyskeamba@email.dk

German Consulate in Aalborg, Denmark., Denmark
Honorary Consulate of Germany in Aalborg
Rings Mabler, Danmarksgade 58-64, 9000 Aalborg
City Aalborg, Denmark.
Phone (0045) 98 12 56 33
Fax (0045) 98 12 41 03
Email rings@rings.dk

German Consulate in Allinge, Denmark., Denmark
Honorary Consulate of Germany in Allinge, Denmark.
c/o Bornholms Sommerhus Udlejning, Sverigesvej 2, 3770 Allinge, Danmark.
City Allinge, Denmark.
Phone (0045) 56 48 05 70
Fax (0045) 56 48 04 70
Email konsulat@bsu.dk

German Consulate in Aarhus, Denmark
Honorary Consulate of Germany in Aarhus
Havnegade 4, 8000 Aarhus C.
City Aarhus
Phone (0045) 86 18 25 88
Fax (0045) 86 18 25 22
Email konsul.de@mail.dk

German Consulate in Haderslev, Denmark., Denmark
Honorary Consulate of Germany in Haderslev, Denmark.
Dencon Foods A/S, Finlandsvej 16, 6100 Haderslev.
City Haderslev, Denmark.
Phone (0045) 74 53 18 28
Fax (0045) 74 53 19 50
Email denconfoods@denconfoods.dk

German Consulate in Ilulissat, Denmark
Consulate General of Japan in of Germany in Denmark
Greenland Tours Elke Meissner, Box 160, 00299 Ilulissat / Graanland
City Ilulissat
Phone (00299) 94 44 22
Fax (00299) 94 45 11
Email greenland.tours@greennet.gl

German Consulate in Middelfart, Denmark, Denmark
Honorary Consulate of the Federal Republic of Germany in Middelfart, Denmark.
Honorary Consulate of the Federal Republic of Germany in Strandvejen 5, 5500 , Middelfart, Denmark
City Middelfart, Denmark
Phone (0045) 64 41 54 01
Fax (0045) 64 41 53 01
Email middelfart@dan-bunkering.dk

German Consulate in Naestved, Denmark, Denmark
Honorary Consulate of the Federal Republic of Germany in Naestved, Denmark.
Scan-Trans Chartering K/S, Vestre Kaj 6, 4700 Naestved.
City Naestved, Denmark
Phone (0045) 55 72 20 00
Fax (0045) 55 77 17 05
Email denmark@scan-trans.com

German Consulate in Nykabing, Denmark, Denmark
Honorary Consulate of the Federal Republic of Germany in Denmark
Induperm A/S, Kobenhavnsvej 1, 4800 Nykabing / Falster
City Nykabing, Denmark
Phone (0045) 54 86 02 00
Fax (0045) 54 86 03 89
Email induperm@induperm.dk

German Embassy in Santo Domingo, Dominican Republic
Embassy of Germany in the Dominican Republic
Alemania, Apartado 1235, Santo Domingo, Dominican Republic
City Santo Domingo
Phone 565-8811
Fax (001809) 542 89 55
Website http://www.santo-domingo.diplo.de
Email embal@verizon.net.do

German Consulate in Puerto Plata, Dominican Republic, Dominican Republic
Honorary Consulate of the Federal Republic of Germany in Puerto Plata, Dominican Republic
Calle Villanueva esq. John F. Kennedy, Edificio Abraxas 2do nivel, Puerto Plata.
City Puerto Plata, Dominican Republic
Phone (001 809) 5 86 69 95
Fax (001 809) 5 86 42 49
Email consulaleman@verizon.net.do

German Embassy in Quito, Ecuador
German Embassy in Quito, Ecuador
Edificio Citiplaza, Avenida Naciones Unidas, Republica de El Salvador, priso 14, Quito
City Quito
Phone 593 2 297 28 20
Fax 593 2 297 08 15
Website http://www.quito.diplo.de/
Email info@quito.diplo.de

German Consulate in Guayaquil, Ecuador, Ecuador
Honorary Consul of the Federal Republic of Germany in Guayaquil, Ecuador
Avenida Las Monjas No. 10, Edificio Berlin, Guayaquil.
City Guayaquil, Ecuador
Phone (0059 34) 220 68 67 / (0059 34) 220 68 68
Email consuladoaleman@investamar.com.ec

German Consulate in Manta, Ecuador, Ecuador
Honorary Consulate of the Federal Republic of Germany in Manta, Ecuador
Av. 102, Los Esteros, Manta.
City Manta, Ecuador
Phone (00593 5) 292 35 77
Fax (00593 5) 292 43 51
Email wrharten@hotmail.com

German Embassy in Cairo, Egypt
Embassy of Germany in Cairo, Egypt
2, Sh. Hassan Sabri, Zamalek
City Cairo
Phone (00202) 739-9600
Fax (00202) 736-0530
Website http://www.kairo.diplo.de/
Email germemb@tedata.net.eg
Office Hours Sunday - Wednesday: 8:00 am to 12:00 am (visitors) Sunday - Thursday: 8:00 am to 11:00 am (passports and legalisations)

German Consulate in Alexandria, Egypt, Egypt
Honorary Consulate of the Federal Republic of Germany in Alexandria, Egypt
Leader Group Shipping Services, 9 El Fawatem Street, Mazarita. Alexandria
City Alexandria, Egypt
Phone (0020 3) 486 75 03
Fax (0020 3) 484 09 77
Email germconsulate@leadergroup.net

German Consulate in Hurghada, Egypt, Egypt
Honorary Consulate of the Federal Republic of Germany in Hurghada, Egypt
Honorary Consulate of the Federal Republic of Germany, 365, El Gabal El Shamali, Hurghada, Red Sea. Egypt
City Hurghada, Egypt
Phone (0020 65) 344 36 05 / (0020 65) 344 57 34
Fax (0020 65) 344 36 05
Email ely@access.com.eg

German Embassy in San Salvador, El Salvador
Embassy of Germany in El Salvador
77a Av. Norte, esqu. 7a Calle Poniente 3972, Colonia Escalon, San Salvador
City San Salvador
Phone (00503) 22 47 00 00
Fax (00503) 22 47 00 99
Website http://www.sansalvador.diplo.de
Email zreg@sans.diplo.de

German Embassy in London, England
Embassy of the Federal Republic of Germany in England
23 Belgrave Square, SW1X 8PZ
City London
Phone 020 7824 1300
Fax 020 7824 1449
Website http://www.london.diplo.de/Vertretung/london/en/02/__Botschaft.html
Email visa@lond.diplo.de

German Consulate in Edinburgh, England
Consulate of the Federal Republic of Germany
16 Eglinton Crescent, EH12 5DG

City Edinburgh
Phone 0131 337 2323
Fax 0131 346 1578
Website http://www.edinburgh.diplo.de/Vertretung/edinburgh/en/Startseite.html
Email visa@lond.diplo.de
Office Hours Monday to Friday, 09.00 - 11.30

German Embassy in Edinburgh, England
German Embassy in Edinburgh
16 Eglinton Crescent, EH12 5DG
City Edinburgh
Phone 0131 337 2323
Fax 0131 346 1578
Website http://germany.embassyhomepage.com/

German Embassy in Asmara, Eritrea
German Embassy in Eritea
Warsay Street, Saba Development Building, Asmara., Asmara
City Asmara
Phone 291 1 18 66 70
Fax 291 1 18 69 00
Website http://www.asmara.diplo.de
Email info@asmara.diplo.de
Details ---

German Embassy in Tallinn, Estonia
German Embassy in Estonia
Toom-Kuninga 11, 15048
City Tallinn
Phone 372 627 53 00
Fax 372 627 53 04
Website http://www.tallinn.diplo.de
Email tallinn@germany.ee

German Embassy in Addis Ababa, Ethiopia
German Embassy in Ethiopia
Khabana, Woreda 12, Kabele 20
City Addis Ababa
Phone 251 1 55 04 33
Fax 251 1 55 13 11
Website http://www.addis-abeba.diplo.de
Email german.emb.addis@telecom.net.et

German Consulate in Suva, Fiji, Fiji
Honorary Consulate of the Federal Republic of Germany in Suva, Fiji
Williams & Gosling LTD, Suva.
City Suva, Fiji
Phone (00679 33) 126 33
Fax (00679 33) 003 67
Email davea@wgfiji.com.fj

German Embassy in Helsinki, Finland
Embassy of Germany in Helsinki, Finland
Krogiuksentie 4b, 00340 Helsinki, Finland
City Helsinki
Phone (+358) (9) 458 580
Fax (+358) (9) 45 85 82 58
Website http://www.helsinki.diplo.de

Email info@helsinki.diplo.de

German Consulate in Joensuu, Finland, Finland
Honorary Consulate of the Federal Republic of Germany in Joensuu, Finland
Broman Group Oy, Tulliportinkatu 50, 80130 Joensuu
City Joensuu, Finland
Phone (00358 13) 2 54 41 41 / (00358 44) 0 33 02 01 Mobile
Fax (00358 13) 2 54 41 99
Email harri.broman@bromangroup.fi

German Consulate in Jyväskylä, Finland, Finland
Honorary Consulate of the Federal Republic of Germany in Jyväskylä, Finland
c/o Wirtschaftsförderungsgesellschaft der Region , Jyväskylä(JYKES), Sepänkatu 4, 3. Stock, 40100 Jyväskylä, Finnland.
City Jyväskylä, Finland
Phone (00358 14) 65 21 01 / (00358 14) 65 21 04
Fax (00358 14)65 21 29
Email ritva.nirkkonen@jykes.fi

German Consulate in Mariehamn, Finland, Finland
Honorary Consulate of the Federal Republic of Germany in Mariehamn, Finland
Norra Esplanadgatan 4 B, 22100 Mariehamn
City Mariehamn, Finland
Phone (00358 18) 2 70 70
Fax (00358 18) 1 26 70
Email gustaf.erikson@geson.aland.fi

German Consulate in Mikkeli, Finland, Finland
Honorary Consulate of the Federal Republic of Germany in Mikkeli, Finland
Kölikaari 23 B, 50170 Mikkeli
City Mikkeli, Finland
Phone (00358 15) 36 08 28
Fax (00358 15) 760 09 50
Email aulis.leva@reimari.net

German Consulate in Oulu, Finland, Finland
Honorary Consulate of the Federal Republic of Germany in Oulu, Finland
c/o Pörhön Autoliike Oy, Nuottasaarentie 6, 90400 Oulu
City Oulu, Finland
Phone (00358 20) 762 40 01
Fax matti.porho@porho.fi

German Consulate in Rauma, Finland, Finland
Honorary Consulate of the Federal Republic of Germany in Rauma, Finland
Oy Rauma Stevedoring Ltd., Hakunintie 23, 26101 Rauma
City Rauma, Finland
Phone (00358 2) 831 24 58 / (00358 40) 588 30 37 (Mobile)
Fax (00358 2) 831 24 44
Email werner.turtscher@raumasteve.fi

German Consulate in Rovaniemi, Finland
Honorary Consulate of the Federal Republic of Germany in Rovaniemi,Finland
Hotelli Olos, 99300 Muonio, Finnland
City Rovaniemi
Phone (00358 16) 53 61 11 / (00358 400) 63 69 69 (Mobile)
Fax (00358 16) 53 61 02

German Consulate in Turku, Finland, Finland
Honorary Consulate of the Federal Republic of Germany in Turku, Finland
Kuntoutusyhtymä-Rehab Group Oy, Juhana Herttuan puistokatu 23, 20100 Turku
City Turku, Finland
Phone (00358 2) 445 45 01
Fax (00358 2) 445 45 20
Email pekka.niemi@saga.fi

German Consulate in Vaasa, Finland, Finland
Honorary Consulate of the Federal Republic of Germany in Vaasa, Finland
Vaasan Käyttöauto, Rantamaantie 4, 65350 Vaasa
City Vaasa, Finland
Phone (00358 6) 315 63 10
Fax (00358 6) 315 63 02
Email teemu.elopuro@kayttoauto.fi

German Embassy in Paris, France
Embassy of Germany in Paris, France
28, rue Marbeau, 75116
City Paris
Phone 01 - 53 83 45 00
Fax 01 40 67 93 53 und 01 53 83 46 50
Website http://www.amb-allemagne.fr/
Email info@amb-allemagne.fr

German Consulate in Lyon, France, France
Consulate General of Germany in Lyon, France
33, Boulevard des Belges, 69458 Lyon Cedex 06
City Lyon, France
Phone (0033 4) 72 69 98 98
Fax (0033 4) 72 43 06 94
Email consualyon@9business.fr

German Consulate in Marseille, France, France
Consulate General of Germany in Marseille, France
338, Avenue du Prado, 13295 Marseille Cedex 08
City Marseille, France
Phone (0033 491) 16 75 20
Fax (0033 491) 16 75 28
Website http://http://www.marseille.diplo.de
Email generalkonsulat.marseille@tiscali.fr

German Consulate in Strasbourg, France, France
Consulate General of Germany in Strasbourg, France
6, Quai Mullenheim, 67000 Strasbourg
City Strasbourg, France
Phone (0033 3) 88 24 67 00
Fax (0033 3) 88 75 79 82
Website http://www.strassburg.diplo.de
Email info@strassburg.diplo.de

German Consulate in Bordeaux, France, France
Consulate of the Federal Republic of Germany in Bordeaux, France
377, Boulevard du Président Wilson, 33200 Bordeaux-Caudéran
City Bordeaux, France
Phone (0033 5) 56 17 12 22
Fax (0033 5) 56 42 32 65
Website http://www.bordeaux.diplo.de

Email info@bordeaux.diplo.de

German Consulate in Avignon, France, France
Honorary Consulate of the Federal Republic of Germany in Avignon, France
c/o Automobile Club Vauclusien, 185, Route des Rémouleurs, Z.I. La Courtine , Mourre Frais, 84095 Avignon Cedex 9
City Avignon, France
Phone (0033 4) 90 86 28 71
Fax (0033 4) 90 27 14 29
Email automobile.club.84@wanadoo.fr

German Consulate in Bastia, France, France
Honorary Consulate of the Federal Republic of Germany in Bastia, France
c/o Socodipha, 20600 Furiani (Société Corse de Distribution Pharmaceutique),, Zone Industrielle RN 193, 20200 Bastia.
City Bastia, France
Phone (0033 4) 95 33 03 56
Fax (033 4) 95 33 88 89
Email jean-jacques.bozzano@wanadoo.fr

German Consulate in Brest, France, France
Honorary Consulate of the Federal Republic of Germany in Brest, France
105, Rue de Siam, 29200 Brest
City Brest, France
Phone (0033 2) 98 43 32 53
Fax (0033 2) 98 44 64 07
Email mda@infini.fr

German Consulate in Montpellier, France
Honorary Consulate of the Federal Republic of Germany in Montpellier, France
Maison des Rélations Internationales, Esplanade Charles, de Gaulle, 34000 Montpellier (Parking Corum)
City Montpellier
Phone (0033 4) 67 60 75 46
Fax (0033 4) 67 64 29 77
Website http://Martinand@numericable.fr

German Consulate in Nantes, France
Honorary Consulate of the Federal Republic of Germany in Nantes, France
24, rue du Marché Commun, 44332 Nantes
City Nantes
Phone (0033 2) 51 89 05 34 / (0033 6) 07 67 15 74
Fax (0033 2) 40 52 18 90
Email domiwit@wanadoo.fr

German Consulate in Nice, France
Honorary Consulate of the Federal Republic of Germany in Nice, France
'Le Minotaure', 5e étage, 34, av. Henri Matisse, 06200 Nice
City Nice
Phone (0033 4) 93 83 55 25
Fax (0033 4) 93 83 05 50

German Consulate in Perpignan, France
Honorary Consulate of the Federal Republic of Germany in Perpignan, France
6, av. des Pervenches, 66000 Perpignan
City Perpignan
Phone (0033 4) 68 35 60 84
Fax (0033 4) 468 35 60 84
Email b.planes@wanadoo.fr

German Consulate in Reims, France
Honorary Consulate of the Federal Republic of Germany in Reims, France
42ter, rue de Capucins, 51100 Reims
City Reims
Phone (0033 3) 26 47 12 34
Fax (0033 3) 26 88 42 56
Email christian-lefebvre@wanadoo.fr

German Consulate in Rennes, France
Honorary Consulate of the Federal Republic of Germany in Rennes, France
CCI de Rennes, 2, avenue de la Préfecture CS 64204, 35042 Rennes Cedex 1
City Rennes
Phone (0033 2) 99 33 66 66
Fax (0033 2) 99 33 24 28

German Consulate in Rouen, France
Honorary Consulate of the Federal Republic of Germany in Rouen, France
43, rue Jean Lecanuet, 76000 Rouen
City Rouen
Phone (0033 2) 35 88 16 52
Fax (0033 2) 35 15 17 80
Email consulatallemagnerouen@laposte.net

German Consulate in Toulouse, France
Honorary Consulate of the Federal Republic of Germany in Toulouse, France
24 rue de Metz, 31000 Toulouse
City Toulouse
Phone (0033 5) 61 52 35 56 / (0033 5) 62 27 50 50
Fax (0033 5) 61 52 35 56
Email consulallem.tlse@wanadoo.fr

German Consulate in Guadeloupe, France, France
Honorary Consulate of the Federal Republic of Germany in Guadeloupe, France
c/o ETS Claude Blandin, Immeuble entre Deux Mers, Zac Moudong Sud, 97122 , Baie-Mahault
City Guadeloupe, France
Phone (00590 590) 38 93 93
Fax (00590 590) 26 83 16
Email consul.allemagne@ecb.gp

German Embassy in Libreville, Gabon
German Embassy in Gabon
Boulevard de l'Independance, Immeuble les Frangipaniers, Libreville
City Libreville
Phone 241 76 01 88/ (00241) 74 27 90
Fax 241 72 40 12
Email amb-allemagne@inet.ga
Details ---

German Embassy in Tbilissi, Georgia
German Embassy in Georgia
c/o Sheraton Metechi Palace Hotel, Telawi Str. 20, 0103 Tbilissi (Tiflis), , Georgien
City Tbilissi
Phone (00995 32) 44 73 00
Fax (00995 32) 91 15 21
Website http://www.tiflis.diplo.de
Email info@tiflis.diplo.de
Details ---

German Embassy in Accra, Ghana
German Embassy in Ghana
No. 6 Ridge Road, North Ridge, Accra
City Accra
Phone 233 21 24 10 82
Fax 233 21 22 13 47
Website http://www.accra.diplo.de
Email info@accra.diplo.de
Details ---

German Embassy in Athens, Greece
German Embassy in Greece
Karaoli & Dimitiou 3, Athens
City Athens
Phone 30 210 7 28 51 11
Fax 30 210 7 25 12 05
Website http://www.athen.diplo.de
Email german-embassy@otenet.gr
Details ---

German Consulate in Thessaloniki, Greece, Greece
Consulate General of the Federal Republic of Germany in Thessaloniki, Greece
Odos Karolou Diehl 4 a, 546 23 Thessaloniki, P.O Box 10515, 541 10 Thessaloniki, Greece
City Thessaloniki, Greece
Phone (0030 2310) 25 11 20 / (0030 2310) 25 11 30
Fax (0030 2310) 24 03 93
Email gkthess@otenet.gr

German Consulate in Igoumenitsa, Greece, Greece
Honorary Consul of the Federal Republic of Germany in Igoumenitsa, Greece
Ethiniki Antistsis 48, 46100 Igoumenitsa
City Igoumenitsa, Greece
Phone (0030 266 50) 234 93
Fax (0030 266 50) 248 47
Email HK-igoumenitsa@linos-travel.gr

German Consulate in Korfu, Greece, Greece
Honorary Consul of the Federal Republic of Germany in Korfu, Greece
Ethiniki Antistsis 48, 46100 Igoumenitsa
City Korfu, Greece
Phone (0030 266 10) 36826
Fax (0030 266 10) 36826
Email gisdakis@infoware.gr

German Consulate in Patras, Greece, Greece
Honorary Consul of the Federal Republic of Germany in Patras, Greece
Odos Mesonos 98, 262 21 Patras
City Patras, Greece
Phone (0030 26 10) 22 19 43
Fax (0030 26 10) 62 10 76
Email abageo@otenet.gr

German Consulate in Crete, Greece, Greece
Honorary Consulate of the Federal Republic of Germany in Crete, Greece
Paraliakí, Stassi Nr. 13, 73014 Chania - Agia Marina, P.O Box Paraliakí, Stassi Nr. 13, 73014 Chania
City Crete, Greece
Phone (0030 282 10) 688 76

Fax (0030 282 10) 688 76

German Consulate in Samos, Greece, Greece
Honorary Consulate of the Federal Republic of Germany in Samos, Greece
Pythagorasplatz 20, 831 00 Samos/Samou
City Samos, Greece
Phone (0030 227 30) 252 70
Fax (0030 227 30) 272 60
Email kapnoull@otenet.gr

German Consulate in St. George's, Grenada
Honorary Consul of the Federal Republic of Germany in Grenada
Fontenoy, St. George's, P.O Box 216, St. George's, Grenada
City St. George's
Phone (001473)440 72 60 / (001473)409 72 60 (Mobile)
Fax 473 443-2155
Email bluebeard@caribsurf.com

German Embassy in Guatemala, Guatemala
Embassy of Germany in Guatemala
20 calle 6-20, Edificio Plaza Maritima, Zona 10, Ciudad de Guatemala, P.O Box 87a, Ciudad de Guatemala, Guatemala
City Guatemala
Phone (00502) 23 64 67 00
Fax (00502) 23 33 69 06
Website http://www.guatemala.diplo.de
Email embalemana@intelnet.net.gt
Office Hours 09:00 AT 12:00 HOURS
Details ---

German Embassy in Conakry, Guinea, Guinea
Embassy of Germany in Conakry, Guinea
P.O. Box Auswartiges Amt, Deutsche Botschaft Conakry, 10113
City Conakry, Guinea
Phone +224-41.15.06 / -45.15.08
Fax +224-45.22.17
Website http://www.conakry.diplo.de/
Email amball@sotelgui.net.gn

German Consulate in Georgetown, Guyana, Guyana
Honorary Consul of the Federal Republic of Germany in Georgetown, Guyana
24 Water Street, Georgetown
City Georgetown, Guyana
Phone (011592) 227 33 44 / (011592) 227 33 50
Fax (011592) 226 18 81
Email chris@jf-ltd.com

German Embassy in Port-au-Prince, Haiti, Haiti
Embassy of Germany in Port-au-Prince, Haiti
2, Impasse Claudinette, Bois Moquette, Pétion-Ville, Port-au-Prince, Haiti, P.O Box 1147, Port-au-Prince, Haiti
City Port-au-Prince, Haiti
Phone (00509) 257 61 31 / (00509) 256 41 31
Fax (00509) 257 41 31
Email amballemagne@hainet.net

German Embassy in Tegucigalpa, Honduras
German Embassy in Honduras
Contiguo al Edificio Los Jarros, Boulevard Morazan, P.O. Box 3145, Tegucigalpa, D.C., Honduras
City Tegucigalpa
Phone 504 232 31 61 /(00504) 232 31 62
Fax 504 239 90 18
Website http://www.tegucigalpa.diplo.de
Email embalema@amnettgu.com
Details ---

German Consulate in San Pedro Sula, Honduras, Honduras
Honorary Consulate of the Federal Republic of Germany in San Pedro Sula, Honduras
6 y 7 Avenida NO, Circunvalación, Local Nº 10, San Pedro Sula
City San Pedro Sula, Honduras
Phone (00504) 553 12 44
Fax (00504) 553 18 68

German Embassy in Budapest, Hungary
German Embassy in Hungary
Uri utca 64-66, Budapest
City Budapest
Phone 36 1 488 35 00/ (0036 1)488 35 67
Fax 36 1 488 35 05
Website http://www.budapest.diplo.de
Email info@deutschebotschaft-budapest.hu

German Consulate in Pecs, Hungary
Honorary Consul of the Federal Republic of Germany in Hungary
Megye u. 21, 7621 Pecs.
City Pecs
Phone (0036 72) 21 27 00
Fax (0036 72) 21 27 77
Email dhcpecsh@dravanet.hu

German Embassy in Reykjavik, Iceland
German Embassy in Iceland
Laufasvegur 31, Reykjavik
City Reykjavik
Phone 354 530 11 00
Fax 354 530 11 01
Website http://www.reykjavik.diplo.de
Email info@reykjavik.diplo.de
Details ---

German Consulate in Ísafjördur, Iceland, Iceland
Honorary Consul of the Federal Republic of Germany in Ísafjördur, Iceland
Seljalandsvegur 73, 400 Ísafjördur
City Ísafjördur, Iceland
Phone (00354) 450 45 00
Fax (00354) 450 45 22
Email thorsteinn.johannesson@fsi.is

German Consulate in Seydisfjördur, Iceland, Iceland
Honorary Consul of the Federal Republic of Germany in Seydisfjördur, Iceland
Túngata 16, 710 Seydisfjördur, Iceland
City Seydisfjördur, Iceland
Phone (00354) 472 14 02 / (00354) 472 13 39 (private)
Fax (00354) 472 12 41

Email adolfgullberg@eldhorn.is

German Embassy in New Delhi, India
German Embassy in New Delhi, India
No. 6/50G, Shanti Path, Chanakyapuri, 110021
City New Delhi
Phone (0091-11) 44199 199
Fax (0091-11) 2687 31 17
Website http://www.new-delhi.diplo.de/Vertretung/newdelhi/en/02/Embassy.html
Email info@new-delhi.diplo.de
Office Hours Mon - Thu: 8:00 - 17:00 Hrs. Fri: 8:00 - 14:00 Hrs.

German Consulate in Chennai, India
German Consulate in Chennai, India
No. 9 Boat Club Road, P.O.Box 3110, Chennai 600 028, India
City Chennai
Phone (0091 44) 24 30 16 00
Fax (0091 44) 24 34 92 93
Website http://www.chennai.diplo.de
Email info@germanconsulatechennai.org
Office Hours Monday - Friday 08.00 to 11.30 hrs

German Consulate in Kolkata, India
Consulate of Germany in Kolkata, India
1 Hastings Park Road, Alipore, P.O. Box 16711, Kolkata 700 027, India
City Kolkata
Phone +91-(0)33-2479 1141/ 1142/ 2150, 2439 8906
In case of emergencies: +91-(0) 98310 16091
Fax +91-(0)33-2479 3028
Website http://www.kalkutta.diplo.de
Email gerconsu@vsnl.com

German Consulate in Mumbai, India
Consulate of Germany in Mumbai, India
'Hoechst House', 10th Floor, Nariman Point, 193 Backbay Reclamation, Mumbai 400 021, India
City Mumbai
Phone (+91-22) 22832422; In case of emergency: (0091) 9821016877
Fax (+91-22) 22025493
Website http://www.germanconsulatemumbai.org
Email info@mumbai.diplo.de
Office Hours Monday - Friday: 9:00 a.m. to 12:00 noon

German Consulate in Goa, India, India
Honorary Consul of the Federal Republic of Germany in Goa, India
Cosme Matias Menezes Pvt. Ltd., Rua de Ourem, Panaji, 403 001, Goa
City Goa, India
Phone (0091 832) 223 55 26
Fax (0091 832) 222 34 41
Email conhongoa@sancharnet.in

German Embassy in Jakarta, Indonesia
Embassy of Germany in Jakarta, Indonesia
1 Jl. M.H. Thamrin 1, Jakarta 10310, Indonesia
City Jakarta
Phone outside Indonesia: (+62-21) 398 55 000
inside Indonesia: (021) 398 55 000
Fax outside Indonesia: (+62-21) 390 1757
inside i

Website http://www.jakarta.diplo.de
Email germany@rad.net.id
Office Hours Monday 07.15 hrs until 15.30 hrs
Tuesday through Thursday 07.15 hrs until 15.45 hrs
Friday 07.15 hrs until 13.00 hrs
Details ---

German Consulate in Sanur, Bali. Indonesia, Indonesia
Honorary Consul of the Federal Republic of Germany in Sanur, Bali. Indonesia
Jalan Pantai Karang 17, Batujimbar-Sanur/Bali, P.O Box 100, Denpasar/Bali, Indonesia
City Sanur, Bali. Indonesia
Phone (0062 361) 28 85 35
Fax (0062 3 61) 28 88 26
Email germanconsul@bali-ntb.com

German Consulate in Jalan Samanhudi 16, Medan 20152, Indonesia
Honorary Consul of the Federal Republic of Germany in Medan, Indonesia
Jalan Pantai Karang 17, Batujimbar-Sanur/Bali, P.O Box 100, Denpasar/Bali, Indonesia
City Jalan Samanhudi 16, Medan 20152
Phone (0062 61) 456 80 06
Fax (0062 61) 456 32 56
Email congermdn@nusa.net.id

German Consulate in Surabaya, Indonesia, Indonesia
Honorary Consul of the Federal Republic of Germany in Surabaya, Indonesia
Jl. Dr. Wahidin 27, Surabaya 60264
City Surabaya, Indonesia
Phone (0062 31) 563 18 71
Fax (0062 31) 563 18 72
Website http://germany@sby.dnet.net.id

German Embassy in Teheran, Iran, Iran
Embassy of the Federal Republic of Germany in Teheran, Iran
Ferdowsi Ave., No 320-324, Teheran
City Teheran, Iran
Phone (0098 21) 39 99 00 00
Fax (0098 21) 39 99 18 90
Website http://www.teheran.diplo.de
Email nfo@teheran.diplo.de

German Embassy in Baghdad, Iraq, Iraq
Embassy of the Federal Republic of Germany in Baghdad, Iraq
Mahala 609, Street 3 / House Nr. 53, Baghdad-Hay Al-Mansour
City Baghdad, Iraq
Phone (00964 1) 543 14 70 / (00964 1) 543 58 40
Fax (00964 1) 543 58 40
Website http://www.bagdad.diplo.de
Email info@bagdad.diplo.de

German Embassy in Dublin, Ireland
German Embassy in Ireland
31 Trimleston Avenue, Booterstown, Blackrock/Co
City Dublin
Phone 353 1 269 30 11
Fax 353 1 269 39 46
Website http://www.dublin.diplo.de
Email germany@indigo.ie

Office Hours Monday to Friday 08.30 - 12.00 Visasection: 08.30 - 11.30 other consular matters: 08.30 - 12.00
Details ---

German Embassy in Tel Aviv, Israel
Embassy of Germany in Tel Aviv, Israel
3, Daniel Frisch St., 19. Stock, 64731 Tel Aviv, Israel
City Tel Aviv
Phone 03-6931 313 / (00972 3) 693 13 12
Fax 03-6969 217
Website http://www.tel-aviv.diplo.de
Email ger_emb@mail.netvision.net.il
Office Hours Monday through Thursday: 8:00 - 16:00 Friday and Holidays: 8:00 - 12:30

German Consulate in Haifa, Israel, Israel
Honorary Consul General of the Federal Republic of Germany in Haifa, Israel
98 Hanassi Ave., Haifa 34455, P.O Box 100,6240, 31061 Haifa, Israel
City Haifa, Israel
Phone (00972 4) 838 14 08
Fax (00972 4) 837 13 53
Email consulate@pappelaw.com

German Consulate in Eilat, Israel, Israel
Honorary Consul of the Federal Republic of Germany in Eilat, Israel
Neviot 5, 88000 Eilat, P.O Box 100, 4061, 88140 Eilat, Israel
City Eilat, Israel
Phone (00972 8) 637 45 36
Fax (00972 8) 634 27 61
Email barbaras@eilatcity.co.il

German Embassy in Rome, Italy
Embassy of Germany in Rome, Italy
Via San Martino della Battaglia, 4, 00185 Rome, Italy
City Rome
Phone +39 06 49213-1
Fax +39 06 44 52 672 /(0039 06) 49 21 33 19
Website http://www.rom.diplo.de
Email info@rom.diplo.de

German Consulate in Milan, Italy, Italy
Consulate General of Germany in Milan, Italy
Via Solferino 40, 20121 Milano
City Milan, Italy
Phone (0039 02) 623 11 01
Fax (0039 02) 655 42 13
Website http://www.mailand.diplo.de
Email info@mailand.diplo.de

German Consulate in Naples, Italy, Italy
Consulate General of Germany in Naples, Italy
Via Crispi 69, 80121 Napoli
City Naples, Italy
Phone (0039 081) 248 85 11
Fax (0039 081) 761 46 87
Website http://www.neapel.diplo.de
Email info@neapel.diplo.de

German Consulate in Bologna, Italy, Italy
Honorary Consulate of the Federal Republic of Germany in Bologna, Italy
Viale Risorgimento 7, 40136 Bologna
City Bologna, Italy
Phone (0039 051) 339 90 14
Fax (0039 051)339 50 56
Email consgermbologna@yahoo.it

German Consulate in Cagliari, Italy, Italy
Honorary Consulate of the Federal Republic of Germany in Cagliari, Italy
Via R. Garzia 9, 09126 Cagliari
City Cagliari, Italy
Phone (0039 070) 30 72 29
Fax (0039 070) 307299
Email germancons.cagliari@tiscali.it

German Consulate in Florence, Italy, Italy
Honorary Consulate of the Federal Republic of Germany in Florence, Italy
Corso die Tintori 3, 50122 Firenze
City Florence, Italy
Phone (0039 055) 234 35 43
Fax (0039 055) 247 62 08

German Consulate in Genova, Italy, Italy
Honorary Consulate of the Federal Republic of Germany in Genova, Italy
Ponte Morosini 41/1, 16126 Genova
City Genova, Italy
Phone (0039 010) 271 59 69
Fax (0039 010) 271 59 66
Email germanhoncons@ge.cosulich.it

German Consulate in Messina, Italy, Italy
Honorary Consulate of the Federal Republic of Germany in Messina, Italy
Via S. Sebastiano 13, 98122 Messina
City Messina, Italy
Phone (0039 090) 67 17 80
Fax (0039 090) 67 17 80
Email honorarkonsulmessina@hotmail.com

German Consulate in Palermo, Italy, Italy
Honorary Consulate of the Federal Republic of Germany in Palermo, Italy
Viale Scaduto 2/d, 90144 Palermo
City Palermo, Italy
Phone (0039 091) 34 25 75 / (0039 091) 625 46 60
Fax (0039 091) 34 70 34
Email tortorici.lex@virgilio.it

German Consulate in Rimini, Italy, Italy
Honorary Consulate of the Federal Republic of Germany in Rimini, Italy
Viale Trieste 3/E, 47037 Rimini
City Rimini, Italy
Phone (0039 0541) 2 77 84
Fax (0039 0541) 2 77 84

German Consulate in Trieste, Germany, Italy
Honorary Consulate of the Federal Republic of Germany in Trieste, Germany
Via Beccaria, 8 - III. Stock, 34133 Trieste
City Trieste, Germany

Phone (0039 040) 36 90 71
Fax (0039 040) 36 43 96
Email hk.brd-ts@libero.it

German Consulate in Turin, Italy, Italy
Honorary Consulate of the Federal Republic of Germany in Turin, Italy
Corso Vittorio Emanuelle II 98, 10121 Torino
City Turin, Italy
Phone (0039 011) 53 10 88
Fax (0039 011) 53 10 88

German Consulate in Venice, Italy, Italy
Honorary Consulate of the Federal Republic of Germany in Venice, Italy
San Marco, Campo S. Angelo 3816, 30124 Venezia
City Venice, Italy
Phone (0039 041) 5 23 76 75
Fax (0039 041) 5 22 76 55
Email consolatodigermania.ve@tin.it

German Embassy in Abidjan, Cote D'Ivoire, Ivory Coast
Embassy of Germany in Abidjan, Cote d'Ivoire
39, Boulevard Hassan II (Boulevard de la Corniche), Abidjan-Cocody
City Abidjan, Cote d'Ivoire
Phone (00225) 22 44 20 30
Fax (00225) 22 44 20 41
Website http://www.abidjan.diplo.de
Email d.bo.abj@africaonline.co.ci

German Embassy in Kingston, Jamaica
German Embassy in Jamaica
10 Waterloo Road (P. O. Box 444), Kingston 10, Jamaica
City Kingston
Phone +1876 926 67 28
Fax +1876 929 82 82
Website http://www.kingston.diplo.de
Email germanemb@cwjamaica.com
Office Hours Office hours January - August, November and December:
Monday and Thursday: 7.30 am - 4.30 pm
Tuesday and Wednesday: 7.30 am - 3.00 pm
Friday: 7.30 am - 2.30 pm
Office hours September and October:
Monday and Thursday: 7.30 am - 3.45 pm
Tuesday, Wednesday and Friday: 7.30 am - 2.30 pm

German Embassy in Tokyo, Japan
German Embassy in Japan
4-5-10, Minami-Azabu, Minato-ku, Tokyo 106-0047, Japan
City Tokyo
Phone (0081 3) 57 91 77 00
Fax (0081 3) 57 91 77 73
Website http://www.tokyo.diplo.de
Email info@tokyo.diplo.de

German Consulate in Osaka, Japan, Japan
Consulate General of the Federal Republic of Germany in Osaka, Japan
Umeda Sky Building, Tower East, 35th Fl. , 1-1-88-3501, Oyodonaka, Kita-ku, Osaka, Japan
City Osaka, Japan
Phone (0081 6) 64 40 50 70

Fax (0081 6) 64 40 50 80
Website http://www.osaka-kobe.diplo.de
Email info@osaka-kobe.diplo.de

German Consulate in Fukui, Japan, Japan
Honorary Consul of the Federal Republic of Germany in Fukui, Japan
Terute 1-I-16, Fukui 910-0024
City Fukui, Japan
Phone (0081 776) 21 60 00
Fax (0081 776) 27 77 78
Email kono@hqs.ono-group.co.jp

German Consulate in Fukuoka, Japan, Japan
Honorary Consul of the Federal Republic of Germany in Fukuoka, Japan
c/o Saibu Gas Kabushiki Kaisha, 1-17-1 Chiyo, Hakata-ku, Fukuoka 812-8707
City Fukuoka, Japan
Phone (0081 92) 633 22 11
Fax (0081 92) 633 22 91

German Consulate in Hiroshima, Japan, Japan
Honorary Consul of the Federal Republic of Germany in Hiroshima, Japan
Hiroshima Dentetsu KK, Naka-ku, Higashisenda-cho 2-9-29, Hiroshima 730-8610
City Hiroshima, Japan
Phone (0081 82) 242 35 11
Fax (0081 82) 242 35 85

German Consulate in Kobe, Japan, Japan
Honorary Consul of the Federal Republic of Germany in Kobe, Japan
651-0087 Kobe, Chuo-ku, Goko-dori 8, Kobe Kokusai Kaikam 17 F
City Kobe, Japan
Phone (0081 78) 230 81 51
Fax (0081 78) 230 81 51

German Consulate in Nagoya, Japan, Japan
Honorary Consul of the Federal Republic of Germany in Nagoya, Japan
c/o Chubu Denryoku K.K. , Toshin-cho 1, Higashi-ku, Nagoya-shi 461-8680
City Nagoya, Japan
Phone (0081 52) 951 82 11
Fax (0081 52) 973 31 83

German Consulate in Sapporo, Japan, Japan
Honorary Consul of the Federal Republic of Germany in Sapporo, Japan
1-2, Odori-higashi, Chuo-ku, Sapporo 060-8677
City Sapporo, Japan
Phone (0081 11) 251 11 11 / (0081 11) 251 22 36
Fax (0081 11) 242 50 51
Email burodeshksp@epmail.hepco.co.jp

German Consulate in YURTEC,4-1-1 Tsutsujigaoka Miyagino-ku ,Sendai, Japan
Honorary Consul of the Federal Republic of Germany in Sendai, Japan
1-2, Odori-higashi, Chuo-ku, Sapporo 060-8677
City YURTEC,4-1-1 Tsutsujigaoka Miyagino-ku ,Sendai
Phone (0081 22) 296 21 11
Fax (0081 22) 296 20 11

German Embassy in Amman, Jordan, Jordan
Embassy of the Federal Republic of Germany in Amman, Jordan
Benghasi Street 25, Jabal Amman, P.O Box 183, 11118 Amman, Jordan.
City Amman, Jordan
Phone (00962 6) 593 03 51 / (00962 6) 593 03 67
Fax (00962 6) 592 94 13
Website http://www.amman.diplo.de
Email germaemb@wanadoo.jo

German Embassy in Almaty, Kazakhstan
German Embassy in Kazakhstan
Ulitza Furmanova 173, Almaty
City Almaty
Phone (007 32 72) 50 61 60 / (007 32 72) 50 70 43
Fax (007 3272) 50 62 76
Website http://www.almaty.diplo.de
Email info@almaty.diplo.de
Details ---

German Embassy in Nairobi, Kenya
German Embassy in Kenya
Ludwig Krapf House , Riverside Drive 113 , Nairobi Kenya
City Nairobi
Phone (00254 20) 426 21 00
Fax (00254 20) 426 21 29
Website http://www.nairobi.diplo.de
Email info@nairobi.diplo.de
Details ---

German Consulate in Mombasa, Kenya, Kenya
Honorary Consul of the Federal Republic of Germany in Mombasa, Kenya
Bank of India Building 2. Stock, Nkrumah Road, Mombasa, P.O Box 86779, Mombasa, Kenia
City Mombasa, Kenya
Phone (00254 41) 222 87 81
Fax (00254 41) 231 45 04
Email mombasa@germanconsul.com

German Embassy in Kuwait
Embassy of the Federal Republic of Germany in Kuwait
Abdullah Al-Salem, Area 1, Ave. 14, Branch of Nusf Al-Yousef Street, Villa 13,, Kuwait
Phone (00965) 2 52 08 57 / (00965) 2 52 07 56
Fax (00965) 2 52 07 63
Website http://www.kuwait.diplo.de
Email info@kuwait.diplo.de

German Embassy in Bishkek, Kyrgyzstan
German Embassy in Kirgyzstan
Ul. Razzakowa 28
City Bishkek
Phone 996 312 66 66 24
Fax 996 312 66 02 07
Website http://www.bischkek.diplo.de/Vertretung/bischkek/ru/Startseite.html
Email info@bischkek.diplo.de
Details ---

German Embassy in Vientiane, Laos
German Embassy in Laos
Rue Sokpalouang 26, Vientiane

City Vientiane
Phone 856 21 31 21 10
Fax 856 21 31 43 22
Website http://--
Email info@vien.diplo.de
Details ---

German Embassy in Riga., Latvia
German Embassy in Latvia
Raina Bulv. 13, Riga.
City Riga.
Phone 371 7 22 90 96
Fax 371 7 82 02 23
Website http://www.riga.diplo.de
Email mailbox@deutschebotschaft-riga.lv
Details ---

German Embassy in Beirut, Lebanon
German Embassy in Lebanon
B.P. 11-2820 Riad El-Solh, Beirut 1102 2110, Lebanon
City Beirut
Phone (00961 4) 91 44 44
Fax (00961 4) 91 44 50
Website http://www.beirut.diplo.de
Email info@beirut.diplo.de
Office Hours Mondays to Fridays from 10.00 am to 12:00 pm
Mondays to Thursdays from 02:00 pm to 03:00 pm

German Consulate in Maseru, Lesotho, Lesotho
Honorary Consul of the Federal Republic of Germany in Maseru, Lesotho
70c Maluti Road, Maseru West
City Maseru, Lesotho
Phone (00266) 22 33 22 92 / (00266) 22 33 29 83
Fax (00266) 22 33 41 98

German Embassy in Monrovia, Liberia, Liberia
Embassy of the Federal Republic of Germany, Tubman Boulevard, Monrovia, Liberia
Tubman Boulevard, Monrovia
City Monrovia, Liberia
Phone (00231) 643 83 65

German Embassy in Tripoli, Libya, Libya
Embassy of the Federal Republic of Germany in Tripoli, Libya
Sharia Hassan el Mashai, Tripoli
City Tripoli, Libya
Phone (00218 21) 444 85 52 / (00218 21) 333 05 54
Fax (00218 21) 444 89 68
Website http://www.tripolis.diplo.de
Email info@tripolis.diplo.de

German Consulate in Schaan, Liechtenstein, Liechtenstein
Honorary Consulate of the Federal Republic of Germany in Schaan, Liechtenstein
Bendererstraße 2, FL 9494 Schaan
City Schaan, Liechtenstein
Phone (00423) 262 04 62
Fax (00423) 232 00 89
Email zeller@hkzeller.li

German Embassy in Vilnius, Lithuania
German Embassy in Lithuania
Sierakausko Gatve 24/8, Vilnius
City Vilnius
Phone (00370 5) 210 64 00
Fax (00370 5) 210 64 46
Website http://www.deutschebotschaft-wilna.lt
Email germ.emb@takas.lt
Details ---

German Embassy in Luxembourg, Luxembourg
Embassy of Germany in Luxembourg, Luxembourg
20-22, avenue Emile Reuter, L- 2420 Luxemburg
City Luxembourg
Phone (00 352) 45 34 45-1
Fax (00 352) 45 56 04
Website http://www.luxemburg.diplo.de
Email deutschebotschaft@luxe.auswaertiges-amt.de
Office Hours Montag bis Freitag 09.00 - 12.00 Uhr

German Embassy in Skopje, Macedonia
German Embassy in Macedonia
59, Ul. Lerinska
City Skopje
Phone (00389 2) 309 39 00
Fax (00389 2) 309 38 99
Website http://www.skopje.diplo.de
Email dtboskop@unet.com.mk
Details ---

German Embassy in Antananarivo, Madagascar
German Embassy in Madagascar
101, Rue du Pasteur Rabeony Hans, Antananarivo
City Antananarivo
Phone 261 20 222 38 02
Fax 261 20 222 66 27
Website http://www.antananarivo.diplo.de
Email amballem@wanadoo.mg

German Embassy in Lilongwe, Malawi
German Embassy in Malawi
Convention Drive (Capital City), Lilongwe
City Lilongwe
Phone 265 1 77 25 55
Fax 265 1 77 02 50
Website http://www.lilongwe.diplo.de
Email info@lilongwe.diplo.de
Details ---

German Embassy in Kuala Lumpur, Malaysia
German Embassy in Malaysia
26th Floor Menara Tan&Tan, Jalan Tun Razak, 50400
City Kuala Lumpur
Phone 60 3 21 42 96 66
Fax (0060 3) 21 61 98 00
Website http://www.kuala-lumpur.diplo.de
Email contact@german-embassy.org.my

German Embassy in Bamako, Mali
German Embassy in Mali
Badalabougou Est, rue 14, porte 334, Bamako
City Bamako
Phone 223 2 22 32 99 / (00223)222 37 15
Fax 223 2 22 96 50
Website http://www.bamako.diplo.de
Email allemagne.presse@afribone.net.ml

German Embassy in Sliema, Malta
German Embassy in Malta
Il-Piazzetta, Tower Road, P.O. Box 48, Marsa GPO 01, Malta
City Sliema
Phone 356 2260 4000
Fax 356 2134 1271
Website http://www.valletta.diplo.de
Email info@valletta.diplo.de

German Embassy in Lamentin, Martinique, Martinique
Honorary Consulate of the Federal Republic of Germany in Lamentin, Martinique
c/o ETS Blandin, Centre Acajou, Z.I. Les Mangles, 97232 Lamentin
City Lamentin, Martinique
Phone (00596 596) 42 79 21
Fax (00596 596) 50 98 94
Email consul.allemagne@ecb.gp

German Embassy in Mauritania

P.O. Box 372, Nouakchott, Mauritania.
Phone (0022 2) 525 17 29 / (0022 2) 525 10 32
Fax (0022 2) 525 17 22
Email Embassy of Germany in Mauritania

German Embassy in Mexico City, Mexico
Embassy of Germany in Mexico City, Mexico
Lord Byron No. 737, Col. Polanco Chapultepec, 11560 México, D.F., P.O Box M-10792, 0600 México, D.F. Mexico
City Mexico City
Phone (01 55) 5283 22 00
Fax (01 55) 5281 25 88
Website http://www.mexiko.diplo.de
Email info@embajada-alemana.org.mx

German Consulate in Veracruz, Mexico, Mexico
Honorary Consulate of Germany in Veracruz, Mexico
World Trade Center, Blvd. Adolfo Ruinz Cortínez 3497, Col. Ylang Ylang, , 94290 Boca del Río, Ver.
City Veracruz, Mexico
Phone (01-229) 927 0656
Fax (0052 229) 104 67 81
Email consulaleman-ver@rembermex.com.mx

German Consulate in Chihuahua, Mexico, Mexico
Honorary Consulate of Germany in Chihuahua, Mexico
Ave. del Campestre No. 175, Col. Club Campestre, 31213 Chihuahua/Chih
City Chihuahua, Mexico
Phone (0052 614) 411 27 62 / (0052 614) 424 29 91
Fax (0052 614) 411 27 62
Email klauskientzle@hotmail.com

German Consulate in Guadalajara, Mexico, Mexico
Honorary Consulate of Germany in Guadalajara, Mexico
Casa Wagner de Guadalajara, S.A., Ave. Madero 215, Col. Centro, 44100 Guadalajara, Jal., P.O. Box 1-107, 44100 Guadalajara, Jalisco. Mexico.
City Guadalajara, Mexico
Phone (0052 33) 36 13 96 23
Fax (0052 33) 35 86 56 91
Email consuladoaleman@axtel.net

German Consulate in Mazatlán, Mexico, Mexico
Honorary Consulate of Germany in Mazatlán, Mexico
Av. Playa Gaviotas 212, Zona Dorada, 82110 Mazatlán, Sinaloa
City Mazatlán, Mexico
Phone (0052 669) 914 93 10 / (0052 669) 916 59 80
Fax (0052 669) 914 34 22
Email consulado_alemania_mazatlan@yahoo.com

German Consulate in Monterrey, Mexico, Mexico
Honorary Consulate of Germany in Monterrey, Mexico
Proa Consultores, S.C., Rio Rosas 400 Sur, Local 12, , Planta Pista Colonia del Valle, 66220 San Pedro Garza García
City Monterrey, Mexico
Phone (0052 81) 83 35 17 84 / (0052 81) 83 78 60 78
Fax (0052 81) 83 35 54 38
Email konsulat@prodigy.net.mx

German Consulate in Puebla, Mexico, Mexico
Honorary Consulate of Germany in Puebla, Mexico
Distribudora O'Farrill Puebla S.A. de C.V, Av. Hermanos Serdan No. 231,, Col. Aquiles Serdan, 72140 Puebla, Pue.
City Puebla, Mexico
Phone (0052 222) 248 16 33 / (0052 222)248 18 80
Fax (0052 222) 230 34 58
Email kolm56@hotmail.com

German Consulate in Queretaro, Mexico, Mexico
Honorary Consulate of Germany in Queretaro, Mexico
Ave. Carrillo Puerto 303, 76130 Santiago de Queretaro, Qro.
City Queretaro, Mexico
Phone (01442) 217 00 00
Fax (01442) 217 04 83
Email cbauer@bamsa.com.mx

German Consulate in Tampico, Mexico, Mexico
Honorary Consulate of Germany in Tampico, Mexico
Heroes del Canonero # 228 - Piso # 2, Edificio 'La Campana', 89000 Tampico
City Tampico, Mexico
Phone (0052 833) 212 90 40
Fax (0052 833) 212 20 23

German Consulate in Acapulco, Mexico, Mexico
Honorary Consulate of the Federal Republic of Germany in Acapulco, Mexico
Antón de Alaminos No. 26, Casa Tres Fuentes, Col. Costa Azul, 39850 Acapulco/Gro
City Acapulco, Mexico
Phone (0052 744) 484 18 60 / (0052 744) 484 96 80
Fax (0052 744) 484 38 10
Email mario@susannapalazuelos.com

German Consulate in Cancun, Mexico, Mexico
Honorary Consulate of the Federal Republic of Germany in Cancun, Mexico
Punta Conoca No. 36, SM 24, 77509 Cancún, Quintana Roo, P.O Box 100, 77500 Cancún, Quintana Roo., Mexico.
City Cancun, Mexico
Phone (0052 998) 884 53 33 / (0052 998) 884 15 98
Fax (0052 998) 887 12 83
Email konsul_d@yahoo.com.mx

German Consulate in Merida, Mexico, Mexico
Honorary Consulate of the Federal Republic of Germany in Merida, Mexico
Calle 49 No 212 entre 30 y 32, San Antonio Cucul, 97116 Mérida, Yucatan
City Merida, Mexico
Phone (0052 999) 944 32 52
Fax (0052 999) 944 32 52
Email konsulat@jerommel.de

German Embassy in Chisinau, Moldova
German Embassy in Moldava
Str. Maria Cibotari 35
City Chisinau
Phone 373 2 20 06 00
Fax 373 2 23 46 80
Website http://www.chisinau.diplo.de
Email info@chisinau.diplo.de
Details ---

German Consulate in Monte Carlo, Monaco, Monaco
Honorary Consulate of the Federal Republic of Germany in Monte Carlo, Monaco
'Le Roc Fleuri', 2 chemin du Ténao, MC 98000 Monaco
City Monte Carlo, Monaco
Phone (00377) 97 97 49 65
Fax (00377) 97 77 51 53
Email dieterspaethe@libello.com

German Consulate in Ulaanbaatar, Mongolia, Mongolia
Embassy of Germany in Ulaanbaatar, Mongolia
Straße der Vereinten Nationen, 210613 Ulaanbaatar., P.O Box 708, 210613 Ulan-Bator, Mongolia
City Ulaanbaatar, Mongolia
Phone (00976 11) 32 33 25 / (00976 11) 32 39 15
Fax (00976 11) 32 39 05
Email germanemb_ulanbator@mongol.net

German Embassy in Rabat, Morocco, Morocco
Embassy of Germany in Rabat, Morocco
7, Zankat Madnine, Rabat, P.O Box 235, 10001 Rabat, Morocco
City Rabat, Morocco
Phone (00212 37) 68 91 00
Fax (00212 37) 70 68 51
Website http://www.rabat.diplo.de
Email amballma@mtds.com

German Consulate in Agadir, Morocco, Morocco
Honorary Consulate of the Federal Republic of Germany in Agadir, Morocco
6, Rue de Madrid, Sec. Résidentiel, 80 000 Agadir
City Agadir, Morocco
Phone (00212 28) 84 10 25

Fax (00212 28) 84 09 26
Email conshono@menara.ma

German Embassy in Maputo, Mozambique, Mozambique
Embassy of Germany in Maputo, Mozambique
Rua Damião de Góis 506, Maputo
City Maputo, Mozambique
Phone (00258 21) 48 27 00 / (00258 21) 49 27 14
Fax (00258 21) 49 28 88
Website http://www.maputo.diplo.de
Email germaemb@tvcabo.co.mz

German Embassy in Yangon, Myanmar, Myanmar
Embassy of the Federal Republic of Germany in Yangon, Myanmar
9 Bogyoke Aung San Museum Road, Bahan Township, Rangoon (Yangon) 11201, P.O Box 12, Rangoon (Yangon) 11181, Myanmar.
City Yangon, Myanmar
Phone (0095 1) 54 89 51 / (0095 1) 54 89 52
Fax (0095 1) 54 88 99
Email post@botschaftrangun.net.mm

German Embassy in Windhoek, Namibia
German Embassy in Namibia
Sanlam Centre, 6/F Independence Ave
City Windhoek
Phone 264 61 27 31 00 / (00264 61) 27 31 33
Fax 264 61 22 29 81/ (00264 61) 27 31 18
Website http://www.windhuk.diplo.de
Email germany@iway.na
Details ---

German Embassy in Kathmandu, Nepal, Nepal
Embassy of the Federal Republic of Germany in Kathmandu, Nepal
Gyaneshwar, Kathmandu, P.O Box 226, Kathmandu, Nepal.
City Kathmandu, Nepal
Phone (00977 1) 441 27 86 / (00977 1) 441 65 27
Fax (00977 1) 441 68 99
Website http://www.kathmandu.diplo.de
Email info@kathmandu.diplo.de

German Embassy in The Hague, Netherlands
German Embassy in Holland
Groot Hertoginnelaan 18-20, The Hague
City The Hague
Phone 31 70 342 06 00
Fax 31 70 342 06 66
Website http://www.den-haag.diplo.de
Email ambduits@euronet.nl
Details ---

German Consulate in Amsterdam, Netherlands, Netherlands
Consulate General of Germany in Amsterdam, Netherlands
Honthorststraat 36-38, 1071 DG Amsterdam, P.O Box 75500, 1070 AM Amsterdam, Netherlands
City Amsterdam, Netherlands
Phone (0031 20) 574 77 00
Fax (0031 20) 676 69 51
Website http://www.duitse-ambassade.nl
Email duitscon@euronet.nl

German Consulate in Arnhem, The Netherlands, Netherlands
Honorary Consulate of the Federal Republic of Germany in Arnhem, The Netherlands
'Velperpoort', Velperweg 1, 6824 BZ Arnhem, P.O Box 111, 6800 AC Arnhem, Netherlands
City Arnhem, The Netherlands
Phone (0031 26) 365 55 44
Fax (0031 26) 365 55 00
Email c.janssen@arnhem.dirkzwager.nl

German Consulate in Eindhoven, Netherlands, Netherlands
Honorary Consulate of the Federal Republic of Germany in Eindhoven, Netherlands
c/o Holland van Gijzen Advocaten en Notarissen, Prof. Dr. Dorgelolaan 14, 5613, AM Eindhoven, P.O. Box 3, 5600 AA Eindhoven, Netherlands.
City Eindhoven, Netherlands
Phone (0031 40) 262 65 28
Fax (0031 40) 262 65 81
Email louis.deterink@hollandlaw.nl

German Consulate in Enschede, Netherlands, Netherlands
Honorary Consulate of the Federal Republic of Germany in Enschede, Netherlands
Hengelosestraat 585, NLD 7521 AG Enschede
City Enschede, Netherlands
Phone (0031 53) 484 98 49
Fax (0031 53) 484 98 99
Email p.h.m.teriele@hetnet.nl

German Consulate in Groningen, Netherlands, Netherlands
Honorary Consulate of the Federal Republic of Germany in Groningen, Netherlands
Leonard Springerlaan 15, 9727 KG Groningen, Netherlands, P.O Box 134, 9700 AC Groningen, Netherlands
City Groningen, Netherlands
Phone (0031 50) 520 58 63
Fax (0031 50) 525 12 10
Email amjvogd@vesta.nl

German Consulate in Leeuwarden, Netherlands, Netherlands
Honorary Consulate of the Federal Republic of Germany in Leeuwarden, Netherlands
Beursplein 1, 8911 BE Leeuwarden, P.O Box 397, BD Leeuwaarden, Netherlands
City Leeuwarden, Netherlands
Phone (0031 58) 299 44 99
Fax (0031 58) 299 45 95
Email a.offringa@worldonline.nl

German Consulate in Maastricht, Netherlands, Netherlands
Honorary Consulate of the Federal Republic of Germany in Maastricht, Netherlands
Parkweg 20, 6212 XN Maastricht, P.O Box 5770, 6202 MH Maastricht, Netherlands
City Maastricht, Netherlands
Phone (0031 43) 326 33 03
Fax (0031 43) 325 69 89
Email l.murk@macintosh.nl

German Consulate in Middelburg, Netherlands, Netherlands
Honorary Consulate of the Federal Republic of Germany in Middelburg, Netherlands
Markt 65 a, 4331 LK Middelburg, P.O Box 12, 4493 ZG Kamperland, Netherlands
City Middelburg, Netherlands
Phone (0031 118) 62 44 06 / (0031 113) 37 43 79
Fax (0031 113) 37 34 69
Email koeveringe.h.van@roompot.nl

German Consulate in Curacao, Netherlands
Honorary Consul of the Federal Republic of Germany in Netherlands
Kaya Kooyman 48, Willemstad, Curacao N.A, P.O Box 3062 Willemstad, Curacao, N.A
City Curacao
Phone (00599 9) 461 38 70
Fax (00599 9) 461 50 86
Email bkooyman@kooymannv.com

German Consulate in Rotterdam, Netherlands
German Consulate in Rotterdam, Netherlands
Jufferstraat 9 , Rotterdam, Netherlands, 3011
City Rotterdam
Phone +31-10-282-3333
Fax +31-10-412-3892
Email jppeterson@peterson.nl

German Consulate in New Caledonia, New Caledonia
Honorary Consulate of the Federal Republic of Germany in New Caledonia
19, rue de la Gazelle, Magenta, 98804 Nouméa Cedex, P.O Box 15122, 98804 Nouméa Cedex, Nouvelle Calédonie
City New Caledonia
Phone (00687) 26 16 81
Fax (00687) 26 16 81
Email w.forster@lagoon.nc

German Embassy in Wellington, New Zealand
Embassy of the Federal Republic of Germany in Wellington, New Zealand
90-92 Hobson Street, Thorndon, Wellington 6011, PO Box 1687, Wellington 6140
City Wellington
Phone (0064 4) 473 60 63
Fax (0064 4) 473 60 69
Website http://http://www.wellington.diplo.de/
Email info@wellington.diplo.de
Office Hours Office hours: 7.30 a.m.-4.15 p.m., Mon-Thurs; 7.30 a.m.-3 p.m., Fri Additional Office hours: 8 a.m.-12 noon., Mon-Fri (Consular)

German Consulate in Auckland, New Zealand
Consulate of the Federal Republic of Germany - Auckland
Level 11, 41 Shortland Street Auckland 1010, Private Bag 92093, Auckland, 1142
City Auckland
Phone (09) 375 8718
Fax (09) 365 5218
Email German.Consulate@heskethhenry.co.nz
Office Hours 10 a.m.‼ 12 noon

German Consulate in Christchurch, New Zealand
Consulate of the Federal Republic of Germany - Christchurch
5 Wairarapa Terrace, Christchurch 8014
City Christchurch
Phone (03) 355 7014
Fax (03) 344 6278
Email info@giesen.co.nz
Office Hours By appointment

German Embassy in Managua, Nicaragua
Embassy of Germany in Managua, Nicaragua
P.O. Box. 29

City Managua
Phone (00 505) 266 3917/266 3918/266 7500/266 7944
Fax (00 505) 266 7667
Email diploger@tmx.com.ni

German Embassy in Lagos, Nigeria
Embassy of German in Nigeria, Lagos Office
15, Walter Carrington Crescent, Victoria Island, P.O. Box 728
City Lagos
Phone +234 (1) 261 1011
Fax +234 (1) 261 1173
Email gembassylagos@micro.com.ng
Office Hours Office Hours: 07:30 h - 15:00 h Visa Applicants: 07:00 h - 09:00 h

German Embassy in Oslo, Norway
German Embassy in Norway
Oscarsgate 45
City Oslo
Phone 47 23 27 54 00
Fax 47 22 44 76 72
Email post@deutschebotschaft.no
Details ---

German Embassy in Muscat, Oman
German Embassy in Oman
near Al-Nahda Hospital, Stadtteil Ruwi, (P.O. Box 128), Ruwi, PC 112, Muscat, Oman
City Muscat
Phone (+968) 24 83 24 82
Fax (+968) 24 83 56 90
Email info@maskat.diplo.de

German Embassy in Islamabad, Pakistan
German Embassy in Pakistan
Ramna 5, Diplomatic Enclave
City Islamabad
Phone 92 51 227 94 30
Fax 92 51 227 94 36
Email pregerem@isb.paknet.com.pk
Details ---

German Consulate in Karachi, Pakistan
General Consulate of Germany in Karachi, Pakistan
92 - A/7, Block - 5, Clifton Karachi
City Karachi
Phone (++92- 21) 5873782-83, 5870234
Fax (++92-21) 5874009
Email consgerm@cyber.net.pk

German Embassy in Panama City, Panama
Embassy of Germany in Panama City, Panama
Edificio Bancomer, Piso 6, CLS 50 y 53, Apartado 4228 Zona 5, Mail to: P.O. Box 0832-0536 World Trade Center
City Panama City
Phone (00 507) 263 7733/263 7991/264 1147/263 4677
Fax (00 507) 223 66 64
Email germpanama@cwp.net.pa

Office Hours -
Details -

German Embassy in Pretoria, South Africa
German Embassy in Sudafrica
180 Blackwood St., Arcadia, Pretoria
City Pretoria
Phone 27 12 427 89 00
Fax 27 12 343 94 01
Email GermanEmbassyPretoria@gonet.co.za

German Embassy in Seoul, South Korea
German Embassy in South Korea
Yongsan-Gu, Tongbingo-Dong, 308-5 Seoul
City Seoul
Phone 82 2 748 41 14
Fax 82 2 748 41 61
Website http://www.gembassy.or.kr
Email dboseoul@kornet.net
Details ---

German Embassy in Seoul, South Korea
Embassy of the Federal Republic of Germany in South Korea
Yongsan-Gu, Tongbingo-Dong 308-5, Seoul 140-816, P.O Box 1289, Seoul 100-612, South Korea
City Seoul
Phone (0082 2) 748 41 14
Fax (0082 2) 748 41 61
Website http://www.seoul.diplo.de
Email dboseoul@kornet.net

German Consulate in Pusan, South Korea, South Korea
Honorary Consul of the Federal Republic of Germany in Pusan, South Korea
12th Floor, Korean Express Building 83-85, Jungang-dong-4-ga, Jung-Gu, Pusan
City Pusan, South Korea
Phone (0082 51) 441 41 12
Fax (0082 51) 441 41 13

German Embassy in Colombo, Sri Lanka
Embassy of Germany in Colombo, Sri Lanka
No. 40, Alfred House Avenue, Colombo-03, Sri Lanka
City Colombo
Phone 94 1 580431
Fax 94 1 580440
Website http://www.germanembassy-colombo.lk
Email germaemb@sltnet.lk
Office Hours 9.00-12.00 Monday- Friday

German Embassy in Khartum, Sudan
German Embassy in Sudan
53 Baladia St., Block No. 8 D, Plot No. 2, Kahrtum
City Khartum
Phone 249 11 77 79 90
Fax 249 11 77 76 22
Email germanembassy-sudan@gmx.net

German Embassy in Stockholm, Sweden
Embassy of Germany in Stockholm, Sweden
Skarpogatan 9, Box 27832, 115 93 Stockholm, Sweden

City Stockholm
Phone (+46) (8) 6 70 15 00
Fax (+46) (8) 670 15 72
Website http://www.stockholm.diplo.de
Email info@german-embassy.se

German Embassy in Bern, Switzerland
German Embassy in Switzerland
Willadingweg 83, 3006 Bern, Switzerland
City Bern
Phone 41 31 359 41 11
Fax 41 31 359 44 44
Website http://www.deutsche-botschaft.ch
Email post@deutsche-botschaft.ch
Office Hours 09.00-12.00

German Embassy in Damascus, Syria
German Embassy in Syria
Abdulmunen Al- Riad St., Corner Ebla St., Damascus
City Damascus
Phone 963 11 3 32 38 00
Fax 396 11 3 32 38 12
Website http://www.deutschebotschaft-damaskus.org

German Embassy in Dushanbe, Tajikistan
German Embassy in Tajikistan
Warsobskaja 16, Dushanbe
City Dushanbe
Phone 992 372 21 21 89
Fax 992 372 24 03 90
Email deutschebotschaftduschanbe@tajnet.com

German Embassy in Dar-es Salaam, Tanzania
German Embassy in Tanzania
Umoja House, Mirambo Street, Dar-es Salaam
City Dar-es Salaam
Phone 255 22 211 74 09
Fax 255 22 211 29 44
Website http://www.german-embassy-daressalam.de
Email german.emb.dar@raha.com

German Embassy in Bangkok, Thailand
Embassy of Germany in Bangkok, Thailand
9 South Sathorn Road, Bangkok 10120, Thailand
City Bangkok
Phone 66 2 287 90 00
Fax 66 2 287 17 76, 66-2285-6232
Website http://www.bangkok.diplo.de/Vertretung/bangkok/de/Startseite.html
Email info@german-embassy.or.th, rk@german-embassy.or.th
Office Hours (Montag bis Freitag, 09.00 - 11.30)

German Consulate in Chiang Mai, Thailand
Consulate of Germany in Chiang Mai, Thailand
199/163 Moo 3, Baan Nai Fun 2, Kan Klong Chonpratan Road, Tambon Mae Hia, Amphoe Muan, Chiang Mai 50100, Thailand
City Chiang Mai
Phone (+66) (53) 83 87 35
Fax (+66) (53) 83 87 35

Email dekonsul@loxinfo.co.th
Office Hours 09.00 - 12.00

German Embassy in Lome, Togo
German Embassy in Togo
Boulevard de la Republique, B.P. 1175, Lome, Togo
City Lome
Phone (+228) 221 23 70
Fax (+228) 222 18 88
Email ambaltogo@cafe.tg

German Embassy in Port Of Spain, Trinidad & Tobago
German Embassy in Trinidad & Tobago
7-9 Marli Street, Port of Spain
City Port of Spain
Phone 1868 628 16 30
Fax 1868 628 52 78
Website http://www.germanemb-portofspain.de
Email germanemb@carib-link.net
Details ---

German Embassy in Tunis, Tunisia
German Embassy in Tunisia
1, Rue el Hamra, Mutueville, Tunis
City Tunis
Phone 216 71 78 64 55
Fax 216 71 78 82 42
Website http://www.tunis.diplo.de
Email info@tunis.diplo.de

German Consulate in Djerba, Tunisia
norary Consul of the Federal Republic of Germany in Tunisia
8, Rue Béchir Sfar, Houmt Souk, 4180 Djerba
City Djerba
Fax (00216 75) 75 77 68
Email info@djerba-thermalisme.com

German Embassy in Ankara, Turkey
German Embassy in Ankara, Turkey
114 Atatürk Bulvari, Kavaklidere, 06540 Ankara, Turkey
City Ankara
Phone (0090 312) 455 51 00
Fax (90 312) 455 53 37
Website http://www.ankara.diplo.de
Email info@ankara.diplo.de

German Consulate in Istanbul, Turkey
General Consulate of the Federal Republic of Germany in Turkey
Inonu Caddesi 16-18, Istanbul.
City Istanbul
Phone (0090 212) 3 34 61 00
Fax (0090 212) 249 99 20
Website http://www.istanbul.diplo.de/
Email info@istanbul.diplo.de

German Consulate in Izmir, Turkey
General Consulate of the Federal Republic of Germany in Turkey
Ataturk Caddesi 260, 35220 Izmir

City Izmir
Phone (0090 232) 488 88 88
Fax (0090 232) 488 88 74
Website http://www.izmir.diplo.de/
Email info@izmir.diplo.de

German Consulate in Antalya, Turkey
Consulate of Germany in Turkey
Yesilbahce Mahallesi, (Yeni Narenciye Yolu), 1447 , Sokak, B.Gürkanlar Apt., Kat 5, No. 14, 07050
City Antalya
Phone (0090 242) 314 11 01, 314 11 02
Fax (0090 242) 321 69 14
Website http://www.antalya.diplo.de/
Email info@antalya.diplo.de

German Consulate in Adana, Turkey
Honorary Consul of the Federal Republic of Germany in Turkey
Paksoy A. S., Karatas Yolu No.: 184, 01120 Adana
City Adana
Phone (0090 322) 311 43 53, 311 48 30
Fax (0090 322) 311 44 01
Email ipaksoy@paksoy.com.tr

German Consulate in Bodrum, Turkey
Honorary Consul of the Federal Republic of Germany in Turkey
Acikkirlar Mevkii Yeni Karsisi Zeytindali Sodak No: , 15, Bitez-Bodrum
City Bodrum
Phone (0090 252) 316 56 08, 316 48 02
Fax (0090 252) 316 46 28
Email gulay_kaman@hotmail.com

German Consulate in Bursa, Turkey
Honorary Consul of the Federal Republic of Germany in Turkey
Ottomantur, Cemal Nadir Cad. 6/3, 16371 Bursa
City Bursa
Phone (0090 224) 221 00 21, 221 00 99
Fax (0090 224) 221 89 48, 222 35 97
Email honorarkonsul@ottomantur.com

German Consulate in Edirne, Turkey
Honorary Consul of the Federal Republic of Germany in Turkey
Balikpazari Cad. Of Sitesi, C Blok D. 2, Kaleici, 22020
City Edirne
Phone (0090 284) 213 55 63
Fax (0090 284) 213 10 61
Email dursunoglu_ercan@hotmail.com

German Consulate in Erzurum, Turkey
Honorary Consul of the Federal Republic of Germany in Turkey
Cumhuriyet Cad. 29/1, 25100 Erzurum.
City Erzurum
Phone (0090 442) 234 12 19, 235 22 50
Fax (0090 442) 233 66 00
Email ykuskay@yahoo.com, kuskay@ttnet.net.tr

German Consulate in Gaziantep, Turkey
Honorary Consul of the Federal Republic of Germany in Turkey
Gazi Mahhallesi Zübeyde Hanim Bulvari No. 54/b, Sehitkamil, 27160 Gaziantep

City Gaziantep
Phone (0090 342) 336 14 00
Fax (0090 342)336 14 02
Email okara@selcukgroup.com

German Consulate in Kayseri, Turkey
Honorary Consul of the Federal Republic of Germany in Turkey
Organize Sanayi Bölgesi 23. Cadde No.32, Kayseri.
City Kayseri
Phone (0090 352) 321 34 74
Fax (0090 352) 321 36 76
Email info@censoy.com

German Consulate in Trabzon, Turkey
Honorary Consul of the Federal Republic of Germany in Turkey
Gazipasa Caddesi, Saruhan Ishani Kat 1, Trabzon.
City Trabzon
Phone (0090 462) 323 08 24
Fax (0090 462) 323 28 27
Email ihsanalioglu@superonline.com

German Embassy in Ashgabat, Turkmenistan
German Embassy in Turkmenistan
Hotel Sheraton Four Points AK Altin Plaza, Magtumguly Street, Pobedy Park, Hydyr Derjajew-Street, 74, Ashgabat
City Ashgabat
Phone 99 312 36 35 15
Fax 99 312 36 35 22
Email info@aschgabat.diplo.de

German Embassy in Kampala, Uganda
Embassy of Germany in Uganda
Plot 15, Philip Road, Kalolo, Kampala
City Kampala
Phone 256 41 50 11 11
Fax 256 41 50 11 15
Website http://www.kampala.diplo.de/
Email info@kampala.diplo.de
Office Hours Monday and Friday 08.00 ‼ 14.00 Tuesday to Thursday 08.00 ‼ 17.00 Open to Public: Monday to Friday 09.00 ‼ 12.00 Scholarship enquiries: Tuesday to Thursday 09.00 - 11.30

German Embassy in Kiev, Ukraine
German Embassy in Ukraine
Wul. Bohdana, Chmelnyzkoho 25, 01901 Kiev
City Kiev
Phone 380 44 2 47 68 00
Fax 380 44 2 47 68 18
Website http://www.kiew.diplo.de/
Email info@kiew.diplo.de

German Consulate in Donezk, Ukraine
General Consulate of the Federal Republic of Germany
Prospekt Mira 15, Büro 71, 83015 Donezk
City Donezk
Phone (00380 62) 343 45 47
Fax (00380 62) 343 45 48
Email info@donezk.diplo.de

German Consulate in Donezk, Ukraine
Honorary Consul of the Federal Republic of Germany in Ukraine
Wul. Artema 58, 83000 Donezk
City Donezk
Phone (00380 62) 345 17 17
Fax (00380 62) 345 17 15
Email viktor.kalashnikov@siemens.com

German Consulate in Lemberg, Ukraine
Honorary Consul of the Federal Republic of Germany in Ukraine
Wulyzja Wynnytschenka 6, 79008 Lviv
City Lemberg
Phone (00380 322) 75 71 02, 75 33 14, 75 33 24
Fax (00380 322) 75 71 02, 75 33 14, 75 33 24
Email notar@lviv.farlep.net

German Consulate in Odessa, Ukraine
Honorary Consul of the Federal Republic of Germany in Ukraine
9, Lanzheronovskayastr., office 17, 65026 Odessa
City Odessa
Phone (00380 48) 777 89 03
Email odessa@hkd.in.ua

German Embassy in Abu Dhabi, United Arab Emirates
German Embassy in United Arab Emirates
Towers at the Trade Center, West Tower, 14th Floor, Abu Dhabi Mall, P.O. Box 2591
City Abu Dhabi
Phone +971-2-6446693 or +971-50-6216291
Fax +971-2-6446942 or +971-2-6449425
Website http://www.abu-dhabi.diplo.de
Email info@abu-dhabi.diplo.de
Office Hours Sundays to Thursdays: 9.00 a.m. to 12.00 p.m. After hours visa applications can only be handed in at prior appointment.
Details Ambassador: H.E. Klaus-Peter Brandes

German Consulate in Dubai, United Arab Emirates
Consulate General of the Federal Republic of Germany in Dubai
Khalid Bin Al Waleed Road, New Sharaf Building, , Near Bur Juman Center, Dubai
City Dubai
Phone (00971 4) 397 23 33
Fax (00971 4) 397 22 25
Website http://www.dubai.diplo.de/
Email info@dubai.diplo.de

German Embassy in London, United Kingdom
German Embassy in London, United Kingdom
23 Belgrave Square, London SW1X 8PZ, United Kingdom
City London
Phone 44 20 78 24 13 00
Fax 44 20 78 24 14 35
Website http://www.london.diplo.de
Email info@london.diplo.de

German Embassy in Washington DC, United States
Embassy of the Federal Republic of Germany
4645 Reservoir Road NW, 20007-1998
City Washington DC
Phone (1 202) 298 4000

Fax (1 202) 298 4249, 333 26 53
Website http://www.germany.info/Vertretung/usa/en/Startseite.html
Email info@washington.diplo.de
Office Hours 8:30 a.m. to 5 p.m., Monday-Thursday 8:30 a.m. to 3:30 p.m. on Fridays

German Consulate in Atlanta, United States
Consulate of Germany in Georgia, United States
Marquis Two Tower, Suite 901, 285 Peachtree Center Avenue, N.E., Atlanta, Georgia 30303-1221
City Atlanta
Phone (404) 659-4760
Fax (001 404) 659 12 80
Website http://www.atlanta.diplo.de/
Email info@atlanta.diplo.de
Office Hours Monday - Friday : 9:00 a.m. to 12:00 p.m. (noon)
Details Consul General of the Federal Republic of Germany: Lutz Hermann Gorgens Ph.D.

German Consulate in Boston, United States
Consulate of Germany in Boston, Mass., United States
Three Copley Place, Suite 500, Boston, MA 02116
City Boston
Phone (617) 369-4900; (617) 369-4934
Fax (617) 369-4940
Website http://www.boston.diplo.de
Email info@boston.diplo.de
Office Hours Monday - Friday: 09.00 a.m. - 12.00 p.m.
new visa applications will be accepted untill 11.30 a.m.

German Embassy in Arizona, United States
Embassy of Germany in Arizona, United States Of America
007 East Missouri Ave. Phoenix, AZ 85014
City Arizona
Phone 602-264-2545

German Consulate in Chicago, United States
Consulate General of the Federal Republic of Germany in Chicago, IL
676 North Michigan Avenue, Suite 3200, Chicago, IL 60611
City Chicago
Phone (001 312) 202 04 80
Fax (001 312) 202 04 66
Website http://www.chicago.diplo.de/
Email info@chicago.diplo.de
Office Hours Monday - Friday: 9 AM - 12 noon
Details Consul General Onno Huckmann is Germany's representative in the Midwest.

German Consulate in Houston, United States
Consulate General of the Federal Republic of Germany in Houston, TX
1330 Post Oak Blvd., Suite 1850, Houston, TX 77056-3018
City Houston
Phone (001 713) 627 77 70
Fax (001 713) 627 05 06
Website http://www.houston.diplo.de/
Email info@houston.diplo.de
Office Hours Monday-Thursday, 7:45 a.m.- 4:00 p.m., and Friday, 7:30 a.m.- 1:30 p.m. Consular Section If you would like to contact our visa section, please call Monday-Thursday between 2:00 and 3:30 p.m.

German Consulate in Los Angeles, United States
Consulate General of the Federal Republic of Germany in Los Angeles, CA
6222 Wilshire Boulevard, Suite No. 500, Los Angeles, CA 90048.

City Los Angeles
Phone (001 323) 930 27 03
Fax (001 323) 930 28 05
Website http://www.los-angeles.diplo.de/
Email info@los-angeles.diplo.de
Office Hours Passport Applicants: Monday-Thursday - 8:30 am - 11:30 am and 1:30 pm - 3:30 pm Friday: 8:30 am - 11:30 am Visa Applicants Monday-Friday - 8:00 am - 11:00 am Other Consular Services Monday-Friday - 8:00 am - 11:00 am Office Hours - Consulate General Monday-Thursday - 8:00 am - 4:00 pm Friday - 8:00 am - 1:00 pm

German Consulate in Miami, United States
Consulate General of the Federal Republic of Germany in Miami, FL
100 N. Biscayne Blvd. Suite 2200, Miami, Florida, 33132
City Miami
Phone (001 305) 358 02 90
Fax (001 305) 358 03 07
Website http://www.miami.diplo.de/
Email info@miami.diplo.de
Office Hours Monday - Thursday: 8:30 am - 4:30 pm Friday: 8:30 am - 2pm
Details German Consul General Klaus Ranner is Germany's representative to the State of Florida, the Commonwealth of Puerto Rico and the US Virgin Islands

German Consulate in New York, United States
Consulate General of the Federal Republic of Germany in New York, NY
871 United Nations Plaza, (1st Avenue between 48th and 49th Street), New York, NY 10017
City New York
Phone (212) 610 9700
Fax (212) 940 0402
Website http://www.new-york.diplo.de/
Email info@new-york.diplo.de
Office Hours Monday - Friday 9am - 12 noon
Details The Consul General: Dr. Horst Freitag

German Consulate in San Francisco, United States
Consulate General of the Federal Republic of Germany in San Francisco, CA
1960 Jackson Street, San Francisco, CA 94109
City San Francisco
Phone (001 415) 775 10 61
Fax (001 415) 775 01 87
Website http://www.san-francisco.diplo.de/
Email info@san-francisco.diplo.de
Office Hours Monday - Friday 9:00 am - 12:00 noon
Details The German Consulate General in San Francisco is headed by Consul General Peter Rothen.

German Consulate in Albuquerque, United States
Honorary Consul of the Federal Republic of Germany in Albuquerque, NM
4801 Lang N. E. # 110, Albuquerque, NM 87109
City Albuquerque
Phone (001 505) 798 25 67
Fax (001 505) 796 96 01
Email mesersmith@aol.com

German Consulate in Anchorage, United States
Honorary Consul of the Federal Republic of Germany in Anchorage, AK
425 'G' Street, Suite 650, Anchorage, AK 99501
City Anchorage
Phone (001 907) 2 74 65 37
Fax (001 907) 2 74 87 98
Email bcg@alaska.net

German Consulate in Birmingham, United States
Honorary Consul of the Federal Republic of Germany in Birmingham, AL
c/o Alabama Germany Partnership, 500 Beacon , Parkway West, Birmingham, AL 35209.
City Birmingham
Phone Parkway West, Birmingham, AL 35209.
Fax (001 205) 943 47 80
Email alabamagermany@earthlink.net

German Consulate in Buffalo, United States
Honorary Consul of the Federal Republic of Germany in Buffalo, NY
140 Pearl Street Suite 100, Buffalo, NY 14202
City Buffalo
Phone (001 716) 848 12 56
Fax (001 716) 819 46 33
Email ckoelbl@hodgsonruss.com

German Consulate in Charlotte, United States
Honorary Consul of the Federal Republic of Germany in Charlotte, NC
Carolinas International Connection, 3808 Pomfret , Lane, Charlotte, NC 28211.
City Charlotte
Phone (001 704) 3 77 03 62
Fax (001 704) 4 23 81 42
Email kgwconsulting@aol.com

German Consulate in Cincinnati, United States
Honorary Consul of the Federal Republic of Germany in Cincinnati, OH
Department of Germanic Languages and Literatures, , University of Cincinnati, Old Chemistry Building 734, , Clifton Avenue, Cincinnati, OH 45221-0372.
City Cincinnati
Phone (001 513) 5 56 27 56
Fax (001 513) 5 56 19 91
Email richard.schade@uc.edu

German Consulate in Cleveland, United States
Honorary Consul of the Federal Republic of Germany in Cleveland, OH
Roetzel & Adress, 1375 E. Ninth Street,, One Cleveland Center, 10th Floor, Cleveland, OH 44114
City Cleveland
Phone (001 216) 623 01 50
Fax (001 216)623 01 34
Email dthimmig@ralaw.com

German Consulate in Dallas, United States
Honorary Consul of the Federal Republic of Germany in Dallas, TX
Hart & Power, Attorneys-at-Law, , 325 N. St. Paul St. # 2300, Dallas, TX 75201-3873.
City Dallas
Phone (001 214) 748 85 00
Fax (001 214) 761 17 00
Email whart@hart-power.com

German Consulate in Denver, United States
Honorary Consul of the Federal Republic of Germany in Denver, CO
621, 17th Street, Suite 811, Denver, CO 80293
City Denver
Phone (001 303) 2 79 15 51
Fax (001 303) 2 95 00 72
Email bleisejd@ecentral.com

German Consulate in Des Moines, United States
Honorary Consul of the Federal Republic of Germany in Des Moines, IA
115 South Howard Street, Indianola, IA 50125-0357.
City Des Moines
Phone (001 515) 961 25 09, 961 59 70
Fax (001 515) 9 61 59 70
Email schlenkerm@dybb.com

German Consulate in Detroit, United States
Honorary Consul of the Federal Republic of Germany in Detroit, MI
Oakland County, Executive Office Building, 2100 , Pontiac Lake Road, Building 41 West, Waterford, MI 48328.
City Detroit
Phone (001 248) 858 40 90
Fax (001 248) 452 20 39
Email migermany@comcast.net

German Consulate in Greenville, United States
Honorary Consul of the Federal Republic of Germany in Greenville, SC
1784 Poplar Drive, Greer, SC 29651.
City Greenville
Phone (001 864) 879 93 34, 3139437 (Mobile)
Fax (001 864) 879 27 27
Email wstromberg@triadsales.com

German Consulate in Indianapolis, United States
Honorary Consul of the Federal Republic of Germany in Indianapolis, In
1525 North Ritter Avenue Indianapolis, IN 46219.
City Indianapolis
Phone (001 317) 359 54 67
Fax (001 317) 322 40 95
Email sschumacher@lutheranfamily.org

German Consulate in Jackson, United States
Honorary Consul of the Federal Republic of Germany in Jackson, MS
c/o AmSouth Bank, 49 Eastbrooke Street, Jackson, MS 39216.
City Jackson
Phone (001 601) 3 54 82 83
Fax (001 601) 3 54 81 92
Email EBarneyR@aol.com, 784516@skytel.com

German Consulate in Kansas, United States
Honorary Consul of the Federal Republic of Germany in Kansas City, KS
8014 State Line, # 203 Leawood, KS 66208.
City Kansas
Phone (001 913) 6 42 51 34
Fax (001 913) 6 42 53 48
Email wbs11@mindspring.com

German Consulate in Las Vegas, United States
Honorary Consul of the Federal Republic of Germany in Las Vegas, NV
4815 W Russell Road, Suite 10 J, Las Vegas, NV 89118.
City Las Vegas
Phone (001 702) 873 67 17
Fax (001 702) 873 96 94
Email consul@vegasresidences.com

German Consulate in Louisville, United States
Honorary Consul of the Federal Republic of Germany in Louisville, KY
Wyatt, Terrant & Coms, 500 W. Jefferson Street, , Suite 2800, Louisville, Kentucky 40202-2898.
City Louisville
Phone (001 502) 562 72 96
Fax (001 502) 589 03 09
Email mblackwell@wyattfirm.com

German Consulate in Naples, United States
Honorary Consul of the Federal Republic of Germany in Naples, FL
5621 Strand Boulevard, Suite 105 Naples, Fl 34109.
City Naples
Phone (001 239) 596 60 20
Fax (001 239) 596 60 51
Email nhenning@henning-law.com

German Consulate in Nashville, United States
Honorary Consul of the Federal Republic of Germany in Nashville, TN
Sun trust Building, 201 Fourth Avenue North, , Suite 1420, Nashville, TN 37219.
City Nashville
Phone (001 615) 251 54 47 (Direct), 251 54 44 (central)
Fax (001 615) 251 54 53
Email dberry@hubbardberry.com

German Consulate in New Orleans, United States
Honorary Consul of the Federal Republic of Germany in New Orleans, LA
Leake, Andersson & Mann, 1100 Poydras Street, , Energy Center, Suite 1700, New Orleans, LA 70163-1701.
City New Orleans
Phone (001 504) 585 75 00
Fax (001 504) 585 77 75
Email pandersson@leakeandersson.com

German Consulate in Oklahoma, United States
Honorary Consul of the Federal Republic of Germany in Oklahoma, OK
5801 North Broadway, Suite 120, Oklahoma City, OK 73118.
City Oklahoma
Phone (001 405) 842 01 00
Fax (001 405) 848 82 48
Email lcraft@wigginprop.com

German Consulate in Philadelphia, United States
Honorary Consul of the Federal Republic of Germany in Philadelphia, PA
One Penn Center, Suite 340, 1617 John F. Kennedy Blvd, Philadelphia, PA 19103.
City Philadelphia
Phone (001 215) 568 55 73
Fax (001 215) 665 03 75
Email honconsulphila@aol.com

German Consulate in Phoenix, United States
Honorary Consul of the Federal Republic of Germany in Phoenix, AZ
1007 East Missouri Avenue, Phoenix, Arizona 85014-2663.
City Phoenix
Phone (001 602) 264 25 45
Fax (001 602) 265 44 28
Email GermanConsulAZ@aol.com

German Consulate in Pittsburgh, United States
Honorary Consul of the Federal Republic of Germany in Pittsburgh, PA
c/o K&L Gates LLP, 210 Sixth Avenue, Pittsburgh, PA 15222
City Pittsburgh
Phone (001 412) 355 67 77
Fax (001 412) 355 65 01
Email david. murdoch@klgates.com

German Consulate in Portland, United States
Honorary Consul of the Federal Republic of Germany in Portland, OR
200 SW Market Street, Suite 1695, Portland, OR 97201.
City Portland
Phone (001 503) 222 04 90, 225 69 24
Fax (001 503) 221 05 64
Email ghoffmann1@aol.com

German Consulate in Salt Lake, United States
Honorary Consul of the Federal Republic of Germany in Salt Lake City, UT
Kirton & Mc Conkie, 1800 Eagle Gate Tower,, 60 East South Temple, Salt Lake City, UT 84111-1004.
City Salt Lake
Phone (001 801) 3 21 48 07
Fax (001 801) 3 21 48 93
Email cdahlquist@kmclaw.com

German Consulate in San Antonio, United States
Honorary Consul of the Federal Republic of Germany in San Antonio, TX
2201 Tower Life Building, 310 South St. Mary's Street, , San Antonio, TX 78205.
City San Antonio
Phone (001 210) 226 17 88
Fax (001 210) 226 20 65
Email mastholte@aol.com

German Consulate in San Diego, United States
Honorary Consul of the Federal Republic of Germany in San Diego, CA
1947 Camino Vida Roble, Suite 108,, Carlsbad, CA
City San Diego
Phone (001 760) 918 02 65
Fax (001 760) 918 04 04
Email german_consulate_sandiego@yahoo.com

German Consulate in Seattle, United States
Honorary Consul of the Federal Republic of Germany in Seattle, WA
7853 S. E. 27th Street, Suite 180,, Mercer Island, WA 98040.
City Seattle
Phone (001 206) 230 51 38
Fax (001 206) 236 5162
Email petrahwalker@gmail.com

German Consulate in United States
Honorary Consul of the Federal Republic of Germany in St. Louis, MO
330 Wenneker Drive,, St. Louis, MO 63124.
Phone (001 314) 567 46 01
Fax (001 314) 567 11 01
Email st-louis@hk-diplo.de

German Consulate in Virginia Beach, United States
Honorary Consul of the Federal Republic of Germany in Virginia Beach, VA
536 Viking Drive, Virginia Beach, VA 23450, USA.
City Virginia Beach
Phone (001 757) 486 91 67
Fax (001 757) 486 91 41
Email peter.mueller@stihl.us

German Embassy in Montevideo, Uruguay
Embassy of Germany in Uruguay
La Cumparsita 1417/1435, Plaza Alemania, Montevideo
City Montevideo
Phone 598 2 902 52 22
Fax 598 2 902 34 22
Website http://www.montevideo.diplo.de/
Email info@montevideo.diplo.de, info@embajadaalemana-montevideo.info
Office Hours Monday - Thursday 7:45am - 12:30pm, 1pm - 4:45pm Friday 7:45am - 1:45 pm

German Embassy in Tashkent, Uzbekistan
German Embassy in Uzbekistan
Sharaf Rashidov Kochasi 15, Taschkent 700017.
City Tashkent
Phone 998 71 120 84 40
Fax 998 71 120 66 93 , 120 84 50, 120 84 85
Website http://www.taschkent.diplo.de/
Email info@taschkent.diplo.de

German Embassy in Vatican City, Vatican
Embassy of Germany to the Vatican City
Via di Villa Sacchetti 4-6, 00197 Roma
City Vatican City
Phone (0039 06) 80 95 11
Fax (0039 06) 80 95 12 27
Website http://www.vatikan.diplo.de

German Embassy in Caracas, Venezuela
Embassy of Germany in the Venezuela
Avenida Eugenio Mendoza (Principal de la Castellana) , y Avenida Jose Angel Lamas, Edif. La Castellana, 10, Stock - La Castellana, Caracas
City Caracas
Phone (0058 212) 219 25 00
Fax (0058 212) 201 00 41
Website http://www.caracas.diplo.de/
Email info@caracas.diplo.de, embajadaalemanacara@cantv.net

German Consulate in Maracaibo, Venezuela
Honorary Consul of the Federal Republic of Germany in Maracaibo
Avda. 3 F No. 69-26, Sector Bellas Artes, 4002, Maracaibo, Edo. Zulia
City Maracaibo
Phone (0058 261) 791 14 16, 792 29 55, 793 00 53, Cel: (0058 416) 662 73 10
Fax (0058 261) 792 29 54
Email herrmann@cantv.net

German Consulate in Porlamar, Venezuela
Honorary Consul of the Federal Republic of Germany in Porlamar
Hotel Hilton & Suites, Lobby Hotel Hilton Suites,, Calle Los Uveros, Urb. Costa Azul Porlamar, Edo. Nueva Esparta.
City Porlamar

Phone (0058 295) 262 84 75, (0058 414) 789 40 05
Fax (0058 295) 262 84 75
Email haciendax@cantv.net

German Consulate in Cristobal, Venezuela
Honorary Consul of the Federal Republic of Germany in Cristobal
Carrera 3 con Calle 4, Centro Colonial Dr. Toto , Gonzales,p. 1, Of.7, San Cristobal/Edo. Tachira
City Cristobal
Phone (0058 276) 343 62 18, 344 19 06, (0058 414) 704 07 70
Fax (0058 276) 344 19 06
Email kmargeit@hotmail.com

German Embassy in Hanoi, Vietnam
German Embassy in Vietnam
29, Tran Phu, Hanoi
City Hanoi
Phone (0084 4) 38 43 02 45, 38 43 02 46, 38 45 38 36, 38 45 38 37
Fax 84 4 845 38 38
Website http://www.hanoi.diplo.de/
Email info@hanoi.diplo.de

German Consulate in Ho Chi Minh, Vietnam
Consulate General of the Federal Republic of Germany in Ho Chi Minh
126 Nguyen Dinh Chieu - Q. 3
City Ho Chi Minh
Phone (0084 8) 38 29 19 67
Fax (0084 8) 38 23 19 19
Website http://www.ho-chi-minh-stadt.diplo.de/
Email info@ho-chi-minh-stadt.diplo.de
Office Hours Monday to Friday 8.30 am to 11.00 am

German Embassy in Sana, Yemen
German Embassy in Yemen
Near Hadda Road, Outer Ring Road, Sana
City Sana
Phone 967 1 41 31 74
Fax 967 1 41 31 79
Email germembasanaa@y.net.ye

German Embassy in Lusaka, Zambia
German Embassy in Zambia
United Nations Avenue, Stand No. 5209, Lusaka
City Lusaka
Phone 260 1 25 06 44
Fax 260 1 25 40 14
Website http://www.germanembassy-lusaka.org
Email geremblusaka@zamtel.zm

German Embassy in Harare, Zimbabwe
German Embassy in Zimbabwe
30, Ceres Road, Avondale, Harare, Zimbabwe
City Harare
Phone 263 4 30 86 55
Fax 263 4 30 34 55
Email germemb@ecoweb.co.zw

WORLD CONSTITUTION AND CITIZENSHIP LAWS HANDBOOK LIBRARY

Constitution, citizenship, immigration, migration - strategic information, government programs, laws and regulations and more...

Price: $149 each

Afghanistan Constitution and Citizenship Laws Handbook
Albania Constitution and Citizenship Laws Handbook
Algeria Constitution and Citizenship Laws Handbook
Angola Constitution and Citizenship Laws Handbook
Antigua and Barbuda Constitution and Citizenship Laws Handbook
Antilles (Netherlands) Constitution and Citizenship Laws Handbook
Argentina Constitution and Citizenship Laws Handbook
Armenia Constitution and Citizenship Laws Handbook
Aruba Constitution and Citizenship Laws Handbook
Australia Constitution and Citizenship Laws Handbook
Austria Constitution and Citizenship Laws Handbook
Azerbaijan Constitution and Citizenship Laws Handbook
Bahamas Constitution and Citizenship Laws Handbook
Bahrain Constitution and Citizenship Laws Handbook
Bangladesh Constitution and Citizenship Laws Handbook
Barbados Constitution and Citizenship Laws Handbook
Belarus Constitution and Citizenship Laws Handbook
Belgium Constitution and Citizenship Laws Handbook
Belize Constitution and Citizenship Laws Handbook
Benin Constitution and Citizenship Laws Handbook
Bermuda Constitution and Citizenship Laws Handbook
Bhutan Constitution and Citizenship Laws Handbook
Bolivia Constitution and Citizenship Laws Handbook
Bosnia and Herzegovina Constitution and Citizenship Laws Handbook
Botswana Constitution and Citizenship Laws Handbook
Brazil Constitution and Citizenship Laws Handbook
Brunei Constitution and Citizenship Laws Handbook
Bulgaria Constitution and Citizenship Laws Handbook
Burkina Faso Constitution and Citizenship Laws Handbook
Burundi Constitution and Citizenship Laws Handbook
Cambodia Constitution and Citizenship Laws Handbook
Cameroon Constitution and Citizenship Laws Handbook
Canada Constitution and Citizenship Laws Handbook
Cape Verde Constitution and Citizenship Laws Handbook
Cayman Islands Constitution and Citizenship Laws Handbook

Central African Republic Constitution and Citizenship Laws Handbook
Chad Constitution and Citizenship Laws Handbook
Chile Constitution and Citizenship Laws Handbook
China Constitution and Citizenship Laws Handbook
Colombia Constitution and Citizenship Laws Handbook
Comoros Constitution and Citizenship Laws Handbook
Congo Constitution and Citizenship Laws Handbook
Congo, Democratic Republic Constitution and Citizenship Laws Handbook
Cook Islands Constitution and Citizenship Laws Handbook
Costa Rica Constitution and Citizenship Laws Handbook
Cote d'Ivoire Constitution and Citizenship Laws Handbook
Croatia Constitution and Citizenship Laws Handbook
Cuba Constitution and Citizenship Laws Handbook
Cyprus Constitution and Citizenship Laws Handbook
Czech Republic Constitution and Citizenship Laws Handbook
Denmark Constitution and Citizenship Laws Handbook
Djibouti Constitution and Citizenship Laws Handbook
Dominica Constitution and Citizenship Laws Handbook
Dominican Republic Constitution and Citizenship Laws Handbook
Ecuador Constitution and Citizenship Laws Handbook
Egypt Constitution and Citizenship Laws Handbook
El Salvador Constitution and Citizenship Laws Handbook
Equatorial Guinea Constitution and Citizenship Laws Handbook
Eritrea Constitution and Citizenship Laws Handbook
Estonia Constitution and Citizenship Laws Handbook
Ethiopia Constitution and Citizenship Laws Handbook
Falkland Islands Constitution and Citizenship Laws Handbook
Faroes Islands Constitution and Citizenship Laws Handbook
Fiji Constitution and Citizenship Laws Handbook
Finland Constitution and Citizenship Laws Handbook
France Constitution and Citizenship Laws Handbook
Gabon Constitution and Citizenship Laws Handbook
Gambia Constitution and Citizenship Laws Handbook
Georgia Constitution and Citizenship Laws Handbook
Germany Constitution and Citizenship Laws Handbook
Ghana Constitution and Citizenship Laws Handbook
Gibraltar Constitution and Citizenship Laws Handbook
Global Constitution and Citizenship Laws Handbook
Greece Constitution and Citizenship Laws Handbook
Greenland Constitution and Citizenship Laws Handbook
Grenada Constitution and Citizenship Laws Handbook
Guam Constitution and Citizenship Laws Handbook
Guatemala Constitution and Citizenship Laws Handbook
Guinea Constitution and Citizenship Laws Handbook
Guinea-Bissau Constitution and Citizenship Laws Handbook
Guyana Constitution and Citizenship Laws Handbook
Haiti Constitution and Citizenship Laws Handbook
Honduras Constitution and Citizenship Laws Handbook
Hungary Constitution and Citizenship Laws Handbook
Iceland Constitution and Citizenship Laws Handbook
India Constitution and Citizenship Laws Handbook

Indonesia Constitution and Citizenship Laws Handbook
Iran Constitution and Citizenship Laws Handbook
Iraq Constitution and Citizenship Laws Handbook
Ireland Constitution and Citizenship Laws Handbook
Israel Constitution and Citizenship Laws Handbook
Italy Constitution and Citizenship Laws Handbook
Jamaica Constitution and Citizenship Laws Handbook
Japan Constitution and Citizenship Laws Handbook
Jersey Constitution and Citizenship Laws Handbook
Jordan Constitution and Citizenship Laws Handbook
Kazakhstan Constitution and Citizenship Laws Handbook
Kenya Constitution and Citizenship Laws Handbook
Kiribati Constitution and Citizenship Laws Handbook
Korea, North Constitution and Citizenship Laws Handbook
Korea, South Constitution and Citizenship Laws Handbook
Kosovo Constitution and Citizenship Laws Handbook
Kurdistan Constitution and Citizenship Laws Handbook
Kuwait Constitution and Citizenship Laws Handbook
Kyrgyzstan Constitution and Citizenship Laws Handbook
Laos Constitution and Citizenship Laws Handbook
Latvia Constitution and Citizenship Laws Handbook
Lebanon Constitution and Citizenship Laws Handbook
Lesotho Constitution and Citizenship Laws Handbook
Liberia Constitution and Citizenship Laws Handbook
Libya Constitution and Citizenship Laws Handbook
Liechtenstein Constitution and Citizenship Laws Handbook
Lithuania Constitution and Citizenship Laws Handbook
Luxembourg Constitution and Citizenship Laws Handbook
Macao Constitution and Citizenship Laws Handbook
Macedonia,Constitution and Citizenship Laws Handbook
Madagascar Constitution and Citizenship Laws Handbook
Madeira Constitution and Citizenship Laws Handbook
Malawi Constitution and Citizenship Laws Handbook
Malaysia Constitution and Citizenship Laws Handbook
Maldives Constitution and Citizenship Laws Handbook
Mali Constitution and Citizenship Laws Handbook
Malta Constitution and Citizenship Laws Handbook
Man Constitution and Citizenship Laws Handbook
Marshall Islands Constitution and Citizenship Laws Handbook
Mauritania Constitution and Citizenship Laws Handbook
Mauritius Constitution and Citizenship Laws Handbook
Mayotte Constitution and Citizenship Laws Handbook
Mexico Constitution and Citizenship Laws Handbook
Micronesia Constitution and Citizenship Laws Handbook
Moldova Constitution and Citizenship Laws Handbook
Monaco Constitution and Citizenship Laws Handbook
Mongolia Constitution and Citizenship Laws Handbook
Morocco Constitution and Citizenship Laws Handbook
Mozambique Constitution and Citizenship Laws Handbook
Myanmar Constitution and Citizenship Laws Handbook
Namibia Constitution and Citizenship Laws Handbook

Nauru Constitution and Citizenship Laws Handbook
Nepal Constitution and Citizenship Laws Handbook
Netherlands Constitution and Citizenship Laws Handbook
New Zealand Constitution and Citizenship Laws Handbook
Nicaragua Constitution and Citizenship Laws Handbook
Niger Constitution and Citizenship Laws Handbook
Nigeria Constitution and Citizenship Laws Handbook
Northern Mariana Islands Constitution and Citizenship Laws Handbook
Norway Constitution and Citizenship Laws Handbook
Oman Constitution and Citizenship Laws Handbook
Pakistan Constitution and Citizenship Laws Handbook
Palau Constitution and Citizenship Laws Handbook
Palestine (West Bank & Gaza) Constitution and Citizenship Laws Handbook
Panama Constitution and Citizenship Laws Handbook
Papua New Guinea Constitution and Citizenship Laws Handbook
Paraguay Constitution and Citizenship Laws Handbook
Peru Constitution and Citizenship Laws Handbook
Philippines Constitution and Citizenship Laws Handbook
Pitcairn Islands Constitution and Citizenship Laws Handbook
Poland Constitution and Citizenship Laws Handbook
Portugal Constitution and Citizenship Laws Handbook
Qatar Constitution and Citizenship Laws Handbook
Romania Constitution and Citizenship Laws Handbook
Russia Constitution and Citizenship Laws Handbook
Rwanda Constitution and Citizenship Laws Handbook
Saint Kitts and Nevis Constitution and Citizenship Laws Handbook
Saint Lucia Constitution and Citizenship Laws Handbook
Saint Vincent and The Grenadines Constitution and Citizenship Laws Handbook
Samoa (Western) Constitution and Citizenship Laws Handbook
Sao Tome and Principe Constitution and Citizenship Laws Handbook
Saudi Arabia Constitution and Citizenship Laws Handbook
Senegal Constitution and Citizenship Laws Handbook
Serbia Constitution and Citizenship Laws Handbook
Seychelles Constitution and Citizenship Laws Handbook
Sierra Leone Constitution and Citizenship Laws Handbook
Singapore Constitution and Citizenship Laws Handbook
Slovakia Constitution and Citizenship Laws Handbook
Slovenia Constitution and Citizenship Laws Handbook
Solomon Islands Constitution and Citizenship Laws Handbook
Somalia Constitution and Citizenship Laws Handbook
South Africa Constitution and Citizenship Laws Handbook
Spain Constitution and Citizenship Laws Handbook
Sri Lanka Constitution and Citizenship Laws Handbook
St. Helena Constitution and Citizenship Laws Handbook
St. Pierre & Miquelon Constitution and Citizenship Laws Handbook
Sudan Constitution and Citizenship Laws Handbook
Suriname Constitution and Citizenship Laws Handbook
Swaziland Constitution and Citizenship Laws Handbook
Sweden Constitution and Citizenship Laws Handbook
Switzerland Constitution and Citizenship Laws Handbook
Syria Constitution and Citizenship Laws Handbook

Taiwan Constitution and Citizenship Laws Handbook
Tajikistan Constitution and Citizenship Laws Handbook
Tanzania Constitution and Citizenship Laws Handbook
Thailand Constitution and Citizenship Laws Handbook
Togo Constitution and Citizenship Laws Handbook
Tonga Constitution and Citizenship Laws Handbook
Trinidad and Tobago Constitution and Citizenship Laws Handbook
Tunisia Constitution and Citizenship Laws Handbook
Turkey Constitution and Citizenship Laws Handbook
Turkmenistan Constitution and Citizenship Laws Handbook
Turks & Caicos Constitution and Citizenship Laws Handbook
Tuvalu Constitution and Citizenship Laws Handbook
Uganda Constitution and Citizenship Laws Handbook
Ukraine Constitution and Citizenship Laws Handbook
United Arab Emirates Constitution and Citizenship Laws Handbook
United Kingdom Constitution and Citizenship Laws Handbook
United States Constitution and Citizenship Laws Handbook
Uruguay Constitution and Citizenship Laws Handbook
Uzbekistan Constitution and Citizenship Laws Handbook
Vanuatu Constitution and Citizenship Laws Handbook
Vatican City Constitution and Citizenship Laws Handbook
Venezuela Constitution and Citizenship Laws Handbook
Vietnam Constitution and Citizenship Laws Handbook
Virgin Islands, British Constitution and Citizenship Laws Handbook
Wake Atoll Constitution and Citizenship Laws Handbook
Wallis & Futuna Constitution and Citizenship Laws Handbook
Western Sahara Constitution and Citizenship Laws Handbook
Yemen Constitution and Citizenship Laws Handbook
Zambia Constitution and Citizenship Laws Handbook
Zimbabwe Constitution and Citizenship Laws Handbook

www.ingramcontent.com/pod-product-compliance
Lightning Source LLC
LaVergne TN
LVHW080030210926
848481LV00011B/3145